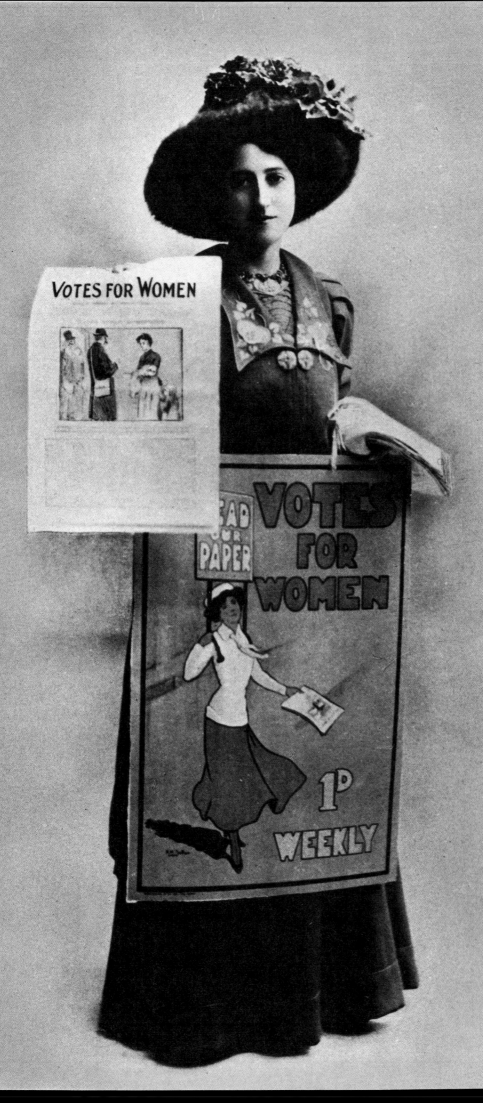

SHOULDER TO SHOULDER

A DOCUMENTARY BY MIDGE MACKENZIE

ALFRED A. KNOPF · 1975

THIS IS A BORZOI BOOK PUBLISHED BY ALFRED A. KNOPF, INC.

Copyright © 1975 by Midge Mackenzie
All rights reserved under International and Pan-American Copyright Conventions.
Published in the United States by Alfred A. Knopf, Inc., New York.
Distributed by Random House, Inc., New York.
Published in Great Britain by Penguin Books Ltd, London.

Library of Congress Cataloging in Publication Data
Main entry under title: Shoulder to shoulder.
1. Women — Suffrage — Great Britain — History — Sources. I. Mackenzie, Midge.
JN979.S5   324′.3′0941   74–25426
ISBN 0–394–49734–1
ISBN 0–394–73070–4 pbk.

The publishers and I are grateful to the following
for permission to reproduce material:
The Longman Group Ltd, for excerpts from *The Suffragette Movement*,
by E. Sylvia Pankhurst;
Victor Gollancz, for material from *My Part in a Changing World*, by Emmeline Pethick-Lawrence;
Edward Arnold Ltd, for excerpts from *Memories of a Militant*, by Annie Kenney;
The Society of Authors on behalf of the Bernard Shaw Estate,
for *Press Cuttings*, by Bernard Shaw;
Arthur Barker Ltd, for material from *Laugh a Defiance*, by Mary Richardson;
Hutchinson Publishing Group Ltd, for excerpts from *Unshackled*,
by Dame Christabel Pankhurst, and *The Home Front*, by E. Sylvia Pankhurst;
Gay and Hancock Ltd, for material from *The Suffragette*, by E. Sylvia Pankhurst;
Macmillan Publishing Co., Inc., New York, for material from *Monstrous Regiment*,
by David Mitchell (copyright ©1965 by David Mitchell).

Manufactured in the United States of America
First American Edition

For my grandmother Anne Charlotte Haimes
and her children

CONTENTS

ACKNOWLEDGMENTS

I would like to thank the many individuals who have shared my enthusiasm for this subject and have worked with me on this book; most especially my editor, Carol Brown Janeway, who has nurtured this project with all its complexities through every stage of production to completion. The art director, Bob Scudellari, for his original design concepts. Louise Fili, the designer, with whom I worked daily for over three months, for her friendship, aesthetics, and sensitive design. Stephen Prockter, the photographer, for his painstaking reproduction of the over fifteen hundred pictures from the archives that we made our final selection from. Jonathan Lumley for the photographic printing. Ellen McNeilly for mixing the inks, choosing the paper, and personally supervising the printing of this book in Kansas with Maxwell Dunleavy. Sally Waitkins, for her help in all departments. Also my friends in New York who have given me generous hospitality, and a home away from home, during the design stages of this book; my thanks to Jan and Lynne Hodenfield, Lina Delano, Richard Johnson, Bob Sann, and Fran Sears.

In London, to Frank Cvitanovich, who has lived with me, our son, the book, and the television series for the last seven years, my love and thanks for his enduring patience and encouragement at all times. Also my friends in London who have scrutinised various stages of the manuscript and lent their support to this project: Ethel de Keyser, Estella Weldon, Dr. M. E. White, and Lynne Hutton-Williams. My agent, Deborah Rogers; Peter Carson of Allen Lane, who commissioned this book; and Eleo Gordon.

My thanks to Enid Goulden Bach, the niece of Emmeline Pankhurst, for arranging for me to meet and interview Grace Roe, Una Duval, Lilian Lenton, and other surviving members of the Women's Social and Political Union.

I would like to thank Mrs. Prohaska and the staff of the London Museum for their help in locating early suffrage letters, manuscripts, pamphlets, and pictures from their archives. Also for their permission to reproduce this material. I would also like to thank Mr. Goosens and all the staff at the British Museum Newspaper Library at Colindale, who patiently dealt with my numerous requests as I researched all the daily newspapers and magazines for this book. Also my good friend Matthew Hoffman for assisting me in this research. My thanks as well to Dinah Brooke for picture research at the International Instituut voor Sociale Geschiedenis in Amsterdam.

The material in this book represents the basis of my story outline for the television series *Shoulder to Shoulder,* produced by Georgia Brown, Verity Lambert, and myself for the BBC and Warner Brothers. I would like to thank both Georgia Brown and Verity Lambert for the unique experience we shared in dramatising and re-creating the lives of these exceptional women. I would also like to thank the writers, Alan Plater, Douglas Livingston, Ken Taylor, and Hugh Whitemore; the directors, Moira Armstrong and Waris Hussein; as well as the actresses for their fine performances, especially Siân Phillips, Angela Down, Patricia Quinn, Judy Parfitt, Georgia Brown, Shiela Allen, Maureen Pryor, and Sheila Ballantyne.

Although it is impossible to list all the names of the many talents that combined to produce the television series and this book, my thanks go to all of you.

Countess Markievicz

INTRODUCTION

I have an abiding interest in history and most especially in women's history. In March 1968, when I was filming the Golden Jubilee of Women's Suffrage in London, I became fascinated by the whole story of how the vote was won. Enquiring more deeply into the subject, I discovered this feat had been almost successfully erased from the history books. The women who fought for the vote had vanished from our history. Their writings were long since out of print and their newspapers buried in archives. As a result, the winning of votes for women is usually erroneously attributed to women's work during the 1914-1918 war, with little or no serious reference to the militant campaign that preceded this wartime period.

The Women's Social and Political Union (W.S.P.U.), founded by Emmeline Pankhurst and her daughters Christabel and Sylvia, was the first and largest militant suffrage group in England. Their challenge to the Government lasted from 1903 to 1914 and involved not merely speechmaking and peaceful agitation but appalling physical hardship, brutality, beatings, forcible feeding, danger—and even death. These events were recorded almost day by day by the Suffragettes themselves in diaries, letters, memoirs, speeches, and in the national Press as well as in their own magazines, *Votes for Women* and *The Suffragette.*

The violent struggle throughout the nineteenth century by succeeding generations of working men to win themselves the vote created the political climate out of which emerged the W.S.P.U. It is important to know that by the late 1880's, when Emmeline Pankhurst was campaigning as a young married woman for the vote, only approximately 4.5 million men in England and Wales, out of a total population of 27.5 million, were empowered to vote.

The Women's Social and Political Union represents a most important factor of women's hidden history. The vast majority of us are unaware of the great struggles, achievements, and writings of the feminist movement in the early twentieth century. These women of principle and passion were fighting one of the most important—and continuing—battles for human liberty. Although still being carried on today in the "New Wave" of feminism, as far as most women are concerned the contest is taking place in a historical vacuum.

I feel that the evolution of the totally free woman in our society will be possible only when we repossess the true dignity of our history and re-integrate it into our lives. Only then will we be able to move beyond this particular struggle, instead of being condemned to repeat it with each succeeding generation. The knowledge that my grandmother's contemporaries were not just good wives, mothers, housekeepers, and cooks but rather a generation of potentially revolutionary freedom fighters gives a new dimension to their lives and a new strength to mine.

When I read later accounts of the Suffragette movement, I felt that their authors had denied the movement its spirit and its soul. They seemed to take a consciously impersonal stand and in no way to reflect the feelings and commitment of the women involved. After meeting with some of the surviving militants—Grace Roe, Lilian Lenton, Una Duval, and Alice Paul—and listening to their stories of this great struggle, I resolved to make my own attempt to redress the balance.

It was as a documentary film-maker that I worked on this book, combining the original experiences of the Suffragettes as expressed in their own words with the images that were available to me from the newspapers and magazines of this period as well as from personal photographs in the archive collections. The text has of necessity been edited throughout from the original, and condensed; but what is revealed here are the perspectives of the Suffragettes themselves, undistorted by my own opinions.

Prior to 1914, it was the militant vanguard, the Women's Social and Political Union, that revitalised the question of votes for women with its tactics of political confrontation and the immense publicity that ensued. Though over one thousand members of the W.S.P.U. were imprisoned, they were, in fact, a tiny minority of the women in England involved in the fight for the vote. Their actions scandalised the more traditional, non-militant suffragist groups, but these same organisations increased their membership dramatically during the W.S.P.U. campaign.

I do find it necessary to comment on the chapters that deal with the 1914-1918 war. These are particularly important because they show the gradual disintegration of the Suffragette movement as such. The war made the split between Sylvia Pankhurst and the women who were revolutionary socialists and Emmeline and Christabel Pankhurst, Millicent Garrett Fawcett, and the conservative feminists irreparable. As elsewhere, I have tried to report back with the factual chronicles of events as recorded by the women themselves, by the Press, and as they appear in Parliamentary annals.

In 1916, Millicent Garrett Fawcett challenged the Government on behalf of the National Union of Women's Suffrage Societies to grant the vote to women. By this time, the bargaining power of the N.U.W.S.S. was greatly strengthened by both the size of their membership and the war work that women were doing. It also seemed more acceptable for the Government to negotiate with and grant the vote to the non-militants than for it to surrender openly to the W.S.P.U.'s threat of resumed post-war militancy.

Though the W.S.P.U. policy during the war years reflected an unwavering co-operation with the Government, there was still the threat that, should the Government not recognise this vital service and deny women the vote, militancy would certainly be resorted to once again. The social changes created by the war in the lives of the women both in the factories and at the French Front and the proof it gave that women could serve their country equally with men meant that support for the vote for women had now become almost universal.

However, the final granting of the vote in 1918 was restricted to women over thirty who could fulfill certain property requirements. The reason for this was that women were a majority and the Government was afraid the balance of political power would be seriously affected if, like men, all women over twenty-one could vote. Therefore, though over 8 million women registered to vote in the first election and seventeen female candidates stood for Parliament, the only woman elected was Countess Markievicz in Dublin. A dedicated Suffragette and Irish revolutionary, she refused to take an oath of loyalty to the English Crown and thereby forfeited her seat in the House of Commons.

By 1928, when all women over twenty-one had attained their voting rights, the questions of social and political equality that had been raised by the Suffragettes were no longer considered important or significant. The new woman, the flapper of the twenties, seemed totally free compared to her Edwardian counterpart; but the superficial permissiveness of society disguised a fundamental lack of progress towards true freedom and equality. The vote had always been thought of by the Suffragettes as symbolising only the beginning of wide-ranging changes in the lives of all women. However, achievement of the goal of votes for women, which had once united so many women, remained an empty victory until a "New Wave" of feminism broke through in the sixties.

Midge Mackenzie
New York
April 27, 1975

SHOULDER TO SHOULDER

THE MAKING OF A MILITANT

EMMELINE PANKHURST: Those men and women are fortunate who are born at a time when a great struggle for human freedom is in progress. It is an added good fortune to have parents who take a personal part in the great movements of their time. I am glad and thankful that this was my case.

One of my earliest recollections is of a great bazaar which was held in my native city of Manchester, the object of the bazaar being to raise money to relieve the poverty of the newly emancipated negro slaves in the United States. My mother took an active part in this effort, and I, as a small child, was entrusted with a lucky bag by means of which I helped to collect money.

Young as I was—I could not have been older than five years—I knew perfectly well the meaning of the words "slavery" and "emancipation." From infancy I had been accustomed to hearing pro and con discussions of slavery and the American Civil War. Although the British Government finally decided not to recognise the Confederacy, public opinion in England was sharply divided on the questions both of slavery and of secession.

Broadly speaking, the propertied classes were pro-slavery, but there were many exceptions to the rule. Most of those who formed the circle of our family friends were opposed to slavery, and my father, Robert Goulden, was always a most ardent abolitionist. He was prominent enough in the movement to be appointed on a committee to meet and welcome Henry Ward Beecher when he arrived in England for a lecture tour. Mrs. Harriet Beecher Stowe's novel, *Uncle Tom's Cabin*, was so great a favourite with my mother that she used it continually as a source of bedtime stories for our fascinated ears. Those stories, told almost fifty years ago, are as fresh in my mind to-day as events detailed in the morning's papers. Indeed they are more vivid, because they made a much deeper impression on my consciousness. I can still definitely recall the thrill I experienced every time my mother related the tale of Eliza's race for freedom over the broken ice of the Ohio River, the agonising pursuit, and the final rescue at the hands of the determined old Quaker. Another thrilling tale was the story of a negro boy's flight from the plantation of his cruel master. The boy had never seen a railroad train, and when, staggering along the unfamiliar railroad track, he heard the roar of an approaching train, the clattering car-wheels seemed to his strained imagination to be repeating over and over again the awful words, "Catch a nigger—catch a nigger—catch a nigger—" This was a terrible story, and throughout my childhood, whenever I rode in a train, I thought of that poor runaway slave escaping from the pursuing monster.

These stories, with the bazaars and the relief funds and subscriptions of which I heard so much talk, I am sure made a permanent impression on my brain and my character. They awakened in me the two sets of sensations to which all my life I have most readily responded: first, admiration for that spirit of fighting and heroic sacrifice by which alone the soul of civilisation is saved; and next after that, appreciation of the gentler spirit which is moved to mend and repair the ravages of war.

I never lost that first impression, and it strongly affected my attitude toward events which were occurring around my childhood.

Manchester is a city which has witnessed a great many stirring episodes, especially of a political character. Generally speaking, its citizens have been liberal in their sentiments, defenders of free speech and liberty of opinion. In the late sixties there occurred in Manchester one of those dreadful events that prove an exception to the rule. This was in connection with the Fenian Revolt in Ireland. There was a Fenian riot, and the police arrested the leaders. These men were being taken to the gaol in a prison van. On the way the van was stopped and an attempt was made to rescue the prisoners. A man fired a pistol, endeavouring to break the lock of the van door. A policeman fell, mortally wounded, and several men were arrested and were charged with murder. I had been spending the afternoon with a young playmate, and my brother had come after tea to escort me home. As we walked through the deepening November twilight he talked excitedly of the riot, the fatal pistol shot, and the slain policeman. I could almost see the man bleeding on the ground, while the crowd swayed and groaned around him.

The rest of the story reveals one of those ghastly blunders which justice not infrequently makes. Although the shooting was done without any intent to kill, the men were tried for murder and three of them were found guilty and hanged. A certain Saturday afternoon stands out in my memory, as on my way home from school I passed the prison where I knew the men had been confined. I saw that a part of the prison wall had been torn away, and in the great gap that remained were evidences of a gallows recently removed. I was transfixed with horror, and over me there swept the sudden conviction that hanging was a mistake—worse, a crime. It was my awakening to one of the most terrible facts of life—that justice and judgment lie often a world apart.

"What a Pity She Wasn't Born a Lad"

I relate this incident of my formative years to illustrate the fact that the impressions of childhood often have more to do with character and future conduct than heredity or education. I tell it also to show that my development into an advocate of militancy was largely a sympathetic process. I have not personally suffered from the deprivations, the bitterness and sorrow which bring so many men and women to a realisation of social injustice. My childhood was protected by love and a comfortable home. Yet, while still a very young child, I began instinctively to feel that there was something lacking, even in my own home, some false conception of family relations, some incomplete ideal.

This vague feeling of mine began to shape itself into conviction about the time my brothers and I were sent to school. The education of the English boy, then as now, was considered a much more serious matter than the education of the English boy's sister. My parents, especially my father, discussed the question of my brothers' education as a matter of real importance. My education and that of my sister were scarcely discussed at all. Of course we went to a carefully selected girls' school, but beyond the facts that the head mistress was a gentlewoman and that all the pupils were girls of my own class, nobody seemed concerned. A girl's education at that time seemed to have for its prime object the art of "making home attractive"—presumably to migratory male relatives. It used to puzzle me to understand why I was under such a particular obligation to make home attractive to my brothers. We were on excellent terms of friendship, but it was never suggested to them as a duty that they make home attractive to me. Why not? Nobody seemed to know.

The answer to these puzzling questions came to me unexpectedly one night when I lay in my little bed waiting for sleep to overtake me. It was a custom of my father and mother to make the round of our bedrooms every night before going themselves to bed. When they entered my room that night I was still awake, but for some reason I chose to feign slumber. My father bent over me, shielding the candle flame with his big hand. I cannot know exactly what thought was in his mind as he gazed down at me, but I heard him say, somewhat sadly, "What a pity she wasn't born a lad."

My first hot impulse was to sit up in bed and protest that I didn't want to be a boy, but I lay still and heard my parents' footsteps pass on toward the next child's bed. I thought about my father's remark for many days afterward, but I think I never decided that I regretted my sex. However, it was made quite clear that men considered themselves superior to women, and that women apparently acquiesced in that belief.

I found this view of things difficult to reconcile with the fact that both my father and my mother were advocates of equal suffrage.

I was fourteen years old when I went to my first suffrage meeting. Returning from school one day, I met my mother just setting out for the meeting, and I begged her to let me go along. She consented, and without stopping to lay my books down I scampered away in my mother's wake. The speeches interested and excited me, especially the address of the great Miss Lydia Becker, who was the Susan B. Anthony of the English movement, a splendid character and a truly eloquent speaker. She was the secretary of the Manchester committee, and I had learned to admire her as the editor of the *Women's Suffrage Journal*, which came to my mother every week. I left the meeting a conscious and confirmed suffragist.

When I was fifteen years old I went to Paris, where I was entered as a pupil in one of the pioneer institutions in Europe for the higher education of girls. This school, one of the founders of which was Mme. Edmond Adam, a distinguished literary figure, was situated in a fine old house in the Avenue de Neuilly. It was under the direction of Mlle. Marchef-Girard, a woman distinguished in education, and who afterward was appointed government inspector of schools in France. Mlle. Marchef-Girard believed that girls' education should be quite as thorough and even more practical than the education boys were receiving at that time. She included chemistry and other sciences in her courses, and in addition to embroidery she had her girls taught bookkeeping. Many other advanced ideas prevailed in this school, and the moral discipline which the pupils received was, to my mind, as valuable as the intellectual training. Mlle. Marchef-Girard held that women should be given the highest ideals of honour. Her pupils were kept to the strictest principles of truth-telling and candour. Myself she understood and greatly benefited.

I was between eighteen and nineteen when I finally returned from school in Paris and took my place in my father's home as a finished young lady. I sympathised with and worked for the woman suffrage movement, and came to know Dr. Richard Marsden Pankhurst, whose work for woman suffrage had never ceased. It was Dr. Pankhurst who drafted the first enfranchisement bill, known as the Women's Disabilities Removal Bill and introduced into the House of Commons in 1870 by Mr. Jacob Bright. The bill advanced to its second reading by a majority vote of thirty-three, but it was killed in committee by Mr. Gladstone's peremptory orders. Dr. Pankhurst acted as counsel for the Manchester women, who tried in 1868 to be placed on the register as voters. He also drafted the bill giving married women absolute control over their property and earnings, a bill which became law in 1882.

I think we cannot be too grateful to the group of men and women who, like Dr. Pankhurst, in those early days lent the weight of their honoured names to the suffrage movement in the trials of its struggling youth. These men did not wait until the movement became popular, nor did they hesitate until it was plain that women were roused to the point of revolt. They worked all their lives with those who were organising, educating, and preparing for the revolt which was one day to come. Unquestionably those pioneer men suffered in popularity for their feminist views. Some of them suffered financially, some politically. Yet they never wavered.

My marriage with Dr. Pankhurst took place in 1879 and lasted through nineteen happy years. Often I have heard the taunt that suffragists are women who have failed to find any normal outlet for their emotions, and are therefore soured and disappointed beings. This is probably not true of any suffragist, and it is most certainly not true of me. My home life and relations have been as nearly ideal as possible in this imperfect world. About a year after my marriage my daughter Christabel was born, and in another eighteen months my second daughter Sylvia came. Two other children followed* and for some years I was rather deeply immersed in my domestic affairs.

I was never so absorbed with home and children, however, that I lost interest in community affairs. Dr. Pankhurst did not desire that I should turn myself into a household machine. It was his firm belief that society as well as the family stands in need of women's

* Henry Francis Robert (d. 1888) and Adela Constantia Mary; a second son, Harry, was born in 1889.

G.W. Allen

PIER AVENUE.
CLACTON ON SEA

An early holiday portrait of Emmeline Pankhurst's daughters: (left to right) Sylvia, Adela, and Christabel

services. So while my children were still in their cradles I was serving on the executive committee of the Women's Suffrage Society, and also on the executive board of the committee which was working to secure the Married Women's Property Act. This act having passed in 1882, I threw myself into the suffrage work with renewed energy. A new reform act, known as the County Franchise Bill, extending the suffrage to farm labourers, was under discussion, and we believed that our years of educational propaganda work had prepared the country to support us in a demand for a women's suffrage amendment to the bill. For several years we had been holding the most splendid meetings in cities all over the kingdom. The crowds, the enthusiasm, the generous response to appeals for support, all these seemed to justify us in our belief that women's suffrage was near.

The Liberal Party was in power in 1884, and a great memorial was sent to the Prime Minister, the Right Honourable William E. Gladstone, asking that a women's suffrage amendment to the County Franchise Bill be submitted to the free and unbiased consideration of the House. Mr. Gladstone curtly refused, declaring that if a women's suffrage amendment should be carried, the Government would disclaim responsibility for the bill. The amendment was submitted nevertheless, but Mr. Gladstone would not allow it to be freely discussed, and he ordered Liberal Members to vote against it. What we call a whip was sent out against it, a note virtually commanding party members to be on hand at a certain hour to vote against the women's amendment. Undismayed, the women tried to have an independent suffrage bill introduced, but Mr. Gladstone so arranged Parliamentary business that the bill never even came up for discussion.

One of the shrewdest acts of Mr. Gladstone's career was his disruption of the suffrage organisation in England. He accomplished this by substituting "something just as good," that something being Women's Liberal Associations. Beginning in 1881 in Bristol, these associations spread rapidly through the country and, in 1887, became a National Women's Liberal Federation. The promise of the Federation was that by allying themselves with men in party politics, women would soon earn the right to vote.

As far as I am concerned, I did not delude myself with any false hopes in the matter. I was present when the Women's Liberal Federation came into existence. Mrs. Gladstone presided, offering the meeting many consolatory words for the absence of "our great leader," Mr. Gladstone, who of course had no time to waste on a gathering of women. At Mrs. Jacob Bright's request I joined the Federation. At this stage of my development I was a member of the Fabian Society, and I had considerable faith in the permeating powers of its mild socialism. But I was already fairly convinced of the futility of trusting to political parties. Even as a child I had begun to wonder at the *naïve* faith of party members in the promises of their leaders. I well remember my father returning home from political meetings, his face aglow with enthusiasm. "What happened, Father?" I would ask, and he would reply triumphantly, "Ah! We passed the resolution."

"Then you'll get your measure through the next session," I predicted.

"I won't say that," was the usual reply. "Things don't always move as quickly as that. But we passed the resolution."

Well, the suffragists, when they were admitted into the Women's Liberal Federation, must have felt that they had passed their resolution. They settled down to work for the party and to prove that they were as capable of voting as the recently enfranchised farm labourers. Of course a few women remained loyal to suffrage. They began again on the old educational lines to work for the cause. Not one woman took counsel with herself as to how and why the agricultural labourers had won their franchise. They had won it, as a matter of fact, by burning hay-ricks, rioting, and otherwise demonstrating their strength in the only way that English politicians can understand. The threat to march a hundred thousand men to the House of Commons unless the bill was passed played its part also in securing the agricultural labourer his political freedom. But no woman suffragist noticed that. As for myself, I was too young politically to learn the lesson then.

In 1885, a year after the failure of the third women's suffrage bill, my husband, Dr. Pankhurst, stood as the Liberal candidate for Parliament in Rotherhithe, a riverside constituency of London. I went through the campaign with him, speaking and canvassing to the best of my ability. Dr. Pankhurst was a popular candidate, and unquestionably would have been returned but for the opposition of the Irish Home-Rulers. Charles Parnell was in command, and his settled policy was opposition to all Liberal candidates. So, in spite of the fact that Dr. Pankhurst was a staunch upholder of home rule, the Parnell forces were solidly opposed to him, and he was defeated. I remember expressing considerable indignation, but my husband pointed out to me that Parnell's policy was absolutely right. With his small party he could never hope to win home rule from a hostile majority, but by constant obstruction he could in time wear out the Government, and force it to surrender. That was a valuable political lesson, one that years later I was destined to put into practice.

The following year found us living in London, and, as usual, interesting ourselves with labour matters and other social movements. It was a time of tremendous unrest, of labour agitations, of strikes and lockouts. It was a time also when a most stupid reactionary spirit seemed to take possession of the Government and the authorities. The Salvation Army, the Socialists, the trade-unionists—in fact, all bodies holding outdoor meetings—were made special objects of attack. As a protest against the policy a Law and Liberty League was formed in London, and an immense Free Speech meeting was held in Trafalgar Square. I was present at this meeting, which resulted in a bloody riot between the police and the populace. The Trafalgar Square Riot is historic, and it did much to establish the right of free speech for English men. English women are still contending for that right.

In 1893, we returned to our Manchester home, and I again took up the work of the Suffrage Society. At my suggestion the members began to organise their first out-of-door meetings, and we continued these until we succeeded in working up a great meeting that filled Free Trade Hall, and overflowed into and crowded a smaller hall near at hand. This marked the beginning of a campaign of propaganda among working people, an object which I had long desired to bring about.

And now began a new and, as I look back on it, an absorbingly interesting stage of my career. Our leaders in the Liberal Party had advised the women to prove their fitness for the Parliamentary franchise by serving in municipal offices, especially the unsalaried offices. A large number of women had availed themselves of this advice, and were serving on Boards of Guardians, on school boards, and in other capacities. My children now being old enough for me to leave them with competent nurses, I was free to join these ranks. A year after my return to Manchester I became a candidate for the Board of Poor Law Guardians.* Several weeks before, I had contested unsuccessfully for a place on the school board. This time, however, I was elected, heading the poll by a very large majority.

When I came into office I found that the law was being very harshly administered. The old board had been made up of the kind of men who are known as rate savers. They were guardians, not of the poor but of the rates, and, as I soon discovered, not very astute guardians even of money. For instance, although the inmates were being very poorly fed, a frightful waste of food was apparent. Each inmate was given each day a certain weight

---

* The Board of Poor Law Guardians disburses for the poor the money coming from the Poor Rates (taxes), and some additional moneys allowed by the local Government board, whose president is a Cabinet Minister. The Board has control of the institution we call the workhouse.

of food, and bread formed so much of the ration that hardly anyone consumed all of his portion. In the farm department pigs were kept on purpose to consume this surplus of bread, and as pigs do not thrive on a solid diet of stale bread the animals fetched in the market a much lower price than properly fed farm pigs. I suggested that, instead of giving a solid weight of bread in one lump, the loaf be cut in slices and buttered with margarine, each person being allowed all that he cared to eat. The rest of the board objected, saying that our poor charges were very jealous of their rights, and would suspect in such an innovation an attempt to deprive them of a part of their ration. This was easily overcome by the suggestion that we consult the inmates before we made the change. Of course the poor people consented, and with the bread that we saved we made puddings with milk and currants, to be fed to the old people of the workhouse. These old folks I found sitting on backless forms, or benches. They had no privacy, no possessions, not even a locker. The old women were without pockets in their gowns, so they were obliged to keep any poor little treasures they had in their bosoms. After I took office we gave the old people comfortable Windsor chairs to sit in, and in a number of ways we managed to make their existence more endurable.

These, after all, were minor benefits. But it does gratify me when I look back and remember what we were able to do for the children of the Manchester workhouse. The first time I went into the place I was horrified to see little girls seven and eight years old on their knees scrubbing the cold stones of the long corridors. These little girls were clad, summer and winter, in thin cotton frocks, low in the neck and short sleeved. At night they wore nothing at all, night dresses being considered too good for paupers. The fact that bronchitis was epidemic among them most of the time had not suggested to the guardians any change in the fashion of their clothes. There was a school for the children, but the teaching was of the poorest order. They were forlorn enough, these poor innocents, when I first met them. In five years' time we had changed the face of the earth for them. We had bought land in the country and had built a cottage system home for the children, and we had established for them a modern school with trained teachers. We had even secured for them a gymnasium and a swimming-bath. I may say that I was on the building committee of the board, the only woman member.

The trouble is, as I soon perceived after taking office, the law cannot, in existing circumstances, do all the work, even for children, that it was intended to do. We shall have to have new laws, and it soon became apparent to me that we can never hope to get them until women have the vote. During the time I served on the board, and for years since then, women guardians all over the country have striven in vain to have the law reformed in order to ameliorate conditions which break the hearts of women to see, but which apparently affect men very little. I have spoken of the little girls I found scrubbing the workhouse floors. There were others at the hateful labour who aroused my keenest pity. I found that there were pregnant women in that workhouse, scrubbing floors, doing the hardest kind of work, almost until their babies came into the world. Many of them were unmarried women, very, very young, mere girls. These poor mothers were allowed to stay in the hospital after confinement for a short two weeks. Then they had to make a choice of staying in the workhouse and earning their living by scrubbing and other work, in which case they were separated from their babies; or of taking their discharges. They could stay and be paupers, or they could leave—leave with a two-week-old baby in their arms, without hope, without home, without money, without anywhere to go. What became of those girls, and what became of their hapless infants?

I thought I had been a suffragist before I became a Poor Law guardian, but now I began to think about the vote in women's hands not only as a right but as a desperate necessity.

Squalid Streets

SYLVIA PANKHURST: Often I went on Sunday mornings with my father to the dingy streets of Ancoats, Gorton, Hulme, and other working-class districts. Standing on a chair or a soap-box, pleading the cause of the people with passionate earnestness, he stirred me, as perhaps he stirred no other auditor, though I saw tears on the faces of the people about him. Those endless rows of smoke-begrimed little houses, with never a tree or a flower in sight, how bitterly their ugliness smote me! Many a time in spring, as I gazed upon them, those two red may trees in our garden at home would rise up in my mind, almost menacing in their beauty; and I would ask myself whether it could be just that I should live in Victoria Park, and go well fed and warmly clad, whilst the children of these grey slums were lacking the very necessities of life. The misery of the poor, as I heard my father plead for it, and saw it revealed in the pinched faces of his audiences, awoke in me a maddening sense of impotence; and there were moments when I had an impulse to dash my head against the dreary walls of those squalid streets.

In Manchester the situation was acute. Under the stirring energies of Dr. Pankhurst, a committee for the relief of the unemployed was formed. Offices were opened and collectors were sent into the streets, funds were advertised for, and subscriptions acknowledged in the *Manchester Guardian*. Food was distributed from twelve noon to two p.m. daily to all comers, no questions being asked.

On Saturdays I went with my mother to help with the distribution, heartsick at the grim sight of those hungry thousands waiting in the bitter cold to receive that meagre aid.

In May 1895, Dr. Pankhurst had accepted the invitation of the I.L.P.* to be its Parliamentary candidate for Gorton, an industrial district on the outskirts of Manchester. The general election took place in July.

---

* In January 1893, the Independent Labour Party was formed, uniting the many Labour and Socialist societies including the Social Democratic Federation, the Fabian Society, the Scottish Labour Party, and several trade organisations. Keir Hardie, who had been elected as a Member of Parliament for West Ham (South) in 1892 as an Independent Labour candidate, was elected Chairman of the newly formed Independent Labour Party. The party declared their primary objective to be the "collective ownership and control of the means of production, distribution and exchange."

Mrs. Pankhurst went to Liverpool to plead with T. P. O'Connor for the Irish vote. He replied: "We have nothing but admiration for your husband, but we cannot support the people he is mixed up with." Thus, as in Rotherhithe ten years before, the Irish Party officially refused its support to the man who, of all candidates, had been first and most staunch in upholding their demands.

I went canvassing with Mrs. Pankhurst; all the people had something kind to say about "the Doctor"; but many of them added they would not vote for him this time, as he had no chance now; but next time he would get in. They seemed to regard the election as a sort of game, in which it was important to vote on the winning side. At an open-air meeting in Openshaw I stood at my mother's side as she spoke to the people from the soap-box: "You put me at the top of the poll [*Mrs. Pankhurst was elected to the Board of Poor Law Guardians*]; will you not vote for the man who has taught me all I know?" Her voice broke; she was almost in tears, and so was I; yet I could not believe that Father, of whom everyone spoke with love; Father, so great and good, could be defeated by this unknown Mr. Hatch. On the evening of the poll I went with my mother through the dark streets to the public-houses, where she implored men with glistening eyes and thirsty lips to come out to vote. How terrible I thought it, this thought-destroying drink!

The result of the poll was: Hatch 5,865, Pankhurst 4,261; and the election expenses: Hatch £1,375, Pankhurst £342. At the I.L.P. meeting after the count, the Doctor was smiling and gay, and declared a great victory for progress had been won. I wept throughout his speech. He rallied me kindly: "There is life in the old bird yet!" When we got home Mrs. Pankhurst told me, though without anger, that I had "disgraced the family" by my tears.

Next day she hired a pony and trap, and drove off alone to the Colne Valley to help Tom Mann in his contest there. Returning through Gorton when all was over she was stoned by Tory roughs, who that Saturday night had celebrated their victory by revelry in public-houses. Tired as she was, her nerve was unshaken. We children were awed by the thought that she had passed through great peril.

The Death of Dr. Pankhurst

Christabel was seventeen. I heard her telling some friends at the Clarion Cycling Club that she wanted to find an easy job which would occupy her from about ten a.m. to four in the afternoon. I listened in consternation, hoping she spoke in jest. I wanted life to be a great adventure, in which every shred of one's energy would be poured into some chosen work of beauty and value. Mrs. Pankhurst was anxious that Christabel should perfect her French; she arranged with Mme. Dufaux to exchange daughters for a year. Mrs. Pankhurst was to take Christabel to Geneva. She looked forward with pleasure and excitement to the visit to her old friend; dressmaking went on for weeks, in preparation.

At the last moment the Doctor could scarcely bear to let his wife go. He was always sad when she was away, as she often was in the evenings at meetings now; always restless if she were late in returning.

"Look after Father!" my mother exhorted me as she left that day. I took the charge very seriously.

He left his chambers on Saturdays at noon, and that day I went to meet him and bring him home. It was his habit to grasp one's upper arm in his hand as he walked beside one, for in the days of his youth it was not good form to walk arm in arm. To be gripped thus held for me, as I often told him, a suggestion of being under compulsion, and I would draw his hand down to my wrist, so that our two arms were folded together. Thus we came home that lovely summer day. . . .

He rose suddenly from the mid-day meal, taking a strawberry from the dish, perhaps to allay my anxiety. "Serve the children," he said to me, and left the room. I followed him presently, and found him, not in the library as I expected, but in my mother's yellow drawing-room, huddled uncomfortably in a small armchair, his every line denoting agony.

"You are not well, Father. Shall I go for Doctor X?"

"No, leave me; it is nothing."

Next morning the awful change in him shocked me. I ran immediately, without consulting him, to find our doctor.

Dr. X came at last. He sent me away during the examination. . . .

"What is the matter with Father?" I searched the ashen face of Dr. X to find an answer before his slow lips opened: "He will soon be better; do not worry."

Oxygen cylinders arrived; I stood by the bed holding out the india-rubber tube for my father to inhale from it. At times he had his usual lucidity; at times his mind wandered in delirium. He seemed helpless as a little child.

He was struggling for breath, but he waved aside the red tube of the oxygen I held toward him. "No, not that," and then: "I am sorry, I thought you were offering me a cherry."

What was the matter with Father? The maddening question seethed within me as I stood holding the tube, striving to soothe and comfort him, striving to allay the excitement which seemed to consume his waning strength, telling him the doctor was just coming; he was not late; he was not detained; he would come; he would come immediately; no, there was not long to wait. . . . Then suddenly he would turn to me in anxious solicitude, urging me almost in his old tones: "You must not stand; you are tired. Do not distress yourself; you must rest." The effort to restrain my grief seemed turning me to stone.

Sunday wore on. Sunday night passed. Still we fought the same desperate, agonizing fight. Mother must not see him like this! We must get him better before she comes.

Some time during Monday night Father sent me away to rest; he would take no denial. I slept. It was morning when I woke. I hastened to his room. Adela and Harry had been brought to his side. I had kept them away and begged them to go to school as usual on Monday—"Like good little dears, to keep the house quite quiet for Father." They gazed with awe at his changed face. Ellen, the housemaid, took them silently away.

The time crept on, and as I stood holding the tube, which seemed a line of life to him, he turned away his head as though to gaze at something. The cook crossed herself, murmuring a prayer. I went to the other side of the bed to see his face. . . . The skies were crashing down, the world was reeling. . . .

Father was dead.

She came in the small hours of Wednesday morning. Dear, brave Mother; she held me in her arms. "Mother, I did not send for you; I did not get a doctor till Sunday." She uttered no complaint, she only tried to soothe me; but nothing could stem the agony of my self-reproach.

Returning in the belief that Harry was ill and that the doctor had worded his telegram to minimise her anxiety, she had read the news in the black-bordered evening paper in the train, and had cried out in the shock of her grief. People in the railway carriage had asked her: "Are you Mrs. Pankhurst?" and offered such poor comfort as they might.

The following Saturday we went to Brooklands Cemetery with Father. They laid his coffin upon an open bier covered with wreaths. A great procession of the many movements he had worked in, the thousands who loved him came with us. The streets were lined with people as we passed. I gazed at my mother, sitting opposite me in the carriage, beautiful and strangely young, as though the years since her marriage had fallen from her. "The widow and the fatherless," a voice seemed to be sounding in my ears. What poignant words!

Bruce Glaster, beside the grave, spoke tenderly. The sky was a glorious blaze of radiance; but our life was broken.

"Faithful and true and my loving comrade"—Mother chose these words of Walt Whitman Father had read to us to be graven upon his headstone.

Mrs. Pankhurst was brave; she had work to do; we should have nothing to live on now. She could not bear to be alone; she must always have one of us beside her. Henceforth I slept with her. Sleepless nights we had; our sorrows and our worries we talked out together, often through half the night. The housekeeping became my charge: I could make the money go further than she.

EMMELINE PANKHURST: In 1898 I suffered an irreparable loss in the death of my husband. His death occurred suddenly and left me with the heavy responsibility of caring for a family of children, the eldest only seventeen years of age. I resigned my place on the Board of Guardians, and was almost immediately appointed to the salaried office of Registrar of Births and Deaths in Manchester.

It was my duty as Registrar of Births and Deaths to act as chief census officer of my district; I was obliged to receive all returns of births and deaths, record them, and send my books quarterly to the office of the Registrar-General. My district was in a working-class quarter, and on this account I instituted evening office hours twice a week. It was touching to observe how glad the women were to have a woman registrar to go to. They used to tell me their stories, dreadful stories some of them, and all of them pathetic with that patient and uncomplaining pathos of poverty. Even after my experience on the Board of Guardians, I was shocked to be reminded over and over again of the little respect there was in the world for women and children. I have had little girls of thirteen come to my office to register the births of their babies, illegitimate, of course. In many of these cases I found that the child's own father or some near male relative was responsible for her state. There was nothing that could be done in most cases. The age of consent in England is sixteen years, but a man can always claim that he thought the girl was over sixteen. During my term of office a very young mother of an illegitimate child exposed her baby, and it died. The girl was tried for murder and was sentenced to death. This was afterward commuted, it is true, but the unhappy child had the horrible experience of the trial and the sentence "to be hanged by the neck, until you are dead." The wretch who was, from the point of view of justice, the real murderer of the baby received no punishment at all.

I needed only one more experience after this one, only one more contact with the life of my time and the position of women, to convince me that if civilisation is to advance at all in the future, it must be through the help of women, women freed of their political shackles, women with full power to work their will in society. It was rapidly becoming clear to my mind that men regarded women as a servant class in the community, and that women were going to remain in the servant class until they lifted themselves out of it. I asked myself many times in those days what was to be done. I had joined the Labour Party, thinking that through its councils something vital might come, some such demand for the women's enfranchisement that the politicians could not possibly ignore. Nothing came.

CHRISTABEL PANKHURST: Knowledge of what was happening at home came to me only by letter, for by Mother's wish I remained in Switzerland waiting to hear what she wished me to do.

Plans for each of the family were considered. Sylvia's future was decided by her gift for painting and by the studentship she obtained at the Manchester School of Art. Adela, for the time being at least, had teaching in view, and Harry was at the grammar school.

As to my own future, I did not know of anything I should like to do and my role was, as the eldest child, to help Mother, as the letters of condolence I received expressed it, and as I myself recognised. Mother's first idea for her own business activity had been

Christabel Pankhurst

dressmaking, suggested by her own flair for good dressing.

Mother had come to feel a distinct prejudice against professional careers and to regard an anonymous business as more compatible with freedom of opinion. So failing any strong preference on my part, her suggestion was that I should be her right hand in the business which she was preparing to start.

She decided finally that this should be a shop, selling artistic wares, silks, cushions, and the rest. She wanted me to continue to improve my French a little longer, and then to return to help her in this venture. It was with resignation, rather than with enthusiasm, that I viewed my future, for I felt no aptitude for business. But I could suggest no practicable alternative. In any case, the time and circumstances were far too sad and grave for the assertion of likes or dislikes. Nothing seemed to matter very much, anyhow, and if one could be of some use that would be all to the good.

Mother summoned me and I went home. A home so changed! It had been midsummer when I went away. When I returned, summer had gone. So it was in our life and home. All was now in the minor key, depressed, forlorn. Mother was in eclipse—heroic as ever, and energetic in her doings, but wan, and with a tragic look that never quite left her. She wanted a fuller occupation, work being ever her recourse in sorrow. She hoped that in the business she might build something that would benefit her children and provide an occupation for me. Her former experience was useful and she soon had all in working order. The new home routine established itself and Mother was ever fortunate in those who served her.

Sylvia, all this time, had been distinguishing herself at the School of Art and the two youngest children were pursuing their course.

I began my work as Mother's right hand. Morning after morning saw me in the tram, reading the newspaper on the way to business, one of very few girls so travelling at that hour in those pre-war days. Mother would follow me later after her official duties closed.

My resolves were good but as time went on I felt more and more unqualified for this avocation. Business was not good for me and I was not good for business. Perhaps I ought to have forced myself to take an interest in my task; yet if I had, subsequent events might have pursued a very different course.

Mother, seeing my unhappy case, suggested some classes at the University. These were, at once, a great mitigation. I had not time to take a full course of lectures leading to a degree, so took logic under Professor Alexander and another course or two. Those lectures were my gateway to a future so filled with inspiring thoughts and activity that I came to reckon myself the happiest person on earth. I found my aim in life.

Dashing to lectures and away again, I had no real touch with the University, but one late afternoon meeting I managed to attend. The Vice-Chancellor, Sir Alfred Hopkinson, spoke on the poets and politics, and a discussion followed. I had had not the faintest intention of saying a word; yet, to my own surprise, the discourse and the debate stirred a thought in me and the thought would out. I rose and rather nervously uttered a sentence or two. "Who is that?" the Vice-Chancellor asked the graduate sitting beside him, and in his closing remarks he referred in a very kind way to my maiden speech, saying: "As one speaker has well said, it is after all the attitude of mind of the poet. . . ."

Miss Esther Roper descended from the platform at the close of the meeting and overtook me. She was secretary of the North of England Society for Woman Suffrage, and one of the committee of the National Union of Women's Suffrage Societies led by Mrs. Fawcett. Miss Roper and her friend Eva Gore-Booth, secretary of the Manchester Women's Trade Council, played an important part in the final phase of the suffrage movement.

Miss Roper and Miss Gore-Booth insisted that the working woman needed the vote as a weapon of self-defence, just as much as did the working man. This argument had gained a new force because of the movement for men's labour representation in Parliament which developed into the Labour Party. Women's labour representation was even more needful, urged Miss Roper and Miss Gore-Booth, because of the terribly low wages of working women.

I joined their respective committees and fought many a battle by their side, with a view to getting woman suffrage recognised as a question of urgent practical importance from the industrial point of view. This was a stage in my political apprenticeship of great and lasting value, and I owed much to the example and sympathy of these two friends. I had been reared in the suffrage cause and the principle of equality had been lived out in our home. In fact, it was the sharp contrast between practical suffragism in the home circle and the inequality I saw meted out to women in general in the outer world that made me see in the suffrage cause one, not of merely academic interest, but of stern practical importance.

Here, then, was an aim in life for me—the liberation of politically fettered womanhood.

One decision I came to firmly; it was that this vote question must be settled. Mine was the third generation of women to claim the vote and the vote must now be obtained. To go on helplessly pleading was undignified. Strong and urgent demand was needed. Success must be hastened or women's last political state would be worse than their first.

SYLVIA PANKHURST: That summer the building the I.L.P. had erected in memory of Dr. Pankhurst at Hightown in Salford was completed. I was invited to decorate the lecture hall, and gladly entered upon the task.

Whilst I was working on the decorations at the Pankhurst Hall, a part of the building was already in use. I learnt, with astonishment, that women were not permitted to join that branch of the I.L.P. The reason given was that a social club, open to men who were not members of the I.L.P., but closed to all women, was attached to the branch. The excuses made for this state of affairs were worse than the fact itself, and aroused so much indignation in my family that they proved the last straw which caused Mrs. Pankhurst to decide on the formation of a new organisation of women.

DEEDS, NOT WORDS

EMMELINE PANKHURST: All these years my daughters had been growing up. All their lives they had been interested in women's suffrage. Christabel and Sylvia, as little girls, had cried to be taken to meetings. They had helped in our drawing-room meetings in every way that children can help. As they grew older we used to talk together about the suffrage, and I was sometimes rather frightened by their youthful confidence in the prospect, which they considered certain, of the success of the movement. One day Christabel startled me with the remark: "How long you women have been trying for the vote. For my part, I mean to get it."

Was there, I reflected, any difference between trying for the vote and getting it? There is an old French proverb, "If youth could know; if age could do." It occurred to me that if the older suffrage workers could in some way join hands with the young, unwearied, and resourceful suffragists, the movement might wake up to new life and new possibilities. After that I and my daughters together sought a way to bring about that union of young and old which would find new methods, blaze new trails. At length we thought we had found a way.

It was on October 10, 1903, that I invited a number of women to my house in Nelson Street, Manchester, for purposes of organisation. We voted to call our new society the Women's Social and Political Union, partly to emphasise its democracy, and partly to define its object as political rather than propagandist. We resolved to limit our membership exclusively to women, to keep ourselves absolutely free from any party affiliation, and to be satisfied with nothing but action on our question. "Deeds, not Words" was to be our permanent motto.

Now, the old suffragists had long since given up hope of obtaining a Government suffrage bill, but they clung to a hope that a private Member's bill would sometime obtain consideration. Every year, on the opening day of Parliament, the association sent a deputation of women to the House of Commons, to meet so-called friendly Members and consider the position of the women's suffrage cause. The ceremony was of a most conventional, not to say farcical character. The ladies made their speeches and the Members made theirs. The ladies thanked the friendly Members for their sympathy, and the Members renewed their assurances that they believed in women's suffrage and would vote for it when they had an opportunity to do so. Then the deputation, a trifle sad but entirely tranquil, took its departure, and the Members resumed the real business of life, which was support of their parties' policies.

Such a ceremony as this I attended soon after the founding of the W.S.P.U. Sir Charles M'Laren was the friendly Member who presided over the gathering, and he did his full duty in the matter of formally endorsing the cause of women's suffrage. He assured the delegation of his deep regret, as well as the regret of numbers of his colleagues, that women so intelligent, so devoted, etc., should remain unenfranchised. Other Members did likewise. The ceremonies drew to a close, but I, who had not been asked to speak, determined to add something to the occasion.

"Sir Charles M'Laren," I began abruptly, "has told us that numbers of his colleagues desire the success of the women's suffrage cause. Now every one of us knows that at this moment the Members of the House of Commons are balloting for a place in the debates. Will Sir Charles M'Laren tell us if any Member is preparing to introduce a bill for women's suffrage? Will he tell us what he and the other Members will pledge themselves to *do* for the reform they so warmly endorse?"

Of course, the embarrassed Sir Charles was not prepared to tell us anything of the kind, and the deputation departed in confusion and wrath. I was told that I was an interloper, an impertinent intruder. Who asked me to say anything? And what right had I to step in and ruin the good impression they had made? No one could tell how many friendly Members I had alienated by my unfortunate remarks.

I went back to Manchester and with renewed energy continued the work of organising for the W.S.P.U.

In the spring of 1904 I went to the annual conference of the Independent Labour Party, determined if possible to induce the Members to prepare a suffrage bill to be laid before Parliament in the approaching session. Although I was a member of the National Administrative Council and presumably a person holding some influence in the party, I knew that my plan would be bitterly opposed by a strong minority, who held that the Labour Party should direct all its efforts toward securing universal adult suffrage for both men and women.

After considerable discussion, the National Council decided to adopt the original Women's Enfranchisement Bill, drafted by Dr. Pankhurst, and advanced in 1870 to its second reading in the House of Commons. The Council's decision was approved by an overwhelming majority of the conference.

The new session of Parliament, so eagerly looked forward to, met on February 13, 1905. I went down from Manchester, and with my daughter Sylvia, then a student at the Royal College of Art, South Kensington, spent eight days in the Strangers' Lobby of the House of Commons, working for the suffrage bill. We interviewed every one of the Members who had pledged himself to support a suffrage bill when it should be introduced, but we found not one single Member who would agree that his chance in the ballot, if he drew such a chance, should be given to introducing the bill. Every man had some other measure he was anxious to further. Mr. Keir Hardie had previously given us his pledge, but his name, as we had feared, was not drawn in the ballot. We next set out to interview all the men whose names had been drawn, and we finally induced Mr. Bamford Slack, who held the fourteenth place, to introduce our bill. The fourteenth place was not a good one, but it served, and the second reading of our bill was set down for Friday, May 12, the second order of the day.

This being the first suffrage bill in eight years, a thrill of excitement animated not only our ranks but all the old suffrage societies. Meetings were held, and a large number of petitions circulated. When the day came for consideration of our bill, the Strangers' Lobby could not hold the enormous gathering of women of all classes, rich and poor, who flocked to the House of Commons. It was pitiful to see the look of hope and joy that shone on the faces of many of these women.

The bill that occupied the first order of the day was one providing that carts travelling along public roads at night should carry a light behind as well as before. We had tried to induce the promoters of this unimportant little measure to withdraw it in the interests of our bill, but they refused. We had tried also to persuade the Conservative Government to

Sylvia Pankhurst in her studio

Annie Kenney

Schmidt   26. Victoria St.
                       Manchester.

give our bill facilities for full discussion, but they also refused. So, as we fully anticipated, the promoters of the Roadway Lighting Bill were allowed to "talk out" our bill.* They did this by spinning out the debate with silly stories and foolish jokes. The Members listened to the insulting performance with laughter and applause.

When news of what was happening reached the women who waited in the Strangers' Lobby, a feeling of wild excitement and indignation took possession of the throng. Seeing their temper, I felt that the moment had come for a demonstration such as no old-fashioned suffragist had ever attempted. I called upon the women to follow me outside for a meeting of protest against the Government. We swarmed out into the open, and Mrs. Wolstenholme-Elmy, one of the oldest suffrage workers in England, began to speak. Instantly the police rushed into the crowd of women, pushing them about and ordering them to disperse. We moved on as far as the great statue of Richard Coeur de Lion that guards the entrance to the House of Lords, but again the police intervened. Finally the police agreed to let us hold a meeting in Broad Sanctuary, very near the gates of Westminster Abbey. Here we made speeches and adopted a resolution condemning the Government's action in allowing a small minority to talk out our bill. This was the first militant act of the W.S.P.U. It caused comment and even some alarm, but the police contented themselves with taking our names.

CHRISTABEL PANKHURST: W.S.P.U. business was done at weekly meetings and all present subscribed what they could to the funds. Mother supplied the rest of the money needed. Militancy was not part of the programme in those early days. Our work was still entirely peaceful and educational, being designed to prove to the public women's need of the vote and to rouse women to insist that the political parties, including the new Labour Party, should take practical and speedy action in our cause.

Heavy work it was to travel hither and thither, to Lancashire, and Cheshire, and the West Riding of Yorkshire, watching occasion, and taking it, to bring woman suffrage to the fore, at public meetings, at trade union gatherings, at lecture and debating societies, in parks and fair grounds, and at street corners. "Won't you speak on some *other* subject than the vote?" would be the appeal, but the answer was always adamantly: No. We did not speak for speaking's sake. If we could not have a say on the great and vital cause, then we would rather stay comfortably at home.

The Oldham Trades Council asked me to address a meeting, and as my subject was the vote, women were to be present. When I had spoken, three eager, vividly intelligent girls, with shining eyes, came up to me. They were Annie Kenney and her sisters.

ANNIE KENNEY: I heard Miss Pankhurst and Miss Billington speak. Miss Pankhurst was more hesitating, more nervous than Miss Billington. She impressed me, though. She was most impersonal and full of zeal. Miss Billington used a sledge-hammer of logic and cold reason—she gave me the impression that she was a good debater. I liked Christabel Pankhurst: I was afraid of Theresa Billington.

Before I knew what I had done I had promised to work up a meeting for Miss Pankhurst among the factory women of Oldham and Lees. I walked to the station with her, and before we separated she had asked me to spend the following Saturday afternoon with them at their home in Nelson Street, Manchester.

The following week I lived on air; I simply could not eat; I wanted to be quiet and

---

* In order for a vote to be taken on a private Member's bill it is necessary for a minimum of two hours' debating to take place. In this case the suffrage bill was the second bill of the day; the Members of Parliament by extending the debate on the Roadway Lighting Bill ensured that the suffrage bill was automatically disqualified through insufficient debating time remaining and therefore successfully "talked it out."

alone. I did not feel elated or excited. A sense of deep stillness took possession of me. It was as though half of me was present; where the other half was I never asked. For the first time in my life I experienced real loneliness. I instinctively felt that a great change had come.

When Saturday arrived I was a little excited. I rushed home, changed my clothes, fled to the station, and later found myself at the door at Nelson Street.

I was shown into a large drawing-room, very artistically furnished, and Christabel introduced me to her mother. Mrs. Pankhurst had the gift of putting you at your ease immediately. I liked her, but all the time I was drawn to Christabel. She sat very quietly in a corner. She had a way of looking vacant, as though she were thousands of miles away, but I discovered later that all the time she was making indelible mental notes about me that were never erased.

We discussed the forthcoming meeting in Oldham, fixed the date, and Christabel drafted the handbill. I had decided to ask the choirmaster to let the choir sing as an attraction. When everything was settled it was getting late, and I had a long way to go to my home, so I departed.

The night of the meeting arrived. I had persuaded a sister to take the chair for Miss Pankhurst, but my future leader insisted on my promising to say a few words. It was a stroke of good fortune that the choir turned up, as they were the only audience we had to address, save Alice Hurst and another friend! There was no living interest in the question.

This meeting made the link stronger between Christabel and myself. Every Saturday I found myself at Nelson Street, and one day I was surprised to hear that they had arranged a meeting at Tib Street, at which I had to speak. Tib Street is just off Market Street, famous for its Labour and unemployed meetings.

I pleaded for exemption, but it was not granted, and I found myself at about seven o'clock at night, mounted on a temporary platform, addressing the crowd. What I said I do not remember. I suppose I touched on Labour, the unemployed, children, and finally summed up the whole thing by saying something about Votes for Women. This was my first public speech.

Both my mother and my father were Lancashire people. My birthplace was in Lancashire, in a small cottage in the village of Springhead. The village is in a valley surrounded by the Pennine Hills. I was Mother's fifth child and appeared on the scene on a September day, the thirteenth of the month, in 1879. I was in a hurry, as the correct month was November. I suffered for this rash act, as I was a weakling, wrapped in cotton-wool, for about a year. I was once told that the lesson I had to learn in life was patience. If that is true, I can only say I began life very badly indeed!

I went to the village school when I was five. My younger sister took me, as she was much older in wisdom and common sense than I. She must have been four years of age. She had always a keen sense of responsibility, and was conscientious in all her actions—I was just the opposite.

When I was ten years of age a change came into my life. My mother announced to me that I was to work in a factory. I was to join the army of half-timers; to work in the factory half the day and attend school the other half.

I received the news with mixed feelings. I was glad to escape the hated school lessons, which were a burden to me, but I had a fear of the new life. I felt a little proud, and it was a change.

When I was thirteen I left school. My education was finished, my school knowledge was nil. I could not do arithmetic; I was a bad writer; geography was Greek to me; the

Sir Edward Grey

only thing I liked was poetry. I discovered that anything I really liked I could learn without effort; it just came.

I then joined the great masses whose lives were spent spinning and weaving cotton. I was a full-timer. I rose at five o'clock in the morning. I had to be in the factory just before six, and I left at five-thirty at night.

Summer 1905

EMMELINE PANKHURST: In Lancashire there is an institution known as the Wakes, a sort of travelling fair where they have merry-go-rounds, Aunt-Sallies, and other festive games, side-shows of various kinds, and booths where all kinds of things are sold. Every little village has its Wakes-week during the summer and autumn, and it is the custom for the inhabitants of the villages to spend the Sunday before the opening of the Wakes walking among the booths in anticipation of to-morrow's joys. On these occasions the Salvation Army, temperance orators, venders of quack medicines, pedlars, and others, take advantage of the ready-made audience to advance their propaganda. At Annie Kenney's suggestion we went from one village to the other, following the Wakes and making suffrage speeches. We soon rivalled in popularity the Salvation Army, and even the tooth-drawers and patent-medicine pedlars.

The Women's Social and Political Union had been in existence two years before any opportunity was presented for work on a national scale. The autumn of 1905 brought a political situation which seemed to us to promise bright hopes for women's enfranchisement. The life of the old Parliament, dominated for nearly twenty years by the Conservative Party, was drawing to an end, and the country was on the eve of a general election in which the Liberals hoped to be returned to power.

October 13, 1905

Now, repeated experiences had taught us that the only way to attain women's suffrage was to commit a Government to it. In other words, pledges of support from candidates were plainly useless. They were not worth having. The only object worth trying for was pledges from responsible leaders that the new Government would make women's suffrage a part of the official programme. We determined to address ourselves to those men who were likely to be in the Liberal Cabinet, demanding to know whether their reforms were going to include justice to women. We laid our plans to begin this work at a great meeting to be held in Free Trade Hall, Manchester, with Sir Edward Grey as the principal speaker.

Annie Kenney and my daughter Christabel were charged with the mission of questioning Sir Edward Grey.

VOTES FOR WOMEN

CHRISTABEL PANKHURST: Good seats were secured for the Free Trade Hall meeting. The question was painted on a banner in large letters, in case it should not be made clear enough by vocal utterance. How should we word it? "Will you give women suffrage?"—we rejected that form, for the word "suffrage" suggested to some unlettered or jesting folk the idea of suffering. "Let them suffer away!"—we had heard the taunt. We must find another wording and we did! It was so obvious and yet, strange to say, quite new. Our banner bore this terse device: WILL YOU GIVE VOTES FOR WOMEN? Thus was uttered for the first time the famous and victorious battle-cry: "Votes for Women!"

Busy with white calico, black furniture stain and paint-brushes, we soon had our banner ready, and Annie Kenney and I set forth to victory, in the form of an affirmative Liberal answer, or to prison. We knew only too well that the answer we longed for would be refused. "We shall sleep in prison tonight," said I to Mother. Her face was drawn and cold when I said goodbye. Our action was really hers. She accepted the responsibility of a militant policy, which she knew must be continued until victory. She considered, as we two young ones who went into the fray that night naturally did not quite so deeply consider, its effect upon our own lives. She realised that her official post, with its present emoluments and future pension, was at stake; she foresaw a day, which later arrived, when she would have to choose between surrendering that position and giving up the militant campaign which she believed politically necessary for the enfranchisement of women. It was for Mother an hour of crisis. She stood utterly alone in the world, so far as this decision to militancy was concerned. Reckoning the cost in advance, Mother prepared to pay for it, for women's sake. The loss might be all hers, but the gain would be theirs.

The Free Trade Hall was crowded. The sky was clear for a Liberal victory—save for a little cloud no bigger than a woman's hand! Calm, but with beating hearts, Annie and I looked at the exultant throng we must soon anger by our challenge. Their cheers as the speakers entered gave us the note and pitch of their emotion. Speech followed speech.

Annie as the working woman—for this should make the stronger appeal to Liberals—rose first and asked: "Will the Liberal Government give votes to women?" No answer came. I joined my voice to hers and our banner was unfurled, making clear what was our question. The effect was explosive! The meeting was aflame with excitement. Some consultation among chairman and speakers ensued and then the Chief Constable of Manchester, Sir Robert Peacock, genial and paternal in manner, made his way to us and promised us, on behalf of the platform, an answer to our question after the vote of thanks had been made. We accepted the undertaking and again we waited. We gave him our question in writing. The vote of thanks was carried. Sir Edward Grey rose to reply without one word in answer to our question! The bargain thus broken on his side, we were free to renew our simple question: "Will the Liberal Government give votes to women?"

Violence answered our demand for justice. Yet better violence than jeers, sneers, or silent contempt. Equality was ours that night, we felt, for the force used against us proved that our question was a thrust which had touched the new Government-to-be in a vital spot. The meeting was in frenzy.

Outside the auditorium and behind the scenes, we were in the grip of policemen and surrounded by stewards. The matter must not, I knew, stay where it was. What we had done must be made a decisive act of lasting import. We must, in fact, bring the matter into Court, into prison. For simply disturbing the meeting I should not be imprisoned. I must use the infallible means of getting arrested, I must "assault the police." But how was I to do it? The police seemed to be skilled to frustrate my purpose. I could not strike them, my arms were being held. I could not even stamp on their toes—they seemed able to prevent that. Yet I must bring myself under arrest. The vote depended upon it. There could be no compromise at that moment of crisis. Lectures on the law flashed to my mind. I could, even with all limbs helpless, commit a technical assault and so I found myself arrested and charged with "spitting at a policeman." It was not a real spit but only, shall we call it, a "pout," a perfectly dry purse of the mouth. At the police station they sent us home without bail, adjuring us to appear next morning at the police court. Next morning we found that the long, long newspaper silence as to woman suffrage was broken. [*Christabel Pankhurst was sentenced to one week's imprisonment and Annie Kenney to three days.*]

"To Prison We Went"

ANNIE KENNEY: I remember very little of my life in prison. Being my first visit to gaol, the newness of the life numbed me. I do remember the plank bed, the skilly, the prison clothes. I also remember going to church and sitting next to Christabel, who looked very coy and pretty in her prison cap. She took my hand tenderly and just held it, as though I were a lost child being guided home. She guessed my feelings of strangeness, and no doubt I looked lonely and troubled.

I scarcely ate anything all the time I was in prison, and Christabel told me later that she was glad when she saw the back of me, it worried her to see me looking pale and vacant.

None of my family had the faintest idea I was in prison until they read the news in the papers. Two of my sisters paid me a visit, and asked if they might pay the fine and give me my release—it was thoughtful of them not to pay it before asking me. I said No, our policy being "Prison, or Votes for Women," and at the moment I felt I might be in prison all my life.

The day of my release was a happy and exciting day for me. Members of the choir were waiting to welcome me, two of my girl friends from the factory, two sisters, and many strangers. A telegram had come from the overlooker at the factory during my absence, demanding my immediate return, but I of course had been in prison when it arrived.

Mrs. Pankhurst greeted me by saying, "Annie, as long as I have a home you must look upon it as yours. You will never have to return to factory life."

MANCHESTER EVENING CHRONICLE
Friday, October 20, 1905

MISS PANKHURST'S RELEASE FROM STRANGEWAYS
PRISON GATE DEMONSTRATION
MOTHER AND DAUGHTER IN TEARS

When the great gates of Strangeways Gaol swung back and the prison had disgorged its fair prisoner, Miss Christabel Pankhurst, soon after daybreak this morning, the curtain was rung down on another act of a drama, the last of which will be presented at the Free Trade Hall, with Mr. J. Keir Hardie in the chief part, this evening.

In "Women's Rights" two heroines were introduced, Miss Christabel Pankhurst and Miss Annie Kenney, and the ladies here ran for a week the gauntlet of public criticism with mixed results.

It will be remembered that the ladies plied the Liberal leaders with questions having reference to the Parliamentary franchise for women, and that as a result of a refusal of Sir Edward Grey and the Chairman of the meeting to be drawn a disturbance was created, and the women were ejected, and later arrested for obstruction outside the building.

At the police court Miss Pankhurst was fined half a guinea for assaulting the police officers by hitting them in the mouth and spitting in their faces, and five shillings for obstruction, or in default seven days. Miss Kenney was fined five shillings, or three days.

Rather than pay the fine the ladies elected to undergo the imprisonment and Miss Kenney was released on Monday morning. During the week-end an effort was made by Mr. Winston Churchill, M.P., and others to purchase the prisoners' freedom, but it failed.

Miss Pankhurst's period expired this morning, and at an early hour the precincts of the prison presented an animated appearance.

She has of late gained considerable notoriety by her enthusiastic advocacy on the platform of women's rights, and friends came from near and far with floral bouquets ready to present to the ex-prisoner on her release.

By seven o'clock about two hundred people had collected, a large number of whom were females. Amongst those present were Dr. and Mrs. Garrett, Mr. and Mrs. John Harker, Mr. J. Bramley, Mr. and Mrs. Drummond, Mrs. Mitchell (Ashton-under-Lyne), Mrs. Morrisey (Salford), Miss Gore-Booth, Miss Billington, Miss Annie Kenney, Mrs. King May, and Miss Bowton, of the Women's Trades and Labour Council.

The officials of the prison seemed curiously amused at the numerous friends of their charge.

EXIT THE HEROINE
At five minutes past seven the ponderous gates were opened, and slowly there emerged in the half light a procession of fallen sisters, with their shawls drawn tightly over their heads, one hugging a baby. As they were eyed by the waiting crowd the coverings were drawn closer round their pale pinched faces, and they slunk out of sight as quickly as their legs would carry them, no doubt glad enough to be free.

In another minute the people's patience had its reward when Miss Christabel, with light step and smiling face, appeared from the gloomy portals. She was hailed with a great cheer and instantly surrounded by a host of male and female admirers, who must have embarrassed the maid by their greeting.

First to greet and embrace the fair prisoner was her mother, Mrs. Pankhurst. It was an affecting scene. Miss Pankhurst fell into the arms of her mother, and the two wept with joy after having been parted for a whole week. The ex-prisoner's friends then closed round her, and presented her with beautiful bunches of chrysanthemums and lilies of the valley. As soon as she could break away from her admirers Miss Pankhurst called out, "I will go in again for the same cause. Don't forget the vote for women." Mrs. Pankhurst asked the people not to forget the principle for which her daughter had suffered. They must press forward and never rest, especially the women, until the vote had been secured.

The party then boarded a cab and drove away amidst the cheers of the crowd.

RESOLUTIONS OF SYMPATHY

This morning's post brought shoals of congratulations and sympathy, and Miss Pankhurst found upon arrival at her home in Nelson Street, where a hot breakfast was prepared and a number of friends ready to receive her, scores of unopened letters.

One of the first letters to be read was from the Nelson Co-operative Women's Guild, enclosing a strongly worded protest against the conduct shown toward Miss Pankhurst and Miss Kenney by the Liberal leaders and the authorities. It condemned the action of Sir Edward Grey.

Mr. Herbert Burrows (London) wrote heartily congratulating the women on the stand they had taken and on their pluck and determination. "This is a time when all women should stand shoulder to shoulder for the great principle. I wish I could be with you at the great meeting to-night."

Mrs. Pankhurst also received a congratulatory and sympathetic message from one of the foremost lawyers in Scotland.

MISS PANKHURST INTERVIEWED

Over breakfast our "Evening Chronicle" representative had a short chat with Miss Pankhurst.

"I have not, as you see, had time to go through my correspondence, or to read the adverse criticism," she went on.

"With regard to my imprisonment. Well, I really haven't anything much to say. Prison is not a bed of roses," said Miss Pankhurst, laughingly, "and I have just had the ordinary treatment meted out to me. Anyhow, I don't want to make much of that. Say, 'I've been in prison,' and that my health has been fairly good under the circumstances.

"I have been doing the ordinary prison work, serving, scrubbing, and cell-cleaning, but mind you say that I don't complain in the least.

"A visiting justice came to see me on Monday and tried to persuade me to allow my fine to be paid. That is all the communication I have had with the outside world during the week.

"With regard to the defence of my position, I shall have something to say about it at the meeting this evening," continued Miss Pankhurst. "The magistrates did not treat me fairly. I was not allowed to refer to the meeting in the hall or the conduct of the officials, although Mr. Bell, who prosecuted for the police, made a great deal of the proceedings inside the building."

Miss Pankhurst was naturally very pleased to be at liberty, and once more amongst her friends. She thinks that after this evening's demonstration another complexion will be put on the unfortunate conflict with the authorities. Her last words were, "Don't forget to say that I am a more ardent and enthusiastic supporter of the franchise for women than I was before—if possible."

"JUST LIKE THE LIBERALS"

Miss Pankhurst is simply burning with indignation at the conduct of the Liberal officials. "Why," she asks, "if we were disorderly in the meeting, did not the police charge us for that offence? As a matter of fact, we were bundled out into the street before the officers were set upon us, and this allowed the Liberals to wipe their hands of us which, of course, they were anxious to do." And then she added as an afterthought, "It is just like the Liberals.

"We just want to know from the Liberal Party, yea, or nay, as to whether it is their intention to give women the vote if they are returned to office. If it would get us the vote I should be ready to go to prison again at any time."

Christabel Pankhurst and Annie Kenney

CHRISTABEL PANKHURST: Mother, then, and home, and all the news! Not an echo from the outside world had penetrated the prison walls and we knew nothing of how things had turned out. Mother had had the brunt of it to bear—being in prison was easy and peaceful, compared to what she had to bear. Anger, criticism, had run high. We had known that must happen. Mother and I had together faced it, before we took the fateful step of forcing the Liberal leaders to fight or give votes to women.

We had certainly broken the Press silence on votes for women, that silence which, by keeping women uninformed, had so largely smothered and strangled the movement. The newspaper silence had, at the same time, protected politicians from criticism of their offences, omissive and commissive, against the suffrage cause.

Mother's heroine's heart was needed in those first critical hours. It is not so easy now to realise the position in which she then stood. A widow, with still dependent children, risking (and eventually losing) her income and future pension in the Government service, Mother had stood firm against a world. From the blow she thus struck with her own hand at her position and fortune, there might have been no recovery, especially in those days. She faced the risk and took it—for women's sake.

December 21, 1905

EMMELINE PANKHURST: We determined that from that time on the little "Votes for Women" banners should appear wherever a prospective member of the Liberal Government rose to speak, and that there should be no more peace until the women's question was answered. We clearly perceived that the new Government, calling themselves Liberal, were reactionary so far as women were concerned, that they were hostile to women's suffrage, and would have to be fought until they were conquered, or else driven from office.

On December 21 a great meeting was held in Royal Albert Hall, London, where Sir Henry Campbell-Bannerman, surrounded by his Cabinet, made his first utterance as Prime Minister. Previous to the meeting we wrote to Sir Henry and asked him, in the name of the Women's Social and Political Union, whether the Liberal Government would give women the vote. We added that our representatives would be present at the meeting, and we hoped that the Prime Minister would publicly answer the question. Otherwise we should be obliged publicly to protest against his silence.

Of course Sir Henry Campbell-Bannerman returned no reply, nor did his speech contain any allusion to women's suffrage. So, at the conclusion, Annie Kenney, whom we had smuggled into the hall in disguise, whipped out her little white calico banner, and called out in her clear, sweet voice: "Will the Liberal Government give women the vote?"

At the same moment Theresa Billington let drop from a seat directly above the platform a huge banner with the words: "Will the Liberal Government give justice to working women?" Just for a moment there was a gasping silence, the people waiting to see what the Cabinet Ministers would do. They did nothing. Then in the midst of uproar and conflicting shouts, the women were seized and flung out of the hall.

This was the beginning of a campaign the like of which was never known in England, or, for that matter, in any other country. If we had been strong enough we should have opposed the election of every Liberal candidate, but being limited both in funds and in members we concentrated on one member of the Government, Mr. Winston Churchill.

We attended every meeting addressed by Mr. Churchill. We heckled him unmercifully; we spoiled his best points by flinging back such obvious retorts that the crowds roared with laughter. We lifted our little white banners from unexpected corners of the hall, exactly at the moment when an interruption was least desired. Sometimes our banners were torn from our hands and trodden under foot. Sometimes, again, the crowds were with us, and we actually broke up the meeting. We did not succeed in defeating Mr. Churchill, but he was returned by a very small majority, the smallest of any of the Manchester Liberal candidates.

We Carry the Fight to London

January 1906

EMMELINE PANKHURST: We decided that the next step must be to carry the fight to London, and Annie Kenney was chosen to be organiser there. With only two pounds [*less than five dollars*] in her pocket the intrepid girl set forth on her mission.

ANNIE KENNEY: I packed my little wicker basket, put the two pounds safely in my purse—it was the only money I possessed—and started my journey to London. When I had paid my fare I had one pound and a few shillings change.

On my arrival in London I was met by Miss Sylvia Pankhurst, who was the only representative the new movement had in London. We went to her rooms, which were also to be my future home for many weeks. It was a small house, 45 Park Walk, Chelsea.

The following night she took me to speak at a meeting which was attended by the very poorest women in Canning Town. The Labour men had lent them the room. Sylvia and I told them all the wonderful things that would happen to them once women got the vote. Poverty would be practically swept away; washing would be done by municipal machinery! In fact, Paradise would be there once the vote was won! I honestly believed every word I said. I had yet to learn that Nature's works are very slow but very sure. Experience is indeed the best though the sternest teacher. Poor East End women, we gave them something to dream about, and a hope in the future, however distant that future might be.

SYLVIA PANKHURST: My life was changed. It became a matter of course to write Annie's letters and convey her hither and thither, introducing her as the mill girl who had gone to prison for a vote. I had been so horribly nervous when I went to sell my designs, but as soon as it was a question of agitating for a cause, my nervousness was gone. When all the letters were done, and I took up a book for a brief half-hour's delight before going to bed, she would sit at my feet and demand to be read to, and particularly that I should pick out favourite little snatches of verse for her to learn; from Tennyson: "A flock of sheep that leisurely pass by"; from Shelley: "Rarely, rarely comest thou, Spirit of Delight!" Parts of his "To a Skylark," or of Keats's "Ode to a Nightingale."

She had come without instructions; what should she do to rouse London? It was easy for me to decide that we should follow all the other popular movements by holding a meeting in Trafalgar Square, and a procession of the East London women in the unemployed movement at the opening of Parliament. I sent her to notify the police. She met me in the evening with the news that the Square was not available that day. I went at once to Keir Hardie for advice. He told us to engage the Caxton Hall for our meeting, and promised to induce a friend to pay for the hall and the handbills to advertise it.

Annie Kenney now spent most of her time in the East End. We formed a London Committee of the W.S.P.U., consisting of ourselves, my aunt, Mary Clarke, and the landlady, Mrs. Roe.

When Mrs. Pankhurst came up to London, and found we had taken a hall holding seven hundred people, and announced a procession, she was angered by my temerity, and declared the whole thing would be a ridiculous fiasco. Yet since the affair had been advertised, there could be no drawing back, and her optimism soon made the best of it. Just then Flora Drummond turned up from Manchester, having begged her fare from friendly I.L.P. members there. Here was another lively pair of legs to run hither and thither, chalking the pavements and delivering handbills. She borrowed a typewriter from the Oliver Company, and thus imparted a business-like appearance to our correspondence. She too was packed in at Park Cottage, and Mrs. Martel, who now got in touch with us, was also accommodated. The Press began to hover around the house; the *Daily Mail* had already christened us the "Suffragettes."

February 19, 1906

EMMELINE PANKHURST: How we worked, distributing handbills, chalking announcements of the meeting on pavements, calling on every person we knew and on a great many more we knew only by name, canvassing from door to door!

At length the opening day of Parliament arrived, and on that day occurred the first suffrage procession in London. I think there were between three and four hundred women in that procession, poor working women from the East End, for the most part, leading the way in which numberless women of every rank were afterward to follow. My eyes were misty with tears as I saw them, standing in line, holding the simple banners which my daughter Sylvia had decorated, waiting for the word of command. Of course our procession attracted a large crowd of intensely amused spectators. The police, however, made no attempt to disperse our ranks, but merely ordered us to furl our banners. There was no reason why we should not have carried banners but the fact that we were women, and therefore could be bullied. So, bannerless, the procession entered Caxton Hall. To my amazement it was filled with women, most of whom I had never seen at any suffrage gathering before.

Our meeting was most enthusiastic, and while Annie Kenney was speaking, to frequent applause, the news came to me that the King's Speech (which is not the King's at all, but the formally announced Government programme for the session) had been read, and that there was in it no mention of the women's suffrage question. As Annie took her seat I arose and made this announcement, and I moved a resolution that the meeting should at once proceed to the House of Commons to urge the Members to introduce a suffrage measure. The resolution was carried, and we rushed out in a body and hurried toward the Strangers' Entrance. It was pouring rain and bitterly cold, yet no one turned back, even when we learned at the entrance that for the first time in memory the doors of the House of Commons were barred to women. We sent in our cards to members who were personal friends, and some of them came out and urged our admittance. The police, however, were obdurate. They had their orders. The Liberal Government, advocates of the people's rights, had given orders that women should no longer set foot in their stronghold.

Pressure from Members proved too great, and the Government relented to the extent of allowing twenty women at a time to enter the lobby. Through all the rain and cold those hundreds of women waited for hours their turn to enter. Some never got in, and for those of us who did there was small satisfaction. Not a member could be persuaded to take up our cause.

Out of the disappointment and dejection of that experience I yet reaped a richer harvest of happiness than I had ever known before. Those women had followed me to the House of Commons. They had defied the police. They were awake at last. They were prepared to do something that women had never done before—fight for themselves. Women had always fought for men, and for their children. Now they were ready to fight for their own human rights. Our militant movement was established.

February 1906

EMMELINE PETHICK-LAWRENCE: Mrs. Pankhurst called on me at this time, because Keir Hardie had told her that in me she would find a practical and useful colleague who could develop in London the new society which she had founded in Manchester—the Women's Social and Political Union. She went back to Sylvia disappointed. "She will not help, she has so many interests." Then Annie Kenney was sent to me by Keir Hardie.

She burst in upon me one day in her rather breathless way and threw all my barriers down. I might have been a life-long friend by the complete trust in me that she showed and by the conviction that she expressed that the only thing needed to bring the movement to complete and speedy success in London was my co-operation.

There was something about Annie that touched my heart. She was very simple and she seemed to have a whole-hearted faith in the goodness of everybody that she met. She told me her version of what had happened at Sir Edward Grey's meeting in the Free Trade Hall, for it was she, with Christabel Pankhurst, who had made the scene which had shocked and horrified the conventional world. She went on to tell me that because Christabel could do nothing further for the suffrage movement until she had obtained the LL.B. degree, Annie herself felt that she must leave Manchester and come to rouse London, as she herself expressed it. The education authorities of Owens College had threatened to expel Christabel after her prison experience and had finally made it an absolute condition that she should take no part in political action until after she had completed her period of studentship.

"How do you want me to help you, Annie?" I asked. "Mr. Keir Hardie told me to ask you to be our national treasurer," said Annie, speaking as if by rote. "Your treasurer!" I exclaimed. "What funds have you?" "That is just the trouble," said Annie, simply. "I have spent the money already and I have had to go into debt. I do not understand money, it worries me; that is why I have come to you for your help. You need not decide at once," she went on hastily, no doubt seeing my lack of enthusiasm for the job. "We have a committee at Park Walk to-morrow, and you will meet Sylvia Pankhurst, the honorary secretary, and the others, and will hear a lot more about it then. You will come, won't you?" I gave my promise because I could not repulse her wistful eagerness.

It was by a very extraordinary sequence of incidents that I, who am not of a revolutionary temperament, was drawn into a revolutionary movement like the Women's Social and Political Union. The first thing that drew me to it was the story of the imprisonment of the two girls who had raised the suffrage issue at the memorable meeting in Manchester. Then I was touched by the appeal of Annie Kenney and made the promise to go to this pathetic little committee that talked so bravely of their plan to rouse London but seemed so helpless.

March 1906

SYLVIA PANKHURST: We now felt that our next move must be to secure an interview with the Prime Minister, and we therefore wrote to Sir Henry Campbell-Bannerman asking him to receive a deputation from our Union. He replied that he could not spare the time to see us. Our answer was that, owing to the urgency of the question, we could take no refusal, and that a number of our members would call upon him at the official residence, No. 10 Downing Street, on the morning of March 2.

On presenting themselves at the door of the official residence, the deputation from the Women's Social and Political Union were told that Sir Henry Campbell-Bannerman could receive no one, as he had been ill and was still confined to his room.

We therefore decided that another attempt must be made to interview him, and after waiting until he had made a complete recovery and was again able to take his part in the House of Commons debates, a larger deputation, consisting of several members of our committee and some thirty other women, made their way to Downing Street about ten o'clock on the morning of March 9. They again asked to see the Prime Minister and the doorkeeper promised to give their message to the secretary. After they had been waiting for three quarters of an hour two men came out and said to them, "You had better be off; you must not stand on this doorstep any longer." The women explained that they were waiting for a reply but were abruptly told that there was no answer and the door was rudely shut in their faces.

Angered by this, Miss Irene Miller immediately seized the knocker and rapped sharply at the door. Then the two men appeared again and one of them called to a policeman on the other side of the road, "Take this woman in charge." The order was at once obeyed, and Miss Miller was marched away to Cannon Row police station. Spurred on by this event Mrs. Drummond, exclaiming that nothing should prevent her from seeing the Prime Minister, darted forward and pulled at the little brass knob in the middle of the door. As she did so, she discovered that the little knob, instead of being a bell, as she had imagined, was something very different indeed, for suddenly the door opened wide. Without more ado she rushed in and headed straight for the Cabinet Council Chamber, but before she could get there she was caught, thrown out of the house, and then taken in custody to the police station. Meanwhile Annie Kenney began to address the gathering crowd, but the man who had first called the policeman again looked out and said, "Why don't you arrest that woman? She is one of the ring-leaders. Take her in charge." Then she was dragged away to join her companions.

The three women were detained at Cannon Row for about an hour. Then a police inspector told them that a message to set them at liberty had been sent by the Prime Minister, who wished them to be informed that he would receive a deputation from the Women's Social and Political Union, either individually or in conjunction with other women's societies. Of course we published Sir Henry Campbell-Bannerman's promise. Shortly afterward, two hundred Members of Parliament, drawn from every party, petitioned Sir Henry to fix an early date for receiving some of their number in order that they might urge upon him the necessity for an immediate extension of the franchise to women. He then formally announced that on May 19 he would receive a joint deputation both from Members of Parliament representing the signatories to this petition and all the organised bodies of women in the country who were desirous of obtaining the suffrage.

WOMEN WHO WANT a VOTE ARRESTED

"Divide! Divide!"

April 25, 1906

SYLVIA PANKHURST: Meanwhile Mr. Keir Hardie had secured a place for a Women's Suffrage Resolution, which was to be discussed in the House of Commons on this evening. Though a resolution is only an expression of opinion and can have no practical legislative effect, this was considered important because it was realised that if the new Parliament were to show a substantial majority in its support, the women's claim that the Government should deal with the question would be greatly strengthened.

Looking down through the brass grille, from behind which women are alone permitted to listen to the debates in Parliament, we saw that the House was crowded as is usual only at important crises, and that both the Government and Opposition front benches were fully occupied. The Resolution, "That in the opinion of this House it is desirable that sex should cease to be a bar to the exercise of the Parliamentary franchise," was moved and seconded in short speeches in order that the opponents should have no least excuse for urging that there had been no time for their own side to be fairly heard. Then Mr. Cremer rose to speak in opposition. His speech was grossly insulting to women and altogether unworthy of a Member of the People's House of Representatives. Both by his words, his voice and gestures he plainly showed his entire view of women to be degraded and indeed revolting.

Above: Flora Drummond and Annie Kenney arrested by the police outside the Prime Minister's residence, March 9, 1906

**REPORT OF THE SPEECH BY THE RT. HON. WILLIAM RANDALL CREMER, M.P.
FOR SHOREDITCH, HAGGERSTON
House of Commons Debates, Vol. 155, Series 4**

"He had always contended that if once they opened the door and enfranchised ever so small a number of females, they could not possibly close it, and that it ultimately meant adult suffrage.

"The government of the country would therefore be handed over to a majority who would not be men, but women. Women are creatures of impulse and emotion and did not decide questions on the ground of reason as men did.

"He was sometimes described as a woman-hater, but he had had two wives, and he thought that was the best answer he could give to those who called him a woman-hater. He was too fond of them to drag them into the political arena and to ask them to undertake responsibilities, duties and obligations which they did not understand and did not care for.

"What did one find when one got into the company of women and talked politics? They were soon asked to stop talking silly politics, and yet that was the type of people to whom hon. Members were invited to hand over the destinies of the country.

"It was not only because he thought that women were unfitted by their physical nature to exercise political power, but because he believed that the majority of them did not want it and would vote against it, that he asked the House to pause before they took the step suggested by the hon. Member for Merthyr Tydfil. He believed that if women were enfranchised the end could be disastrous to all political Parties. He therefore asked the House to pause before it took a step from which it never could retreat."

SYLVIA PANKHURST: Willie Redmond, brother of John Redmond, the leader of the Irish Party, then indignantly protested against the tone of Mr. Cremer's speech, crying fervently that he himself had always believed in women's suffrage because, all his life, he had been opposed to slavery in any form, and declaring that "any of God's creatures who are denied a voice in the Government of their country are more or less slaves," and that "men have no right to assume that they are so superior to women, that they alone have the right to govern."

All through the debate everyone was waiting for a declaration from the Government. At last Mr. Herbert Gladstone, the Home Secretary, rose to speak, but his words were vague and evasive, and whilst not absolutely excluding the possibility of the Government's taking the matter up, he certainly made no promise on their behalf.

At ten minutes to eleven Mr. Samuel Evans rose with the obvious intention of talking the Resolution out and, as eleven o'clock, the hour for closing the debate, drew nearer, whilst spinning out his remarks by means of some very doubtful jokes, he kept turning round, every now and then, to look at the clock. Our eyes were also eagerly fixed upon the timepiece. Every moment one woman or another stretched across and asked Mrs. Pankhurst whether the demonstration of protest should begin, but her answer was always that there was "time yet," and that we must wait.

At last someone looked round and saw that the police were already in the gallery and we realised that we were to be taken away in order that the Resolution might be talked out without our having an opportunity to protest. Irene Miller could no longer be restrained. She called out loudly, "Divide! Divide!" as they do in the House of Commons, and "We refuse to have our Resolution talked out." Then we all followed suit, and Theresa Billington thrust a little white flag bearing the words "Votes for Women" through the historic grille. It was a relief to thus give vent to the feelings of indignation which we had been obliged to stifle during the whole of the evening, and though we were dragged roughly out of the gallery, it was with a feeling almost of triumph that we cried shame upon the men who had wasted hours in useless talk and pitiful and pointless jokes.

"WE ARE NOT SATISFIED!"

EMMELINE PETHICK-LAWRENCE: A successful little procession accompanied our deputation to the Prime Minister, including a body of women textile workers who came from Lancashire and Cheshire, and a group of working women from the East End. Annie Kenney was attired on this occasion as a Lancashire mill girl, her hair in a plait on her back, her head covered with a shawl, clogs instead of shoes on her feet. One of the most touching figures in the procession was old Mrs. Wolstenholme-Elmy, who had worked all her life in the old suffrage movement. She must have been pretty as a young woman, for although very fragile and weak, her complexion was still lovely and she had little grey curls that framed her pink and white face. She was so tiny and so tottery that it seemed as if a breath of wind would blow her away, but she insisted on walking in the procession and was as keen and as eager as the youngest. Mrs. Pankhurst was the speaker for our deputation, and beside her walked Keir Hardie. We marched to the Foreign Office, where we all assembled.

Sir Charles M'Laren introduced the deputation. He arranged that there should be eight speakers, and the first was to be Miss Emily Davies, LL.B., one of the two women who in 1866 had handed John Stuart Mill the first petition for woman suffrage ever presented to Parliament. Mrs. Pankhurst had come from Manchester and was told that she would be the final speaker for the deputation. Over 260,000 women were represented—Suffragists, Co-operators, Temperance Workers, Textile Workers, Liberals, Socialists. A petition was also presented by 1,530 women university graduates. The large room was crowded—the atmosphere was tense.

The Prime Minister listened to the eight speakers with attention. Then he rose to reply. He made a long speech in which he expressed his approval of our demand, his belief that if granted it would benefit the whole country. But though he spoke as a supporter, he struck a dismal note at the end and said that as his Cabinet was opposed, it would never do to make any pledge. Keir Hardie, in a gracious little speech of thanks to the Prime Minister, made it quite clear that women could not be expected to accept his statement as final. He alluded to a favourable statement made recently by Mr. Balfour* of his personal support of our demand, and said that with the leaders of both parties in agreement and with so many members eager to support them, "it could not be beyond the wit of statesmanship" to find ways and means for the enfranchisement of women before the present Parliament came to a close. At this suggestion the Prime Minister sadly and solemnly shook his head. After the resolution of thanks had been seconded, Mrs. Wolstenholme-Elmy, who had not been placed on the list of speakers, rose, and in a small, quavering voice spoke of her many years of work, and protested against further delay. Although she could not be heard very well, her age and her record won the silent and attentive respect of all, including the Prime Minister himself. It was a touching little scene. Sir Henry did not strengthen his statement in his reply to the vote of thanks but advised us to "go on converting the country." When he had finished, Annie Kenney sprang a surprise. Jumping up on her seat and standing so that she could be seen by all, she cried to the Prime Minister: "Sir, we are not satisfied! The agitation will go on."

SYLVIA PANKHURST: Then we dispersed to meet again at three o'clock in Trafalgar Square.

On this ground, consecrate to the discontented and the oppressed, under that tall column topped by the statue of the fighting Nelson and on that wide plinth, flanked by the four crouching lions, the first big open-air women's suffrage meeting in London was held. By three o'clock more than seven thousand people had assembled. I well remember every detail of the scene. In my mind's eye I can clearly see the Chairman, my mother, with her pale face, her quiet dark clothes, her manner, calm as it always is on great occasions, and her quiet-sounding but far-reaching voice with its plaintive minor chords. I can see beside her the strangely diverse group of speakers: Theresa Billington in her bright-blue dress, strongly built and up-standing, her bare head crowned with those brown coils of wonderfully abundant hair. I see Keir Hardie, in his rough brown homespun jacket, with his deep-set, honest eyes, and his face full of human kindness, framed by the halo of his silver hair. Then Mrs. Wolstenholme-Elmy, fragile, delicate, and wonderfully sweet, with her face looking like a tiny bit of finely modelled, finely tinted porcelain, her shining dark-brown eyes and her long grey curls. Standing very close to her is Annie Kenney, whose soft bright hair falls loosely from her vivid, sensitive face, and hangs down her back in a

---

* Arthur James Balfour, first Earl of Balfour (1848–1930), was at this time Unionist leader of the opposition in the Commons, having served as Prime Minister, 1902–1905.

Annie Kenney and Mrs. Wolstenholme-Elmy

long plait, just as she wore it in the cotton mill. Over her head she wears a grey shawl as she did in Lancashire, and pinned to her white blouse is a brilliant red rosette, showing her to be one of the marshals of the procession, whilst her dark-blue serge skirt just shows the steel tips of her clogs. How beautiful they are, these two women, as hand clasped in hand they stand before us!—one rich in the mellow sweetness of a ripe old age which crowns a life of long toil for the common good; the other filled with the ardour of a chivalrous youth; both dedicated to a great reform. But now, Annie Kenney speaks. She stands out, a striking, almost startling, figure, against the blackened stone-work of the plinth and speaks with a voice that cries out for the lost childhood, blighted hopes and weary, over-burdened lives of the women workers whom she knows so well.

May 21, 1906: Daily Mirror

MRS. WOLSTENHOLME-ELMY: When you have enthusiasm for a great cause you know you have discovered eternal youth. I have been fighting for this cause half my life, and yet I am as enthusiastic as when I started. Of course, I feel disappointed today. We all feel disappointed, for the Prime Minister's words showed that he had little real sympathy with our movement. I sometimes wonder whether we are not as far off as we were forty years ago. I shall go on fighting still. Even an old woman can do something when she is in earnest.

June 19, 1906

EMMELINE PETHICK-LAWRENCE: We had been explicitly informed by the Prime Minister that the obstacle to our demand for the vote was the hostility of members of the Cabinet, so we began to consider what means could be taken, other than the practice of heckling them when they came before the public, to induce them to change their mind. As Mr. Asquith, the Chancellor of the Exchequer, was the most notorious opponent, we considered that he ought to receive our attention. We had discovered that in an autograph book Mr. Asquith had recorded that his favourite maxim was "Taxation and Representation must go together." Yet he showed no reluctance to tax women, who were the unrepresented half of the people.

The Rt. Hon. Herbert Henry Asquith

We wrote to Mr. Asquith asking him to receive a deputation from our Society. He replied that it was his rule to refuse all deputations not directly connected with his office as Chancellor. This reply gave an excellent opportunity for a reasoned letter making it quite clear that we considered that voteless women had a more direct and logical claim on the Chancellor, who was immediately responsible for taxing them, than upon any other member of the Government. To this letter the Chancellor made no reply. The secretary therefore wrote again to say that a small deputation would call on him at his house at 20 Cavendish Square to enlarge on the point. The appointment was named at ten o'clock on Tuesday, June 19.

When the deputation called shortly before ten o'clock, he had escaped. So far the plan had gone much as we expected. But another deputation visited him two days later, and this time it was a larger one. Part of it came from the East End of London. About thirty working women marched in procession to Cavendish Square, where they were met by a strong body of police who told them to go back. Full of the traditional fear of "the policeman," these women trembled but stood their ground. The police began to push and threaten and in the end to rain blows upon the defenceless little crowd. Miss Billington protested and was taken into custody. Annie Kenney put out her hand to ring the bell of No. 20 but her arm was seized and she was arrested. An elderly working woman, Mrs. Sparborough, who supported her aged husband and herself by needlework, saw some ladies laughing, and protested: "Don't do that," she said, "this is a serious matter." She was pounced upon and arrested. So was also another working woman who was lame—Mrs. Knight.

All the charges against these three broke down in court except that of being in Cavendish Square with intent to see Mr. Asquith. But the magistrate demanded that they should bind themselves to keep the peace for twelve months. Upon refusal to enter into this bond he declared that the alternative was six weeks in prison. To prison they went.

June 30, 1906

On the last day of the month, Christabel Pankhurst took her LL.B. degree with first-class honours.* She had already taken the prize for International Law. In July she came to London and became at once political secretary of the Women's Social and Political Union. She stayed with us in our flat at Clement's Inn, and the visit lasted for five years. My husband and I became aware of the "flair" for political affairs which was Christabel's unique and special gift at this time. She was, as her mother said, "a born politician"—not, of course, in the superficial sense, but in her instinctive insight into the heart of a political problem, and

* At Owens College, Manchester.

Christabel Pankhurst

in the certainty and conviction that resulted from that insight: so that she could never be deflected by any reasoning, however specious, from the line of policy that in her judgment was the right one. It was astonishing to come in contact with a mind politically mature in a girl so simple and unpretentious. It was Christabel who had been the first to originate and carry out the first line of militant action—that of the determined questioning of Cabinet Ministers whenever they appeared on the public platforms; she had been obliged to leave Annie Kenney to carry into effect the second line of action, that of attempting to interview the Prime Minister by standing on the doorstep of his private residence—a line of action which developed subsequently in the attempt of deputations to enter the House of Commons. Now that she was the political secretary of the W.S.P.U. she thought out the third line of militant action—the active intervention of the militants at all by-elections in opposition to Government candidates, irrespective of what their personal declared views of woman suffrage might be.

It is impossible to realise the almost universal disapproval that met the declaration of this line of action. Many of our own members were opposed to it. True to her practice of leading the way before calling on others to follow, Christabel, on learning that there was to be a by-election at Cockermouth, went off herself alone to initiate her policy. From the outset she made it quite clear that she was entering the field purely to attack the Liberal candidate as a representative of the existing Government, obdurate in their refusal to give votes to women, and she emphasised the fact that she did not care whether the electors voted Tory or Labour, so long as they kept the Liberal out. Imagine the consternation and anger of the Labour Party that one who for years had been a member of the Independent Labour Party should take this line! It was a great shock! As for the Liberals, they were furious that we should make no distinction between friend and foe. I doubt if at that time they could have understood Christabel's ruthless logic, even if they had been less personally involved. In brief, it amounted to this: "We have had 'life-long' supporters of women's enfranchisement in the House of Commons for forty years. They have done nothing to advance our cause. Now we see that they are helpless to do anything. They must obey the Government whip. They are only political counters in the party game. Why waste energy in differentiating between these counters—personal supporters or non-supporters—they are all alike, counters that will be used to uphold the Government which resists our just demand."

Sylvia Pankhurst returned to her studies at the Royal College of Art and resigned her position on the W.S.P.U. committee. Mrs. Edith How-Martyn, a science graduate of London University, and Mrs. Despard were appointed jointly to the committee to replace her.

The Sinews of War
Autumn 1906

CHRISTABEL PANKHURST: We were now installed in the office at Clement's Inn, which for the next six years was to be our stronghold. Adjacent to Fleet Street, it was highly convenient for the newspapers, which were ever interested in the militant movement.

Never lose your temper with the Press or the public is a major rule of political life. We never made that mistake. We liked the public, we even liked the Press. At any rate the journalists who interviewed us or reported our meetings seemed to us to be quite sympathetic and we suspected that their copy was touched up in newspaper offices by those who had no first-hand knowledge of the movement, and that they themselves were perhaps under instruction "not to encourage it." Yet even exaggerated and distorted reports, which made us seem more terrible than we really were, told the world this much—that we wanted the vote and were resolved to get it.

The sinews of war were coming in. Our honorary treasurer was unrivalled in her rare courage to ask others to give, as well as to give herself, and our campaign fund mounted phenomenally. This was financial militancy, which to the very last the Government, even by the threat to proceed against our individual subscribers, could not defeat. The contributors to the W.S.P.U. funds included most of the surviving suffrage pioneers of the earliest days. Some of the very richest women in the country were also among the contributors. Yet the W.S.P.U. workers themselves received very little. None were paid, apart from the clerical staff, unless they were taking definite organising responsibility. Speakers were not paid and there was no pay for militant action. No one, therefore, was in the movement for personal advantage. The funds were mainly spent on rent and the other expenses of the campaign, printing and the like. Not the least generous of our subscribers were in fact our organisers, who cheerfully and self-regardlessly received so little money and gave so great service.

Parliament reassembled in the autumn of 1906. The militants were there to make to the Prime Minister their demand for the vote. Received instead by his spokesman, they were given a negative reply, and on making speeches of protest they were ejected from the building and several—Mrs. Pethick-Lawrence, Mrs. How-Martyn, Annie Kenney, Theresa

Above: A meeting of the W.S.P.U. in Emmeline Pethick-Lawrence's apartment, Clement's Inn, London: (left to right) Christabel Pankhurst, Jessie Kenney, Mrs. Martel, Emmeline Pankhurst, and Mrs. Despard

Billington, Mary Gawthorpe, Sylvia, Adela, and last, but far from least, Mrs. Cobden-Sanderson—were sent to prison. The daughter of Richard Cobden* imprisoned by a Liberal Government! This was the strongest evidence of their real illiberalism. Had other women of Liberal name and fame followed the fine example of Cobden's daughter, the Government could have been driven to surrender.

October 1906

SYLVIA PANKHURST: On October 23, Parliament re-assembled for the autumn session. A large number of our women made their way to the House of Commons on that day, but the Government had again given orders that only twenty women at a time were to be allowed in the Lobby. All women of the working class were rigorously excluded. My mother and Mrs. Pethick-Lawrence were among those who succeeded in gaining an entrance. They at once sent in for the Chief Liberal Whip and requested him to ask the Prime Minister, on their behalf, whether he proposed to do anything to enfranchise the women of the country during the session, either by including the registration of qualified women in the provisions of the Plural Voting Bill then before the House, or by any other means. The Liberal Whip soon returned with a refusal from the Government to hold out the very faintest hope that the vote would be given women at any time during their term of office.

On hearing this, Mrs. Pankhurst and Mrs. Pethick-Lawrence returned to their comrades and consulted with them. The women had received a direct rebuff, and they felt that they must now act in such a way as to prove that the Suffragettes would no longer quietly submit to this perpetual ignoring of their claims. They therefore decided to hold a meeting of protest, not outside in the street, but just there, in the Lobby of the House of Commons. Mary Gawthorpe mounted one of the settees close to the statue of Sir Stafford Northcote and began to address the crowd of visitors who were waiting to interview various Members of Parliament. The other women closed up around her, but in the twinkling of an eye dozens of policemen sprang forward, tore the tiny creature from her post and swiftly rushed her out of the Lobby. Instantly Mrs. Despard stepped into the breach; but she also was roughly dragged away. Then followed Mrs. Cobden-Sanderson and many others, but each in her turn was thrust outside and the order was given to clear the Lobby. Mrs. Pankhurst was thrown to the ground in the outer entrance hall and many of the women, thinking that she was seriously hurt, closed round her refusing to leave her side. Crowds were now collecting in the roadway, and the women who had been flung out of the House attempted to address them but were hurled away.

Meanwhile, some of the poor women who had marched from the East End and who had been denied admission to the Lobby were resting their tired limbs on the stone benches in the long entrance hall, and after Mrs. Cobden-Sanderson had made her attempt to speak and had been hustled away, she seated herself quietly beside these women and began to talk with them. Shortly afterward a young policeman came up and abruptly ordered her away and, as she did not go, he seized her and dragged her to the police station.

The next morning the women were brought up at Rochester Row police court before Mr. Horace Smith.

He said that each of the ten defendants must enter into her own recognisances to keep the peace for six months and must find a surety for her good behaviour in £10, and that

* Richard Cobden (1804–1865), politician, was the chief public spokesman for the repeal of the Corn Laws, which taxed imported grain and raised the domestic price of food in England. Between 1839 and 1846 he became a prominent figure in British politics, devoting most of his energies to the repeal of the Corn Laws, which he maintained were both economically disastrous and morally wrong. He entered Parliament in 1841, and was one of the revered founders of the modern Liberal party.

if she failed to do this, she must go to prison for two months in the second division.* The women at once protested against this mockery of a trial, and raising a banner bearing the words "Women should vote for the laws they obey and the taxes they pay" declared that they would not leave the dock until they had been allowed the right to which all prisoners were entitled, namely that of making a statement in their own defence. But Mr. Horace Smith cared nothing for the justice of what they said; he merely called the police and the women were forcibly removed.

The police court authorities now announced to those of us who were waiting in the witness room that the case was over and that our friends had been taken to Holloway. I can scarcely express our feelings of indignation. It seemed, indeed, terrible that ten upright, earnest women should have been thus hustled off to prison, without a word from their friends, after a trial lasting less than half an hour.

Some protesting, others filled with silent consternation, the women turned to go, but I, myself, felt that I could not leave without a single word of rebuke to those who had conducted the proceedings against us so shamefully. I therefore returned to the door of the inner court and asked to be admitted. "It is all over," said the doorkeepers, "there is nothing to interest you now," but I walked quickly past them and entered the court. It was quite a small room; one could easily make oneself heard without raising one's voice, and as shortly as I could, I told the magistrate how women had been refused admittance whilst the trial was in progress, and how some who had actually taken their seats had been tricked into leaving. I pointed out to him that as it was customary to allow the general public, and especially friends of the prisoners, to be present in court, it was grossly unfair to refuse to do so in this case, and likely to destroy confidence in the justice of the trial. I was explaining that even the women who had wished to testify as voluntary witnesses had been kept out of the court, when the magistrate interrupted me saying, "There is no truth in any of your statements. The court was crowded."

I was then seized by two policemen, dragged across the outer lobby and flung into the street. Here a great mass of people had assembled and I felt that I ought not to go away without telling them something of the cause for which we were fighting and of the very scanty justice which had been doled out to our women. I tried to speak to them, though I had been rendered almost breathless by the violent manner of my ejection, and only to those who were near me could I make myself heard. In a moment, I hardly knew how or why, I was again seized by the policeman and dragged back into the court house. Soon afterward I found myself in the dock before Mr. Horace Smith, and was charged with causing an obstruction and with the use of violent and abusive language. I protested against the latter half of the charge and it was immediately withdrawn. At greater length than on the first occasion, I was then able to describe all that had happened within the precincts of the court. Many of our friends and members, on hearing that all was not over, had returned and from amongst them I called as witnesses to the truth of my statement Mrs. Cobden-Unwin, Mrs. Cobden-Sickert, and a number of other ladies, but their testimony was ignored and I was found guilty and sentenced either to pay a fine of £1 or to undergo fourteen days' imprisonment in the third and lowest class. Of course I chose the latter alternative, and was taken to join my comrades in the cells.

The following day we were removed to the cells which we were to occupy during the remainder of our imprisonment. Many of the ordinary cells are exactly like the reception cells, but the cell into which I was now put was smaller, but better lit than the reception

---

* Imprisonment within the first division denoted political prisoner status and carried certain privileges. Imprisonment in the second and third divisions was normally reserved for the criminal class, and inmates were treated with much greater severity and required to perform menial work or even hard labour.

cell, for it had a larger window and there was a small electric light bulb attached to the wall instead of the recessed gas jet. Hanging on a nail in the wall was a large round badge made of yellow cloth bearing a number of the cell and the letter and the number of its block in the prison. I was told to attach this badge to a button on my bodice, and henceforth, like the other prisoners, I was called by number of my cell, which happened to be twelve.

Suppose yourself to be one of the third-class prisoners. Like them you will follow the same routine. Each morning whilst it is still quite dark you will be awakened by the tramp of heavy feet and the ringing of bells; then the light is turned on. You wash in the tiny basin and dress hurriedly. Soon you hear the rattle of keys and the noise of iron doors. The sound comes nearer and nearer until it reaches your own door. The wardress flings it open and orders sharply, "Empty your slops, twelve!" You hasten to do so, and return at the word of command.

Then, just as you have been shown, you roll your bed. The first sheet is folded in four, then spread out on the floor, and rolled up from one end, tightly like a sausage. The second sheet is rolled round it, and round this, one by one, the blankets and quilt. You must be careful to do this very neatly or you are certain to be reprimanded.

Next clean your tins. You have three pieces of rag with which to do this. Two of them are frayed scraps of brown serge, like your dress, and the other is a piece of white calico. These rags were probably not new and fresh when you came here, but had been well used by previous occupants of the cell. Folded up in these rags you will find a piece of bath-brick. You have been told to rub this bath-brick on the stone floor until you have scoured off a quantity of its dust. Then you take one of the brown rags and soap this on the yellow cake which you use for your own face. Then with the soapy rag you rub over one of the tins, and this done, dip the rag into the brick dust which is lying on the floor and rub it onto the soapy tin. Then you rub it again with the second brown rag and polish with the white calico one that remains. You must be sure to make all the tins very bright.

Presently the door opens and shuts again. Someone has left you a pail of water; with it you must scrub the stool, bed, and table, and wash the shelves. Then scrub the floor. All this ought to be done before breakfast, but unless you are already experienced in such matters it will take you very much longer.

Before you have done your task there comes again the jangling of keys and clanging of iron doors. Then, "Where's your pint, twelve?" You hand it out, spread your little cloth, and set your plate ready. Your pint pot is filled with gruel (oatmeal and water without any seasoning), and six ounces of bread are thrust upon your plate. Then the door closes. Now eat your breakfast, and then, if your cleaning is done, begin to sew. Perhaps it is a sheet you have to do. Of these, with hem top and bottom and mid seam, the minimum quantity which you must finish, as you will learn from your "Labour Card," is fifteen per week.

At half-past eight it is time for chapel. The officer watches you take your place in line among the other women. They all wear numbered badges like yours, and are dressed as you are.

Every now and then the wardress cries out that someone is speaking, and as you march along there is a running fire of criticism and rebuke. "Tie up your cap string, twenty-seven. You look like a cinder-picker. You must learn to dress decently here." "Hold up your head, number thirty." "Hurry up, twenty-three." In the chapel it is your turn. "Don't look about you, twelve." In comes the clergyman. He reads the lessons and all sing and pray together.

Can they really be criminals, all these poor sad-faced women? How soft their hearts are. How easily they are moved. If there is a word in the services which touches the experience of their lives, they are in tears at once. Anything about children, home, affection,

Emmeline and Frederick Pethick-Lawrence outside the law courts

a word of pity for the sinner, or of striving to do better—any of these things they feel deeply. Singing and the sound of the organ make them cry. Many of them are old, with shrunken cheeks and scant white hair. Few seem young. All are anxious and careworn. They are broken down by poverty, sorrow, and overwork. Think of them going back to sit, each in her lonely cell, to brood for hours on the causes which brought her here, wondering what is happening to those she loves outside, tortured, perhaps, by the thought that she is needed there. How can these women bear the slow-going, lonely hours?

October 24, 1906: Holloway Prison

EMMELINE PETHICK-LAWRENCE: I was, as a reaction from unusual excitement, terribly depressed. It seemed to me that I was in my grave, forgotten by the world. I passed another sleepless night, and the next day one of the officials probably reported to the doctor, and he must have 'phoned my husband and told him that I was seriously ill, for he and my father came at once, armed with a message from Mrs. Pankhurst that she wished me to give the undertaking, which would automatically release me at once, not to engage in militant action for six months. I was taken to the Governor's private room, where they awaited me. I felt too near the edge of a nervous collapse to refuse. I left the prison with them, and the next day my husband took me to Italy and left me with friends there while he returned at once to London, for in the few days that had elapsed since the demonstration in Parliament, he had taken my place as treasurer and was obliged to cope with a mass of business.

My imprisonment was the incident that brought him finally to devote all his manifold powers to a cause which needed the help that a trained mind like his could give. Every demonstration that ended with arrest and imprisonment made enormous demands upon him in addition to the normal business of the day. He was the person with whom the police were glad to deal, especially later when the numbers of arrested persons sometimes ran into hundreds. Since there was no adequate accommodation in the police court, bail had to be found for every one and suitable arrangements made for their attendance the next morning. The news had to be broken to the families of those concerned, and if anxious and bewildered relatives suddenly turned up next day, he had to answer enquiries and make what arrangements he could to satisfy them. This was not all. Volunteers, many of them from the provinces, had never been inside a police court and had no notion of what was expected from them: he undertook the task of seeing them one by one and instructing them how to deal with their defence.

But for my husband to take on my specific work at a time when he was subjected to acute personal anxiety on my account was a severe test. In the midst of it all he was called to speak at a hastily arranged protest meeting. Determined that the emotion of the gathering should not go to waste, when his turn came he said: "It is not a question of how much do you feel, but how much are you going to *do*? I am going to give ten pounds to the W.S.P.U. for every day of my wife's sentence, and I should like to know who will follow my example." Thereupon many promises were made and a large amount raised to provide more organisers for the campaign. The newspapers, always on the *qui vive* to guy the suffrage movement, seized upon this utterance to twist its meaning. They made a huge joke of it—the poor man was so glad to be free of his tiresome Suffragette wife that he was prepared to pay up ten pounds for every day that she was kept in prison!

Round the whole world went that joke, and I encountered it later in many a distant country. My mother said: "A pity Fred put it like that!" But I knew that it was an inspiration. Nothing could have served better the purpose that we had at heart, which was to get to all peoples the news that women in Britain were in revolt.

It became a tag: **Ten pounds a day**
He said he'd pay
To keep this face
In Holloway.

So read the placard that took the prize for the wearer at a Fancy Dress Ball in Covent Garden.

November 1906

SYLVIA PANKHURST: Amongst people of all parties, there was a growing feeling that the imprisoned Suffragettes should receive the treatment due to political offenders. The Liberals, large numbers of whom knew her personally, found an especial difficulty in reconciling themselves to the idea that Richard Cobden's daughter should be thrown into prison and treated by a Liberal Government as though she had been a drunkard or a pickpocket. Protests against the treatment of the Suffragettes daily became more and more insistent, and at last, on October 31, Mr. Gladstone changed his mind and ordered—or as he put it, "intimated his desire"—that the suffrage prisoners should be transferred to the first class.

On the eighth day of our imprisonment my cell door was flung open suddenly and the matron announced that an order had come from the Home Office to say that I was to be transferred to the first class. I was then hurriedly bustled out of my cell and a few minutes afterward as, in charge of a wardress, I was staggering along the passage carrying my brush and comb, the sheets that I was hemming, and all my bed linen, I met my comrades going in the same direction.

We were ushered into a row of rather dark cells adjoining each other in an old part of the prison which is chiefly occupied by prisoners on remand who have not yet been tried. On consulting the prison rules, however, I found that first-class misdemeanants are entitled to exercise their profession whilst in prison, if their doing so does not interfere with the ordinary prison regulations. I, therefore, applied to the Governor to be allowed to have pen, pencils, ink, and paper, and after a day's waiting my request was granted. For me prison had now lost the worst of its terrors because I had congenial work to do.

On November 6 my sentence came to an end, and the newspaper representatives were all eager to hear from me what the inside of Holloway was like. I was thus able to make known exactly what the conditions of imprisonment had been both before and after our transfer to the first division and to show that even under the new conditions, the treatment of the Suffragettes was very much more rigorous than that applied to men political prisoners in this and other countries.

Public sympathy was still daily turning more and more to the side of the Suffragettes and when a by-election became necessary at Huddersfield, Mr. Herbert Gladstone decided to release Mrs. Cobden-Sanderson and her colleagues, though they had served but half their sentences, and, on November 24, they were set free after one month's imprisonment. They were not only welcomed with enthusiasm by their fellow militant Suffragettes, but a dinner was given in their honour by Mrs. Fawcett and the older non-militant suffragists at the Savoy Hotel.

Believing that it was to the Huddersfield by-election that they owed their unexpected freedom, a number of the released prisoners at once hurried off to the constituency where Mrs. Pankhurst and a band of other women were strenuously working against the Government and had already become the most popular people in the election.

Though the train by which the prisoners arrived was more than two hours late, they were welcomed at the station by cheering crowds, and found that a great meeting of women, which had been called for the due time of their arrival, was still patiently waiting to hear them speak.

The three candidates, Liberal, Unionist, and Labour, were now, because of its extraordinary popularity, all anxious to be known as supporters of women's suffrage and they went about wearing the white Votes for Women buttons of the W.S.P.U. Mr. Sherwell, the Liberal, tried to sidetrack the Suffragettes' appeal to the electors to vote against him because he was the nominee of the Government by constantly announcing that he was in favour of women's suffrage, and that the Liberal Party was the best of all parties for women.

The following handbill issued from his committee rooms:

MEN OF HUDDERSFIELD, DON'T BE MISLED BY SOCIALISTS, SUFFRAGETTES, OR TORIES. VOTE FOR SHERWELL.

Polling took place on November 28, and when the votes were counted, it was found that the Liberal poll as recorded at the general election had been reduced by 540. The figures were:

Arthur Sherwell (Liberal)   **5,762**
T. R. Williams   (Labour)   **5,422**
J. Foster Fraser   (Unionist)   **4,844**

"RISE UP, WOMEN"

CHRISTABEL PANKHURST: The spirit of the movement was wonderful. It was joyous and grave at the same time. Self seemed to be laid down as the women joined us. Loyalty, that greatest of the virtues, was the keynote of the movement—first to the cause, then to those who were leading, and member to member. Courage came next, not simply physical courage, though so much of that was present, but still more the moral courage to endure ridicule and misunderstandings and harsh criticism and ostracism. There was a touch of the "impersonal" in the movement that made for its strength and dignity. Humour characterised it, too, in that our militant women were like the British soldier who knows how to joke and smile amid his fighting and trials.

If only the Liberal leaders had also been, like the Suffragettes, gifted with a sense of humour!

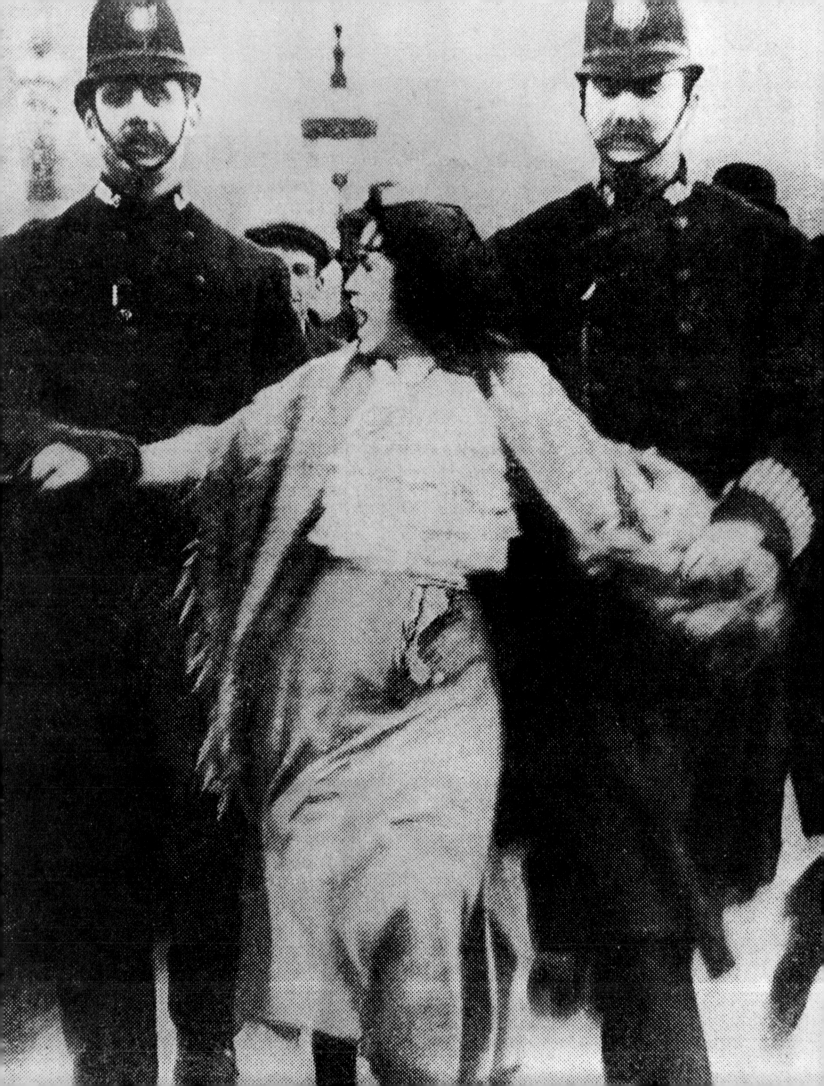

Jessie Kenney as she tried to gain admittance to Mr. Asquith's meeting on December 10, 1909,
disguised as a telegraph boy

CHRISTABEL PANKHURST: Campaigns in London were increasing our membership by enabling us to reach the women whose interest had been roused by the militant action of the past months. The weekly Hyde Park meetings near the Reformer's Tree were a great recruiting ground. It was a great thing to notice the faces in every audience and to enlist in our ranks the women of promise. There would be a light in the eye, a set of the mouth, and an expression of the face. "She is one of ours: she has the makings in her."

A great discovery was Mrs. Tuke, who for the longer part of the W.S.P.U.'s existence was honorary secretary. Mr. and Mrs. Pethick-Lawrence had met and greatly liked her on their homeward voyage from South Africa, whence she was returning after the death out there of her husband, a young army officer. Mrs. Pethick-Lawrence invited her to luncheon, I being also a guest. She came, still in mourning, gentle and beautiful, the last woman in the world, it might have been supposed, to join the militant movement. Yet when, after luncheon, I remarked: "I must go now and chalk pavements for a meeting," what did she say but "I'll come and chalk pavements too!" I knew, then, that she was of the right stuff and all the more as she did her chalking with such a will, and laughed when a rude errand boy called her youthful self "You old fool!" From that day onward she was one of us.

Clement's Inn, our headquarters, was a hive seething with activity. Mother and Mrs. Tuke had their honorary secretaries' office. Mrs. Pethick-Lawrence and her assistant, Mrs. Sanders, treasured the money in their offices. The large general office housed Miss Kerr and a battalion of secretaries and typists, with place for voluntary workers and a corner for tea. My own office adjoined it and next to this was Jessie Kenney's office, where, with the aid of Miss Hambling, plans for pestering Cabinet Ministers were laid and the most diversified measures were taken. Press-cuttings and reference books were housed beyond. General Flora Drummond's office was full of movement. As department was added to department, Clement's Inn seemed always to have one more room to offer. And so on, daily, weekly, monthly, yearly! All the time, watching, attacking, defending, moving, and counter-moving! It was indeed a question of "I shall not cease from mental fight." Yet how glorious those Suffragette days were! To lose the personal in a great impersonal is to live!

SYLVIA PANKHURST: Many women who had long felt that there was "something wrong" with the position of their sex, but had not realised that the possession of the Parliamentary franchise could do anything to remove the disabilities both of law and custom from which they suffered, were now being awakened by the much-talked-of militant tactics to a knowledge of what the vote could do for them. Moreover, many who for years had been nominal adherents of the suffrage movement, now began to feel that if some other women cared so passionately for the cause that they were prepared to throw aside all the usual conventions of good manners and to thrust themselves forward to meet ridicule, scandalous abuse, ill usage and imprisonment, it was surely time that they too should make sacrifices. But most of them as yet thought only of bolstering up and stirring to new activity the old National Union of Women's Suffrage Societies, for they still looked upon the militant women as a rather dreadful body of fanatics who could have no notion either of systematic organisation or the prudent laying-out of money. Therefore, on February 9, 1907, three days before the opening of Parliament, a crowd of the non-militants assembled close to the Achilles statue at Hyde Park Corner. It was a dismal wet Saturday afternoon, but in spite of the rain and the muddy streets a procession of women half a mile in length was formed and marched steadily on to attend meetings in Exeter Hall in the Strand and in Trafalgar Square. This procession was afterward known as the "Mud March."

First Women's Parliament

February 13, 1907

EMMELINE PANKHURST: The campaign of 1907 began with a Women's Parliament, called together in Caxton Hall, to consider the provisions of the King's Speech, which had been read in the national Parliament on the opening day of the session, February 12. The King's Speech, as I have explained, is the official programme for the session. When our Women's Parliament met at three o'clock on the afternoon of the thirteenth we knew that the Government meant to do nothing for women during the session ahead.

I presided over the women's meeting, which was marked with a fervency and a determination of spirit at that time altogether unprecedented. A resolution expressing indignation that woman suffrage should have been omitted from the King's Speech, and calling upon the House of Commons to give immediate facilities to such a measure, was moved and carried. A motion to send the resolution from the hall to the Prime Minister was also carried. The slogan "Rise up, women!" was cried from the platform, the answering shout coming back as from one woman, "Now!" With copies of the resolution in their hands, the chosen deputation* hurried forth into the February dusk, ready for Parliament or prison, as the fates decreed.

Suddenly a body of mounted police came riding up at a smart trot, and for the next five hours or more, a struggle, quite indescribable for brutality and ruthlessness, went on.

The horsemen rode directly into the procession, scattering the women right and left. But still the women would not turn back. Again and again they returned, only to fly again and again from the merciless hoofs. Some of the women left the streets for the pavements, but even there the horsemen pursued them, pressing them so close to walls and railings that they were obliged to retreat temporarily to avoid being crushed. Other strategists took refuge in doorways, but they were dragged out by the foot police and were thrown directly in front of the horses. Still the women fought to reach the House of Commons with their resolution. They fought until their clothes were torn, their bodies bruised, and the last ounce of their strength exhausted. Fifteen of them did actually fight their way through those

---

* A deputation (which usually comprised no more than thirteen individuals) was a device used by the women's suffrage movement to avoid breaking the English law that prohibited large assemblies within a one-mile radius of the Houses of Parliament. Many such deputations could thus approach Parliament without technically violating the law.

Above: W.S.P.U. meeting at Caxton Hall

hundreds on hundreds of police, foot and mounted, as far as the Strangers' Lobby of the House. Here they attempted to hold a meeting, and were arrested. Outside, many more women were taken into custody. It was ten o'clock before the last arrest was made, and the square cleared of the crowds. After that the mounted men continued to guard the approaches to the House of Commons until the House rose at midnight.

The next morning fifty-seven women and two men were arraigned, two and three at a time, in Westminster police court. Christabel Pankhurst was the first to be placed in the dock. She tried to explain to the magistrate that the deputation of the day before was a perfectly peaceful attempt to present a resolution, which, sooner or later, would be presented and acted upon. She assured him that the deputation was but the beginning of a campaign that would not cease until the Government yielded to the women's demand. "There can be no going back for us," she declared, "and more will happen if we do not get justice."

The magistrate, Mr. Curtis Bennett, who was destined later to try women for that "more," rebuked my daughter sternly, telling her that the Government had nothing to do with causing the disorders of the day before, that the women were entirely responsible for what had occurred, and finally, that these disgraceful scenes in the street must cease—just as King Canute told the ocean that it must roll out instead of in. "The scenes can be stopped in only one way," replied the prisoner. His sole reply to that was, "Twenty shillings or fourteen days." Christabel chose the prison sentence, and so did all the other prisoners. Mrs. Despard, who headed the deputation, and Sylvia Pankhurst, who was with her, were given three weeks in prison.

March 1907

EMMELINE PANKHURST: Of course the raid, as it was called, gave the Women's Social and Political Union an enormous amount of publicity, on the whole, favourable publicity. The newspapers were almost unanimous in condemning the Government for sending mounted troops out against unarmed women. Angry questions were asked in Parliament, and our ranks once more increased in size and ardour. The old-fashioned suffragists, men as well as women, cried out that we had alienated all our friends in Parliament; but this proved to be untrue. Indeed, it was found that a Liberal member, Mr. Dickinson, had won the first place in the ballot, and had announced that he intended to use it to introduce a women's suffrage bill. More than this, the Prime Minister, Sir Henry Campbell-Bannerman, promised to give the bill his support. For a time, a very short time, it is true, we felt that the hour of our freedom might be at hand, that our prisoners had perhaps already won us our precious symbol—the vote.

March 8, 1907

Soon, however, a number of professed suffragists in the House began to complain that Mr. Dickinson's bill, practically the original bill, was not "democratic" enough, that it would enfranchise only the women of the upper classes—to which, by the way, most of them belonged. That this was not true had been proved again and again from the municipal registers, which showed a majority of working women's names as qualified householders. The contention was but a shallow excuse, and we knew it. Therefore we were not surprised when Sir Henry Campbell-Bannerman departed from his pledge of support, and allowed the bill to be talked out.

Second Women's Parliament

March 20, 1907

EMMELINE PANKHURST: Twelve days later the second Women's Parliament assembled, in the afternoon. As before, we adopted a resolution calling upon the Government to introduce an official suffrage measure, and again we voted to send the resolution from the hall to the Prime Minister. Lady Harberton was chosen to lead the deputation, and instantly hundreds of women sprang up and volunteered to accompany her. This time the police met the women at the door of the hall, and another useless, disgraceful scene of barbarous, brute-force opposition took place. Something like one thousand police had been sent out to guard the House of Commons from the peaceful invasion of a few hundred women. All afternoon and evening we kept Caxton Hall open, the women returning every now and again, singly and in small groups, to have their bruises bathed, or their torn clothing repaired. As night fell the crowds in the street grew denser, and the struggle between the women and the police became more desperate. Lady Harberton, we heard, had succeeded in reaching the entrance to the House of Commons, nay, had actually managed to press past the sentries into the lobby, but her resolution had not been presented to the Prime Minister. She and many others were arrested before the police at last succeeded in clearing the streets, and the dreadful affair was over.

The next day, in Westminster police court, the magistrate meted out sentences varying from twenty shillings or fourteen days to forty shillings or one month's imprisonment.

Within these first months of the year 1907 the English Government sent to prison one hundred and thirty women whose "militancy" consisted merely of trying to carry a resolution from a hall to the Prime Minister in the House of Commons. Our crime was called obstructing the police. It will be seen that it was the police who did the obstructing.

It may be asked why neither of these deputations was led by me personally. The reason was that I was needed in another capacity, that of leader and supervisor of the suffrage forces in the field to defeat Government candidates at by-elections. On the night of the second "riot," while our women were still struggling in the streets, I left London for Hexham in Northumberland, where by our work the majority of the Liberal candidate was reduced by a thousand votes. Seven more by-elections followed in rapid succession.

Above: Annie Kenney leads a W.S.P.U. demonstration during a by-election campaign.

Our by-election work was such a new thing in English politics that we attracted an enormous amount of attention wherever we went.* It was our custom to begin work the very hour we entered a town. If, on our way from the station to the hotel, we encountered a group of men, say, in the market-place, we either stopped and held a meeting on the spot, or else we stayed long enough to tell them when and where our meetings were to be held, and to urge them to attend. The usual first step, after securing lodgings, was to hire a vacant shop, fill the windows with suffrage literature, and fling out our purple, green, and white flag.† Meanwhile, some of us were busy hiring the best available hall. If we got possession of the battle-ground before the men, we sometimes "cornered" all the good halls and left the candidate nothing but schoolhouses for his indoor meetings. Truth to tell, our meetings were so much more popular than theirs that we really needed the larger halls. Often, a candidate with the Suffragettes for rivals spoke to almost empty benches. The crowds were away listening to the women.

We met with some pretty rough horse-play, and even with some brutality, in several by-elections, but on the whole we found the men ready, and the women more than ready, to listen to us. We tamed and educated a public that had always been used to violence at elections.

After a summer spent in strengthening our forces, organising new branches, holding meetings—something like three thousand of these between May and October—invading meetings of Cabinet Ministers—we managed to do that about once every day—electioneering, and getting up huge demonstrations in various cities, we arrived at the end of the year.

* As a result of this policy the W.S.P.U. became a national organisation. In every part of England where they campaigned, a nucleus of local women would become active in the by-election campaign and form a W.S.P.U. branch.
† Emmeline Pethick-Lawrence selected colours to represent the W.S.P.U.—purple, white, and green. Purple represented justice, white purity, and green hope.

Mrs. Martel and Emmeline Pankhurst during a by-election campaign

In the last months of the year, I directed several hotly contested by-elections, at one of which I met with one of the most serious misadventures of my life.

This by-election was held in the division of Mid-Devon, a stronghold of Liberalism. In fact, since its creation in 1885, the seat has never been held by any except a Liberal Member. The constituency is a large one, divided into eight districts. The population of the towns is a rough and boisterous one, and its devotion, blind and unreasoning, to the Liberal Party has always reflected the rude spirit of the voters.

We held meetings twice a day, calling upon the voters to "beat the Government in Mid-Devon, as a message that women must have votes next year." Although some of the meetings were turbulent, we were treated with much more consideration than either of the candidates, who, not infrequently, were howled down and put to flight. Often the air of their meetings was thick with decayed vegetables and dirty snowballs. We had some rather lively sessions, too. Once, at an outdoor meeting, some young roughs dragged our lorry round and round until it seemed that we must be upset, and several times the language hurled at us from the crowd was quite unfit for me to repeat. Still, we escaped actual violence until the day of the election, when it was announced that the Unionist candidate had won the seat by a majority of 1,280. We knew instantly that the deepest resentment of the Liberals would be aroused, but it did not occur to us that the resentment would be directed actively against us.

After the declaration at the polls, my companion, Mrs. Martel, and I started to walk to our lodgings. Some of our friends stopped us, and drew our attention to the newly elected Unionist Member of Parliament, who was being escorted from the polling place by a strong guard of police. We were warned that our safety demanded an immediate flight from the town. I laughingly assured our friends that I was never afraid to trust myself in a crowd, and we walked on. Suddenly we were confronted by a crowd of young men and boys, clay-cutters from the pits on the edge of town. These young men, who wore the red rosettes of the Liberal Party, had just heard of their candidate's defeat, and they were mad with rage and humiliation. One of them pointed to us, crying: "They did it! Those women did it!" A yell went up from the crowd, and we were deluged with a shower of clay and rotten eggs. We were not especially frightened, but the eggs were unbearable, and to escape them we rushed into a little grocer's shop close at hand. The grocer's wife closed and bolted the door, but the poor grocer cried out that his place would be wrecked. I did not want that to happen, of course, so I asked them to let us out by the back door. They led us out the

Mrs. Martel and Emmeline Pankhurst leaving Newton Abbot
after they were attacked

door, into a small back yard which led into a little lane, whence we expected to make our escape. But when we reached the yard we found that the rowdies, anticipating our move, had surged round the corner, and were waiting for us.

They seized Mrs. Martel first, and began beating her over the head with their fists, but the brave wife of the shopkeeper, hearing the shouts and the oaths of the men, flung open the door and rushed to our rescue. Between us we managed to tear Mrs. Martel from her captors and get her into the house. I expected to get into the house, too, but as I reached the threshold a staggering blow fell on the back of my head, rough hands grasped the collar of my coat, and I was flung violently to the ground. Stunned, I must have lost consciousness for a moment, for my next sensation was of cold, wet mud seeping through my clothing. Sight returning to me, I perceived the men, silent now, but with a dreadful, lowering silence, closing in a ring around me. In the centre of the ring was an empty barrel, and the horrid thought occurred to me that they might intend putting me in it. A long time seemed to pass, while the ring of men slowly drew closer. I looked at them, in their drab clothes smeared with yellow pit-clay, and they appeared so underfed, so puny and sodden, that a poignant pity for them swept over me. "Poor souls," I thought, and then I said suddenly, "Are none of you *men?*" Then one of the youths darted toward me, and I knew that whatever was going to happen to me was about to begin.

At that very moment came shouts, and a rush of police who had fought their way through hostile crowds to rescue us. Of course the mob turned tail and fled, and I was carried gently into the shop, while the police guarded for two hours, before it was deemed safe for us to leave in a closed motor-car. It was many months before either Mrs. Martel or I recovered from our injuries.

September 1907

EMMELINE PETHICK-LAWRENCE: The Women's Social and Political Union when it was first formed had adopted a constitution framed on the lines of that of the Labour Party, to which the Pankhursts and all the original members in Manchester belonged.

The first national conference of delegates was due to take place this month, but some months before this date differences of thought and opinion had begun to manifest themselves amongst some of the members. The Union had grown very rapidly since the foundation of the London headquarters in 1906, and to cope with its demands organiser after organiser had been added to the staff. They were appointed because of their great courage and eloquence, and their ability to control and dominate crowds.

As September approached, it became evident that some influential people who had been attracted by the movement wished to frame a constitution that would substitute the principle of democratic control for that of individual leadership. It seemed to them reasonable and right that, following the practice of other organisations, the W.S.P.U. branches should be accorded the power to criticise and, if they could secure a majority, to amend the policies and the programme of the movement.

But there was another aspect of this question, an aspect acutely realised at headquarters. Newcomers were pouring into the Union. Many of them were quite ill-informed as far as the realities of the political situation were concerned. Christabel, who possessed in a high degree a flair for the intricacies of a complex political situation, had conceived the militant campaign as a whole. In her mind it drew its justifications from the frustrations of fifty years. These frustrations, she maintained, were not due to natural causes, but were directly due to the extremely adroit tactics of successive Governments that had enabled them to avoid dealing with the question. If the suffrage movement was ever to rise from the grave where politicians had laid it, tactics equally adroit needed to be employed. She never doubted that the tactics she had evolved would succeed in winning a cause which, as far as argument or reason was concerned, was intellectually won already. She dreaded all the old plausible evasions and she feared the ingrained inferiority complex in the majority of women. Thus she could not trust her mental offspring to the mercies of politically untrained minds. Moreover, the very fact that militant action involved individual sacrifice imposed heavy responsibilities upon the leaders of the campaign. Individuals who were ready to make the sacrifice that militancy entailed had to be sustained by the assurance of complete unity within the ranks. I agreed with this view of the situation, although I felt that it would be a difficult one to sustain in the conference. The issue to be raised was that of "democracy." It was an irony that this question of principle should come up in a political union which was to win votes for women. It became evident that, young as the militant movement was, it had to meet a crisis the solution of which would influence its future history.

While these clouds had been slowly gathering at headquarters Mrs. Pankhurst was conducting a campaign of meetings in the north. She knew nothing of the difficulties of the position until she returned to London on the eve of the conference. I shall never forget the gesture with which she swept from the board all the "pros and the cons" which had caused us sleepless nights. "I shall tear up the constitution," she declared. This intrepid woman when apparently hemmed in by difficulties always cut her way through them.

The next day at the conference she asserted her position as founder of the Union, declared that she and her daughter had counted the cost of militancy, and were prepared to take the whole responsibility for it, and that they refused to be interfered with by any kind of constitution. She called upon those who had faith in her leadership to follow her, and to devote themselves to the sole end of winning the vote. This announcement was met with a dignified protest from Mrs. Despard. These two notable women presented a great contrast, the one aflame with a single idea that had taken complete possession of her, the other upheld by a principle that had actuated a long life spent in the service of the people.

Mrs. Despard calmly affirmed her belief in democratic equality and was convinced that it must be maintained at all costs. Mrs. Pankhurst claimed that there was only one meaning to "democracy," and that was equal citizenship in a State, which could only be attained by inspired leadership. She challenged all who did not accept the leadership of herself and her daughter to resign from the Union that she had founded, and to form an organisation of their own.

Thereupon Mrs. Despard, Mrs. How-Martyn and Miss Billington and their followers formed a separate organisation, the Women's Freedom League. The severance was always referred to as "The Split."

October 1907

EMMELINE PETHICK-LAWRENCE: My husband and I launched our paper, *Votes for Women*, and became its co-editors. Its first standing paragraph was as follows:

> To the brave women who to-day are fighting for freedom: to the noble women who all down the ages kept the flag flying and looked forward to this day without seeing it: to all women all over the world of whatever race or creed or calling, whether they be with us or against us in this fight, we dedicate this paper.

Suffragettes in Chains January 17, 1908

SYLVIA PANKHURST: Because vigorous militancy was the order of the day, the Press teemed with articles upon the abstract question of Votes for Women and with notices of the doings of the Suffragettes. "SUFFRAGETTES IN DOWNING STREET," "CABINET BAITING AS THE LATEST RUSE," "SUFFRAGETTES IN CHAINS." These and others of the same nature were the startling headlines that one saw in the evening papers on January 17 and in the morning papers of the following day. It was merely that Mrs. Drummond and a number of other members of our Union, knowing that the Cabinet was sitting to decide upon the questions which should find a place in the legislative programme of the forthcoming session, had made an attempt to urge upon them the necessity of dealing with the women's claim.

Whilst Press representatives were congregating in Downing Street, to snapshot the Ministers and to gain material for foolish paragraphs describing their appearance and manner of arrival at the first Cabinet Council of the season, and whilst police were assembling to dance attendance upon the Prime Minister and his colleagues, three or four of the women appeared to demand an interview. The police pulled them aside and the Cabinet Ministers brushed past as they tried to speak, and when they applied at the door of the official residence, no notice was taken. Then Miss New, well knowing that her words would be heard both inside the House and by the crowd that was collecting in the street, began to make a speech explaining what she and her friends had come for. Before beginning, she chained herself to the railings beside the Prime Minister's front door, both symbolically to express the political bondage of womanhood, and for the very practical reason that this device would prevent her being dragged speedily away. Her example was followed by Nurse Olivia Smith and, whilst the police were struggling to break the double set of chains, a taxi-cab drove up and stopped on the opposite side of the street. Suspecting more Suffragettes, some of the constables rushed to the door of the cab which opened on to the pavement. At the same moment, Flora Drummond opened the door on the road side and bounded across to the sacred residence, where, as there was no one to bar her progress and as she now possessed the secret of the little knob in the centre of the door, she was inside and very near to the Council Chamber itself, before a number of men, some of whom she believed to be Cabinet Ministers, rushed upon her, and she was flung out and hurled down the steps. She was then arrested, and shortly afterward she and four of her comrades found themselves before Sir Albert de Rutzen at Bow Street police court charged with disorderly conduct. They were found guilty and, on refusing to be bound over, were sent to prison for three weeks.

Flora Drummond arrested outside the Prime Minister's residence, 10 Downing Street

Third Women's Parliament

February 11, 1908

SYLVIA PANKHURST: When the third Women's Parliament met in Caxton Hall, it did so with all the splendid courage and enthusiasm for militant action that had characterised its predecessors. It was now known that an excellent place in the private Members' ballot had been won, and on the women's bill, by Mr. Stanger, a Liberal, and it was realised that before February 28, when the bill was to come up for second reading, strong pressure must be brought to bear upon the Government to prevent this bill being wrecked as that of Mr. Dickinson had been in the previous year. It was therefore with an added sense of immediate pressing necessity that the women set out unflinchingly for the old hard fight with overwhelming force. The motion to carry the usual resolution to the Prime Minister was moved by Miss Marie Naylor and Miss Florence Haig, both London members of the Union and both Chelsea portrait painters, and then the whole hall seemed to rock with the noise of the cheers as the majority of the women present sprang up to form a deputation.

Large crowds had gathered to see them whilst the police were drawn up on either side of the road, and at one point formed a line across the thoroughfare. The constables pushed and jostled the women for some time without altogether preventing their passage, but at Broad Sanctuary a large contingent of police entirely blocked the way. Undaunted, the women pressed forward, and the crowds, some with the idea of helping the Suffragettes, others from curiosity, pressed forward too. The police charged again and again, and there was grave danger that someone would be trampled under foot. When at last the streets were cleared, it was found that some fifty women had been arrested.

Above: W.S.P.U. supporters outside Westminster police court.
On the right, Mr. Horace Smith, the magistrate who sent the prisoners to gaol

February 12, 1908

EMMELINE PANKHURST: The next morning, when the cases were tried, Mr. Muskett, who prosecuted for the Crown, and who was perhaps a little tired of telling the Suffragettes that these scenes in the streets must cease, and then of seeing them go on exactly as if he had not spoken, made a very severe and terrifying address. He told the women that this time they would be subject to the usual maximum of two months' imprisonment, with the option of a fine of five pounds, but that, in case they ever offended again, the law had worse terrors in store for them. It was proposed to revive, for the benefit of the Suffragettes, an act passed in the reign of Charles II, which dealt with "Tumultuous Petitions, either to the Crown or Parliament." This act provided that no person should dare to go to the King or to Parliament "with any petition, complaint, remonstrance, declaration, or other address" accompanied with a number of persons above twelve. A fine of one hundred pounds, or three months' imprisonment, might be imposed under this law. The magistrate then sentenced all but two of the women to be bound over for twelve months, or to serve six weeks in the second division. Two other women, "old offenders," were given one month in the third division, or lowest class. All the prisoners, except two who had very ill relatives at home, chose the prison sentence.

The next day's session of the Women's Parliament was one of intense excitement, as the women reviewed the events of the previous day, the trials, and especially the threat to revive the obsolete act of Charles II, an act *which was passed to obstruct the progress of the Liberal Party, which came into existence under the Stuarts, and under the second Charles was fighting for its life.* It was an amazing thing that the political descendants of these men were proposing to revive the act to obstruct the advance of the women's cause, fighting for its life under Edward VII and his Liberal Government. At least, it was evidence that the Government were baffled in their attempt to crush our movement. Christabel Pankhurst, presiding, said: "At last it is realised that women are fighting for freedom, as their fathers fought. If they want twelve women, aye, and more than twelve, if a hundred women are wanted to be tried under that act and sent to prison for three months, they can be found."

A black Maria carries Suffragette prisoners from Westminster to Holloway Prison.

CHALLENGE THE GOVERN- MENT

EMMELINE PANKHURST: I had determined that I must be the first person to challenge the Government to carry out their threat to revive the old act of Charles II. I made a long speech to the women that day, telling them something of my experiences of the past months, and how all that I had seen and heard throughout the country had only deepened my conviction of the necessity for women's votes. "I feel," I concluded, "that the time has come when I must act, and I wish to be one of those to carry our resolution to the Parliament this afternoon."

Amid a good deal of excitement and emotion, we chose the requisite thirteen women, who were prepared to be arrested and tried under the Charles II "Tumultuous Petitions" Act. I had not entirely recovered from the attack made upon me in Mid-Devon, and my wrenched ankle was still too sensitive to make walking anything but a painful process. Seeing me begin almost at once to limp badly, Mrs. Drummond, with characteristic, blunt kindness, called to a man driving a dog-cart and asked him if he would drive me to the House of Commons. He readily agreed, and I mounted to the seat behind him, the other women forming in line behind the cart.

We had not gone far when the police, who already surrounded us in great force, ordered me to dismount. Of course I obeyed and walked, or rather limped along, with my companions. They would have supported me, but the police insisted that we should walk single-file. Presently I grew so faint from the pain of the ankle that I called to two of the women, who took hold of my arms and helped me on my way. This was our one act of disobedience to police orders. We moved with difficulty, for the crowd was of incredible size. All around, as far as the eye could see, was the great moving, swaying, excited multitude, and surrounding us on all sides were regiments of uniformed police, foot and mounted. You might have supposed that instead of thirteen women, one of them lame, walking quietly along, the town was in the hands of an armed mob.

We had progressed as far as the entrance to Parliament Square, when two stalwart policemen suddenly grasped my arms on either side and told me that I was under arrest. My two companions, because they refused to leave me, were also arrested, and a few minutes later Annie Kenney and five other women suffered arrest. That night we were released on bail, and the next morning we were arraigned in Westminster police court for trial under the Charles II Act. But, as it turned out, the authorities, embarrassed by our readiness to test the act, announced that they had changed their minds, and would continue, for the present, to treat us as common street-brawlers.

This was my first trial, and I listened, with a suspicion that my ears were playing tricks with my reason, to the most astonishing perjuries put forth by the prosecution. I heard that we had set forth from Caxton Hall with noisy shouts and songs, that we had resorted to the most riotous and vulgar behaviour, knocking off policemen's helmets, assaulting the officers right and left as we marched. Our testimony, and that of our witnesses, was ignored. When I tried to speak in my own defence, I was cut short rudely, and was told briefly that I and the others must choose between being bound over or going to prison, in the second division, for six weeks.

Two days of solitary confinement, broken each day by an hour of silent exercise in a bitterly cold courtyard, and I was ordered to the hospital. There I thought I should be a little more comfortable. The bed was better, the food a little better, and small comforts, such as warm water for washing, were allowed. I slept a little the first night. About midnight I awoke, and sat up in bed, listening. A woman in the cell next mine was moaning in long, sobbing breaths of mortal pain. She ceased for a few minutes, then moaned again, horribly. The truth flashed over me, turning me sick, as I realised that a life was coming into being, there in that frightful prison. A woman, imprisoned by men's laws, was giving a child to the world. A child born in a cell! I shall never forget that night, nor what I suffered with the birth-pangs of that woman, who, I found later, was simply waiting trial on a charge which was found to be baseless.

At last the time came when they gave me back all my things, and let me go free. At the door the Governor spoke to me, and asked me if I had any complaints to make. "Not of you," I replied, "nor of any of the wardresses. Only of this prison, and all of men's prisons. We shall rase them to the ground."

February 28, 1908

CHRISTABEL PANKHURST: While Mother was in prison, a woman suffrage bill, introduced by a private Member, Mr. H. Y. Stanger, passed its second reading in the House of Commons by 271 votes to 92. Our next step was to ask for the Government support without which the bill could go no further. Mr. Herbert Gladstone, a member of the Government, said in the second-reading debate that the predominance of argument alone—and he believed we had won this—was not enough to win the vote. "The time comes," said he, "when political dynamics are far more important than political argument." Alas, we had discovered that: it was the reason why we had taken to militancy.

March 19, 1908

A great event of this year was our Albert Hall meeting, the first woman suffrage meeting ever held there and the largest indoor gathering ever held until then by anybody in support of votes for women. Mother's prison sentence did not expire until after the date appointed for this meeting. Her place was left empty, save for a placard: "Mrs. Pankhurst's Chair." The vast hall was overflowing, many being turned away. Intense determination animated that great throng of women. Thunders of applause broke out as the speakers entered—but they were above all for Mother and the other absent ones.

A Speech Delivered at Albert Hall

CHRISTABEL PANKHURST: The resolution to-day has reference to the bill which is now before Parliament for the enfranchisement of women, and it is our intention during the whole of the present session to press for the enactment of that bill, in order that when the general election comes—and I think that general election is not now far distant—women, as well as men, may have the opportunity of recording their opinions at the polling booth.

Friends, every attempt has been made to make the second reading of that measure a fruitless and ineffective thing; but I think it is in our power to rescue the bill from the difficult position in which it stands, and to compel the Government to carry it into law. When this bill was before the House, we had from Mr. Herbert Gladstone a long speech of advice. What he said was that men had struggled for centuries, since the days of Cromwell, for their rights, but that the fight—it was going on still—was not completely won. Then he said that experience shows that the predominance of argument alone—and he believed that had been attained in the matter of woman suffrage—is not enough to win the political day. "The time comes," says Mr. Gladstone, "when political dynamics are far more important than political argument."

It is upon a recognition of that fact that these new tactics of ours are based. We know that relying solely on argument we wandered for forty years politically in the wilderness. We know that arguments alone are not enough, above all, with a Government like this one, and that political force is necessary. We agree with Mr. Herbert Gladstone that much is to be accomplished by the holding of great meetings like this; that much is to be accomplished by the holding of great meetings like the one that is to be held in Hyde Park on June 21, but we know that there must also be hard and strenuous fighting. To gather at meetings like this is only useful in so far as we can make the Government believe that we, assembled in our thousands, as we are to-night, are prepared to back up words by deeds.

It is because we are recognised to-day as women who are ready to *act* that the movement stands where it stands now. You may not like our methods, some of you, but these methods are a success. You may not like our going to great public meetings, addressed by members of the Government, to demand the enfranchisement of women. Yet I say the women who do these things are the women who are in earnest. If we on this platform were responsible for guiding the destinies of the nation, if it were upon us that lay the guilt of refusing to our fellow-creatures the elementary rights of citizenship, we should be ashamed to protest because some of these wronged people, these disinherited ones, came here to state their grievance and demand their rights. I think the Government, who whine because we do these things, are showing themselves doubly deserving of the contempt of this nation. If they are absolutely bent on defrauding us of our vote, then they must be prepared to play the part of men and face the music.

The effect of our tactics has been to rouse the conscience of the nation, to stir within women a new sense of self-respect, a new sense of the dignity of their sex, and a new hope for the future, to rouse in men a feeling of truer respect for womanhood than this generation of men has ever known. The effect of our tactics has been to hold up the Government of this country not only to the contempt of our own people of this country, but to the contempt of the people of the whole civilised world.

We have held our hands from doing violent acts or criminal deeds. We have shown more self-restraint than men have ever done under similar circumstances. We have broken no moral law. All we have done has been to make ourselves of little esteem. We have been prepared to sacrifice our safety of life and limb. We have been prepared to do these things because we believe in our cause. We say this not to boast of it, but to claim that we have the same spirit that the reformers of all ages have had to show before they could win success. We are not ashamed of what we have done, because, when you have a great cause to fight for, the moment of greatest humiliation is the moment when the spirit is proudest. The women we do pity, the women we think unwomanly, the women for whom we have almost contempt, if our hearts could let us have that feeling, are the women who can stand aside, who take no part in this battle—and perhaps even more; the women who know what the right path is and will not tread it, who are selling the liberty of other women in order to win the smiles and favour of the dominant sex. How true it is that people who have a false end in view fail even to achieve that end! And so these women who are bending their heads beneath oppression, these women who are prepared to play the part of vassals, they are not the women who have the respect of other women; and they are not the women who have the respect of men. We are the women whom men respect to-day; we are the women whose position is more dignified than that of any other women in this country, because if you cannot be recognised as a citizen it is best to be in the front, fighting for a citizen's rights.

We Suffragettes, as you call us, do know the destiny that ought to be that of all in this country. We are proud of all we have been through, and we are proud to think that victory is likely to come soon to us in our crusade. We are fighting the Government to-day in Peckham. We are doing our best to inflict upon them a crushing blow at the poll. The charge has been brought against us that in doing this we are endangering a great measure of social reform, the Licencing Bill. It is not for us to express an opinion upon that measure, though we do say that the evil for which the Government are trying to find a remedy by this bill has a much deeper root than they imagine. But I want you to understand this, that if any harm comes to this Licencing Bill it will not be our fault. It will be the fault of the Government, who rather than see the women of this country enfranchised, will sacrifice every other measure on their programme. Once too often has the crack of the party whip been sounded on our ears. They are always telling us to wait for the vote, because other matters are important. We are deaf to that argument now. We say, bills may come, bills may go, Governments may rise, and Governments may fall, but we are determined to have the franchise. Now, men and women here this evening, we have got to see this

thing through. We mean to have the vote this session. This we know, that if you stand by us we can get it. Disregard the argument that this question must be referred to the electors. There is the great principle that taxation and representation must go together. It has been often enough fought for and won in the past. We don't need to have it thrashed out again in this the twentieth century. I do not think much of any man who says that taxation and representation must go together and yet refuses to give the vote to women. I call upon the men to say to the Government, "Give the women their rights before you face the tribunal of the nation at the next general election."

Men and women, we are fighting a national cause; and let us make a vow to-night that if the Government do not carry the bill before they go to the country, that every one of us, both men and women, men with their votes—women—voteless—shall see to it that upon this issue shall depend the next general election.

On Sunday last we had a demonstration at Peckham, and there was a good deal of disorder, and danger for some of us, but it had the effect of stirring the conscience of men in that audience. I had a letter from a working man, who said that having come to that meeting opposed to our cause, he now understands what it means: "My vote," he said, "is at your service, when the election comes." Friends, we must have such men as that by the thousand in this country! We must let the Government know, and know soon, that unless they are prepared to give us the vote, defeat awaits them when next the country has an opportunity of pronouncing upon their record. Now, women, it depends upon us, and upon how we fight, how soon we shall win. We appeal against the Government to the electors. They are watching us to see how we acquit ourselves. It is not only by appealing to them, it is by showing them that we are in earnest, have made up our minds to be free, that we shall win the support of men. Let women not only pass this resolution, but be prepared to carry it through fire and water till we succeed.

EMMELINE PANKHURST: I walked quietly onto the stage, took the placard out of the chair, and sat down. A great cry went up from the women as they sprang from their seats and stretched their hands toward me. It was some time before I could see them for my tears, or speak to them for the emotion that shook me like a storm.

CHRISTABEL PANKHURST: Those thousands of women were afoot, cheering and cheering again. Mother spoke. The contrast between the quiet, bare, narrow prison cell and this vast hall, this human throng, this vibrance and intensity, was almost overwhelming. Yet she rose as ever to the occasion. Finally she moved the resolution calling upon the Government to adopt and carry into law the Women's Enfranchisement Bill then before Parliament.

March 20, 1908

EMMELINE PANKHURST: The next morning I, with the other released prisoners, drove off to Peckham, a constituency of London, where the W.S.P.U. members were fighting a vigorous by-election. In open brakes we paraded the streets, dressed in our prison clothes, or exact reproductions of them. Naturally, we attracted a great deal of attention and sympathy, and our daily meetings on Peckham Rye, as their common is known, drew enormous crowds. When polling day came our members were stationed at every polling booth, and many men as they came to the booths told us that they were, for the first time, voting "for the women," by which they meant against the Government. That night, amid great excitement, it was made known that the Liberal majority of 2,339 at the last general election had been turned into a Conservative majority of 2,494. Letters poured into the newspapers, declaring that the loss of this important Liberal seat was due almost entirely to the work of the Suffragettes, and many prominent Liberals called upon party leaders to start doing something for women before the next general election.

Mr. Asquith became Prime Minister about Easter time, 1908, on the resignation, on account of ill health, of Sir Henry Campbell-Bannerman. He was a bluntly outspoken opponent of woman suffrage, and it was sufficiently plain to us that no methods of education or persuasion would ever prove successful where he was concerned. Therefore, the necessity of action on our part was greater than ever.

June 1908

CHRISTABEL PANKHURST: Militancy had brought woman suffrage so far into the region of practical politics that a deputation of sixty Liberal Members of the House of Commons waited on Mr. Asquith to ask him to give facilities for the enactment of Mr. Stanger's Woman Suffrage Bill in the current session, or at least in the existing Parliament. Mr. Asquith observed that his own position with regard to woman suffrage was "a delicate one." He had "not reached that state of grace" in which the members of the deputation were "so fully and firmly established." To give, that session, facilities for Mr. Stanger's bill was "wholly out of the question."

As to the remainder of that Parliament, his intention was to introduce an electoral reform measure for men only, and it would clearly be within the competence of the House of Commons to seek, by amendment or extension of this Government bill, to effect the accomplishment of the great purpose they had in view. It was, he said, necessary that a great constitutional change of this kind must have behind it the support of the women of the country, as well as the present electorate.

We wholly objected to this project. We condemned and rejected Mr. Asquith's proposition on grounds set forth in this letter published in *The Times*.

To the Editor of THE TIMES

Sir,—The reply of Mr. Asquith to the deputation of Liberal Members of Parliament confirms the Women's Social and Political Union in their determination to fight against the Government.

In the first place, Mr. Asquith refuses to deal with the question this session, either on his own initiative or by giving facilities to Mr. Stanger's bill. He reverts to the old Liberal policy of delay, the fruits of which we have seen so often before.

In the second place, he now makes it clear that the Government have no intention themselves at any time during the present Parliament of introducing a measure of woman suffrage; and at the same time do intend to introduce a bill dealing with electoral reform for the benefit of men alone.

We are not in the least reassured by his reported statement that a woman suffrage amendment, moved by a private Member, to this bill would not, under certain circumstances, be opposed by the Government, as it is of too negative and vague a character to be of any value. Moreover, the Government cannot shirk direct responsibility in this matter. Nothing short of a definite pledge of action this session will satisfy the Women's Social and Political Union, and unless this is given we shall continue to bring effective pressure on the Government. Our policy of opposing their nominees at by-elections, which has proved so successful in the past, will be vigorously pursued. And if, after our demonstration in Hyde Park on Sunday, June 21, the Government are still obdurate, we shall take it as a signal that further militant action is required to wring from them the necessary reform.

Christabel Pankhurst

SYLVIA PANKHURST: On the Thursday evening before the demonstration, Mrs. Drummond and a dozen other members of the Union set sail for the Houses of Parliament in a steam launch decorated with banners and posters announcing the demonstration. At the little tables on the terrace many members, including Mr. Lloyd George, were entertaining their lady friends at afternoon tea, when the sound of a band playing heralded the Suffragettes' arrival. Everyone crowded to the water's edge as the boat stopped, and Mrs. Drummond began to speak. She invited all Members of Parliament, and especially Cabinet Ministers, to join the women's procession to Hyde Park on the twenty-first of June, assuring them that it was their duty to inform themselves as to the feelings of the people. She twitted the Government who were supposed to be democratic with remaining always behind barred gates under the protection of the police, and urged, "Come to the park on Sunday; you shall have police protection there also, and we promise you that there shall be no arrests."

"POWER BELONGS TO THE MASSES"

EMMELINE PANKHURST: What a day was this Sunday—clear, radiant, filled with golden sunshine! As I advanced, leading, with the venerable Mrs. Wolstenholme-Elmy, the first of the seven processions, it seemed to me that all London had turned out to witness our demonstration. And a goodly part of London followed the processions. When I mounted my platform in Hyde Park, and surveyed the mighty throngs that waited there and the endless crowds that were still pouring into the park from all directions, I was filled with amazement not unmixed with awe. Never had I imagined that so many people could be gathered together to share in a political demonstration. It was a gay and beautiful as well as an awe-inspiring spectacle, for the white gowns and flower-trimmed hats of the women, against the background of ancient trees, gave the park the appearance of a vast garden in full bloom. The bugles sounded, and the speakers at each of the twenty platforms began their addresses, which could not have heard by more than half of the audience.

Notwithstanding this, they remained to the end. At five o'clock the bugles sounded again, the speaking ceased, and the resolution calling upon the Government to bring in an official woman suffrage bill without delay was carried at every platform, often without a dissenting vote. Then, with a three-times-repeated cry of "Votes for Women!" from the assembled multitude, the great meeting dispersed.

We felt that we had answered the challenge in Mr. Gladstone's declaration that "power belongs to the masses," and that through this power the Government could be influenced; so it was with real hope that we despatched a copy of the resolution to the Prime Minister, asking him what answer the Government would make to that unparalleled gathering of men and women.

June 30, 1908

Mr. Asquith replied formally that he had nothing to add to his previous statement—that the Government intended, at some indefinite time, to bring in a general reform bill which *might* be amended to include woman suffrage. Our wonderful demonstration, it appeared, had made no impression whatever upon him.

Now we had reached a point where we had to choose between two alternatives. We had exhausted argument. Therefore, either we had to give up our agitation altogether, as the suffragists of the eighties virtually had done, or else we must act, and go on acting, until the selfishness and the obstinacy of the Government was broken down, or the Government themselves destroyed. Until forced to do so, the Government, we perceived, would never give women the vote.

We realised the truth of John Bright's words, spoken while the reform bill of 1867 was being agitated. Parliament, John Bright then declared, had never been hearty for any reform. The Reform Act of 1832 had been wrested by force from the Government of that day, and now before another, he said, could be carried, the agitators would have to fill the streets with people from Charing Cross to Westminster Abbey. Acting on John Bright's advice, we issued a call to the public to join us in holding a huge demonstration on June 30 outside the House of Commons. We wanted to be sure that the Government saw as well as read of our immense following. A public proclamation from the Commissioner of Police, warning the public not to assemble in Parliament Square and declaring that the approaches to the Houses of Parliament must be kept open, was at once issued.

We persisted in announcing that the demonstration would take place, and I wrote a letter to Mr. Asquith telling him that a deputation would wait upon him at half-past four on the afternoon of June 30. We held the usual Women's Parliament in Caxton Hall, after which Mrs. Pethick-Lawrence, eleven other women, and myself, set forth. We met with no opposition from the police, but marched through cheering crowds of spectators to the Strangers' Entrance to the House of Commons. Here we were met by a large group of uniformed men commanded by Inspector Scantlebury, of the police. The inspector, whom I knew personally, stepped forward and demanded officially, "Are you Mrs. Pankhurst, and is this your deputation?"

"Yes," I replied.

"My orders are to exclude you from the House of Commons."

"Has Mr. Asquith received my letter?" I asked.

For answer the inspector drew my letter from his pocket and handed it to me.

"Did Mr. Asquith return no message, no kind of reply?" I enquired.

"No," replied the inspector.

Emmeline Pankhurst, leading the deputation to the House of Commons, is interviewed by a newspaper reporter, June 30, 1908.
Bottom left: Superintendent Wells escorts Emmeline Pankhurst.
Bottom right: The deputation outside the House of Commons.

We turned and walked back to Caxton Hall, to tell the waiting audience what had occurred. We resolved that there was nothing to do but wait patiently until evening, and see how well the public would respond to our call to meet in Parliament Square.

At eight we went out in groups from Caxton Hall, to find Parliament Square packed with a throng, estimated next day at least one hundred thousand. From the steps of public buildings, from stone copings, from the iron railings of the Palace Yard, to which they clung precariously, our women made speeches until the police pulled them down and flung them into the moving, swaying, excited crowds. Some of the women were arrested, others were merely ordered to move on. Mingled cheers and jeers rose from the spectators. Some of the men were roughs who had come out to amuse themselves. Others were genuinely sympathetic, and tried valiantly to help us to reach the House of Commons. Again and again the police lines were broken, and it was only as the result of repeated charges by mounted police that the people's attacks were repelled. Many Members of Parliament, including Mr. Lloyd George, Mr. Winston Churchill, and Mr. Herbert Gladstone, came out to witness the struggle, which lasted until midnight and resulted in the arrest of twenty-nine women. Two of these women were arrested after they had each thrown a stone through a window of Mr. Asquith's official residence in Downing Street.

This was the first window-breaking in our history. Mrs. Mary Leigh and Miss Edith New, who had thrown the stones, sent word to me from the police court that, having acted without orders, they would not resent repudiation from headquarters. Far from repudiating them, I went at once to see them in their cells, and assured them of my approval of their act. The smashing of windows is a time-honoured method of showing displeasure in a political situation.

October 1908: Women's Social and Political Union Manifesto

Parliament is about to meet to continue the work of legislation.

The bill for the enfranchisement of women, which earlier in the year passed its second reading by a great majority, finds no place in the Government programme, although every effort has been made by women to convince the Cabinet that it is expedient, as well as just, that the disability of sex should be removed without further delay.

Great demonstrations, exceeding in size any ever held in support of any other question, have taken place all over the country.

At the by-elections, the voters have voted against the Government on the issue of votes for women.

To all these manifestations of the people's will, the Government continue blind and deaf.

It is for us who are called the militant women to take further action and to show our determination to break down this obstinate resistance to our just demands.

On October 13 we shall meet in the Caxton Hall, and we have asked those who support our demands to assemble in Parliament Square.

From our meeting in Caxton Hall will be chosen a deputation to go again, as deputations have gone before, to the House of Commons, to enter the House—if possible the Chamber itself—and lay our claim to the vote before the Government and Parliament.

Women have the right, being voteless, to plead their cause in person. We shall insist on that right. . . .

On October 13, in Parliament Square, there will be many thousands of people to see fair play between the women and the Government.

Thousands of our fellow countrywomen, who are unable by their circumstances to take an active part in the fight, are looking to us to obtain for them their political freedom.

All over the world women are gaining hope from our efforts here in England.

Let us then show the world on October 13, 1908, that British women are determined to be free citizens of a free country before the year is out.

Yours, in the women's cause,
Emmeline Pankhurst

"Rush the House"

EMMELINE PANKHURST: Again we resolved to send a deputation to the Prime Minister, and again we invited the general public to take part in the demonstration. We had printed thousands of little handbills bearing this inscription: "Men and Women, Help the Suffragettes to Rush the House of Commons, on Tuesday Evening, October 13, at 7:30."

On Sunday, October 11, we held a large meeting in Trafalgar Square, my daughter Christabel, Mrs. Drummond, and I speaking from the plinth of the Nelson Monument. Mr. Lloyd George, as we afterward learned, was a member of the audience. The police were there, taking ample notes of our speeches. We had not failed to notice that they were watching us daily, dogging our footsteps, and showing in numerous ways that they were under orders to keep track of all our movements. The climax came at noon on October 12, when Christabel, Mrs. Drummond, and I were each served with an imposing legal document which read, "Information has been laid this day by the Commissioner of Police that you, in the month of October, in the year 1908, were guilty of conduct likely to provoke a breach of the peace by initiating and causing to be initiated, by publishing and causing to be published, a certain handbill, calling upon and inciting the public to do a certain wrongful and illegal act, *viz.*, to rush the House of Commons at 7:30 p.m. on October 13 *inst.*"

The last paragraph was a summons to appear at Bow Street police station that same afternoon at three o'clock. We did not go to Bow Street police station. We went instead to a crowded "At Home" at Queen's Hall, where it can be imagined that our news created great excitement.

"The Government's Representatives are now, as I speak, expecting us at Bow Street,

Above: Christabel Pankhurst addresses a meeting in Trafalgar Square, October 11, 1908.

but we have decided that our engagement to meet you here is of far greater importance to us. So we are here, and we shall not go to Bow Street until they come and take us."

The place was surrounded by constables, and the police reporters were on hand to take stenographic reports of everything that was said from the platform. Once an excited cry was raised that a police inspector was coming in to arrest us. But the officer merely brought a message that the summons had been adjourned until the following morning.

It did not suit our convenience to obey the adjourned summons quite so early, so I wrote a polite note to the police, saying that we would be in our headquarters, No. 4 Clement's Inn, the next evening at six o'clock, and would then be at his disposal. Warrants for our arrests were quickly issued, and Inspector Jarvis was instructed to execute them at once. This he found impossible to do, for Mrs. Drummond was spending her last day of liberty on private business, while my daughter and I had retreated to another part of Clement's Inn, which is a big, rambling building. There, in the roof-garden of the Pethick-Lawrences' private flat, we remained all day, busy, under the soft blue of the autumn sky, with our work and our preparations for a long absence. At six we walked downstairs, dressed for the street. Mrs. Drummond arrived promptly, the waiting officers read the warrants, and we all proceeded to Bow Street in cabs. It was too late for the trial to be held. We asked for bail, but the authorities had no mind to allow us to take part in the "rush" which we had incited, so we were obliged to spend the night in the police station.

October 13, 1908

SYLVIA PANKHURST: Mrs. Pankhurst at once claimed her right as an untried prisoner to communicate with the outside world and immediately despatched telegrams to several Members of Parliament. A weary hour or two went by. Then the door of Mrs. Pankhurst's cell was thrown wide open, and the tall, breezy presence of Mr. Murray, Liberal Member of Parliament for East Aberdeenshire, appeared. He was horrified to find the three ladies in these surroundings and, promising to return soon, he hurried to the Savoy Hotel, and there arranged for various comforts to be sent in to the prison. Then he prevailed upon the authorities to allow the three Suffragettes to take their evening meal together and, in an incredibly short space of time, they were ushered into the matron's room.

The bare little place with its dingy walls, its wooden chairs and two deal tables, had been wonderfully transformed. Numbers of tall wax candles had been lighted, the tables were laid with silver, flowers and brightly coloured fruit, and three waiters were ready to serve the prisoners with a most elaborate meal. At the same time, Mr. Murray, with his face wreathed in smiles, was superintending the carrying into the cells of three comfortable beds. The management of the Savoy had thrown themselves into the enterprise with the greatest eagerness and, having acted throughout with almost overwhelming kindness and courtesy, ended by refusing to charge anything at all for what they had provided. As well may be imagined, the three comrades were in no haste to finish the meal and return to the dark and solitary cells.

EMMELINE PETHICK-LAWRENCE: I alone was left of the speakers announced to speak that evening. When I arrived at Caxton Hall some twenty minutes before eight o'clock, I found women waving their tickets despairingly in the road outside. I was incoherently told that a crowd of medical students, several hundreds strong, had rushed the hall and were in possession of all the seats. At this supremely critical moment, in view of the arrest of three of the leaders, this situation was desperate.

I walked onto the platform and was greeted with whistles and calls—I felt in dead calm, the calm of desperation. Then I spoke. I reminded these young fellows that they were Englishmen and believed in fair play. Was it fair play, was it sporting, to interfere with women who were struggling to win the freedom which they already enjoyed, and which had been won for them in the past? Then I appealed to the man who sat nearest the exit. "Will you get up now at once and *go out of that door!*" He got up at once and went. The next in the row followed him and then, row by row, they all filed out as quietly as if they were going to church. There is a long passage from the large Caxton Hall to the entrance to the street, and it must have been a strange sight to see that procession of young men quietly marching. When the passage was cleared the women streamed in and took their places.

The proceedings then began. They took the usual form, except that the feeling was intense because of the news of the arrest of the Pankhursts. The resolution demanded facilities for Mr. Stanger's bill to become law. Eleven women volunteered to take it to the House.

The police evidently had received orders to make no arrests but to take measures to reduce the Suffragettes to exhaustion. Deputation after deputation was escorted by a body-guard of men as far as the police cordon and was hurled back into the crowds. It speaks eloquently of the popularity of the Suffragettes amongst the working-class masses of the people. Had the sympathy of the crowds not been with the Suffragettes they would have been torn to pieces. Exhausted they were, but not prepared to abandon their purpose, and at last the police began to make arrests. As a result of this attempt to "rush the House of Commons" twenty-four women and twelve men were sentenced to three weeks' imprisonment in default of being bound over to keep the peace for twelve months.

October 14, 1908

EMMELINE PANKHURST: The next morning, in a courtroom crowded to its utmost capacity, my daughter rose to conduct her first case at law. She had earned the right to an LL.B. after her name, but as women are not permitted to practise law in England, she had never appeared at the bar in any capacity except that of defendant. Now she proposed to combine the two roles of defendant and lawyer, and conduct the case for the three of us. She began by asking the magistrate not to try the case in that court, but to send it for trial before a judge and jury. We had long desired to take the Suffragettes' cases before bodies of private citizens, because we had every reason to suspect that the police-court officials acted under the direct commands of the very persons against whom our agitation was directed. Jury trial was denied us; but after the preliminary examination was over the magistrate, Mr. Curtis Bennett, allowed a week's adjournment for preparation of the case.

Above: Christabel and Emmeline Pankhurst in the roof garden at Clement's Inn.
Opposite: Flora Drummond, Emmeline and Christabel Pankhurst arrested by Inspector Jarvis
at Clement's Inn

On Trial
October 21, 1908

CHRISTABEL PANKHURST: Mr. Lloyd George and Mr. Herbert Gladstone were requested to attend as witnesses, since the one had been present at the Trafalgar Square meeting and had received a copy of our handbill, and the other had seen the occurrences outside Parliament. They expressed doubt that their evidence would be of use. When I thereupon applied for a subpoena to compel their attendance, Mr. Curtis Bennett suggested and advised the despatch of a second letter to both, and this time they said they would appear.

The day came: the two Ministers were there. The court was packed: the atmosphere was tense. There was the relief of knowing women at that moment of political combat humanly even and equal with men. True, they still held back our vote, but they had to reckon with us as representing womanhood. We were in the dock, but they that day were also there. For the witness-box of the police court was really the dock in that larger and higher court of public opinion, and indeed of history, before which we Suffragettes, the advocates for womanhood, were arraigning these two Ministers and political leaders on the charge of illiberality and injustice.

Mr. Lloyd George was first to enter the witness-box. "Did you hear any violence advocated in Trafalgar Square?" we asked him. "Not except to force an entrance to the House of Commons." "There were no words used so likely to incite to violence as the advice you gave at Swansea that women should be ruthlessly flung out of your meeting?" The witness said he had been, with his small daughter, in the neighbourhood of the House of Commons on October 13. "Did you think it safe to bring this young child?" "Certainly, she was very much amused." "Were you yourself attacked or assaulted in any way?" "No."

"You are aware that we argue that, as we are deprived of a share in the election of Parliamentary representatives, we are entitled to go in person to the House of Commons?" "That was a point put by Mrs. Pankhurst in the speech I heard." "Do you agree with that point of view?" "I should not like to express an opinion."

The magistrate interposed: "It is not for the witness to express an opinion."

Mother put the most telling question of the day, the question in which all others were summed up.

"I want to ask you whether in your opinion the whole of this agitation which women are carrying on—very much against the grain—would be immediately stopped if the constitutional right to vote were conceded to them?" "I should think that is very likely," replied Mr. Lloyd George.

Mr. Herbert Gladstone was rather cheery as he entered the witness-box.

"Did you anticipate that you would be in bodily danger as a consequence of the issue of this bill?" he was asked. "I didn't think of it at all." "Like ourselves you are above such a consideration!"

He thought that, but for the police, the crowd might have done more harm, yet admitted that, taking all our Westminster demonstrations together, very little harm had been done. "Did you say," he was asked, "that it was impossible not to sympathise with the eagerness and passion which have actuated so many women on this subject, that you were entirely in favour of the principle of votes for women, that men had had to fight for their rights from the time of Cromwell and that for the last 130 years the warfare had been perpetual? Did you say that on this question of the franchise, experience had shown that argument alone is not enough to win the political day and that 'there comes a time when political dynamics are far more important than political argument'?" "Yes," was the answer to all these questions.

We thanked the two Cabinet Ministers for acting as witnesses and they departed, leaving us to trial, sentence, and imprisonment.

A long list of witnesses was called for the defence, but the longest trial must have its end and the moment came for the accused to address the magistrate. We had urged that the case go before a jury, but in vain. We had argued, with reference to the dictionaries and to common usage, that the word "rush" implies "haste" and not "violence."

Speech to the Court

EMMELINE PANKHURST: Sir, I want to endorse what my daughter has said, that in my opinion we are proceeded against in this court by malice on the part of the Government. I want to protest as strongly as she has done. I want to put before you that the very nature of your duties in this court—although I wish to say nothing disrespectful to you—makes you perhaps unfitted to deal with a question which is a political question, as a body of jurymen could do. We are not women who would come into this court as ordinary law-breakers, and we feel that it is a great indignity—as have felt all the other women who have come into this court—that for political offences we should come into the ordinary police court. We do not object to that if from that degradation we shall ultimately succeed in winning political reform for the women of this country.

Mrs. Drummond here is a woman of very great public spirit; she is an admirable wife and mother; she has very great business ability, and she has maintained herself, although a married woman, for many years, and has acquired for herself the admiration and respect of all the people with whom she has had business relations. I do not think I need speak about my daughter. Her abilities and earnestness of purpose are very well known to you. They are young women. I am not, sir. You and I are older, and have had very great and very wide experience of life under different conditions. Before you decide what is to be done with us, I should like you to hear from me a statement of what has brought me into this dock this morning.

Mr. Curtis Bennett, magistrate
Mr. Herbert Gladstone, M.P.

Suffragist leaders and their symbolic banners commemorating women of all ages:
1. Mrs. Despard, Women's Freedom League
2. Lady Henry Somerset
3. The Reverend Dr. Anna Shaw
4. Mrs. Israel Zangwill, writer
5. Lady Frances Balfour
6. Beatrice Harraden, writer
7. Cicely Hamilton, dramatist
8. Dr. Garrett Anderson, the first woman physician
9. Mrs. Ayrton, electrical engineer
10. Mrs. Alfred Lyttelton, dramatist

Ever since my girlhood, a period of about thirty years, I have belonged to organisations to secure for women that political power which I have felt essential to bringing about those reforms which women need. I have tried constitutional methods. I have been womanly. When you spoke to some of my colleagues the day before yesterday about their being unwomanly, I felt that bitterness which I know every one of them felt in their hearts. We have tried to be womanly, we have tried to use feminine influence, and we have seen that it is of no use. Men who have been impatient have invariably got reforms for their impatience. And they have not our excuse for being impatient.

Now, while I share in the feeling of indignation which has been expressed to you by my daughter, I have lived longer in the world than she has. Perhaps I can look round the whole question better than she can, but I want to say here, deliberately, to you, that we are here to-day because we are driven here. We have taken this action, because as women—and I want you to understand it is as women we have taken this action—it is because we realise that the condition of our sex is so deplorable that it is our duty even to break the law in order to call attention to the reasons why we do so.

Now, we have tried every way. We have presented larger petitions than were ever presented for any other reform, we have succeeded in holding greater public meetings than men have ever had for any reform, in spite of the difficulty which women have in throwing off their natural diffidence, that desire to escape publicity which we have inherited from generations of our foremothers; we have broken through that. We have faced hostile mobs at street corners because we were told that we could not have that representation for our taxes which men have won unless we converted the whole of the country to our side. Because we have done this, we have been misrepresented, we have been ridiculed, we have had contempt poured upon us. The ignorant mob at the street corner has been incited to offer us violence, which we have faced unarmed and unprotected by the safeguards which Cabinet Ministers have. We know that we need the protection of the vote even more than men have needed it.

Although the Government admitted that we are political offenders, and, therefore, ought to be treated as political offenders are invariably treated, we shall be treated as pickpockets and drunkards; we shall be searched. I want you, if you can, as a man, to realise what it means to women like us. We are driven to do this, we are determined to go on with this agitation, because we feel in honour bound. Just as it was the duty of our forefathers, it is our duty to make this world a better place for women than it is to-day.

I was in the hospital at Holloway, and when I was there I heard from one of the beds near me the moans of a woman who was in the pangs of child-birth. I should like you to realise how women feel at helpless little infants breathing their first breath in the atmosphere of a prison. We believe that if we get the vote we will find some more humane way of dealing with women than that. It turned out that that woman was a remand prisoner. She was not guilty, because she was finally acquitted.

We believe that if we get the vote it will mean better conditions for our unfortunate sisters. We know what the condition of the woman worker is. Her condition is very bad. Many women pass through this court who I believe would not come before you if they were able to live morally and honestly. The average earnings of the women who earn their living in this country are only seven shillings, seven pence a week. There are women who have been driven to live an immoral life because they cannot earn enough to live decently.

We believe your work would be lightened if we got the vote. Some of us have worked, as I have told you, for many years to help our own sex, and we have been driven to the conclusion that only through legislation can any improvement be effected, and that that legislation can never be effected until we have the same power as men have to bring pressure to bear upon our representatives and upon Governments to give us the necessary legislation.

Well, sir, that is all I have to say to you. We are here not because we are law-breakers; we are here in our efforts to become law-makers.

The burly policemen, the reporters, and most of the spectators were in tears as I finished. But the magistrate, who had listened part of the time with his hand concealing his face, still held that we were properly charged in a common police court as inciters to riot. Since we refused to be bound over to keep the peace, he sentenced Mrs. Drummond and myself to three months' imprisonment, and Christabel to ten weeks' imprisonment.

October 22, 1908

My first act on reaching Holloway was to demand that the Governor be sent for. When he came I told him that the Suffragettes had resolved that they would no longer submit to being treated as ordinary law-breakers. In the course of our trial two Cabinet Ministers had admitted that we were political offenders, and therefore we should henceforth refuse to be searched or to undress in the presence of the wardresses. For myself I claimed the right, and I hoped the others would do likewise, to speak to my friends during exercise, or whenever I came in contact with them. The Governor, after reflection, yielded to the first two demands, but said that he would have to consult the Home Office before permitting us to break the rule of silence.

At the end of the second week I decided I would no longer endure it. That afternoon at exercise I suddenly called my daughter by name and bade her stand still until I came up to her. Of course she stopped, and when I reached her side we linked arms and began to talk in low tones. A wardress ran up to us, saying: "I shall listen to everything you say." I replied: "You are welcome to do that, but I shall insist on my right to speak to my daughter." Another wardress had hastily left the yard, and now she returned with a large number of wardresses. They seized me and quickly removed me to my cell, while the other suffrage prisoners cheered my action at the top of their voices. For their "mutiny" they were given three days' solitary confinement, and I, for mine, a much more severe punishment.

For this I was characterised as a "dangerous criminal" and was sent into solitary confinement, without exercise or chapel, while a wardress was stationed constantly at my cell door to see that I communicated with no one.

The Suffragettes marched by thousands to Holloway, thronging the approaches to the prison street. Round and round the prison they marched, singing the "Women's *Marseillaise*" and cheering. Faintly the sound came to our ears, infinitely lightening our burden of pain and loneliness.

The demonstrations, together with a volley of questions asked in the House of Commons, told at last. Orders came from the Home Office that I was to see my daughter, and that we were to be allowed to exercise and to talk together for one hour each day. In addition, we were to be permitted the rare privilege of reading a daily newspaper. Then, on December 22, the day of Christabel's release, orders came that I, too, should be discharged, two weeks before the expiration of my sentence.

At the welcome breakfast given us, as released prisoners, at Lincoln's Inn House, I told our members that henceforth we should all insist on refusing to abide by ordinary prison rules. We did not propose to break laws and then shirk punishment. We simply meant to assert our right to be recognised as political prisoners.

DAILY MIRROR, February 24, 1909

An ingenious, but unsuccessful, attempt to see Mr. Asquith was made by the Suffragettes yesterday. Finding that they could send "human letters," two ladies despatched themselves from the East Strand Post Office, setting off on their journey to Downing Street in charge of a telegraph messenger. One of the "letters" carried a card bearing the words, "To the Right Hon. H. H. Asquith, 10 Downing Street." Though well laid, the plan did not succeed, for when they arrived at the Premier's residence, only the messenger was admitted. After an interval, an official came out with the card, and, notwithstanding the ladies' protest that they had been "paid for," said, "You cannot be delivered here. You must be returned; you are dead letters." The ladies then returned to the post office. The picture shows the "letters," Miss McLellan and Miss Solomon, outside No. 10 Downing Street. The upper portrait is of Miss Solomon, and the lower Miss McLellan.

LADY C. LYTTON

Constance Georgina Lytton was born on February 12, 1869. She was the third child of Robert Lytton, diplomat and poet, the first Earl of Lytton, and his wife, Edith Villiers. Lady Constance spent her childhood in Vienna, Paris, and Lisbon, where her father was in the diplomatic service, and in India, where he was the Viceroy. As Viceroy he proclaimed Queen Victoria Empress of India in Delhi in 1877. Lady Constance was eleven years old when her parents returned from India in 1880 and settled in the family home of Knebworth, Hertfordshire.

In 1887 the family moved to Paris when Lord Lytton became Ambassador. He died in Paris four years later and the family returned to England to unexpected financial misfortune. As a result of this, in 1895 his wife accepted the post of lady-in-waiting to Queen Victoria and after her death continued as lady-in-waiting to Queen Alexandra.

In 1905, when Lady Constance was thirty-six years old, her mother left the court and they moved back to the country to a house at Knebworth. She had been a chronic invalid since infancy, suffering from a weak heart and rheumatism, and she continued to live quietly with her mother in the country.

Lady Constance had a passionate interest in music and when in 1906 she received a small inheritance from her godmother, Lady Bloomfield, she brought members of the Esperance Girls' Club to her village to teach traditional folk dances to the villagers as a lively revival of "joy-giving native arts."

LADY CONSTANCE LYTTON: It was in August-September 1908, at The Green Lady Hostel, Littlehampton, the holiday house of the Esperance Girls' Club, that I met Mrs. Pethick-Lawrence and Miss Annie Kenney. I was two or three days in the house with them without discovering that they were Suffragettes or that there was anything unusual about their lives. But I realised at once that I was face to face with women of strong personality, and I felt, though at first vaguely, that they represented something more than themselves, a force greater than their own seemed behind them. Their remarkable individual powers seemed illumined and enhanced by a light that was apart from them as are the colours and patterns of a stained-glass window by the sun shining through it. I had never before come across this kind of spirituality. I have since found it a characteristic of all the leaders in the militant section of the woman's movement, and of many of the rank and file. I was much attracted by Mrs. Pethick-Lawrence, and became intimate with her at once on the strength of our mutual friendship for Olive Schreiner. We had, besides, many other interests and sympathies in common. The first Sunday that we were together, the girls of the club were asked to come in early that evening so that Jessie Kenney, Annie Kenney's sister, who had only recently been released from Holloway, might tell them of her prison experiences. I then realised that I was amongst Suffragettes. I immediately confessed to them that although I shared their wish for the enfranchisement of women, I did not at all sympathise with the measures they adopted for bringing about that reform. I had, however, always been interested in prisons and recognised from the first that, incidentally, the fact of many educated women being sent to gaol for a question of conscience must do a great deal for prison reform, and I was delighted at this opportunity of hearing first-hand something about the inner life of a prison. I listened eagerly and was horrified at some of the facts recorded. Amongst these I remember specially that the tins in which the drinking water stood were cleaned with soap and brick-dust and not washed out, the tins being filled only once or at most twice in twenty-four hours; the want of air in the cells; the conduct of prison officials toward the prisoners.

Having betrayed my disapproval of the Suffragette "tactics," which seemed to me unjustified, unreasonable, without a sense of political responsibility, and as setting a bad example in connection with a reform movement of such prominence, there was naturally something of coolness and reserve in my further intercourse with Mrs. Pethick-Lawrence and the Kenneys. But before their brief stay at the club came to an end, I achieved a talk with each of the leaders.

One evening, after incessant rain, Annie Kenney and I marched arm-in-arm round the garden under dripping trees. I explained that though I had always been for the extension of the suffrage to women, it did not seem to me a question of prime urgency, that many other matters of social reform seemed more important, and I thought class prejudice and barriers more injurious to national welfare than sex barriers. I was deeply impressed with her reply. She said, in a tone of utmost conviction: "Well I can only tell you that I, who am a working-class woman, have never known class distinction and class prejudice to stand in the way of my advancement, whereas the sex barrier meets me at every turn."

I felt that through Annie Kenney's whole being throbbed the passion of her soul for other women, to lift from them the heavy burden, to give them life, strength, freedom, joy, and the dignity of human beings, that in all things they might be treated fairly with men. I was struck by her expression and argument; it was straightforward in its simplicity, yet there was inspiration about her.

Then Mrs. Pethick-Lawrence and I, during a day's motoring expedition, achieved a rare

**Robert, First Earl of Lytton
The Countess of Lytton**

talk-out. She met all my arguments, all my prejudices and false deductions, with counter-arguments, and above all facts of which I had till then no conception.

I learnt that before resorting to militancy the women's organisations had for many years past succeeded in obtaining a majority of supporters in the House of Commons, and the backing of leading men of both parties. It was startling to realise that the proposed advocacy of such men as Lord Beaconsfield, the late Lord Salisbury, and Mr. Arthur Balfour had not moved the Conservative Party in any way to assist their cause. When the Liberal Government was returned to power in 1906 under the leadership of Sir Henry Campbell-Bannerman, he himself was a declared suffragist, as were all but a few of the men of most influence in his Cabinet, including Mr. Birrell, Mr. Buxton, Mr. John Morley, and Mr. John Burns.

The women had tried repeatedly, and always in vain, every peaceable means open to them of influencing successive Governments. Processions and petitions were absolutely useless. I saw the extreme need of their position, the ineffectiveness of every method hitherto adopted to persuade these professed suffragists to put their theories into practice.

January 1909

I became a member of the Women's Social and Political Union on the twenty-eighth, and I wrote to Mrs. Pethick-Lawrence offering myself for the deputation. I did not tell anybody but her of my decision. On the thirtieth I received her answer, accepting my offer.

February 24, 1909

I went up to London from Homewood, without telling Mother of the plan and actually without saying goodbye to her, as she went out to the village before I started. I wrote her the following letter at King's Cross Station, but it was not posted till later in the day:

Wednesday

My Angel Mother,—I don't know whether I shall post this to you or see you first. I want to have a letter ready.

Don't be startled or afraid. I have something to tell you which—with the help of recent presentiments—you, I know, are half expecting to hear.

If you ever see this letter it will mean that after joining the deputation I have been arrested and shall not see you again until I have been to Holloway. For months I have been planning this letter to you, but now that the time has come, it is not any easier to write for that. Of course, my hope has been all along that I should be able to take you into my confidence, that I should have the perhaps all-undeserved yet heaven-like joy of knowing that though you could not share all my views, yet that you would understand why I held them, and, granted these, you would

further understand my action and the great sacrifice which I know it means to you. My darling Muddy, you will never know, I trust, the pain it is to have to do this thing without your sympathy and help—with, on the contrary, the certainty that it shocks you and hurts you and makes you suffer in numberless ways. Hardly a day has passed but what I have tried to feel my way with you, tried to convert you—not to my theoretic views, difference there does not matter, but to my intended conduct in connection with them. Every day I have failed.

I am no hero, but the thought of other travellers' much worse privations on that road will, I believe, fizzle up my flimsy body enough for what is necessary, and if only I knew you were helping me in your heart I should not, could not, fail, Muddy darling.

You can't forgive me now, but perhaps you will some day. Whatever you feel toward me, whatever I do, I shall still be always

Your most loving and devoted
Con.

I went to 4 Clement's Inn, lunched there with Mrs. Pethick-Lawrence, Christabel, Mrs. Pankhurst, and Mrs. Tuke; Miss Neal came too. She kindly undertook to post my letter to Mother and buy me a brush and comb and toothbrush in case we should be sent to the first division.

I had a cracking headache and felt quite dazed. They kindly put me to lie down in the upstairs rest room boudoir, where Mrs. Pankhurst and Christabel had remained hidden from the police on October 13, 1908.

At about six o'clock we had supper. I ate next to nothing. Miss Elsa Gye, who had been summoned by telegraph to come and assist me through the deputation, was at supper. She was a delightful girl, young and fresh-looking. I had been told that she was just engaged to be married, and I felt it was horrible that she should risk weeks of imprisonment solely because of me.

I had disguised myself by doing my hair in an early Victorian way, so that the police, if on the look-out for me, should not recognise me and so be tempted not to arrest me; for people whose relatives might make a fuss effectively are considered awkward customers.

As we drove to Caxton Hall, it suddenly struck me that I had not sufficiently learnt up my part. "What does one have to do?" I asked. "I suppose I must do something to show that I mean business." "Oh, no," my companion answered, "you needn't bother about what you'll do. It will all be done *to* you. There is only one thing you must remember. It is our business to go forward, and whatever is said to you and whatever is done to you, you must on no account be turned back." That seemed to me at the time, and has seemed to me ever since, to be the essence of our militant tactics.

Miss Gye and I sat in the body of the hall, we had on the "Votes for Women" sashes and were to join the deputation unostentatiously as it left the building.

Many friends had seen and not recognised me, at which I was delighted. Others did recognise me, and seeing I had the sash on, which meant the deputation, they looked immensely surprised.

The following resolution was put to the meeting and carried with acclamation: "That this Parliament of women expresses its indignation that while every measure in the King's Speech vitally affects the interests of their sex, and while heavier financial burdens are to be laid upon woman tax-payers, the Government have not included in the programme for the session a measure to confer the Parliamentary vote upon duly qualified women. The women here assembled call upon the Government to introduce and carry into law this session a measure giving votes to women on the same terms as to men.

"A deputation is hereby appointed, to whom is entrusted the duty of forthwith conveying this resolution to the Prime Minister at the House of Commons and eliciting his reply."

A copy was then handed to each member of the deputation.

Presently the deputation came down from the platform, formed up in couples, headed by Mrs. Pethick-Lawrence, and marched out of the hall. We were thirty women in all. By this time I had a feeling of exhilaration that the moment for my own independent action had come at last.

We had scarcely stepped into the street before we found ourselves hedged in by a ∧-shaped avenue of police, narrowing as we advanced. They asked no questions, said nothing, but proceeded to close upon us from either side. My companion and I kept together. Very soon all breath seemed to have been pressed out of my body, but remembering the order of the day, "Don't be turned back," I tried to hold my ground even when advance was out of the question. Miss Gye, however, soon realised the situation and pulled me back, saying, "We are not yet in Parliament Square; we must manage to get there somehow; let's try another way." The police had forced themselves between the ranks of the deputation, keeping them apart and trying also to sever the couples, but Miss Gye and I managed to regain hold of each other.

Miss Gye and I were, of course, recognisable as members of the deputation by our sashes, and though at first whenever the police or the crowd pushed us apart she managed to return to me, we eventually got completely separated and lost sight of each other.

First when the crowd wedged me up against a policeman, I said to him: "I know you are only doing your duty and I am doing mine." His only answer was to seize me with both his hands round the ribs, squeeze the remaining breath out of my body and, lifting me completely into the air, throw me with all his strength. Thanks to the crowd I did not reach the ground; several of my companions in more isolated parts of the square were thrown repeatedly onto the pavement.

But I gained in the direction of the House nevertheless, always assisted by the crowd. A German lady who was tall, well-built, and of considerable strength managed to keep near me. Three times, after each of the "throws," she came to my help and warded off the crowd while I leant up against some railings, or against her shoulder to recover my breath. Several times I said to her, "I can't go on; I simply can't go on." She answered, "Wait for a little, you will be all right presently." At the time and ever since I have felt most inexpressibly grateful to this stranger-friend.

I found myself at the gates of the Members' Entrance. No crowd was near and only two policemen stood, ordinary-wise, at either side of the gate. They did not seem to be noticing me. I straightened my back to assume as much of a normal appearance as possible. I passed through the gate. At this the policeman nearest to me turned and seized my arm. Expecting to be thrown as before, I tried to hold my ground and said, "Please let me pass," or words to that effect. Another policeman promptly took me by the other arm and I was led off at a great pace.

We seemed to be going a long way. "How shall I ever get back from here," I wondered. Presently there was an alteration in the sounds of our footsteps and in the gestures of the men. I opened my eyes and looked up. Close in front of me, over a doorway, was a blue lamp with the words "Police Station" printed upon it. I knew then that I had been arrested.

It was here, at Cannon Row, that I first tasted the delights of that full, unfettered companionship which is among the greatest immediate rewards of those who work actively in this cause. No drudgery of preliminary acquaintanceship has to be got through, no misdoubting enquiries as to kindred temperaments or interests. The sense of unity and mutual confidence is complete and begins from the first unhesitatingly.

I had made no arrangements as to where I should spend the night, my chief concern having been to keep secret my share in the day's proceedings till they were over. I felt stunned and cold as ice. I was in a sense, of course, satisfied and glad that, at least, I had shared what the other women had endured, but for the first time during that day it had come before me forcibly that, not only the Government, but the general public too were to a great extent responsible for the official treatment of the deputation.

I took a four-wheeler and made for my youngest sister's house in Bloomsbury Square. On the way, by as it seemed a strange coincidence, I passed my eldest sister, who was just emerging from a theatre with a friend. I stopped and spoke to her. She apparently did not notice my dishevelled condition or suspect that I had been with the deputation. She told me that she too was staying in Bloomsbury Square. Arrived there, I found my hostess in bed. I asked her if she could put me up. "You've been with the deputation?" she asked. "Yes." "You've not been arrested yourself?" "Yes." Her look of mingled sympathy and satisfaction was life-giving, I shall never forget it. Both my sisters were immensely kind and helpful. The house was full, and I shared a bed with my eldest sister. All night she kept her strong arm round my heart and steadied my throbbing body which, owing to the attentions of the police, continued to shake all night.

In the morning we telephoned to Mother, supposing she would have received my letter, telling her of the trial at Bow Street that morning, but begging her not to come up for it unless she specially wished to do so. This telephone message was, unfortunately, the first news that reached her of my arrest, and was a great shock to her. She could not have caught a train that would have brought her in time to Bow Street; my eldest sister, Betty, and my brother, Vic, went down to her later in the day. I felt happier than I had done for a long time. I knew that the first news would be the worst to her, that had now reached her, all else would seem unimportant in comparison; the most difficult, most dreaded part of my job was over.

Betty drove with me in a hansom to Bow Street. A considerable crowd was waiting outside the police station; we elbowed our way through them with great difficulty and only by the help of the police, to whom we appealed to ease matters "for one of the accused." I felt dazed with the press of people. Before long I found myself in a sort of loose-box guard-room, or wide passage, where all my fellow-criminals and many of their friends were assembled. Many of my personal friends were there and most heart-gladdeningly kind to

me. I had concocted a short speech, explaining the reasons of my action. I was told it was not very likely that the magistrate would allow me to deliver it; my friends kindly helped me to condense it as much as possible. It consisted of about four short paragraphs, sentences bearing on the reasonableness, justice, and urgency of our demand. I remember nothing of it but these words: "I have been more proud to stand by my friends in their trouble than I have ever been of anything in my life before."

The sentence was one month, with the alternative of being bound over to "keep the peace." I was immensely relieved that there was no fine. At the same time the length of the sentence was a surprise and somewhat of a shock, although I had prepared myself for it. It seemed hardly believable that what I had done was really considered worthy of four weeks in prison.

Eventually we filed out into a courtyard where the prison van, Black Maria, like the hull of a great dead ship, awaited her cargo.

I moved forward after the others. Black Maria looked like a sort of hearse with elephantiasis—warranted to carry many coffins concealed in her body and to bear them to as many graves. She fairly set one shuddering. To get inside her seemed a sort of living death, certainly, most literally, entry into another world. For a moment I hesitated and thought, "Suppose I refuse to get in?" The mere notion called up the forces arrayed against one and made me realise my utter helplessness. The gates, the bolts, locks, and chains, the cells we had just left, the court and magistrate, the high walls all around, the enormous policemen on every hand. The one who stood at the open door of the van said, "Come along, please." His words were civil enough and linked one back to the normal outer world, but his voice and beckoning gesture were authoritative and the sense of physical power seemed to wedge one in.

When the cells were all filled the passage was duly packed with prisoners, standing one against the other like tinned sardines. As the van was not high enough to admit of standing upright, this must have been a most tiring position. Presently there was a final shutting and locking of the outer door, in which was a small grating window, as we know it from the outside. Then followed a rumbling jerk and Black Maria's great overcharged body began her long, jolting drive to Holloway.

We started singing the "Women's *Marseillaise*" and other of our songs. Those in the passage managed to put a scarf with our colours through the ventilator under the coachman's seat, others passed a scarf through the grating window of the door at the opposite end. These feats were, of course, communicated to the whole Maria-ful of us, and the news that the police were allowing the scarves to remain was greeted with much cheering.

I joined in the songs for as long as I could and in the counter-cheering whenever we had a cheer from the streets, but I soon withdrew into the luxury of my solitude. I was exhilarated and happy in mind, but my physical exhaustion was considerable. The physical tax of the deputation and the nervous tax of the trial proceedings had strained my powers to their uttermost. At last I was alone with myself.

When we arrived at the prison we formed up along a passage in the order of our arrest. We were taken in charge by two or three wardresses who, without a word or sign of greeting, went through the routine of taking our names, ages, sentences, etc. Then we were removed into waiting cells, three or four of us to each one. I found myself, to my joy, in a cell with our leader, Mrs. Pethick-Lawrence, Miss Leslie Lawless, and Mrs. Fahey, daughter of the great sculptor Gilbert. Strength came back into my bones with delight at being with Mrs. Pethick-Lawrence. She, having been in the prison before, gave us various directions and advice.

Some time after supper had been let in upon us, the door was again opened and "Lytton" was summoned to an unknown presence. I was conducted to a room where a lady in a bonnet stood waiting to receive me. She was the matron. She told me in a civil and considerate manner that she had a letter for me from my mother which she had been allowed to give to me.

I asked: "Is it not against prison rules that I should have the letter?" She looked surprised, but promptly answered, "We make the rules as the occasion calls for, and you have been allowed to receive this letter." "Will the other suffrage prisoners also be allowed to receive letters?" She hesitated, but eventually said decisively, "No." "Then I am afraid I can't have this letter either." In spite of my effort to conceal it, I think she saw or guessed my great desire to have the letter, for the look in her eyes became very kind and she pleaded with me to take the letter. I shook my head. Then she told me it was within the ordinary rules that she should read the letter to me. I hesitated for a moment; there might be something sacredly private in the letter and it seemed such desecration that strangers should know what my mother felt. Then I glanced at the envelope and realised that it had been officially opened and probably read already. So I agreed. The letter had been written under the agitation of the news about me and was not easily legible in places, so that the matron, although she did her best, could not decipher some passages, and the tension of deferred anxiety as to its contents made my mind and hearing dull from overstrain. As a result, I received the impression that my mother was more angry with me than was actually the case. She did not speak of being ill or broken down herself, and I felt I could bear everything but that; but the imagined degree of her disapproval shadowed the whole of my imprisonment without cause.

On returning to my companions in the waiting cell I told them what had taken place. My mind was filled with thoughts of my mother and I remember no details until the door was again thrown open and a wardress told us to line up in the passage, preparatory to inspection by the medical officer.

After the medical examination we were soon taken off, separately, to the changing room. Here my trinkets, money, watch, the combs in my hair, and everything in my pocket were taken from me and a list made, which I had to sign. I had a great longing to keep my handkerchiefs. A wardress sitting at a desk with a large book on it asked a further string of questions as to age, name, address, place of birth, previous convictions. As I gave Vienna, Austria, for the place of my birth, my father having been in the diplomatic service, I thought how impossible it would have seemed had some seer foretold, at the time of my birth in an official residence, that I was destined to be imprisoned in Holloway as a common criminal.

Mrs. Pethick-Lawrence and I waited together in the passage. Presently a wardress came up to us with a paper in her hand and began reading out the prison rules, which we were told had to be strictly observed under pain of punishment.

We were then led off through various corridors, taken out of doors and into another building, weighed a second time, and taken up a staircase. At the top we were told to remove our shoes and carry them in our hands. In the passage there were cells with locked gates that looked very grim, and locked doors behind them. One door opposite the stairs was open and the gate only closed. This was unlocked for us and we were ushered into a large high room. A fire burned brightly at one end and beds were ranged on either side of the walls. It was evidently a hospital ward. We were shown to the beds nearest the fireplace, on either side of it, and told they would be ours. Mrs. Pethick-Lawrence came over to me and whispered, "They have put us in hospital." The one thing on which my hopes had centred throughout that seemingly eternal day was the prospect of being completely alone at the end of it. Now that was not to be. For the first time I was taken unawares, had made no preparation for the contingency; I felt quite unnerved and could have sobbed like a child. The fact that I was to remain with Mrs. Pethick-Lawrence was my only consolation.

On March 2, as a result of my pleading to be dismissed from the hospital, I was put to sleep in a separate cell along the passage of our ward. This cell had a floor of unpolished wooden boards, contained a fixed iron bedstead, movable washing stand furnished with tin utensils, a wooden chair, a square plank fixed to the wall near the door as a table, and a corner shelf under the window to hold Bible, prayer and hymn book, prayer card, list of rules, salt cellar, toilet paper, slate, and slate pencil.

I was kept in bed that morning until after the rounds of inspection. The Governor was very civil. He urged me to give the required assurance and bind myself over "to be of good behaviour," that I might leave the prison. He asked if I had "considered" my mother. I have no doubt he thought it his duty to talk in this way, and probably he was trying to be kind as well. At the time, however, his insinuation seemed more like a blow in the face. The words rushed to my lips: "If you knew my mother, if you had seen her only once, you would know that it was impossible to risk causing her anxiety without immensely considering it," but I restrained myself and merely said: "I am not the only woman here who has a mother." I remembered that when Mrs. Pankhurst had been imprisoned she had been punished for exchanging a few words with her daughter. The Governor then brought out a stethoscope to examine my heart. This was surprising, as I had not realised that he was a doctor. He urged tonics, but did not insist. Eventually I consented to take maltine and a banana after the mid-day meal, as they were distressed that I was so thin.

I went into the general ward for the greater part of the day. I made my bed and dusted my cell, but was not allowed to wash the floor or clean the tin utensils because of my "heart disease." The quieter nights enabled me to eat more food, and I think I gained in weight and became generally restored to quite normal health. It was obvious that no ordinary prisoner nor Suffragette prisoner would, in my state of health, have been put in hospital, and that I was being kept there either to give me a soft time or for another impenetrable reason. I told the Senior Medical Officer that unless I were allowed to the "other side" I should feel obliged to protest by means which he would probably regret when it was too late.

The days went by with unvarying monotony. Although I had known for several weeks of my decision to go on the deputation and had full time to prepare for a likely imprisonment, I was continually remembering some concern of my home life, the wheels of which would be getting clogged in my absence.

I had determined to begin my strike in real earnest the following week if I failed by reasonable pleadings to get sent to the cells.

I began my strike gently; I knocked off all diet extras, such as the maltine and its accompanying banana or the pudding at the mid-day meal, and kept to the food which would be mine the other side, viz., *Breakfast:* Brown bread, butter, milk. *Mid-day:* Brown bread, potatoes, one vegetable. *Supper:* Brown bread, butter, milk. Both doctors and wardresses talked of the plank bed as one of the hardships likely to be too much for me in the cells, so I took one of the two mattresses from my bed and slept with it on the floor.

My continued appeals to the authorities to treat me as they did my fellow-prisoners and not keep me in hospital now that I was in normal health having proved unavailing, I entered upon the last phase of my strike. I had decided to write the words "Votes for Women" on my body, scratching it in my skin with a needle, beginning over the heart and ending it on my face. My skin proved much tougher than I had expected and the small needle supplied to me for sewing purposes was quite inadequate. I procured another and stronger one for darning my stockings, but neither of them produced the required result. I thought of a hairpin but had only three left of these precious articles and could not make up my mind to spare one. I had the good luck, however, while exercising, to find one, the black enamel of which was already partially worn off. I cleaned and polished it with a stone under my cloak as I walked the round. The next morning before breakfast I set to work in real earnest and, using each of these implements in turn, I succeeded in producing a very fine V just over my heart.

After breakfast I was summoned into the presence of the Governor and given a scolding, but no sentence of punishment was passed and I remained in doubt as to whether my evil deed had been sufficiently impressive. Later on I was taken down to the Senior Medical Officer.

He and the ward superintendent, who ushered me into his presence and exposed the scratched V for his inspection, were evidently much put out. I felt all a craftsman's satisfaction in my job. The V was very clearly and evenly printed in spite of the varying material of its background, a rib-bone forming an awkward bump.

At last he hit on a brilliant idea and said, "If you go on like this we shall have to dismiss you from the prison altogether." I could have congratulated him with both hands for this really understanding remark.

As there were now only ten days before our release I had decided to push through my efforts to get to the cells regardless of all else.

My wound being the nominal ground on which I had been returned to hospital, it had to be treated with official respect.

I was again summoned before the Governor. He looked as if he had an important announcement to make to me. "Do you still wish to leave the hospital?" he asked. I was afraid this might mean my dismissal. "Do you mean going to the other side?" I said. He answered, "Yes." "Rather!" I exclaimed, and could hardly contain myself for surprise and delight. He proceeded to explain: "The weather having changed, the medical officer gives his consent to your being moved to the cells."

The moment of joining my companions was most exhilarating. They were sitting on chairs placed in regular rows, knitting stockings or sewing women's underclothes and men's shirts. I was put into a vacant place about six rows from the front.

Some of them were almost unrecognisably changed by the prison dress, others I was distressed to see looked extremely ill, but, as the news spread amongst them of my presence, they looked my way in turn and gave me a welcoming smile that momentarily changed prison into paradise.

"They That Sow in Tears Shall Reap in Joy"

May 13, 1909

SYLVIA PANKHURST: The Women's Social and Political Union opened in the Prince's Skating Rink, Knightsbridge, a Votes for Women Exhibition in the purple, white, and green. Mrs. Pethick-Lawrence and the Committee of the Union were driven thither by a woman chauffeur in a motor-car for which the Suffragettes had subscribed in order that they might present it to the treasurer on her release from prison. The rink was covered outside with a mass of waving flags in the colours, and inside these also predominated. The theme of the decorations which lined the walls of the great central hall was "They that sow in tears shall reap in joy. He that goeth forth and weepeth, bearing precious seed, shall doubtless come again with rejoicing, bringing his sheaves with him."

The exhibition lasted a fortnight, and at the end of the first week came a great surprise, for a women's drum and fife band, consisting of members of our Union, who had been practising in secret for months past, now dressed in a specially designed uniform of purple, white, and green, formed up in the centre of the rink and with Mrs. Leigh as drum major, marched out playing the *"Marseillaise,"* and then went round the town to advertise the exhibition.

Hundreds of new members were made during the fortnight, and perhaps the smallest part of the whole achievement was that £5,664 was added to the W.S.P.U. campaign fund.

Another effect of the Press coverage of the Suffragettes was that many women artists became aware that the principles of freedom corresponded with their own ideals. Many new suffrage groups were formed, including an Artists' League and the Actresses' Franchise League. The Actresses' Franchise League formed a play committee and a company of players. Only one-act feminist plays were accepted and these were performed throughout England.

Members of the Actresses' Franchise League. Insets:

Ellen Terry, Lilah McCarthy, Gertrude Elliot, Mr. Forbes Robertson

Fourth Women's Parliament   June 29, 1909

EMMELINE PANKHURST: Now we determined to do something still more ambitious; we resolved to test the constitutional right of the subject to petition the Prime Minister as the seat of power. The right of petition, which has existed in England since the earliest known period, was written into the Bill of Rights, which became law in 1689 on the accession of the joint monarchs. According to the Bill of Rights, "It is the right of subjects to petition the King, and all commitments and prosecutions for such petitionings are illegal." The power of the King having passed almost completely into the hands of Parliament, the Prime Minister now stands where the King's majesty stood in former times. Clearly, then, the right of the subject to petition the Prime Minister cannot be legally denied.

Again I called together, on the evening of June 29, a Parliament of Women. Previously I had written to Mr. Asquith stating that a deputation of women would wait on him at the House of Commons at eight o'clock in the evening. I wrote him further that we were not to be refused, as we insisted upon our constitutional right to be received. To my note the Prime Minister returned a formal note declining to receive us.

Our Women's Parliament met at half-past seven that evening, and the petition to the Prime Minister was read and adopted. Then our deputation set forth. Accompanying me as leader were two highly respectable women of advanced years, Mrs. Saul Solomon, whose husband had been Prime Minister at the Cape, and Miss Neligan, one of the foremost of the pioneer educators of England. We three and five other women were preceded by Miss Elsie Howey, who, riding fast, went on horseback to announce our coming to the enormous crowds that filled the streets.

Suffrage prisoners waiting outside Bow Street police court

We were escorted on our way by Inspector Wells, and as we passed, the crowd broke into vociferous cheering, firmly believing that we were after all to be received.

I simply led my deputation on as far as the entrance to St. Stephen's Hall. There we encountered another strong force of police commanded by our old acquaintance, Inspector Scantlebury, who stepped forward and handed me a letter. I opened it and read it aloud to the women. "The Prime Minister, for the reasons which he has already given in a written reply to their request, regrets that he is unable to receive the proposed deputation."

I dropped the note to the ground and said: "I stand upon my rights, as a subject of the King, to petition the Prime Minister, and I am firmly resolved to stand here until I am received."

Inspector Scantlebury turned away and walked rapidly toward the door of the Strangers' Entrance. I turned to Inspector Jarvis, who remained, to several Members of Parliament, and some newspaper men who stood looking on, and begged them to take my message to the Prime Minister, but no one responded, and the inspector, seizing my arm, began to push me away. I now knew that the deputation would not be received and that the old miserable business of refusing to leave, of being forced backward, and returning again and again until arrested, would have to be re-enacted. I had to take into account that I was accompanied by two fragile old ladies, who, brave as they were to be there at all, could not possibly endure what I knew must follow. I quickly decided that I should have to force an immediate arrest, so I committed an act of technical assault on the person of Inspector Jarvis, striking him very lightly on the cheek. He said instantly, "I understand why you did that," and I supposed then that we would instantly be taken. But the other police apparently did not grasp the situation, for they began pushing and jostling our women. I said to the inspector: "Shall I have to do it again?" and he said "Yes." So I struck him lightly a second time, and then he ordered the police to make the arrests.

The matter did not end with the arrest of our deputation of eight women. In recurring deputations of twelve the Suffragettes again and again pressed forward in vain endeavour to reach the House of Commons. In spite of the fact that the crowds were friendly and did everything they could to aid the women, their deputations were broken up by the police and many of the women arrested. By nine o'clock Parliament Square was empty, an enormous force of mounted police having beaten the people back into Victoria Street and across Westminster Bridge. For a short time all looked tranquil, but soon little groups of women, seven or eight at a time, kept appearing mysteriously and making spirited dashes toward the House. This extraordinary procedure greatly exasperated the police, who could not unravel the mystery of where the women came from. As a matter of bygone history the explanation is that the W.S.P.U. had hired thirty offices in the neighbourhood, in the shelter of which the women waited until it was time for them to sally forth. It was a striking demonstration of the ingenuity of women opposing the physical force of men, but it served still another purpose. It diverted the attention of the police from another demonstration which was going on. Other Suffragettes had gone to the official residence of the First Lord of the Admiralty, to the Home Office, the Treasury and Privy Council Offices, and had registered their contempt for the Government's refusal to receive the deputation by the time-honoured method of breaking a window in each place.

One hundred and eight women were arrested that night, but instead of submitting to arrests and trial, the Women's Social and Political Union announced that they were prepared to prove that the Government and not the women had broken the law in refusing to receive the petition.

HUNGER-STRIKE

CHRISTABEL PANKHURST: Now happened something destined to have far-reaching influence on the militant movement, for it led to the adoption of the hunger-strike. One of our members, Miss Wallace Dunlop, an artist of very resourceful mind, entered the House of Commons and stencilled in large letters on the wall of St. Stephen's Hall this aide-mémoire to the Government and Members of Parliament: WOMEN'S DEPUTATION JUNE 29. BILL OF RIGHTS. IT IS THE RIGHT OF THE SUBJECTS TO PETITION THE KING, AND ALL COMMITMENTS AND PROSECUTIONS FOR SUCH PETITIONINGS ARE ILLEGAL.

So sudden was her act that the police could not reach her in time to prevent her. Miss Wallace Dunlop was ejected from the House. Two hours were needed to remove that unwelcome inscription.

"I wrote these words because I thought they were in danger of being forgotten by our legislators and because I intended that they should be indelible," said Miss Wallace Dunlop when charged at Bow Street with "wilful damage," by stencilling on a Parliamentary wall the words of the Bill of Rights. She was sent, in default of paying a fine, to prison for one month.

Miss Wallace Dunlop

Miss Wallace Dunlop, taking counsel with no one and acting entirely on her own initiative, sent to the Home Secretary, Mr. Gladstone, as soon as she entered Holloway Prison, an application to be placed in the first division as befitted one charged with a political offence. She announced that she would eat no food until this right was conceded. Mr. Gladstone did not reply, but after she had fasted ninety-one hours, Miss Wallace Dunlop was set free. She was in an exhausted state, having refused every threat and appeal to induce her to break her fast.*

The stone-throwing case now came on. Miss Ada Cecile Wright's defence of her action explains the motive of all who had made, or would yet make, this form of protest: "I am quite prepared to stand by what I have done. I went to Parliament Square determined that if my leader was again refused permission to present her petition to Mr. Asquith, I would put my protest into a form which would not be forgotten. I do not believe that my action was morally wrong, but I believe that what I did was my duty, because it was a means of calling attention to the present disgraceful state of affairs due to the obstinate action of the Prime Minister in refusing to act justly by the women of the country. If my action was legally wrong I claim that those men who incited me to this act should be with me in this dock today. Mr. Herbert Gladstone ought to be here, who said in the House of Commons that argument was not enough, but that the women will have to use *force majeure* as men had done to obtain the vote. Mr. Haldane ought to be here, who taunted women with using pin-pricks, and asked them why they did not do something serious; Mr. John Burns ought to be here, who said that 'working men had forced open the door at which the ladies were scratching.' If they are not to be sent to prison for inciting me, then I ought not to be sent to prison for taking action far more moderate than their words would suggest."

Arrived at Holloway, the prisoners demanded political prisoner status and after protests of a more vigorous nature, resorted to the hunger-strike. The Government well knew that the prisoners would die rather than yield, and after several days they were, one by one, released as their state of weakness caused alarm.

"Coercion defeated," we said, and declared that we should reserve the right to use the hunger-strike as a protest against the fact of this imprisonment of suffragists, because while it was undoubtedly wrong to deny to suffragists the privileges of political offenders, the greater wrong was to imprison them at all.

July 9, 1909

EMMELINE PANKHURST: My case, coupled with that of the Hon. Mrs. Haverfield, was selected as a test case for all the others, and Lord Robert Cecil was retained for the defence.

I told the magistrate that should he decide that we and not the Government had been

* This was the first hunger-strike in the W.S.P.U. campaign.

guilty of an infraction of the law, we should refuse to be bound over, but should all choose to go to prison.

The magistrate, Sir Albert de Rutzen, an elderly, amiable man, rather bewildered by this unprecedented situation, then gave his decision. He agreed with Mr. Henle and Lord Robert Cecil that the right of petition was clearly guaranteed to every subject, but he thought that when the women were refused permission to enter the House of Commons, and when Mr. Asquith had said that he would not receive them, the women acted wrongly to persist in their demands. He should, therefore, fine them five pounds each, or sentence them to prison for one month in the second division. The sentence would be suspended for the present until learned counsel could obtain a decision from a higher court on the legal point of the right of petition.

I then put in a claim for all the prisoners, and asked that all their cases might be held over until the test case was decided, and this was agreed to.

Lord Robert Cecil again appeared for the defence, and in a masterly piece of argumentation, contended that in England there was and always had been the right of petition, and that the right had always been considered a necessary condition of a free country and a civilised Government. The right of petition, he pointed out, had three characteristics: in the first place, it was the right to petition the actual repositories of power; in the second place, it was the right to petition in person; and in the third place, the right must be exercised reasonably.

"The women," pursued Lord Robert, "had gone to Parliament Square on June 29 in the exercise of a plain constitutional right, and that in going there with a petition they had acted according to the only constitutional method they possessed, being voteless, for the redress of their grievances."

In an address full of bias, and revealing plainly that he had no accurate knowledge

Hunger-striking suffrage prisoners taking exercise in Holloway Prison yard

Alice Paul and Lucy Burns

of any of the events that had led up to the case in hand, the Lord Chief Justice delivered judgment that I and the other women were guilty of an infraction of the law when we insisted on a right to enter the House of Commons. The Lord Chief Justice therefore ruled that our conviction in the lower court had been proper, and our appeal was dismissed with costs.

The decision of the high court was appalling to the members of the W.S.P.U., as it closed the last approach, by constitutional means, to our enfranchisement. Far from discouraging or disheartening us, it simply spurred us on to new and more aggressive forms of militancy.

August 20, 1909

SYLVIA PANKHURST: When Lord Crewe spoke at the great St. Andrew's Hall, Glasgow, Miss Alice Paul succeeded in climbing to the roof and, in the hope of being able to speak to the Cabinet Minister from this point, she lay there concealed for many hours in spite of a downpour of rain. When she was discovered and forced to descend she was heartily cheered for her pluck by a crowd of workmen, one of whom came forward and apologised for having told a policeman of her presence, saying that he had thought she was in need of help.

Later, when the women attempted to force their way into the building, the people needed no urging to lend their aid, and the police who were guarding the entrance were obliged to use their truncheons to beat them back. When the officers of the law attempted to make arrests, the women were rescued from their clutches again and again. Eventually Adela Pankhurst, Lucy Burns, Alice Paul, and Margaret Smith were taken into custody, but even when the gates of the police station were closed upon them, the authorities feared that they would not be able to hold their prisoners, for the crowds shouted vociferously for their release and twisted the strong iron gates. It was only when the women themselves appealed to them that they consented to refrain from further violence.

CHRISTABEL PANKHURST: The Prime Minister and his colleagues were compelled to risk these suffragist encounters, because they had embarked upon a budget-campaign of meetings all over the country, which gave the militants a magnificent opportunity.

Embarrassing as these protests were to Cabinet Ministers, the women who made them paid the greater price, for they risked injury from those who angrily ejected them from meetings and they were in many cases arrested for their part in the demonstrations. Hunger-striking became general, and while this deepened the effect of the women's protests, it involved added suffering and sacrifice.

Unknown woman hunger-striker

Censored!

July 1909

George Bernard Shaw, moved by the horrors of force feeding, wrote a topical sketch called "Press Cuttings" compiled from the editorial columns of the daily papers during the women's war in 1909. It proved to be a biting satire and was banned by the Censor on the grounds that it burlesqued public men: "Mr. Balsquith," the Prime Minister, and "General Mitchener," of the War Office.

The sketch was performed privately at the Court Theatre in July 1909.

PRESS CUTTINGS
By George Bernard Shaw

A TOPICAL SKETCH COMPILED FROM THE EDITORIAL
AND CORRESPONDENCE COLUMNS OF THE DAILY PAPERS
DURING THE WOMEN'S WAR IN 1909

The forenoon of the first of April, three years hence.

General Mitchener is at his writing-table in the War Office, opening letters. On his left is the fireplace, with a fire burning. On his right, against the opposite wall, is a standing desk with an office stool. The door is in the wall behind him, half way between the table and the desk. The table is not quite in the middle of the room: it is nearer to the hearthrug than to the desk. There is a chair at each end of it for persons having business with the General. There is a telephone on the table.

Long silence.

A VOICE FROM THE STREET: Votes for Women!

The General starts convulsively; snatches a revolver from a drawer; and listens in an agony of apprehension. Nothing happens. He puts the revolver back, ashamed; wipes his brow; and resumes his work. He is startled afresh by the entry of an Orderly. This Orderly is an unsoldierly, slovenly, discontented young man.

MITCHENER: Oh, it's only you. Well?

THE ORDERLY: Another one, sir. She's chained herself.

MITCHENER: Chained herself? How? To what? We've taken away the railings and everything that a chain can be passed through.

THE ORDERLY: We forgot the door-scraper, sir. She lay down on the flags and got the chain through before she started hollerin'. She's lyin' there now; and she downfaces us that you've got the key of the padlock in a letter in a buff envelope, and that you'll see her when you open it.

MITCHENER: She's mad. Have the scraper dug up and let her go home with it hanging round her neck.

THE ORDERLY: There is a buff envelope there, sir.

MITCHENER: You're all afraid of these women. *(He picks up the letter.)* It does seem to have a key in it. *(He opens the letter; takes out a key and a note; and reads.)* "Dear Mitch"—Well, I'm dashed!

THE ORDERLY: Yes, sir.

MITCHENER: What do you mean by Yes, sir?

THE ORDERLY: Well, you said you was dashed, sir; and you did look—if you'll excuse my saying it, sir—well, you looked it.

MITCHENER *(who has been reading the letter, and is too astonished to attend to the Orderly's reply)*: This is a letter from the Prime Minister asking me to release the woman with this key if she padlocks herself, and to have her shewn up and see her at once.

THE ORDERLY *(tremulously)*: Don't do it, governor.

MITCHENER *(angrily)*: How often have I ordered you not to address me as governor? Remember that you are a soldier and not a vulgar civilian. Remember also that when a man enters the army he leaves fear behind him. Here's the key. Unlock her and shew her up.

THE ORDERLY: Me unlock her! I dursen't. Lord knows what she'd do to me.

MITCHENER *(pepperily, rising)*: Obey your orders instantly, sir; and don't presume to argue. Even if she kills you, it is your duty to die for your country. Right about face. March.

The Orderly goes out, trembling.

THE VOICE OUTSIDE: Votes for Women! Votes for Women! Votes for Women!

MITCHENER *(mimicking her)*: Votes for Women! Votes for Women! Votes for Women! *(in his natural voice)* Votes for children! Votes for babies! Votes for monkeys! *(He posts himself on the hearthrug and awaits the enemy.)*

THE ORDERLY *(outside)*: In you go. *(He pushes a panting Suffraget into the room.)* The person, sir. *(He withdraws.)*

The Suffraget takes off her tailor-made skirt and reveals a pair of fashionable trousers.

MITCHENER *(horrified)*: Stop, madam. What are you doing? You must not undress in my presence. I protest. Not even your letter from the Prime Minister—

THE SUFFRAGET: My dear Mitchener: I am the Prime Minister. *(He takes off his hat and cloak; throws them on the desk; and confronts the General in the ordinary costume of a Cabinet Minister.)*

MITCHENER: Good heavens! Balsquith!

BALSQUITH *(throwing himself into Mitchener's chair)*: Yes: it is indeed Balsquith. It has come to this: that the only way the Prime Minister of England can get from Downing Street to the War Office is by assuming this disguise; shrieking "Votes for Women"; and chaining himself to your door-scraper. They were at the corner in force. They cheered me. Bellachristina herself was there. She shook my hand and told me to say I was a vegetarian, as the diet was better in Holloway for vegetarians.

MITCHENER: Why didn't you telephone?

BALSQUITH: They tap the telephone. Every switchboard in London is in their hands, or in those of their young men.

MITCHENER: Where on earth did you get the dress? I hope it's not a French dress?

BALSQUITH: Great heavens, no. We're not allowed even to put on our gloves with French chalk. Everything's labelled "Made in Camberwell."

MITCHENER: As a Tariff Reformer, I must say Quite right. (*Balsquith has a strong controversial impulse and is evidently going to dispute this profession of faith.*) No matter. Don't argue. What have you come for?

BALSQUITH: Sandstone has resigned.

MITCHENER (*amazed*): Old Red resigned?

BALSQUITH: Resigned.

MITCHENER: But how? Why? Oh, impossible! the proclamation of martial law last Tuesday made Sandstone virtually Dictator in the metropolis; and to resign now is flat desertion.

BALSQUITH: Yes, yes, my dear Mitchener. I know all that as well as you do: I argued with him until I was black in the face, and he so red about the neck that if I had gone on he would have burst. He is furious because we have abandoned his plan.

MITCHENER: But you accepted it unconditionally.

BALSQUITH: Yes, before we knew what it was. It was unworkable, you know.

MITCHENER: I don't know. Why is it unworkable?

BALSQUITH: I mean the part about drawing a cordon round Westminster at a distance of two miles, and turning all women out of it.

MITCHENER: A masterpiece of strategy. Let me explain. The Suffragets are a very small body; but they are numerous enough to be troublesome—even dangerous—when they are all concentrated in one place—say in Parliament Square. But by making a two-mile radius and pushing them beyond it, you scatter their attack over a circular line twelve miles long. Just what Wellington would have done.

BALSQUITH: But the women won't go.

George Bernard Shaw

MITCHENER: Nonsense: they must go.

BALSQUITH: They won't.

MITCHENER: What does Sandstone say?

BALSQUITH: He says: Shoot them down.

MITCHENER: Of course.

BALSQUITH: You're not serious?

MITCHENER: I'm perfectly serious.

BALSQUITH: But you can't shoot them down! Women, you know!

MITCHENER *(straddling confidently):* Yes you can. Strange as it may seem to you as a civilian, Balsquith, if you point a rifle at a woman and fire it, she will drop exactly as a man drops.

BALSQUITH: But suppose your own daughters—Helen and Georgina—

MITCHENER: My daughters would not dream of disobeying the proclamation. *(As an afterthought)* At least Helen wouldn't.

BALSQUITH: But Georgina?

MITCHENER: Georgina would if she knew she'd be shot if she didn't. That's how the thing would work. Military methods are really the most merciful in the end. You keep sending these misguided women to Holloway and killing them slowly and inhumanly by ruining their health; and it does no good: they go on worse than ever. Shoot a few promptly and humanely; and there will be an end at once of all resistance and of all the suffering that resistance entails.

BALSQUITH: But public opinion would never stand it.

MITCHENER *(walking about and laying down the law):* There's no such thing as public opinion.

BALSQUITH: No such thing as public opinion!!

MITCHENER: Absolutely no such thing. There are certain persons who entertain certain opinions. Well, shoot them down. When you have shot them down, there are no longer any persons entertaining those opinions alive; consequently there is no longer any more of the public opinion you are so much afraid of. Grasp that fact, my dear Balsquith; and you have grasped the secret of government. Public opinion is mind. Mind is inseparable from matter. Shoot down the matter and you kill the mind.

BALSQUITH: But hang it all—

MITCHENER *(intolerantly):* No, I won't hang it all. It's no use coming to me and talking about public opinion. You have put yourself into the hands of the army; and you are committed to military methods. And the basis of all military methods is that when people won't do what they're told to do, you shoot them down.

On November 10, 1909, a "Pageant of Great Women" was presented at the Scala Theatre, London.
The Pageant was written by Cicely Hamilton, arranged by Edith Craig,
and performed by members of the Actresses' Franchise
League and leading suffragists.

Left to right: Nella Powys as Zenobia; Viola Finney as Tsze-Hsi-An; Janette Steer as Queen Elizabeth; Edith Olive as Deborah; Angela Hubbard as Queen Victoria; Mrs. Sam Sothern as Queen Philippa Insets: left, Cicely Hamilton as Christian Davies, Christopher St. John as Hannah Snell; right, Suzanne Sheldon as Catherine the Great, Lina Rathbone as Mary Ann Talbot

FORCIBLE FEEDING

SYLVIA PANKHURST: On this day the Prime Minister was going up to Birmingham to hold a meeting of 10,000 people at the great Bingley Hall. A "bower bedecked" special train was to carry the Cabinet Ministers and Members of Parliament up north straight from their duties in the House, and back again. Tremendous efforts were being made to work up enthusiasm, for at this meeting Mr. Asquith was to throw down his challenge to the House of Lords to proclaim that their power of veto should be abolished, and that the will of the people should prevail. But the Suffragettes were determined that, if the freedom to voice their will were to be confined to half the people alone, there should be no peace in Birmingham for the Prime Minister.

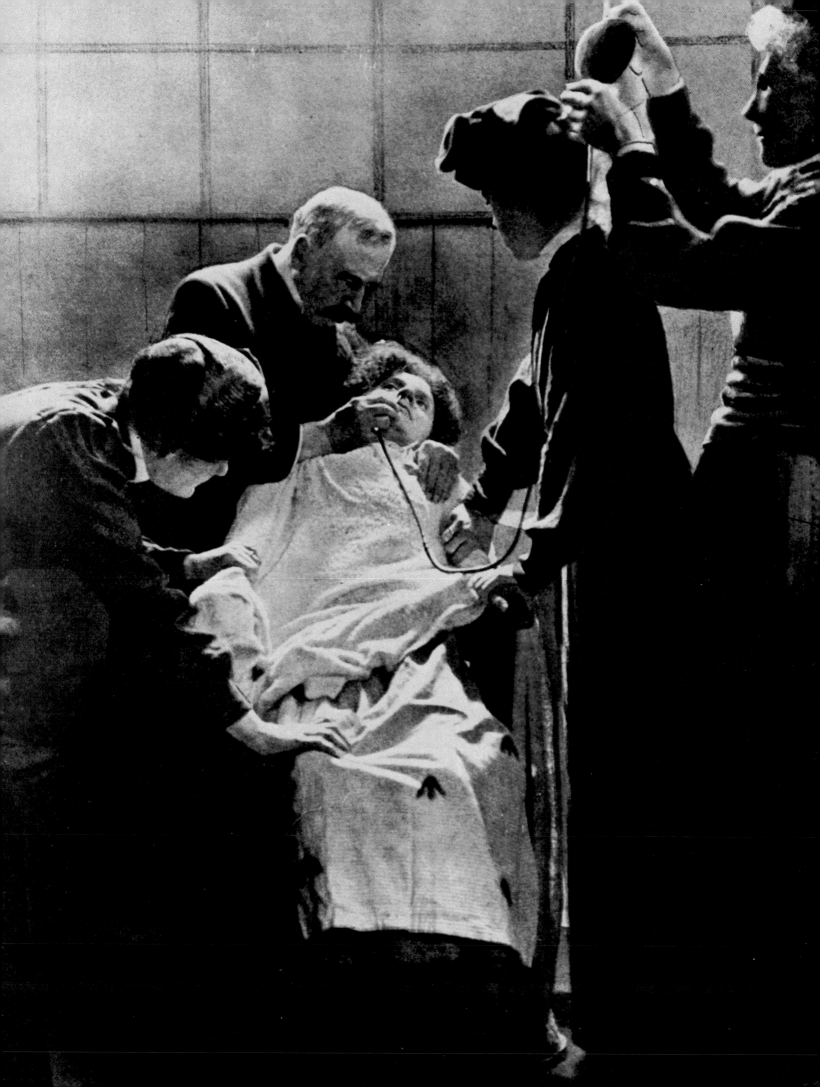

Mary Leigh and her colleagues, who were organising there, began by copying the police methods so far as to address a warning to the public not to attend Mr. Asquith's meeting, as disturbances were likely to ensue, and immediately the authorities were seized with panic. A great tarpaulin was stretched across the glass roof of the Bingley Hall, a tall fire escape was placed on each side of the building, and hundreds of yards of firemen's hoses were laid across the roof. Wooden barriers, nine feet high, were erected along the station platform and across all the leading thoroughfares in the neighbourhood, whilst the ends of the streets both in front and at the back of Bingley Hall were sealed up by barricades. Nevertheless, inside those very sealed-up streets, numbers of Suffragettes had been lodging for days past and were quietly watching the arrangements.

When Mr. Asquith left the House of Commons for his special train, detectives and policemen hemmed him in on every side, and when he arrived at the station in Birmingham, he was smuggled to the Queen's Hotel by a back subway a quarter of a mile in length and carried up in a luggage lift.

Meanwhile, tremendous crowds were thronging the streets and the ticket holders were watched as closely as spies in time of war. They had to pass four barriers and were squeezed through them by a tiny gangway and then passed between long lines of police and amid an incessant roar of "show your ticket." The vast throngs of people who had no tickets and had only come out to see the show surged against the barriers like great human waves, and occasionally cries of "Votes for Women" were greeted with deafening cheers.

Inside the hall there were armies of stewards and groups of police at every turn. The meeting began by the singing of a song of freedom led by a band of trumpeters. Then the Prime Minister appeared. "For years past the people have been beguiled with unfulfilled promises," he declared, but during his speech he was again and again reminded, by men, of the unfulfilled promises which had been made to women; and, though men who interrupted him on other subjects were never interfered with, these champions of the Suffragettes were, in every case, set upon with a violence which was described by onlookers as "revengeful" and "vicious." Thirteen men were maltreated in this way.

Meanwhile, amid the vast crowds outside women were fighting for their freedom. Cabinet Ministers had sneered at them and taunted them with not being able to use physical force. "Working men have flung open the franchise door at which the ladies are scratching," Mr. John Burns had said. So now they were showing that, if they would, they could use violence, though they were determined that, at any rate as yet, they would hurt no one. Again and again they charged the barricades, one woman with a hatchet in her hand, and the friendly people always pressed forward with them. In spite of a thousand police the first barrier was many times thrown down. Whenever a woman was arrested the crowd struggled to secure her release, and over and over again they were successful, one woman being snatched from the constables no fewer than seven times.

Inside the hall Mr. Asquith had not only the men to contend with, for the meeting had not long been in progress when there was a sudden sound of splintering glass and a woman's voice was heard loudly denouncing the Government. A missile had been thrown through one of the ventilators by a number of Suffragettes from an open window in a house opposite. The police rushed to the house door, burst it open, and scrambled up the stairs, falling over each other in their haste to reach the women, and then dragged them down and flung them into the street, where they were immediately placed under arrest. Even whilst this was happening there burst upon the air the sound of an electric motor horn which issued from another house near by. Evidently there were Suffragettes there too. The front door of this house was barricaded and so also was the door of the room in which the women

**Suffrage demonstration outside Bingley Hall,
Birmingham, September 17, 1909**

were, but the infuriated Liberal stewards forced their way through and wrested the instrument from the woman's hands.

No sooner was this effected, however, than the rattling of missiles was heard on the other side of the hall, and on the roof of the house, thirty feet above the street, lit up by a tall electric standard was seen the little agile figure of Mary Leigh, with a tall fair girl beside her. Both of them were tearing up the slates with axes, and flinging them onto the roof of the Bingley Hall and down into the road below—always, however, taking care to hit no one and sounding a warning before throwing. The police cried to them to stop and angry stewards came rushing out of the hall to second this demand, but the women calmly went on with their work. A ladder was produced and the men prepared to mount it, but the only reply was a warning to "be careful" and all present felt that discretion was the better part of valour. Then the fire hose was dragged forward, but the firemen refused to turn it on, and so the police themselves played it on the women until they were drenched to the skin. The slates had now become terribly slippery, and the women were in great danger of sliding from the steep roof, but they had already taken off their shoes and so contrived to retain a foothold, and without intermission they continued "firing" slates. Finding that water had no power to subdue them, their opponents retaliated by throwing bricks and stones up at the two women, but, instead of trying, as they had done, to avoid hitting, the men took good aim at them and soon blood was running down the face of the tall girl, Charlotte Marsh, and both had been struck several times.

At last Mr. Asquith had said his say and came hurrying out of the building. A slate was hurled at the back of his car as it drove away, and then "firing" ceased from the roof, for the Cabinet Minister was gone. Seeing that they now had nothing to fear the police at once placed a ladder against the house and scrambled up to bring the Suffragettes down, and then, without allowing them to put on their shoes, they marched them through the streets, in their stockinged feet, the blood streaming from their wounds and their wet garments clinging to their limbs. At the police station bail was refused and the two women were sent to the cells to pass the night in their drenched clothing.

We knew that Mary Leigh, Charlotte Marsh, and their comrades in the Birmingham prison would carry out the hunger-strike, and, on the following Friday, September 24, reports appeared in the Press that the Government had resorted to the horrible expedient of feeding them by force by means of a tube passed into the stomach. Filled with concern, the committee of the Women's Social and Political Union at once applied both to the prison and to the Home Office to know if this were true but all information was refused.

Statement to Her Solicitor

MRS. MARY LEIGH: On my arrival at Winson Green Gaol on Wednesday afternoon, September 22, I protested against the treatment to which I was subjected and broke the windows in my cell. Accordingly at nine o'clock in the evening I was taken to the punishment cell, a cold dark room on the ground floor—light only shines on very bright days—with no furniture in it. A plank bed was brought in. I was then stripped and handcuffed with the hands behind during the day, except at meals, when the palms were placed together in front. At night they were also placed in front with the palms out. On Thursday food was brought into the cell—potatoes, bread, and gruel—but I did not touch it.

On Thursday afternoon the visiting magistrates came, and I was taken before them, handcuffed. After hearing what I had to say they sentenced me to nine days' close confinement, with bread and water, and to lose forty-two days' remission marks, and pay five shillings damage. The handcuffs were removed at midnight on Thursday by the matron's orders. I still refrained from food. About noon on Saturday I was told the matron wished to speak to me, and was taken to the doctor's room, where I saw the matron, eight wardresses, and two doctors. There was a sheet on the floor and an armchair on it. The doctor said I was to sit down, and I did.

He then said: "You must listen carefully to what I have to say. I have orders from my superior officers" (he had a blue official paper in his hand, to which he referred) "that you are not to be released, even on medical grounds. If you still refrain from food I must take other measures to compel you to take it."

I then said: "I refuse, and if you force food on me I want to know how you are going to do it."

He said: "That is a matter for me to decide."

I said he must prove I was insane, that the Lunacy Commissioners would have to be summoned to prove I was insane, and that he could not perform an operation without the patient's consent. The feeding by the mouth I described as an operation and the feeding by the tube as an outrage. I also said: "I shall hold you responsible, and shall take any measure in order to see whether you are justified in doing so."

He merely bowed and said: "Those are my orders."

I was then surrounded and forced back onto the chair, which was tilted backward. There were about ten persons around me. The doctor then forced my mouth so as to form a pouch, and held me while one of the wardresses poured some liquid from a spoon; it was milk and brandy. After giving me what he thought was sufficient, he sprinkled me with eau de cologne, and wardresses then escorted me to another cell on the first floor, where I remained two days. On Saturday afternoon the wardresses forced me onto the bed and the two doctors came in with them. While I was held down a nasal tube was inserted. It is two yards long, with a funnel at the end; there is a glass junction in the middle to see

Mary Leigh dressed in her uniform as drum major of the W.S.P.U. fife band

if the liquid is passing. The end is put up the right and left nostril on alternate days. Great pain is experienced during the process, both mental and physical. One doctor inserted the end up my nostril while I was held down by the wardresses, during which process they must have seen my pain, for the other doctor interfered (the matron and two of the wardresses were in tears), and they stopped and resorted to feeding me by the spoon, as in the morning. More eau de cologne was used. The food was milk. I was then put to bed in the cell, which is a punishment cell on the first floor. The doctor felt my pulse and asked me to take food each time, but I refused.

On Sunday he came in and implored me to be amenable and have food in the proper way. I still refused. I was fed by the spoon up to Saturday, October 2, three times a day. From four to five wardresses and the two doctors were present on each occasion. Each time the same doctor forced my mouth, while the other doctor assisted, holding my nose on nearly every occasion. On Monday, September 27, I was taken to a hospital cell, where I was fed by spoon in similar fashion. On Tuesday, the twenty-eighth, a feeding cup was used for the first time, and Benger's Food poured into my mouth for breakfast and supper, and beef-tea mid-day.

On Tuesday afternoon I overheard Miss Edwards, on issuing from the padded cell opposite, call out, "Locked in a padded cell since Sunday." I called out to her, but she was rushed into it. I then applied (Tuesday afternoon) to see the visiting magistrates. I saw them, and wished to know if one of our women was in a padded cell, and, if so, said she must be allowed out. I knew she had a weak heart and was susceptible to excitement, and it would be very bad for her if kept there longer. I was told no prisoner could interfere on behalf of another; any complaint on my own behalf would be listened to. I then said this protest of mine must be made on behalf of this prisoner, and if they had no authority to intervene on her behalf, it was no use applying to them for anything. After they had gone I made my protest by breaking eleven panes in my hospital cell. I was then fed in the same way by the feeding cup and taken to the padded cell, where I was stripped of all clothing and a night dress and bed given to me. As they took Miss Edwards out they put me into her bed, which was still warm. The cell is lined with some padded stuff—india-rubber or something. There was no air, and it was suffocating. This was on Tuesday evening.

I remained there until the Wednesday evening, still being fed by force. I was then taken back to the same hospital cell, and remained there until Saturday, October 2, noon, feeding being continued in the same way. On Saturday, October 2, about dinner time, I determined on stronger measures by barricading my cell. I piled my bed, table, and chair by jamming them together against the door. They had to bring some men warders to get in with iron staves. I kept them at bay about three hours. They threatened to use the fire hose. They used all sorts of threats of punishment. When they got in, the chief warder threatened me and tried to provoke me to violence. The wardresses were there, and he had no business to enter my cell, much less to use the threatening attitude. I was again placed in the padded cell, where I remained until Saturday evening. I still refused food, and I was allowed to starve until Sunday noon. Food was brought, but not forced during that interval.

Sunday noon, four wardresses and two doctors entered my cell and forcibly fed me by the tube through the nostrils with milk. Sunday evening, I was also fed through the nostril. I remained in the padded cell until Monday evening, October 4. Since then I have been fed through the nostril twice a day.

The sensation is most painful—the drums of the ears seem to be bursting and there is a horrible pain in the throat and the breast. The tube is pushed down twenty inches. I have to lie on the bed, pinned down by wardresses, one doctor stands up on a chair, holding

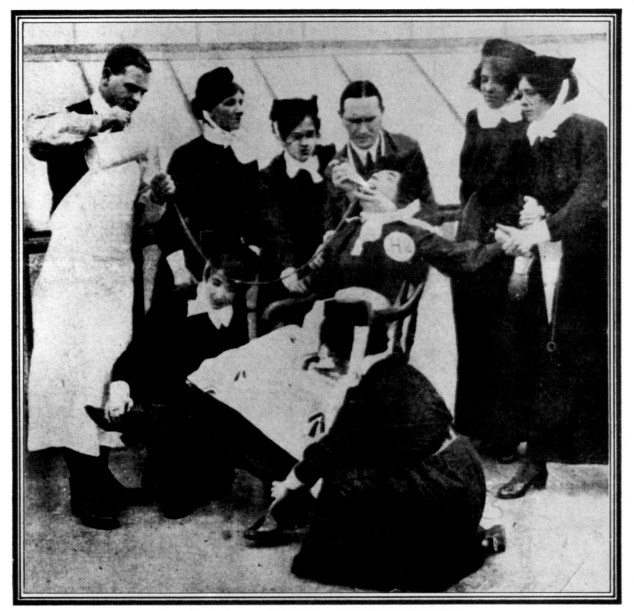

A Daily Sketch photograph depicting a re-enactment of forcible feeding

the funnel end at arm's length, so as to have the funnel end above the level, and then the other doctor, who is behind, forces the other end up the nostrils.

The one holding the funnel end pours the liquid down—about a pint of milk, egg and milk sometimes being used. When the glass junction shows the fluid has gone down, a signal is given; a basin of warm water is put under my chin, and the other doctor withdraws the tube and plunges the end into the water. Before and after use they test my heart and make a lot of examination. The after-effects are a feeling of faintness, a sense of great pain in the diaphragm or breast-bone, in the nose and the ears. The tube must go below the breast-bone, though I cannot feel it below there.

I was very sick on the first occasion after the tube was withdrawn. I have also suffered from bad indigestion. I am fed in this way very irregularly. I have used no violence, though having provocation in being fed by force. I resist and am overcome by weight of numbers. If the doctor does not think the fluid is going down sufficiently swiftly he pinches my nose with the tube in it and my throat, causing me increased pain.

During the previous months, thirty-seven women had been released from prison after hunger-striking. On August 13 the Home Secretary, Herbert Gladstone, had received a letter from Edward VII:

Marienbad 13 VIII 09

Dear Mr. Gladstone,
The King has signed the enclosed submissions as he feels sure you will have seriously considered the advisability of letting these women out of prison.

At the same time His Majesty would be glad to know why the existing methods, which must obviously exist for dealing with prisoners who refuse nourishment, should not be adopted.

His Majesty is inclined to think that this short term of martyrdom is more likely to attract than deter women from joining the ranks of the militant Suffragettes.

Yours very truly,
Ponsonby

Rufford Abbey, Ollerton, Notts.   11 September 1909

Dear Mr. Gladstone,
The King is very glad to learn from your Memorandum that more stringent and precautionary measures are to be taken with regard to the Suffragettes whose behaviour of late has, in many cases, been a public scandal.

I remain
Yours sincerely,
Arthur Davidson

It was after this correspondence with King Edward VII that Herbert Gladstone, the Home Secretary, issued orders that the medical officers at Winson Green Gaol should use force to feed the hunger-striking Suffragette prisoners.

DAILY NEWS, Wednesday, September 29, 1909

(From our Parliamentary Correspondent) WESTMINSTER, Tuesday Night

This afternoon, before Mr. Masterman's courteous replies to questions as to the experiences of the suffragist prisoners in Birmingham, Mr. Keir Hardie's bolts tumble harmless. Even Mr. Snowden is baffled. Mr. Masterman comes forward not to assert a blind authority on the part of the state but to discharge a grave duty to the women themselves. Their lives are sacred, and must be preserved. The officials would be liable for criminal proceedings if these prisoners were to commit suicide by starvation. Yes, they had been induced to take food, and there had been a progressive improvement in their health. No, chains were not necessary to the hospital treatment; female wardresses did what had to be done under the supervision of the doctor. The House cheered the Minister; he had well braved the ordeal.

J. Keir Hardie

DAILY NEWS, September 29, 1909

To the Editor of the DAILY NEWS

Sir,—May I crave the courtesy of your columns to call attention to the latest development in connection with the militant section of the women's suffrage movement?

In reply to a question of mine to-day, Mr. Masterman, speaking on behalf of the Home Secretary, admitted that some of the nine women prisoners now in Winson Green Gaol, Birmingham, had been subjected to "hospital treatment," and admitted that this euphemism meant administering food by force. The process employed was the insertion of a tube down the throat into the stomach and pumping the food down. To do this, I am advised, a gag has to be used to keep the mouth open.

That there is difference of opinion concerning the tactics of the militant Suffragettes goes without saying, but surely there can be no two opinions concerning the horrible brutality of this proceeding? Women, worn and weak by hunger, are seized upon, held down by brute force, gagged, a tube inserted down the throat, and food poured or pumped into the stomach. Let British men think over the spectacle.

I endeavoured to learn from Mr. Masterman under what law, rule, or regulation this thing had been done, but he was unable to say without notice. He admitted, however, that it had been done by order of the Home Office. My information is that there is no such power given to prison authorities save in the case of persons certified to be insane. If this be so, a very serious responsibility rests with the Home Office, and I shall endeavour to find out to-morrow at question time whether it is so or not.

May I add one more remark? I was horrified at the levity displayed by a large section of the Members of the House when the question was being answered. Had I not heard it I could not have believed that a body of gentlemen could have found reason for mirth and applause in a scene which I venture to say has no parallel in the recent history of our country. One of these days we shall learn that Mrs. Leigh or some other of her brave fellow-prisoners has succumbed to the "hospital treatment," as a man did in 1870. I would not envy the position of the Home Secretary or the Government responsible for such a result. Surely the people of these islands will speak out ere our annals are stained by such a tragedy.—Yours, etc.,

J. Keir Hardie
House of Commons, Sept. 27

THE TIMES, October 5, 1909

To the Editor of THE TIMES

Sir,—You allowed one of us a few weeks ago to cite in your columns passages from speeches by Mr. W. E. Gladstone and Mr. John Morley which defined the attitude of the older Liberalism towards political offenders. They held that only "base and degrading crimes" could properly be visited with humiliating punishments, they denounced the forcing of prison dress and other indignities on Irish agitators and produced a formidable list of precedents to show that for many generations it has been the practice of both parties to accord the honours of war to political prisoners. Mr. Herbert Gladstone, in dealing with the suffragist prisoners, persists in his unfilial reading of Liberalism. He insists on classing women who are fighting for an idea with ordinary criminals, and to the hunger-strike he has now replied with the loathsome expedient of the stomach-tube. The women protested against humiliating punishments: he proceeds to make the inflictions of these humiliations possible by a method which, besides being certainly nauseating and probably dangerous, is an unpardonable outrage on human dignity.

To say that the alternative is to abandon all thought of punishing these prisoners is to reason loosely. Two courses are open to Mr. Gladstone. He may release the women after five or six days of total starvation, a punishment which was thought adequate until they happened to choose the Prime Minister as the object of their demonstrations. He may also transfer them to the first division. The stomach-tube is not required in order to render imprisonment possible. It is required in order to make possible punishment in the second and third divisions. We observe that some Liberals are now discovering that persons who have been guilty of violence are not political offenders. But most of our noteworthy political prisoners from Smith O'Brien to Dr. Jameson were leaders in violence incomparably more formidable than anything which these women have yet attempted.

There are, we take it, two main reasons for discriminating in favour of political prisoners. In the first place, they are commonly persons of high character who possess (to use the words which Mr. W. E. Gladstone quoted from Burke) that noble sensitiveness which "feels a stain like a wound." In the second place, no Government party or class can be trusted, without the check of some such tradition as this, to deal fairly with its opponents. After the alternate Whig and Tory proscriptions of the seventeenth century, our forefathers had seen enough of the libertine malice of ignominious punishments. There is evidence, for those who read the Liberal Party Press, that in the present instance the corrosive of party resentment is at work. The oldest of the Liberal dailies has circulated the baseless legend that at Birmingham a deliberate attempt was made to "assassinate" the Prime Minister. Its Parliamentary correspondent has announced that on learning of the sufferings of these women in prison, Liberal Members (who seemed to have laughed at Mr. Hardie's honourable protest) had no room for any emotion save one of sympathy for their "great leader" in his "peril." But the clearest evidence of his vindictive spirit is the Home Secretary's unflagging pursuit of these militant adversaries. Three of the Liverpool demonstrators, who have just emerged from gaol, after the misery and exhaustion of their fast, are now about to be prosecuted for the damage done to the prison furniture to the extent respectively of ls.6d. and 3d. For this they have already been punished in prison. We must say nothing that might prejudice their trial, but it is legitimate to note that when the Home Secretary determined to ignore the traditional maxim "De minimus non curat lex"—"The law does not concern itself about little matters," he can hardly have failed to see the consequences. These women (if found guilty) will again be sentenced, will again reply by a hunger-strike, and will then be tortured by the stomach-tube. There can be no explanation of this pursuit save a determination to break the spirit and degrade the self-respect of women whose real crime is that they have embarrassed the Government, injured it at by-elections, and exposed its chiefs to the just ridicule of the country.

The train of cause and effect is only too clear. At the outset the Government treated the movement with a blind contempt. The movement grew under persecution. Exasperation begat violence, and with suffering came a bravery and a spirit of self-sacrifice which no penalty can crush. The weeks as they pass are bringing us nearer to the phase of mortal tragedy. To our minds the graver responsibility will fall on the members of a nominally democratic party who have turned their backs upon a gallant movement of emancipation....

Lest we should seem in our strictures on Liberalism and its organs in the Press to be guilty of an inconsistency, we wish to take this opportunity of stating that, despite our warm approval of the budget, we have resigned our positions as leader-writers on the DAILY NEWS. We cannot denounce torture in Russia and support it in England, nor can we advocate democratic principles in the name of the party which confines them to a single sex.

We are, Sir, your obedient servants,

H. N. Brailsford

Henry W. Nevinson

"Only Be Thou Strong and Very Courageous"

October 8, 1909

LADY CONSTANCE LYTTON: On this Friday Christabel Pankhurst and I were on our way to Newcastle.

I had made up my mind that I was going to throw a stone—that was as sure as death, but the manner of it was going to be my own; I was equally sure of that. I was not sure of "the stone-throwers." I had vaguely felt that they would have different reasons from mine for this errand, that perhaps, though they could not be more certain than myself, they would mind it less. I had not been in the room with them five minutes before I realised that I was mistaken. I was the "hooligan," if there were one amongst them.

No particular job was given to me. Miss Emily Davison and I were to keep together. It was still early, and first we had to make sure of our stones. We went to the other office to get them. I was doing up mine in brown paper, double thick. "You will not be able to throw those," said the organiser, "if there is the least bit of wind, it will get inside and send them you don't know where." That was true. I found some much thinner paper which kept closely round the stone. I took four or five. On each one I wrote a different thing, I think they were all taken from Mr. Lloyd George's recent speech. I put them into my pockets and went out.

I had not met Miss Davison before, and it was most interesting to hear her experiences. Still, we could neither of us speak nor listen with anything but effort. We decided to go and see what it was like at the Haymarket, a large, open space, where the car with Mr. Lloyd George would probably pass.

We heard cheering in the distance; it was the arrival of Mr. Lloyd George at the theatre, he having driven by another way. My companion began to think that our chance was over until the evening. A feeling came over me that I could not wait any longer, and that somehow or other I must throw my stone. As it would anyhow be but symbolical, it seemed to me one could find an occasion as well here as elsewhere. One thing, however, I was determined upon—it must be more zealously done, more deliberate in its character than the stone-throwing at ordinary windows, which had been done lately. I was determined that when they had me in court my act should inevitably be worse than that of other women. At this moment there was a hurry in the crowd. The police were making a clearing and opening the carriage entrance for a motor-car. We found ourselves on the very edge of the crowd.

As the motor appeared, I whispered to Miss Davison: "Is this any good?" "Not the least in the world," was her reply, "just one of the motors coming back." I knew this, of course, but the instinct was too much for me. To throw a stone against the car as it ran along the side was dangerous, as there were two men in the front. I stepped out into the road, stood straight in front of the car, shouted out, "How can you, who say you back the women's cause, stay on in a Government which refuses them the vote, and is persecuting them for asking it," and threw a stone at the car.

Lady Constance Lytton's stone was aimed low to avoid injuring the chauffeur or passengers. Sir Walter Runciman was in the car, and her stone, wrapped in paper, carried the inscription: "To Lloyd George—Rebellion against tyranny is obedience to God—Deeds, not words."

Lady Constance Lytton in Newcastle shortly before throwing a stone at Sir Walter Runciman's car, October 8, 1909

While in custody at Newcastle Police Station awaiting trial, Lady Constance Lytton wrote to The Times *on behalf of the eleven Suffragettes in custody.*

To the Editor of THE TIMES

Sir,—We ask you to give us our opportunity, before we go through the ordeal awaiting us in Newcastle Prison, of explaining to the public the action which we are now about to take.

We want to make it known that we shall carry on our protest in our prison cells. We shall put before the Government by means of the hunger-strike four alternatives: to release us in a few days; to inflict violence upon our bodies; to add death to the champions of our cause by leaving us to starve; or, and this is the best and only wise alternative, to give women the vote.

We appeal to the Government to yield, not to the violence of our protest, but to the reasonableness of our demand, and to grant the vote to the duly qualified women of the country. We shall then serve our full sentence quietly and obediently and without complaint. Our protest is against the action of the Government in opposing woman suffrage, and against that alone. We have no quarrel with those who may be ordered to maltreat us.

Yours sincerely,

Lily Asquith	Dorothy Shallard
Jane E. Brailsford	Winifred Jones
Kathleen Brown	Constance Lytton
Violet Bryant	Kitty Marion
Ellen Pitfield	Dorothy Pethick
	Ellen W. Pitman

Central Police Station
Newcastle,
October 10, 1909

LADY CONSTANCE LYTTON: I wrote on the wall of my cell my name and the words which rung in my head over and over again, from the Book of Joshua: "Only be thou strong and very courageous."

Who were those for whom we fought? I seemed to hear them in my cell, the defenceless ones who had no one to speak for their hungry need. The sweated workers, the mothers widowed with little children, the women on the streets, and I saw that their backs were bent, their eyes grown sorrowful, their hearts dead without hope. And they were not a few, but thousands upon thousands.

I wrote on the wall:

> To defend the oppressed,
> To fight for the defenceless,
> Not counting the cost.

The magistrates convicted me of "disorderly behaviour with intent to disturb the peace," and bound me over in the sum of fifty pounds and two sureties of twenty-five pounds each, to be enforced for twelve months; in default, one month's imprisonment in the second division. I, of course, had no option of finding sureties for twelve months, and was sentenced to the month's imprisonment. My companion, Miss Davison, was dismissed, as she had literally done nothing.

Mrs. Brailsford, who had struck at the barricade with an axe, was also given the option of being bound over, which she, of course, refused, with the alternative of a month's imprisonment in the second division.

We were put again into a van, but had only a short way to drive. We were shown into a passage of the prison where the Governor came and spoke to us. He was very civil, and begged us not to go on the hunger-strike. Then the matron came, a charming and very refined woman, who walked with a stick, being lame. Miss Davison had headed our little band of twelve; when she was dismissed, Miss Dorothy Pethick, Mrs. Pethick-Lawrence's youngest sister, was our head and spoke for us. Her face had all the beauty that freshness, youth, and grace could give it, and, with it all, for her age—she was twenty-seven—there was a wonderful strength about it. She spoke civilly to the Governor, but in a very determined way. He could not do enough for us. "Don't break your windows—please don't break your windows." "We will not break them if they can open. You must understand that we have come here not to please ourselves; we have pleaded for windows to open in the cells through two years in vain. Now we break the glass to make more sure. It is for the poor things who are shut up in these little cells for weeks and months at a time. Whether they know it or not, their bodies know it—it is all that is bad for them to sleep and live in a room supposed to be ventilated, without a window; and to be given a book, telling them elaborately how a window may be kept open in all weathers by placing a board in front of it on a slant, will not make things any better. And what is more, if you feed us by force, we shall break every window we can lay hands on." "Very well," said the Governor, "choose your own cells; come round and see." Then, with the Governor and matron, we went round. Several cells were shown to us. We were left in some that were small but new—the windows did not open. Finally, Mrs. Brailsford and I were taken to different cells on the ground floor, where we were separated completely from the others.

The first day, Tuesday, was fairly fine. At exercise in the morning we looked around and we noticed some broken glass windows. We shouted "Votes for Women, Hurrah! Hurrah!" but were not sure of any response. They had put our companions into the punishment cells. We were scarcely back in our cells before there were hasty footsteps; they slammed our doors shut, we could only dimly hear the steps as they passed our cells and then above. Soon after we heard shrieks, always coming from the same direction. It seemed as if the others were being fed by force. During about half an hour the sounds were terrible. Then the doctors, two of them, came to us. They had on white jackets, as if they had just come from an operation, as indeed they had. I said to them, "You have been feeding our friends by force?" One of them answered, "Well, yes, we were bound to have a food trial with one or two of them." They felt my pulse, first one, then the other; they felt it over again, then they went out. Mrs. Brailsford and I discussed the feeding of our friends, which had sounded most awful; we did not know what to do. We had, of course, not touched any food since our breakfast in the police-station cells. We ourselves had met with nothing but kindness.

The second morning, Wednesday, October 13, when the doctors came, I stood in the corner of my cell with my arms crossed and my fingers caught in my nostrils and my mouth. It was the best position I knew of for them not to be able to feed me by nose or mouth without having first a considerable struggle. They came, and after I saw that they had no tube I came out from my corner and let them both look at my heart. They thumped, each of them in turn, and felt my pulse as well. Then they appeared to be agreed and went out. I said to them, "You seemed to be puzzled by my heart; I can tell you about it if you like." But they had made up their minds about something, and did not want any help from me.

A wardress came in and announced that I was released, because of the state of my heart! Though this was fairly evident from the visit of the outside doctor, I had not realised it. I gathered my things together and went out. I called to Mrs. Brailsford; she was released too. We were put to wait in the Governor's room; he was not there. We wondered if we were the only two to be released, and if so, why not the others? How about the heart of Nurse Pitman, who was close on sixty, or of Miss Brown, who had only just been released from a recent hunger-strike!

Nurse Pitman and Miss Brown were released the next day. It was not possible to understand for what reason they should have been kept twenty-four hours longer on hunger-strike than Mrs. Brailsford and myself; the only reason that we could see was that our names were known, theirs were not!

Amelia Brown and Alice Paul in court

November 9, 1909

SYLVIA PANKHURST: To-day was Lord Mayor's Day, and, as usual, the Lord Mayor had invited the Cabinet Ministers to a banquet in the Guild Hall. Knowing this, Miss Alice Paul, an American citizen, and Miss Amelia Brown disguised themselves as charwomen, and, carrying buckets and brushes, entered the building with the other cleaners at nine o'clock in the morning. There they hid themselves and waited until the evening, when they took their stand in the gallery outside the banqueting hall. When Mr. Asquith was about to speak, Miss Brown, having carefully selected a pane of the stained-glass window upon which there was no ornament, and which she thought might be easily replaced, stooped down, took off her shoe, and smashed the chosen pane in order that her shout of "Votes for Women" might be heard by those below. Miss Alice Paul also took up the cry. Both women were arrested and afterward sent to prison for one month's hard labour on refusing to pay fines of five pounds and damages of two pounds ten shillings each. They were both forcibly fed and as a result of this Miss Brown was attacked with severe gastritis.

A few days later, on November 13, Mr. Winston Churchill visited Bristol to speak at the Colston Hall. Miss Theresa Garnet, the woman who had been twice through the hunger-strike, and whom the Home Secretary had wrongfully accused of biting, resolved to humiliate Mr. Churchill, both as a member of the Government which preferred rather to imprison women than to enfranchise them and to torture them rather than to extend toward them the ordinary privileges of political prisoners; and also on his own account for his slippery and disingenuous statements in regard to the Votes for Women question.

She therefore met the train by which he was arriving from London and found him on the platform in the midst of a large force of detectives who formed a semi-circle around him. She rushed straight forward, and they either did not, or would not, see her coming, but the Cabinet Minister saw her, he paled and stood there as though petrified, only raising his arm to guard himself. She reached him and with a light riding switch, struck at him three times, saying, "Take that in the name of the insulted women of England." At that he grappled with her, wrested the switch from her hand, and put it in his pocket. Then she was seized and dragged away to prison.

She was charged with assaulting Mr. Churchill, but eventually this charge was withdrawn (presumably because Mr. Churchill knew that he would be subpoenaed as a witness) and, on being accused of having disturbed the peace, was sentenced to one month's imprisonment on refusing to be bound over.

Meanwhile thirty thousand men and women had turned out to help the Suffragettes in their protest around the Colston Hall where Mr. Churchill was speaking, and during the evening four women were arrested, and afterward punished with from two months' hard labour to fourteen days in the second division, whilst several men who had spoken up for them inside the Colston Hall were beaten unmercifully by the stewards. Forcible feeding was resorted to in Bristol Prison also, and handcuffs were used in some cases.

MARY RALEIGH RICHARD-SON

Mary Raleigh Richardson, poet and novelist, was born in Canada. When she was two years old her parents separated and she went to live with her grandfather in Belleville, a small town on the shores of Lake Ontario.

Very little is known of her early life other than her love of outdoor life and sport. She became proficient at "jumping the logs" that floated down the Moira River: "It is no easy thing to keep one's footing on a floating tree trunk and leap from it on to another when it is rolling and pitching in turbulent water." Mary's favourite sport was to drag her sledge to the top of a hill at the foot of which ran a railway track. When a slow freight train came through, Mary, lying flat on her stomach on the sledge, found it was just possible to shoot between the bogies of the long timber wagons as the train was moving past and go careering on through the snow.

Following her grandfather's death when she was fifteen, she travelled with friends to Paris. A year later she moved to London and when she was twenty she joined the Women's Social and Political Union.

MARY RICHARDSON: I was walking down Kingsway when my attention was attracted by a crowd of people round a barrow. It was being pushed along by a youth who was holding something up in his hand. When I got nearer I saw what a pale, delicate-looking fellow he was. But he had a very determined expression and he kept waving a pamphlet with ''Votes for Women'' printed across it. The hostile crowd was trying to overturn his barrow and get at the stacks of literature on it, presumably to tear them up. I felt sorry for the youth—whom I learned afterwards was Mrs. Pankhurst's own son [*Harry*]—and I was so incensed by the treatment he was receiving that I followed and managed to insinuate myself on the edge of the pavement between him and the threatening people. I don't remember what I shouted at them; but I managed to hold them back. When we reached the Strand with the jostling crowd still round us, we turned left and the youth pushed his barrow into Clement's Inn. I went after him. Before I really knew where I was going I found myself in a bare room which had a bench and a long table in it. The sunshine came in through the dusty windows which overlooked the courtyard.

I was suddenly face to face with a plump, pretty young woman who was sitting on the edge of a table. She was Christabel, Mrs. Pankhurst's daughter.

''Good morning,'' she said cheerfully. ''Have you come to help us?'' ''Yes. Yes,'' I muttered uncertainly, ''I should like to help.'' Christabel smiled in a business-like way and waved me towards the door of an inner room, which I entered, still in a kind of daze. It was quite as sparsely furnished as the bigger room had been. A stout little woman with a cheery countenance rose at once from a chair behind a trestle table, thrust out her hand, and clasped mine with warm friendliness. This was the ''General,'' Flora Drummond. She had a broad, lovable Scottish accent. ''So you've decided to join us, eh, lassie?''

''Yes,'' I murmured; and I began to wonder exactly what it was I was joining.

''Sign your name here.'' She pushed a printed paper across the table at me. ''You know what we're out for, do you?'' Except in a most general way I did not know what they were

W.S.P.U. members advertising their newspaper Votes for Women

The "General," Flora Drummond

out for. I knew I was against injustice and the cruelty that had been meted out to the youth who had been distributing the Votes for Women pamphlets. Perhaps the General could see how vague I was, for her next question forced me to make a decision. "Can you go and help at Kilburn?" Kilburn. It seemed as far away as China. "Yes." I roused myself. "I can go to Kilburn."

They were making tea when I arrived; and the cup they offered me was very welcome. My chief, Mrs. Penn-Gaskell, a solicitor's wife, was a large, full-bosomed lady who was evidently accustomed to giving orders and being obeyed. I liked her at once. She greeted me cordially and introduced me to her assistant organiser, Elsa Myers, a girl more like myself, younger and rather forlorn-looking. We listened to what Mrs. Penn-Gaskell had to say as I sipped my tea and ate a farthing bun. She explained how the day's work was usually arranged and outlined the next morning's activities. I nodded, tried to show that I was interested, and continued to drink my tea. Then she turned to me and said, "Your job will be to mind the office in the mornings. Answer questions, if anyone calls. In the afternoons, while Elsa rests, you will distribute handbills."

October 1909

CHRISTABEL PANKHURST: The immense and growing responsibility of her whole movement; the hard work of campaigning at meetings, far beyond her real strength; the constant demand upon her attention, her vigilance, her amiability, her judgment, her inspiration; the imminence of imprisonment and hunger-strike—Mother had all this strain and burden to bear, when she was smitten by a great grief. Harry fell ill with infantile paralysis.

She turned to her friend of many years, Mrs. Stanton Blatch, now living again in New York, and the outcome was her first tour in America.

MRS. STANTON BLATCH: Your mother wrote to me about the illness of Harry, who had been a great favourite of mine. She spoke of her desire to earn some money so as to be able to secure for Harry the best of medical care and asked if I could put her in touch with some reliable lecture bureau.

Without a day's delay I brought her and my mother's former agents into communication and arranged also that the Women's Political Union of America, of which I was president, should give the great militant leader a suitable send-off in the popular auditorium of Carnegie Hall.

America

October 1909

EMMELINE PANKHURST: This month I made my first visit to the United States. I shall never forget the excitement of my landing, the first meeting with the American "reporter," an experience dreaded by all Europeans. In fact the first few days seemed a bewildering whirl of reporters and receptions, all leading up to my first lecture at Carnegie Hall on October 25. The huge hall was entirely filled, and an enormous crowd of people thronged the streets outside for blocks. With me on the stage were several women whom I had met in Europe, and in the chair was an old friend, Mrs. Stanton Blatch, whose early married life had been spent in England. The great crowd before me, however, was made up of strangers, and I could not know how they would respond to my story. When I rose to speak a deep hush fell, but at my first words: "I am what you call a hooligan—" a great shout of warm and sympathetic laughter shook the walls. Then I knew that I had found friends in America. And this all the rest of the tour demonstrated. In Boston the committee met me with a big grey automobile decorated in the colours of our Union, and that night at Tremont Temple I spoke to an audience of 2,500 people all most generous in their responsiveness. In Baltimore professors and students from Johns Hopkins University acted as stewards of the meeting. I greatly enjoyed my visit to Bryn Mawr College and to Rosemary Hall, a wonderful school for girls in Connecticut.

Everywhere I found the Americans kind and keen, and I cannot say too much for the wonderful hospitality they showed me. The women I found were remarkably interested in social welfare. The work of the women's clubs struck me very favourably, and I thought these institutions a perfect basis for a suffrage movement.

On December 8 Emmeline Pankhurst returned from America. She spoke at the Albert Hall the following day.

Above: Emmeline Pankhurst and Mrs. Stanton Blatch

MARY RICHARDSON: The Albert Hall was packed. People were even standing round the topmost galleries under the great dome. From where I stood in the right-hand section of the arena their faces in the shadows were indistinguishable blobs that seemed to stare through the hot light down upon the women's hats in the vast horseshoe gallery below. All the boxes were filled. There was the loud murmur of excited talk all round me. In one of the rows of seats nearby I saw a party of obvious hecklers and tried to keep my eye on them; but my fears on their account vanished completely in the excitement of the tumultuous ovation which greeted Mrs. Pankhurst's and Annie Kenney's appearance on the platform.

The two speakers were entirely different from each other in their approach to an audience. Emmeline Pankhurst's appeal was the more intellectual; she convinced with arguments and left us with an unshakable determination to continue the fight. Annie Kenney, the mill girl, was more emotional. Her words went to our hearts.

During the meeting I edged my way round the aisles until I was standing at the side of the platform, staring up at the speakers, fascinated by their words. In some strange way I was inspired by the atmosphere of the great gathering. "We will fight," I kept repeating to myself. We will fight. I was so spellbound looking up at Mrs. Pankhurst, so lost in my own wild emotions, that I had to be reminded that I was one of those who had to pass round the collection plate to collect funds to carry the "fight" forward. This left me more amazed than ever. As my collection plate began to be piled up with jewellery I realised what devotion and determination there were behind our movement. And when a Chelsea pensioner, who was sitting in the front row, dropped a small bag of copper on my plate—it was mostly farthings—I knew that not only was I a small part of a great resurgence of energy, but that I had enlisted in a holy crusade.

While Emmeline Pankhurst went to America to raise funds for Harry's treatment, Sylvia, who was still continuing her work as an artist, returned to London to nurse her brother.

American suffragists advertise Emmeline Pankhurst's appearance at the Academy of Music, New York

Harry Pankhurst

SYLVIA PANKHURST: I settled down painting by day, writing by night, in a cottage on Cinder Hill near Penshurst. Certainly there was no peace for me, or for anyone else who had touch or sympathy with the militant movement. Keir Hardie came down to see me. He told me that the thought of forcible feeding was making him ill. The levity in the House had surprised and saddened him. "I cannot stay here if it continues," I told him. "I shall have to go to prison to stand by the others." "Of what use to make one more?" he asked me ruefully. "Finish what you are working on at least!" So I resolved. Then a great blow fell.

I returned from my work in the little wood, with my canvas on my back, to find a telegram announcing that my brother was seriously ill. I found him at the nursing home in Pembridge Gardens, completely paralysed from the waist downward, and suffering intolerable agony. He had been obliged to cease work and return to bed the previous day, and had waked in the morning to find himself unable to move. The people with whom he lodged had sent to Mrs. Maclachlan, a member of the W.S.P.U., who lived near, with the message: "Mr. Pankhurst is dying." She had brought him in her car to the nursing home.

Each day Dr. Mills tested the boy's progress. He lay there extended in his nudity, proportioned like the ancient Greeks, lovely as an image of the young Adonis, showing no trace of illness, save only in his clear, smooth pallor. "A beautiful boy," the doctor murmured in shocked distress each day as he left his room. Gradually he recovered the power to move his toes; then that, too, ebbed away. He could raise himself with his arms by a pulley above his head; that was all; pain he felt in all acuteness, but all movement from the waist downward was destroyed for ever.

In his long, sleepless nights of agony he often asked me: "Shall I be able to walk again?" I lied to him faithfully: "Yes, yes." Then, later, when weeks had passed, learning a desperate cunning, I added, as though this were the whole, unpleasant truth I had wished to keep from his knowledge: "You must not be impatient; it will be rather long." Soon I should have to tell his mother that he would never be able even to sit up unaided; to tell her and to warn her: "He must not know it; he is not strong enough to bear it yet."

One night when the pain seemed to be crushing him down, as he told me later, he confided to me his love for "Helen." He had arrived in Manchester for the by-election in April of the previous year. The Suffragette committee rooms were in darkness. "Is Mrs. Drummond here?" he questioned. A voice which made him tremble answered he knew not what. He was in love. . . .

When she appeared to his sight he saw she was of his own age, fair and tall, with a bright little face well poised on a graciously curved throat. He regarded her as the most adorable of beings. Driving the Suffragette four-in-hand at the election, he always contrived a place for her beside him. What days of bliss! But when the election was over she returned to her boarding school at Brighton. He had written to her and received an answer; and once he had gone down there and spent the night on the cliffs, in the hope of catching a glimpse of her. He had seen her for an instant, as she passed by in a troop of girls. Her parents were wealthy, he had been told, and now, more than ever, so sorely stricken, he despaired of ever being able to reach her. I soothed him to rest, determined to bring her to him.

Next morning I telegraphed to Mrs. May. Could she find her? In an hour Helen was with me. I begged her: "Think of him as your young brother. Tell him you love him; he has only three weeks to live." Gallantly she played her part, if part it were. To me, who watched them with anxious absorption, her constant tenderness was very real. All day she sat with him, and at night slept on a sofa to be near the telephone, lest I should summon her. I never did so, but always she was prepared.

Great joy transfigured him, endowing him with extraordinary fortitude; for several days he firmly refused to permit the injection of anodynes, having conceived the idea that they would undermine his character, and render him unworthy of her love. It was with difficulty that Dr. Mills overcame his determination, and only by persuading him that his character would be unharmed. His transcendent happiness comforted the poignancy of my sorrow; he had reached the highest pinnacle of joy. His illness enclosed those two young creatures within a haven of dream; the hard realities of life were shut away. They planned a delightful convalescence; they would go to Venice and take me with them. "Dear Sylvia," they were very kind to her; they called her to sit beside them and share their happiness. She was content; life has no greater gift than this, she told herself. He has achieved the highest point of being: life cannot long endure thus perfect, thus unclouded.

Although the doctors declared his malady increasing, and precluded hope, not one of us could believe this radiant boy was dying. We said it with our lips; our minds refused to know it, until those final days, when all his frame was racked with torture, and only the stifling aid of drugs enabled him to drift into unconsciousness. The end came in the new year—lightly at last, with one small, stifled gasp, as though to wake. . . .*

In those sad and yet precious months of illness his life from childhood passed before me in his talk; his gentle, loyal character, unsullied by flaw or smirch, revealing itself with limpid clearness. Reserve and shyness fell from him; his mind gained in maturity. As though subconscious memories were at work, his gestures and phrases strangely recalled his father. Ever more closely he twined himself about my heart; my life seemed merged in his.

When the great blank fell, some remnants of his glory clung about me.

Mother was broken as I had never seen her, huddled together without a care for her appearance, she seemed an old, plain, cheerless woman. Her utter dejection moved me more than her vanished charm. We rode that sad way in the funeral coaches, stricken with regret— regret that we had not saved our boy. I saw him, beautiful, gentle; little forgotten incidents forcing their way into my mind, of the toddler with flaxen hair, the eager child watching the trains, the schoolboy meeting me on his holidays, the youth with his dreams. We stood in our hopeless impotence beside the grave. The sod fell down. We parted in the misery of our regret.

Before Mrs. Pankhurst left London she asked me to arrange for a headstone, for she and the doctor had never been able to bend themselves to the sad task of placing a stone over their first little son. "Choose something you like," she said; then with insistent passion: "Sylvia, remember, when my time comes, I want to be put with my two boys!"

"Blessed are the pure in heart" were the words I chose to be written over them—for that sweet purity and gentleness was all they had.

* January 5, 1910.

ALIAS JANE WARTON

LADY CONSTANCE LYTTON: I was sent to Liverpool and Manchester to join in working an anti-Government campaign during a general election. Just before I went, there came the news of the barbarous ill-treatment of Miss Selina Martin and Miss Leslie Hall, while on remand in Walton Gaol. They had been refused bail, and, while awaiting their trial, their friends were not allowed to communicate with them. This is contrary to law and precedent for prisoners on remand. As a protest they had started a hunger-strike. They were fed by force, in answer to which they broke the windows of their cells. They were put in irons for days and nights together, and one of them was frog-marched in the most brutal fashion to and from the room where the forcible feeding was performed. These facts they made known to their friends at the police court on the day of their trial.

Mary Gawthorpe
Leslie Hall

I heard, too, of another prisoner in Liverpool, Miss Bertha Brewster, who had been re-arrested after her release from prison, and charged with breaking the windows of her prison cell, which she had done as a protest against being fed by force. She had been punished for this offence while in prison. She did not respond to the summons, and when arrested on a warrant, three and a half months later, she was sentenced to six weeks' hard labour for this offence. I felt a great wish to be in Liverpool, if possible to get public opinion in that town to protest against such treatment of women political prisoners. If I failed in this, I determined myself to share the fate of these women.

When I was in Manchester, Mary Gawthorpe was ill with the internal complaint which has since obliged her to give up work. She saw me in her room one day. We had been distressed beyond words to hear of the sufferings of Selina Martin and Leslie Hall. Mary Gawthorpe said, with tears in her eyes, as she threw her arms round me: "Oh, and these are women quite unknown—nobody knows or cares about them except their own friends. They go to prison again and again to be treated like this, until it kills them!" That was enough. My mind was made up. The altogether shameless way I had been preferred against the others at Newcastle, except Mrs. Brailsford who shared with me the special treatment, made me determine to try whether they would recognise my need for exceptional favours without my name.

I joined the W.S.P.U. again, filling up the membership card as Miss Jane Warton.

I accomplished my disguise in Manchester, going to a different shop for every part of it, for safety's sake. I had noticed several times while I was in prison that prisoners of unprepossessing appearance obtained least favour, so I was determined to put ugliness to the test. I had my hair cut short and parted, in early Victorian fashion, in smooth bands down the side of my face. This, combined with the resentful bristles of my newly cut back hair, produced a curious effect. I wished to bleach my hair as well, but the hairdresser refused point-blank to do this, and the stuff that I bought for the purpose at a chemist's proved quite ineffective. A tweed hat, a long green cloth coat, which I purchased for eight shillings sixpence, a woollen scarf and woollen gloves, a white silk neck-kerchief, a pair of pince-nez spectacles, a purse, a note-bag to contain some of my papers, and my costume was complete. I had removed my initials from my underclothing, and bought the ready-made initials "J.W." to sew on in their stead, but to my regret I had not time to achieve this finishing touch.

Constance Lytton travelled to Liverpool to take part in a W.S.P.U. demonstration outside Walton Gaol.

January 14, 1910

Arrived at Liverpool, and not knowing my way to Walton, I took a cab, and drove out for nearly an hour before reaching my destination. I was already racing hard with daylight and, thanks to a damp fog, it was already quite dark when I arrived there.

We set out for the prison. All through the day I had been dogged by the nightmare thought that I should be too late for the meeting, or for some other reason should be prevented from achieving my purpose. As we neared the place, a crowd of between two and three hundred men and women were following the carriage in which were our speakers. It had been agreed that I should mix with the crowd, not join with the speakers, but at the end of the meeting should have my say from below.

I reminded the audience of how the men of Dundee, when forcible feeding of suffrage prisoners was threatened in that town, had assembled to the number of two thousand and protested against it. How thereupon the hunger-strikers had been released and no forcible feeding to our women had been inflicted in Scotland. Could not Englishmen have done the same? Let the men of Liverpool be the first to wipe out the stain that has been tolerated up till now. We were outside the gaol where these and other barbarities were actually going on. The Home Secretary had denied responsibility and asserted that it rested with the prison officials.

To my surprise, the crowd began to follow me. Again I shouted out to them—"No violence, remember, but call for the Governor and refuse to be dispersed till you have secured the release of the prisoners."

A policeman began leisurely to follow me; there were only two or three of them about. I took to running and urged on the crowd. The police then took hold of me. As for once it was my object above all else to get arrested and imprisoned, I began discharging my stones, not throwing them, but limply dropping them over the hedge into the Governor's garden. One of them just touched the shoulder of a man who had rushed up on seeing me arrested. I apologised to him. Two policemen then held me fast by the arms and marched me off to the police station. The crowd followed me excitedly, and our members gathered round me, appealing for my release and saying that I had done nothing.

Vera Holme, chauffeuse, with A. Flatman, Geraldine Lister, and Georgina Brackenbury during the Cheltenham by-election

Jane Warton was sentenced by the magistrate, Mr. Shepherd Little, to a fortnight in the third division with the option of a fine. Hard labour usually accompanied a sentence in the third division unless stated to the contrary.

I lay in my bed most of the day, for they did not disturb me, and I tried to keep warm, as I felt the cold fearfully. They brought me all my meals the same as usual, porridge in the morning at seven, meat and potatoes mid-day at twelve, porridge at four-thirty. When they were hot I fed on the smell of them, which seemed quite delicious; I said, "I don't want any, thank you," to each meal, as they brought it in. I had made up my mind that this time I would not drink any water, and would only rinse out my mouth morning and evening without swallowing any. I wrote on the walls of my cell with my slate pencil and soap mixed with the dirt of the floor for ink, "Votes for Women," and the saying from Thoreau's *Duty of Civil Disobedience*—"Under a Government which imprisons any unjustly, the true place for a just man (or woman) is also a prison"; on the wall opposite my bed I wrote the text from Joshua, "Only be thou strong and very courageous." That night I dreamt of fruits, melons, peaches, and nectarines, and of a moonlit balcony that was hung with sweetest-smelling flowers, honeysuckle and jessamine, apple-blossom and sweet scented verbena.

Tuesday, January 18, I was visited again by the Senior Medical Officer, who asked me how long I had been without food. I said I had eaten a buttered scone and a banana sent in by friends to the police station on Friday at about midnight. He said, "Oh, then, this is the fourth day; that is too long, I shall have to feed you, I must feed you at once," but he went out and nothing happened till about six o'clock in the evening, when he returned with, I think, five wardresses and the feeding apparatus. He urged me to take food voluntarily. I told him that was absolutely out of the question, that when our legislators ceased to resist enfranchising women then I should cease to resist taking food in prison. He did not examine my heart nor feel my pulse; he did not ask to do so, nor did I say anything which could possibly induce him to think I would refuse to be examined. I offered no resistance to being placed in position, but lay down voluntarily on the plank bed. Two of the wardresses took hold of my arms, one held my head and one my feet. One wardress helped to pour the food. The doctor leant on my knees as he stooped over my chest to get at my mouth. I shut my mouth and clenched my teeth. I had looked forward to this moment with so much anxiety lest my identity should be discovered beforehand, that I felt positively glad when the time had come. The sense of being overpowered by more force than I could possibly resist was complete, but I resisted nothing except with my mouth. The doctor offered me the choice of a wooden or steel gag; he explained elaborately, as he did on most subsequent occasions, that the steel gag would hurt and the wooden one not, and he urged me not to force him to use the steel gag. But I did not speak nor open my mouth, so that after playing about for a moment or two with the wooden one he finally had recourse to the steel. He seemed annoyed at my resistance and he broke into a temper as he pried my teeth with the steel implement. He found that on either side at the back I had false teeth mounted on a bridge which did not take out. The superintending wardress asked if I had any false teeth, if so, that they must be taken out; I made no answer and the process went on. He dug his instrument down onto the sham tooth, it pressed fearfully on the gum. He said if I resisted so much with my teeth, he would have to feed me through the nose. The pain of it was intense and at last I must have given way, for he got the gag between my teeth, when he proceeded to turn it much more than necessary until my jaws were fastened wide apart, far more than they could go naturally. Then he put down my

Elsie Howey

throat a tube which seemed to me much too wide and was something like four feet in length. The irritation of the tube was excessive. I choked the moment it touched my throat until it had got down. Then the food was poured in quickly; it made me sick a few seconds after it was down and the action of the sickness made my body and legs double up, but the wardresses instantly pressed back my head and the doctor leant on my knees. The horror of it was more than I can describe. I was sick over the doctor and wardresses, and it seemed a long time before they took the tube out. As the doctor left he gave me a slap on the cheek, not violently, but, as it were, to express his contemptuous disapproval, and he seemed to take for granted that my distress was assumed. At first it seemed such an utterly contemptible thing to have done that I could only laugh in my mind. Then suddenly I saw Jane Warton lying before me, and it seemed as if I were outside of her. She was the most despised, ignorant, and helpless prisoner that I had seen. When she had served her time and was out of the prison, no one would believe anything she said, and the doctor, when he had fed her by force and tortured her body, struck her on the cheek to show how he despised her! That was Jane Warton, and I had come to help her.

When the doctor had gone out of the cell, I lay quite helpless. The wardresses were kind and knelt round to comfort me, but there was nothing to be done, I could not move, and remained there in what, under different conditions, would have been an intolerable mess. I had been sick over my hair, which, though short, hung on either side of my face, all over the wall near my bed, and my clothes seemed saturated with it, but the wardresses told me they could not get me a change that night as it was too late, the office was shut. I lay quite motionless, it seemed paradise to be without the suffocating tube, without the liquid food going in and out of my body and without the gag between my teeth. Presently the wardresses all left me, they had orders to go, which were carried out with the usual promptness. Before long I heard the sounds of the forced feeding in the next cell to mine. It was almost more than I could bear, it was Elsie Howey, I was sure. When the ghastly process was over and all quiet, I tapped on the wall and called out at the top of my voice, which wasn't much just then, ''No surrender,'' and there came the answer past any doubt in Elsie's voice, ''No surrender.''

Lady Constance Lytton as Jane Warton was forcibly fed a further seven times before her identity was discovered and she was released on "medical grounds" on Sunday, January 23.

A Speech Delivered at the Queen's Hall, January 31, 1910

LADY CONSTANCE LYTTON: I am grateful for your kindness, and I appreciate it as fully and as deeply as any human being can, but let me remind the strangers here that though what I have done is something rather different perhaps to what other women have done, because the circumstances concerning me were different, and because there was something to lay hold rather freshly of the imagination of outsiders; yet they must remember this fact, that thirty-five other women have been treated as I have been treated, and of these women I have suffered almost the least.

People say, what does this hunger-strike mean? Surely it is all folly. If it is not hysteria, at least it is unreasonable. They will not realise that we are like an army, that we are deputed to fight for a cause, and for other people, and in any struggle or any fight, weapons must be used. The weapons for which we ask are simple, a fair hearing; but that is refused us in Parliament, refused us by the Government, refused us in the magistrates' courts, refused us in the law courts. Then we must have other weapons. What do other people choose when they are driven to the last extremity? What do men choose? They have recourse to violence. But what the women of this movement have specially stood out for is that they will not kill, they will not harm while they have other weapons left to them. These women have chosen the weapon of self-hurt to make their protest, and this hunger-strike brings great pressure upon the Government. It involves grave hurt and tremendous sacrifice, but this is on the part of the women only, and does not physically injure their enemies. Can that be called violence and hooliganism? But it is no good taking a weapon and being ready to drop it at the very first provocation, so when the Government retaliated with their unfair methods, with their abominable torture and tyranny of feeding by force, did you expect the women to drop their weapons?

No, of course not. I had been in this movement many months, and although I absolutely approved of the method of getting in our messages by means of stones which did nothing but convey our meaning to the Ministers and to the world, still I felt I could not throw a stone myself. However, as I have told you here before, when I saw the first of these women released—a mere girl—from Birmingham Gaol, I took another view. I went to Newcastle for a protest, meaning to share what these women endured. I went in my own name, and, as you know, I was released after a very short hunger-strike, a heart specialist being called in who examined me for something like a quarter of an hour. I made a tremendous protest. I said that in the same prison where I was, there was a woman, a first offender, who had done much less violence than I had, and she was fed by force without having her heart tested at all. "Whatever you think of the subject," I said, "whatever you think of the militant movement, surely you can see that justice is done between one human being and another!"

I tried all I could, when I came out, and I got others whom I knew to fight that question with truth and exposure, and what did they give us back? Lies, and nothing but lies! Well, I thought, you choose your weapons, I will fight with the same weapon, and you shall take my life, and do with it what you will! So I disguised myself; I changed my personality, and I went and made my protest outside that very gaol where these hideous, abominable things were being done.

It is like describing a hospital scene—and much worse. The doctor and four wardresses came into my cell. I decided to save all my resistance for the actual feeding, and when they pointed to my bed on the floor I lay down, and the doctor did not even feel my pulse. Two wardresses held my hands, one my head. Much as I had heard about this thing, it was infinitely more horrible and more painful than I had expected. The doctor put the steel gag in somewhere on my gums and forced open my mouth till it was yawning wide. As he proceeded to force into my mouth and down the throat a large rubber tube, I felt as though I were being killed—absolute suffocation is the feeling. You feel as though it would never stop. You cannot breathe, and yet you choke. It irritates the throat, it irritates the mucous membrane as it goes down, every second seems an hour, and you think they will never finish pushing it down. After a while the sensation is relieved, then the food is poured down, and then again you choke, and your whole body resists and writhes under the treatment; you are held down, and the process goes on, and, finally, when the vomiting becomes excessive the tube is removed. I forgot what I was in there for, I forgot women, I forgot everything except my own sufferings, and I was completely overcome by them.

What was even worse to me than the thing itself was the positive terror with which I anticipated its renewal. Very soon I thought to try and appeal to that man as a doctor to perform the operation in a better way, but whatever one said or suggested was treated with most absolute contempt.

There was one even worse thing, and that was the moral poisoning, if one may call it that, of one's whole mind. I always closed my eyes. I tried not to see the beings who came to do this thing. I felt it was all too hideous, and I did not wish it imprinted on my eyes. Nevertheless, I got to hate those men and women, I got to hate infinitely more the powers that stood behind them, I got to hate the blindness, the prejudice, in those who turn away and won't look or listen to what is being done under their very eyes. I tried to think of the splendid heroes and heroines since the world began, of all the martyrs, all the magnificent women in this movement, and I felt a tremendous gratitude to them, an admiration which overpowered me.

Then one evening, as I lay on the bed on the floor of my cell, I looked up. There were three panes of clear glass, and on them as the light fell there came shadows of the moulding that looked like three crosses. It brought to my mind the familiar scene of Calvary with its three crosses, and I thought: What did they stand for? One for the Lord Christ who died for sinners, and one for the sinner who was kind, and one for the sinner who had not yet learnt to be kind, and behind those crosses I saw those hateful faces, and the self-righteous, all those hateful institutions of superior goodness and moral blindness of officialdom, of all the injustice done, not only in prison, but in the world outside, and I thought surely it was for these that Christ died and is dying still and will have to die until they begin to see.

This is the most glorious fight that has ever been. Become a member of our Union. It is so easy to do that. Before you leave this hall, say: "I will stand by you whatever the world says, whatever public opinion says, I am for you now, before another minute goes by."

THE TIMES, Thursday, February 10, 1910
PRISON TREATMENT OF WOMAN SUFFRAGISTS

The Home Secretary has caused the following letter to be addressed to a correspondent who called his attention to a leaflet which has been recently circulated with reference to the imprisonment of Lady Constance Lytton at Liverpool:

Home Office, Whitehall, Feb. 9, 1910
Sir,—With reference to your letter of the 28th ult., I am directed by the Secretary of State to say that the statement that Lady Constance Lytton was released from Liverpool Prison only when her identity was discovered is untrue. The release of "Jane Warton" was recommended by the medical officer and authorised by the Secretary of State upon purely medical grounds before her identity with Lady Constance Lytton was suspected by any official either at the Home Office or at the prison.

As regards the allegation that the treatment of "Jane Warton" differed from that of Lady Constance Lytton, I am to inform you that Lady Constance Lytton was released from Newcastle Prison in October last because the medical authorities at that prison considered that, owing to the condition of her heart, the violent resistance which she was expected to offer to the necessary artificial feeding would be attended with risk. Their diagnosis of the case has recently been fully confirmed by the opinion of her own medical attendant.

Upon her reception at Liverpool Prison under the name of "Jane Warton" on the 15th ult., she refused to allow her heart to be examined. From her demeanour and conversation there was no reason to anticipate that she would resist being fed, and the examination of her heart which she allowed the doctor to make before he fed her did not indicate that the operation would involve risk to her health. She was accordingly artificially fed for a few days like any other prisoner who persists in refusing to take food. On the 22nd ult. the medical officer, finding that the injury to her health which was being caused by her persistent refusal to take food could not be prevented by artificial feeding, recommended her discharge on the ground of her state of health, and she was released in accordance with the usual practice in such cases.

The suggestion that any difference in her treatment at the two prisons was due to considerations of social position is entirely without foundation, and the Secretary of State is satisfied, after careful enquiry, that there is no justification whatever for the charges made by Lady Constance Lytton against the officers employed at Liverpool Prison.—I am, Sir, your obedient servant,

Edward Troup

THE TIMES, Wednesday, March 30, 1910
LADY CONSTANCE LYTTON AND THE HOME OFFICE

To the Editor of THE TIMES

Sir,—On February 10 a letter was sent to the Press by Sir Edward Troup, relative to a statement made by my sister Lady Constance Lytton regarding her treatment in Liverpool Prison, in which he declared on behalf of the Home Secretary that there was no foundation for any of the charges which she had made. I am anxious to explain why this official imputation of untruthfulness has hitherto remained unanswered.

Lady Constance was seriously ill at the time as the result of her prison experiences, and unable to defend herself. I therefore undertook the task of vindicating her veracity. Before making any public statement on her behalf, I was anxious to find out what steps had been taken by the Home Office to investigate the matters referred to in her statement, and I hoped by a friendly intervention to secure a full and impartial enquiry into all the circumstances of her treatment by the prison officials.

I have had several communications with the Home Office on the subject, and owing to the retirement of Mr. Gladstone and the appointment of a new Home Secretary they have necessarily been protracted over a considerable period. My attitude throughout has been entirely conciliatory, and the only claim which I have made was that in the interests of justice charges of this nature should be submitted to a full and impartial enquiry, which would, of course, involve a separate examination of both the parties concerned. This claim has been refused by the Home Office on the grounds that the prison officials have been closely interrogated, and that as they deny entirely every one of the charges made, "no useful purpose would be served" by granting my request.

In the absence of such an enquiry as I asked for the matter must be left to the opinion of unbiased minds. I desire, however, to say that nothing which I have been able to learn has in any way shaken my belief in the substantial accuracy of my sister's account. The idea that her charges can be disposed of by the bare denial of the persons against whom they are made is not likely to commend itself to anyone outside the Home Office, and no amount of denial can get over the following facts:

1. Lady Constance Lytton, when imprisoned in Newcastle, after refusing to answer the medical questions put to her and adopting the hunger-strike, received a careful and thorough medical examina-tion, which disclosed symptoms of "serious heart disease," and on these grounds she was released as unfit to submit to forcible feeding.

2. Three months later "Jane Warton," when imprisoned at Liverpool, also refused to answer medical questions or to take prison food. On this occasion she was entered in the prison books as having refused medical examination, and was forcibly fed eight times. Such medical examination as took place during the forcible feeding failed, according to the medical officer's report, to disclose any symptoms of heart disease, and she was eventually released on the grounds of loss of weight and general physical weakness.

These facts are incontrovertible, and though the Home Office is quite satisfied that in both cases the prison officials performed their duty in the most exemplary fashion, your readers will form their own opinions of the justice of a Government Department which brings accusations of untruthfulness against an individual whilst refusing the only means by which the truth can be established.

I am, your obedient servant

LYTTON

In 1912 Lady Constance suffered a severe heart attack and was paralysed on the right side of her body. As militancy continued she still felt compelled to defend and explain the militant suffrage movement and during the years 1912 through 1914 she wrote of her prison experiences. Handicapped by paralysis, she was forced to write with her left hand "slowly and laboriously." Lady Constance Lytton never recovered her health and was nursed by her mother at home until her death on May 22, 1923.

Yours sincerely
Constance Lytton

TRUCE

CHRISTABEL PANKHURST: A truce was declared by Mrs. Pankhurst after the general election early in the year, because she wanted the Government to decide, in an atmosphere of peace and calm, what would be their action in regard to votes for women in the new Parliament.

The general election had made the Liberal and Conservative parties equal in strength. The Government had no longer any majority of their own. The remainder of the House of Commons consisted of Irish Nationalists and forty Labour Members.

The disappearance of the Government's majority was largely, if not mainly, due to the woman suffrage issue. Liberal women had lost their enthusiasm for a Government who would not give them the vote. The earnest and energetic campaign of Mrs. Pankhurst and her followers had stirred the electors to vote against the Government.

With the death of King Edward VII we, with all the country, were in mourning and in sympathy with Queen Alexandra. So in a serious atmosphere of national peace the Conciliation Committee for Woman Suffrage came into being, and a new chapter of suffrage history opened.

Lord Lytton, chairman of the Conciliation Committee, was the brother of the Suffragette prisoner who, as "Jane Warton," had endured the worst suffering such a prisoner could endure, and the honorary secretary, Mr. H. N. Brailsford, was the husband of one who had been imprisoned and had risked the same suffering. They knew, therefore, the spirit and motive of the militant women and their readiness to sacrifice all that life held for them, and even life itself, rather than waver in their fight.

Excepting the chairman and honorary secretary, the Conciliation Committee consisted entirely of Members of the House of Commons. All political parties were represented on the committee, which was able to state that its formation was "welcomed by several members of the Liberal and Conservative front benches and by the chairman of the Labour Party." This object was to press for an early solution to the woman suffrage question, on a plan which members of all political parties might accept as a practicable minimum.

The truce to militancy was from first to last loyally observed by Suffragettes. Non-militant work only was undertaken and this was to culminate in a magnificent procession and demonstration in London, attended by representatives of our whole organisation.

June 14, 1910

EMMELINE PANKHURST: The Conciliation Bill was introduced into the House of Commons by Mr. D. J. Shackleton, and was received with the most extraordinary enthusiasm. The newspapers remarked on the feeling of reality which marked the attitude of the House toward the bill. It was plain that the Members realised that here was no academic question upon which they were merely to debate and to register their opinions, but a measure which was intended to be carried through all its stages and to be written into English law.* The enthusiasm of the House swept all over the kingdom. The medical profession sent in a memorial in its favour, signed by more than three hundred of the most distinguished men and women in the profession. Memorials from writers, clergymen, social workers, artists, actors, musicians were also sent.

June 18, 1910

The Women's Social and Political Union arranged a demonstration in support of the Conciliation Bill, the greatest that had, up to that time, been made. It was a national, indeed an international affair in which all the suffrage groups took part, and its massed ranks were so great that the procession required an hour and a half to pass a given point. At the head marched 617 women, white clad and holding long silver staves tipped with the broad arrow. These were the women who had suffered imprisonment for the cause, and all along the line of march they received a tribute of cheers from the public. The immense Albert Hall,

* The main features of the Conciliation Bill were: to enfranchise every woman possessed of a household qualification to vote for the county or borough in which the qualifying premises are situated; to ensure that marriage not disqualify a woman from being registered as a voter provided husband and wife shall not both be registered as voters in the same constituency. This was an attempt to secure the Parliamentary franchise for a million women.

the largest hall in England, although it was packed from orchestra to the highest gallery, was not large enough to hold all the marchers. Amid great joy and enthusiasm Lord Lytton delivered a stirring address in which he confidently predicted the speedy advance of the bill. The women, he declared, had every reason to believe that their enfranchisement was actually at hand.

July 12, 1910

We feared treachery, but in view of the announcement that the Government had set apart July 11 and 12 for debate on the second reading, we preserved a spirit of waiting calm. July 26 had been fixed as the day for the adjournment of Parliament, and if the bill was voted on favourably on the twelfth there would be ample time to take it through its final stages. When a bill passes its second reading it is normally sent upstairs to a Grand Committee which sits while the House of Commons is transacting other business, and thus the commit-

Above: W.S.P.U. demonstration in support of the Conciliation Bill, June 18, 1910

tee stage can proceed without special facilities. The bill does not go back to the House until the report stage is reached, at which time the third and last reading occurs. After that the bill goes to the House of Lords. A week at most is all that is required for this procedure. A bill may be referred to the whole House, and in this case it cannot be brought up for its committee stage unless it is given special facilities. In our paper and in many public speeches we urged that the Members vote to send the bill to a Grand Committee.

Some days before the bill reached its second reading it was rumoured that Mr. Lloyd George was going to speak against it, but we refused to credit this. Unfair to women as Mr. Lloyd George had shown himself in various ways, he had consistently posed as a staunch friend of women's suffrage, and we could not believe that he would turn against us at the eleventh hour. Mr. Winston Churchill the promoters of the bill also counted upon, as it was known that he had more than once expressed sympathy with its objects. But when the debates began we found both of these ardent suffragists arrayed against the bill. Mr. Churchill, after making a conventional anti-suffrage speech, in which he said that women did not need the ballot, and that they really had no grievances, attacked the Conciliation Bill because the class of women who would be enfranchised under it did not suit him. Some women, he conceded, ought to be enfranchised, and he thought the best plan would be to select "some of the best women of all classes" on considerations of property, education, and earning capacity. These special franchises would be carefully balanced, "so as not on the whole to give undue advantage to the property vote against the wage-earning vote." A more fantastic proposal and one less likely to find favour in the House of Commons could not possibly be imagined. Mr. Churchill's second objection to the bill was that it was anti-democratic! It seemed to us that anything was more democratic than his proposed "fancy" franchises.

Mr. Lloyd George said that he agreed with everything Mr. Churchill had said "both relevant and irrelevant." He made the amazing assertion that the Conciliation Committee that had drafted the bill was a "committee of women meeting outside the House." And that this committee said to the House of Commons not only that they must vote for a women's suffrage bill but "You must vote for the particular form upon which we agree, and we will not even allow you to deliberate upon any other form."

Of course these statements were wholly false. The Conciliation Bill was drafted by men, and it was introduced because the Government had refused to bring in a party measure. The suffragists would have been only too glad to have had the Government deliberate on a broader form of suffrage. Because they refused to deliberate on any form, this private bill was introduced.

The House filled to hear the Prime Minister, Mr. Asquith, speak: "No suffrage measure will be satisfactory which does not give women votes on precisely the same terms as men."
Referring to the militants:

"THOSE WHO TAKE THE SWORD SHALL PERISH BY THE SWORD. A CAUSE WHICH CANNOT WIN ITS WAY TO PUBLIC ACCEPTANCE BY PERSUASION, BY ARGUMENT, BY ORGANISATION, BY PEACEFUL METHODS OF AGITATION, IS A CAUSE WHICH ALREADY, AND IN ADVANCE, HAS PRONOUNCED ON ITSELF ITS OWN SENTENCE OF DEATH."

When the division was taken it was seen that the Conciliation Bill had passed its second reading by a majority of 109, a larger majority than the Government's far-famed budget or the House of Lords Resolution had received. In fact no measure during that Parliament had received so great a majority.

To Hyde Park

July 23, 1910

CHRISTABEL PANKHURST: We were preparing another huge peaceful demonstration. Two processions to Hyde Park, and one hundred and fifty speakers—such was the programme, and it was carried through in triumph.

That vast concourse of men and women were so many friends and allies. A sea of hands went up for the resolution put at forty platforms—a resolution, described by the Press, as "a dialectical hit, both legitimate and effective"—"This meeting rejoices that the Woman Suffrage Bill has passed its second reading by 109 votes, a majority larger than that accorded to the Government's House of Lords veto proposal. The meeting further calls upon the Government to bow to the will of the people as expressed by their representatives in the House of Commons and to provide the facilities necessary to enable the bill to pass into law during the present session of Parliament."

The Commons had spoken. The people had spoken. Nothing imaginable remained to be done to demonstrate public support—or we should have done it. Every peaceful mode of promoting the bill had been put into effect. Militancy was the only thing left, but to militancy we were determined not to resort, so long as there was life and hope left for the bill.

The move was now with the Government. We waited.

Then came the Prime Minister's reply on behalf of the Government. He refused to give time for the passage of the Conciliation Bill.

This reply was not made in the House of Commons, but in a negative intimation conveyed direct to the Conciliation Committee.

The Conciliation Committee again declined to accept as final Mr. Asquith's refusal of facilities. Mrs. Pankhurst decided still to maintain the truce and to continue the peaceful work for facilities, though she now deemed it wise to say that our patience had its limit.

"If they fail to get rid of the Government's veto upon the Conciliation Bill, women themselves must act," she said. "The opposition which the Women's Social and Political Union have offered to the Liberal Government during the past few years will be renewed and redoubled."

BLACK FRIDAY

 EMMELINE PANKHURST: It had been exceedingly difficult, during these troublous days, to hold all the members of the W.S.P.U. to the truce, and when it became perfectly apparent that the Conciliation Bill was doomed, war was again declared. At a great meeting held in Albert Hall, I myself threw down the gage of battle. I said, because I wanted the whole matter to be clearly understood by the public as well as by our members: "This is the last constitutional effort of the Women's Social and Political Union to secure the passage of the bill into law. If the bill, in spite of our efforts, is killed by the Government, then first of all, I have to say there is an end of the truce. If we are met by the statement that there is no power to secure on the floor of the House of Commons time for our measure, then our first step is to say, 'We take it out of your hands, since you fail to help us, and we resume the direction of the campaign ourselves.'"

November 18, 1910

HENRY NEVINSON: In that low, but intense and penetrating voice that reaches to the furthest lines of any audience, Mrs. Pankhurst read the statement on which the future hung. Under conditions for admitting extension of the Bill the Prime Minister had promised facilities, not before March, not for next session, but for "next Parliament." There was a moment's pause while the meeting realised the full meaning of the nonsensical trick attempted upon the women's cause. Miss Christabel Pankhurst rose to explain the significance of the blow that Mr. Asquith had struck under his apparent concession, but her calm and logical explanation was hardly needed. "We had hoped the statement would be satisfactory," she said. "But we will take nothing but next session. The promise for next Parliament is an absurd mockery of a pledge. It is an insult to common sense. We hurl it back upon them. They have been talking of declarations of war. We also declare war from this moment."

Certainly it was war from that moment. One great outburst of indignation and cheering rose, and then Mrs. Pankhurst announced she would lead the deputation to Downing Street, as the House was empty. The movement was incredibly rapid. I think all the deputation came. They formed up in fours without the least confusion. I had the good fortune to march beside the first four, in which Mrs. Pankhurst was, and looking back I could see the deputation extending in a compact body for nearly two hundred yards. Many in the rear carried small purple banners with white lettering. Mrs. Pankhurst's step was so quick that requests came up once or twice against the pace. Nevertheless, passing up Tothill Street, where there was no crowd, we had reached Parliament Square within a quarter of an hour of the committee's reappearance on the platform. There the crowd, awaiting the usual march to the House, perceived us and came running over in large numbers. A few police accompanied the deputation, and they evidently had also expected a march to the House, for when we turned up Parliament Street and had nearly reached the Home Office I saw a superintendent in front hurriedly signal to a body of police, who at once lined up across the entrance of Downing Street, which, I think, had not been closed till then.

They were hardly in time, and they only formed a single cordon, stretching two deep across the entrance from side to side. Maintaining the pace without a check, the leading four of the deputation wheeled to the left, and at once were face to face with that apparently solid line. Mrs. Pankhurst did not pause or slacken for a moment. With that look of silent courage and patient, almost pathetic, determination that everyone now knows so well, she

Members of the W.S.P.U. deputation are arrested on Black Friday.

Police restrain the crowd, on Black Friday, November 18, 1910.
Bottom: A Suffragette breaks through the police line.

Dr. Garrett Anderson and Emmeline Pankhurst

walked straight up against the police, straight into the midst of them. The deputation followed, hesitating no more than she. They pressed forward steadily from behind. I don't know how many of them were there—perhaps three hundred. Only for a moment the cordon stood its ground. Under that pressure right against the centre it struggled, it wavered, and broke. Instantly the women rushed forward through the gap with cries of triumph. The police lost all cohesion. Fighting desperately, in separate little groups or as isolated men, they were driven further and further up the street. Many of the women passed right through them, and got clear up to the Prime Minister's house. But the main body of the conflict never reached much further than halfway, and the advance was there checked by reinforcements which, I think, came out from the Foreign Office courtyard.

At the front the struggle was then for some minutes both piteous and horrible. Against the gathering lines of police the women charged again and again with reckless indifference to blows or the violent pushes that flung them to the ground. Indeed, the whole length of the street from the official residences down to the entrance was now one wild turmoil of struggling men and women, swaying this way and that, the women continually striving to advance, in most cases isolated, and the police continually thrusting them back. The banners were early broken to pieces, and became an extra danger. Every now and then, where a woman fell, those around fell on the top of her, with terrible result. Here I saw one of the most famous doctors rush against the police at the very front. Flung savagely back, she instinctively tidied her scarf and rushed again. Here a writer, equally famous, was caught bodily off her feet and dashed upon the pavement, but being an athlete as well as a writer she fell upon her hands. There a hospital nurse almost succeeded in breaking the renewed line till she was caught by the throat and driven back again into the seething contest.

I cannot specially blame the police, violent and savage though many of them were. Their position under such a Government is difficult and detestable. It was all the more difficult when their lines were broken and they were rolled back in sudden defeat.

EMMELINE PANKHURST: At intervals of two or three minutes small groups of women appeared in the square, trying to join us at the Strangers' Entrance. They carried little banners inscribed with various mottoes, "Asquith Has Vetoed Our Bill," "Where There's a Bill There's a Way," "Women's Will Beats Asquith's Won't," and the like. These banners the police seized and tore in pieces. Then they laid hands on the women and literally threw them from one man to another. Some of the police used their fists, striking the women in their faces, their breasts, their shoulders. One woman I saw thrown down with violence three or four times in rapid succession, until at last she lay only half conscious against the curb, and in a serious condition was carried away by kindly strangers. Every moment the struggle grew fiercer, as more and more women arrived on the scene. Women, many of them eminent in art, in medicine and science, women of European reputation, subjected to treatment that would not have been meted out to criminals, and all for the offence of insisting upon the right of peaceful petition.

This struggle lasted for about an hour, more and more women successfully pushing their way past the police and gaining the steps of the House. Then the mounted police were summoned to turn the women back. But, desperately determined, the women, fearing not the hoofs of the horses or the crushing violence of the police, did not swerve from their purpose.

While all this was going on outside the House of Commons, the Prime Minister was obstinately refusing to listen to the counsels of some of the saner and more justice-loving members of the House. Keir Hardie, Sir Alfred Mondell, and others urged Mr. Asquith to receive the deputation.

The next morning the suffrage prisoners were arraigned in police court. Or rather, they were kept waiting outside the court room while Mr. Muskett, who prosecuted on behalf of the Chief Commissioner of Police, explained to the astounded magistrate that he had received orders from the Home Secretary that the prisoners should all be discharged. Mr. Churchill, it was declared, had had the matter under careful consideration, and had decided that "no public advantage would be gained by proceeding with the prosecution, and accordingly no evidence would be given against the prisoners."

The country was on the eve of a general election, and the Liberal Party needed the help of Liberal women. This fact made the wholesale arrest and imprisonment of great numbers of women, who were demanding the passage of the Conciliation Bill, extremely undesirable from the Government's point of view. The Women's Liberal Federations also wanted the passage of the Conciliation Bill, although they were not ready to fight for it. What the Government feared was that the Liberal women would be stirred by our sufferings into refraining from doing election work for the party. So the Government conceived a plan whereby the Suffragettes were to be punished, were to be turned back and defeated in their purpose of reaching the House, but would not be arrested.

The Government fully realised that it was bad election tactics to be responsible for the imprisonment of women of good character who were struggling for citizenship.

A sympathiser is arrested.

DAILY MIRROR, November 22, 1910
POLICE AND WOMEN

COMPLAINTS OF ROUGHNESS IN DEALING WITH SUFFRAGETTES

The following letter was received yesterday by the Editor of the DAILY MIRROR:

Sir,—I notice in your account of the reception given to the deputation from the W.S.P.U. to the Prime Minister on Friday last it is stated that the police behaved with great good temper, tact, and restraint.

This may have been the case on previous occasions on which deputations have been sent; on the present one it is absolutely untrue.

The women were treated with the greatest brutality. They were pushed about in all directions and thrown down by the police. Their arms were twisted until they were almost broken. Their thumbs were forcibly bent back, and they were tortured in other nameless ways that made one feel sick at the sight.

I was there myself and saw many of these things done. The photographs that were published in your issue of November 19 prove it. And I have since seen the fearful bruises, showing the marks of the fingers, caused by the violence with which these women were treated.

"BANDS OF ROUGHS"

These things were done by the police. There were in addition organised bands of well-dressed roughs who charged backwards and forwards through the deputation like a football team without any attempt being made to stop them by the police; but they contented themselves with throwing the women down and trampling upon them.

As this behaviour on the part of the police is an entirely new departure, it would be interesting to know who issued the instructions that they were to act with such brutality, and who organised the bands of roughs who suddenly sprang up on all sides from nowhere.

The Home Secretary, who does not want women arrested, is credited with the statement that he had devised a new method of putting a stop to deputations. Is this the method?

The women were discharged without a trial by the Secretary of State on the grounds of public policy. Is it public policy that there should be no trial and that the evidence which might otherwise have come out should be suppressed in this way?

Yours faithfully,

C. Mansell-Moullin

Vice-President, Royal College of Surgeons, Consulting Surgeon to the London Hospital

Mary Clarke

The Death of Mary Clarke

SYLVIA PANKHURST: Amongst the seventy-five Suffragettes now in Holloway was Mrs. Pankhurst's sister, Mary Clarke. On ceasing to be Mrs. Pankhurst's deputy in the Registrarship, she had become an organiser for the W.S.P.U., and thereby found release from the regretful memories of an unhappy marriage. Facing the rude violence of the seaside rowdies at Brighton, where she was stationed, she displayed a quiet, persistent courage, which made peculiarly large demands on one so sensitive. Exerting her frail physique to its utmost, she was grievously ill on the eve of Black Friday, and her Brighton comrades had begged her not to go. She had promised to take the easier course of arrest for window-breaking, and had telegraphed to Brighton from the police court: "One month: I am content to pay the price of victory."

Preparing to leave for America, and revising the final chapters of *The Suffragette,** I spent Christmas alone at Linden Gardens. Early on the morning of Boxing Day I saw at the window my mother's face, haggard and drawn. I ran to admit her: "Something has happened!" "Aunt Mary is not very well," she faltered. "She is dead, I know."

Yes; she was dead, our gentle confidante, too frail to weather this rude tide of militant struggle. Released from prison two days before, she had spoken at the welcome luncheon in London, hastened to Brighton to address a welcome meeting there the same night, and returned on Christmas Eve to her brother's house in London. She was with Mrs. Pankhurst and others of the family at the mid-day Christmas dinner, and quietly left the table. When Mrs. Pankhurst went to look for her she found her unconscious. She had burst a blood vessel on the brain.

Stunned by this sudden blow, we spent the next days together, my mother coming to Southampton to see me sail.

Engrossed in work for my book, and desiring no other relaxation than to gaze on the tremendous grandeur of the seas, I paid little attention either to passengers or officers. I remember a sensation of pity for the third-class passengers, coming on board at Queenstown, and made to pause in mid-gangway to have their eyeballs examined by the doctor. On the last day the doctor, who had occasionally spoken a brief word in passing, astonished me by a proposal of marriage, mainly motivated, I gathered, by the desire to save me from the militant movement. That was how it affected some people of protective tendencies. I ques-

* *The Suffragette* (London: Gay & Hancock Limited), by E. Sylvia Pankhurst. A history of the women's militant suffrage movement, 1905–1910.

Sylvia Pankhurst

tioned myself, most searchingly, as to whether I had inadvertently said or done anything to encourage this undue interest in my welfare, but was able to exonerate myself from culpability.

The jagged silhouette of New York City showed like a ruined castle on the horizon. It was intensely cold, with great blocks of ice jamming the harbour. That learned nurse, Lavinia Dock, Mrs. Stanton Blatch, and Mrs. Winters Brannan of the Women's Political Union met me with a flock of Pressmen, who kept me busy with interviews for three entire days. They were exceedingly young, almost like schoolboys, I thought. I received them in relays, four to six at a time. "Don't you take notes?" I asked them, anxious for accurate reports. "We are not stenographers!" they replied indignantly, but I rang for the "bell girl," and sent for notebooks and pencils from the stationer's stall in the hotel. The young men amiably permitted me to suggest the questions and dictate the answers. The result was excellent; the interviews, which appeared all over the country, were so good that whilst the Civic Forum Lecture Bureau had only booked two engagements for me on my arrival, telegrams for dates began pouring in, and during my three months' stay I could satisfy only a small proportion of those who were asking me to speak, though I travelled almost every night, and spoke once, twice, or thrice a day. I had arrived at the height of the interest and sympathy felt by America in the English movement. Everywhere the Press was wholly benign toward me, except in Chicago, where the difference arose from my own action. It happened that I had there a day to spare. I attempted to spend it quietly writing, and to postpone my interviews with the reporters till the morrow. This incensed some of them extremely. Some battered persistently on my door, others invented the most atrocious interviews, which were published with faked photographs in which I appeared an appalling hooligan. A newspaper containing one such caricature was flung over the head of the chambermaid as she entered my room. Seeing it, I capitulated immediately, but the Press men and women did not entirely relent. Arriving after an all-night journey at Des Moines, Iowa, having entirely lost my voice, I was met by a group of women, who told me that at noon I must address the Senate and the House of Representatives in joint convention. The only woman who had previously done so was Susan B. Anthony, on Married Woman's Property, forty years before. I whispered that my voice was gone, but Dr. Dewey, an osteopath, assured me that she would put it right for me, and she absolutely fulfilled her promise in a miraculous manner. A bill to enfranchise the women of Iowa was then pending, and in view of this I felt very deeply the responsibility laid upon me. The Speaker bowed low and led me to the dais to speak; the legislators were cordial. The women assured me I had helped them.

Coronation Year

CHRISTABEL PANKHURST: Never had a year begun in so much hope. It might be Coronation Year for the women's cause as well as for the King and Queen. Cabinet Ministers themselves had bidden us hope for votes this year. Mr. Augustine Birrell had said to a deputation in 1910: "My own strong opinion is that when Parliament meets next year this question will have to be decided." Sir Edward Grey, even while he made himself Mr. Asquith's mouthpiece in denying facilities for the Conciliation Bill in 1910, had said to the suffragists of his constituency that in his opinion facilities ought to be found for the bill "next year." Mr. Runciman, yet another Government Minister, had spoken in the same sense.

The Prime Minister's own pre-election pledge was that "The Government will give facilities in the next Parliament for effecting proceeding with a bill which is so framed as to permit of free amendment." Mr. Lloyd George and Mr. Winston Churchill had therefore no longer any ground for tactics such as they had used against the Conciliation Bill in 1910.

"Keep your word," was all we asked the Government this session. And what a graceful thing it would be to gladden women and set them politically free in Coronation Year!

April 2, 1911

EMMELINE PANKHURST: In April the census was to be taken, and we organised a census resistance on the part of women. According to our law the census of the entire kingdom must be taken every ten years on a designated day. Our plan was to reduce the value of the census for statistical purposes by refusing to make the required returns. Two ways of resistance presented themselves. The first and more important was direct resistance by occupiers who should refuse to fill in the census papers. This laid the resister open to a fine of five pounds or a month's imprisonment, and thus required the exercise of considerable courage. The second means of resistance was evasion—staying away from home during the entire time that the enumerators were taking the census. We made the announcement of this plan and instantly there ensued a splendid response from women and a chorus of horrified disapproval from the conservative public.

In London we gave a great concert at Queen's Hall on census night. Many of us walked about Trafalgar Square until midnight and then repaired to Aldwich skating rink, where we amused ourselves until morning. Some skated while others looked on and enjoyed the admirable musical entertainment that helped to pass the hours. We had with us a number of the brightest stars in the theatrical world, and they were generous in their contributions.

There was a good deal of curiosity to see what the Government would devise in the way of punishment for the rebellious women, but the Government realised the impossibility of taking punitive action, and Mr. John Burns, who, as head of the Local Government Board, was responsible for the census, decided to treat the affair with magnanimity.

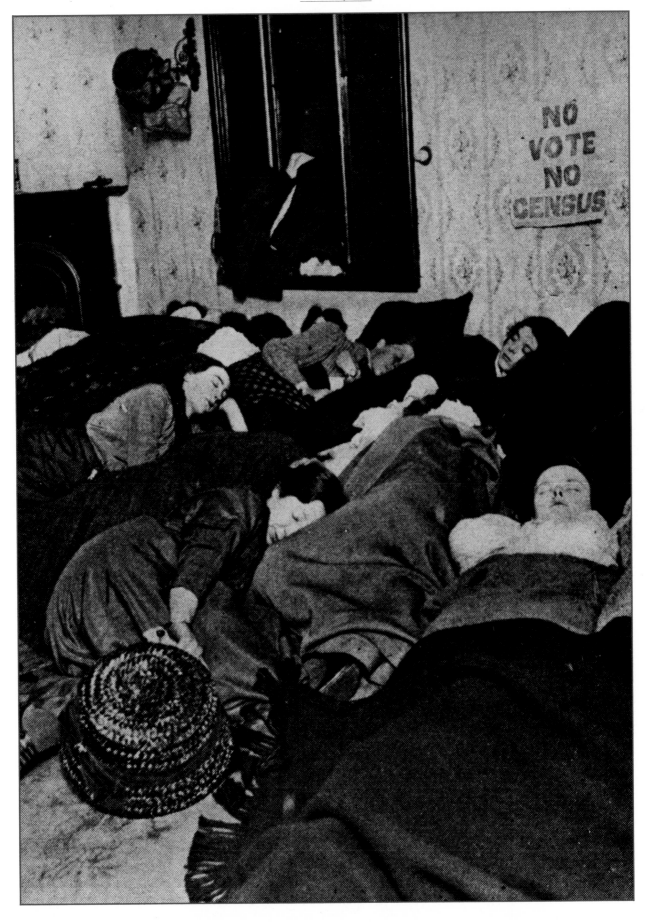

FROM PRISON TO CITIZENSHIP

EMMELINE PETHICK-LAWRENCE:
A suffrage procession that broke all
records walked through the London
streets.

As I walked amongst others at the
head of the procession, I was able, on
reaching our destination, to watch
from the upper windows of the Albert
Hall precincts the advance of that
great army marching five abreast. It
was all deeply moving. To me, naturally enough, the most
significant and beautiful part of the pageant was the
contingent of those who had been in prison. They
marched in white, a thousand strong, each one carrying a
small silver pennant, and in their midst was borne a great
banner depicting a symbolic woman with a broken
chain in her hands and the inscription:
FROM PRISON TO CITIZENSHIP.

THE STANDARD, Thursday, October 5, 1911

MRS. PANKHURST'S DEPARTURE
SPECIAL INTERVIEW
PLANS FOR CANADA AND UNITED STATES

The departure of Mrs. Pankhurst for her autumn campaign in America was the occasion of an informal but enthusiastic "God-speed" at Waterloo yesterday morning, where a large number of members and friends of the Women's Social and Political Union had assembled from an early hour. Mrs. Pankhurst arrived about half-past nine with her daughter, Miss Sylvia Pankhurst, and Miss Pethick, who accompanies her in the present tour.

A large purple, white, and green flag floated in front of the engine, and many of the visitors bore the colours of the movement. Mrs. Pankhurst, who looked remarkably well, wore a dark-blue serge suit, a small felt hat, and a purple and green shot chiffon scarf; while in her bosom was a sprig of ivy-leaf geranium, pinned on personally by Lady Constance Lytton. As the train steamed away from Waterloo at 9:45 a.m. repeated cheers were given, and flags and handkerchiefs were waved enthusiastically.

MRS. PANKHURST INTERVIEWED

"We mean to have the vote next session!" Thus Mrs. Pankhurst outlined, on the eve of her departure for America, the coming campaign of the suffragists, which they finally believe will result in the passing of the Conciliation Bill during the next Parliamentary session. All the organised forces of the Women's Social and Political Union are to be brought to bear on it, and this time the struggle for the vote will not be fought out in Parliament Square, but in the House of Commons itself.

"Prospects have never been so bright," said Mrs. Pankhurst to a *Standard* representative. "The Prime Minister has given us the most definite promises that full facilities shall be given to the Bill, and we are going to make the most of them."

Before the campaign opens, however, the leader of the suffragists is to make a lecture tour in the United States, her second visit to that country, to preach the gospel of "Votes for Women." "I sail," said Mrs. Pankhurst, "to address a round of meetings in most of the important towns in the United States. The greater part of November will be taken up in the Western States. Then I go on to Canada, beginning at Toronto, and expect to be back in England by Christmas."

WOMEN IN IMPERIAL POLITICS

"The chief object of my lecture tour is to further the international suffrage movement and to develop the suffrage question from the Imperial point of view. That is why I am going to Canada. It is time that the women took their place in Imperial politics, and the growing interest in the question of the suffrage for women over there is a good beginning. We want the same political cohesion amongst the women of the Empire as there is amongst the men."

October 1911

EMMELINE PANKHURST: I remember this third visit to the United States with especial pleasure. I was the guest in New York of Dr. and Mrs. Winters Brannan, and through the courtesy of Dr. Brannan, who is at the head of all the city hospitals, I saw something of the penal system and the institutional life of America.

But, after all, in the United States, as in other countries, the problem of the relations between unfranchised women and the State remains unsolved and unsatisfactory. One night my friends took me to that sombre and terrible institution, the Night Court for Women. We sat on the bench with the magistrate, and he very courteously explained everything to us. The whole business was heart-breaking. All the women, with one exception—an old drunkard—were charged with solicitation. Most of them were of high type by nature. It all seemed so hopeless, and it was clear that they were victims of an evil system. Their conviction was a foregone conclusion. The magistrate said that in most cases the reason for their coming there was economic. One case of a little cigar-maker, who said very simply that she only went on the streets when out of work, and that when in work she earned eight dollars a week, was very tragic and touching. I could not keep the night court out of my speeches after that. The whole dreadful injustice of women's lives seemed mirrored in that place.

I went as far west as the Pacific Coast on this visit, spending Christmas Day in Seattle, and for the first time seeing a community where women and men existed on terms of exact equality. It was a delightful experience.

It was in November, when I was in the city of Minneapolis, that a crushing blow descended on the English suffragists. I learned of this through cabled despatches in the newspapers and from private cables, and was so staggered that I could scarcely command myself sufficiently to fill my immediate engagements. This was the news, that the Government had broken their plighted word and had deliberately destroyed the Conciliation Bill. My first wild thought, on hearing of this act of treachery, was to cancel all engagements and return to England, but my final decision to remain afterward proved the right one, because the women at home, without a moment's loss of time, struck the answering blow, guided by that insight which has been characteristic of every act of the members of our Union.

November 17, 1911

EMMELINE PETHICK-LAWRENCE: The Conciliation Bill was, to all purposes, killed by a declaration from the Prime Minister in November of this year that he intended to introduce a manhood suffrage bill in the next session of Parliament.* This was a direct slap in the face to the woman suffrage organisations, for there had been no public demand whatever from men for an extension of the male franchise. Mr. Lloyd George, who openly rejoiced that the Conciliation Bill had been "torpedoed," announced that the bill would be open to an amendment to include women. Probably he had cast himself for the heroic part of becoming the champion of women on the floor of the House. The amendment would be quite impossible to carry, if for no other reason than that it would split the ranks of suffrage supporters who were composed of all parties in Parliament, while it would not

* In England and Wales men were unable to vote who did not fulfil the property qualifications of the Second Reform Act of 1867. They were either young men living at home or lodgers paying less than ten pounds per annum rent in the city boroughs, and in the counties tenants of property rated at less than twelve pounds per annum. In Scotland and Ireland the qualifications were similar.

receive the support of the Liberal Government. I wrote a letter to Mr. Asquith in the following terms:

> Consternation has been caused by your recent announcement that the Government intend to introduce in 1912 a manhood suffrage bill. It has accordingly been decided that a deputation representing the Women's Social and Political Union shall wait upon yourself and the Chancellor of the Exchequer on the evening of Tuesday November 21, for the purpose of demanding that the proposed manhood suffrage bill be abandoned, and in its stead the Government introduce and carry a measure giving equal franchise rights to men and women.

A similar letter was written to Mr. Lloyd George which concluded with the statement that "the deputation refuses to consider the proposition that the enfranchisement of women should depend on an amendment to a Government measure for manhood suffrage."

On many previous occasions Mr. Asquith, as Prime Minister, had met the request to receive a deputation from us with contemptuous refusal. It was significant of the ever-growing pressure of public opinion that this time he consented to receive us and all the various suffrage societies. He appointed Friday, November 17, and stated that Mr. Lloyd George, the Chancellor of the Exchequer, would also be present. Christabel Pankhurst and I were the speakers representing the W.S.P.U. We put the views expressed above in my letter to Mr. Asquith. Representatives of other societies followed, expressing their various opinions on the situation. Mr. Asquith in his reply denied the imputation of bad faith, and declared that he, as a convinced anti-suffragist, could not consent to the Government introducing a woman suffrage bill. But as a House of Commons man he would bend to a majority vote. Mr. Lloyd George denied the political impossibility of an amendment being carried and said that if it were done, we should look very foolish for having said that it was a trick

Members of the suffrage deputation to the Prime Minister outside 10 Downing Street, November 17, 1911
Centre: Emmeline Pethick-Lawrence
Right: Christabel Pankhurst greets a member of the Actresses' Franchise League.

to baulk women. "We shall not mind that if we get the vote," interjected Christabel.

"Miss Pankhurst, in a very able speech," said Mr. Asquith, "used one or two rather strong expressions to which of course I do not take any exception. She talked of terms of peace, presenting, I might say, a pistol in one hand and a dagger in the other at the Government. Mrs. Pethick-Lawrence, too, used some expressions about being tricked and betrayed. Where does the trick come in? I am pointing out to you that the position of the Government is perfectly consistent. I quite understand Miss Pankhurst's position. She says it is our duty ourselves to introduce a bill conferring the franchise on women on the same terms as men. It is an intelligible position, but we have never promised to do anything of the kind. If you ask me why we don't do it, I will tell you once more: I am the head of the Government, and I am not going to make myself responsible for the introduction of a measure which I do not conscientiously believe to be in the best interests of the country."

November 20, 1911

EMMELINE PETHICK-LAWRENCE: Victimised by such trickery, there was only one reply for self-respecting women to make. On the following Monday we had a mass meeting in the Royal Albert Hall at which I made the announcement that, on the following day, I would lead a deputation of protest to the House of Commons. Many hundreds of women came with me and we made a demonstration in Parliament Square.

November 21, 1911

HENRY NEVINSON: Happily it was a fine frosty evening, and the hundreds of police who were stationed around Parliament Square at dusk, and had to remain there till midnight, did not get wet. Nor did the more unhappy detectives, who hung about the W.S.P.U. offices and shops, looking as conspicuously innocent as detectives always do. I passed through the square at seven o'clock. It was already crowded, and a full battalion of police was massed in three companies there, while many hundred more were held in reserve, besides a squadron of mounted police. If force could protect the Members of Parliament, who happened that evening to be discussing the question of mistresses and maids, certainly those domestic gentlemen were secure. One felt that a Member's place is the House.

At Caxton Hall things were busy, as they usually are when "General" Drummond, smiling and imperturbable, is organising events. But, except in the spectators' gallery, the hall was not crowded. The report had gone out that the police would shut and barricade the gates, thus hoping to catch the whole demonstration like birds in a net. It was a fine idea, but in vain is the net laid in the sight of any Suffragette. Means had been provided for breaking through all bolts and bars, and the exit would have been only more interesting. But to avoid the chance of accident large numbers of the volunteers were being sent out quietly in squads of ten at a time to be ready to support the general body in the square. However, no attempt at "bottling in" was made, and the gates of the hall remained as freely open as the vote will be to all male persons under the threatened and detested bill.

At 7:15 Mrs. Pethick-Lawrence and Miss Pankhurst arrived. The platform filled. Mrs. Saul Solomon was there, still suffering from her severe injuries on Black Friday a year ago. Mrs. Cobden-Sanderson, Mrs. Brailsford, Mrs. Mansell-Moullin, Miss Vida Goldstein, Dr. Pethick, and many other distinguished leaders of the movement were there too. At 7:40 Miss Pankhurst took the chair, and in that stirring voice of hers, an excellent thing in warfare, she read the resolution that was to be taken to the House. It dwelt upon two of the main points on which the strength of the Union's opposition in the present situation depends—the insult done to women by the manhood suffrage bill, and the refusal of women to come into their rights on chance divisions taken on a private member's amendment. It therefore called on the Government to withdraw their proposal of manhood suffrage and introduce a bill on terms of equality. Miss Pankhurst supported the resolution in a brief but admirable statement. As usual, she was happy in quoting a great authority, when she recalled the words of Mill, who refused to support manhood suffrage without the grant of an equal right to women, because manhood suffrage alone would only serve as one more rivet to the chains on half the human race.

Mrs. Pethick-Lawrence then spoke with similar brevity, and a few minutes before eight o'clock led the demonstration to the doors, without fuss or delay. She walked alone at their head, the remainder following two deep. Wheeling to the left, they advanced some forty yards down the street, and then came up against the first cordon of police. A struggle began at once and it seemed as though we should get no further. But the object of the police was only to break the demonstration into small parties. Some six or ten were suddenly let through with Mrs. Pethick-Lawrence, and they went on alone. We who came in the second detachment did not see her again, though we hurried up Victoria Street as fast as the crowd would let us. I was told that she was at last arrested after a prolonged effort to break through the thick lines of police drawn across the square opposite Parliament Street.

From the point of view of the police, their manoeuvre was successful. There was no body or weight in it, as in the compact column with which Mrs. Pankhurst broke the police lines across the entrance of Downing Street, just a year before. The parties sent in advance were unable to mass together owing to the crowd; and the parties that followed arrived separate, and could do nothing but throw themselves upon the police in succession, only to be beaten back and defeated in detail. This they did with the utmost courage and resolution, especially at the corner of the square, where the road passes St. Margaret's towards the House. It was there and opposite Parliament Street that the fiercest struggles took place. But even the little groups soon lost all cohesion, being intermingled with the surging crowd, and constantly ridden down and broken up by the mounted police. Nothing more was possible but isolated and individual attacks. The first I could distinguish clearly came from Miss Vera Holme, the Union's redoubtable horsewoman and chauffeur. Dashing straight at a mounted policeman, she seized the horse's bridle, and tried to turn his head against the cordon. She was assisted by another Suffragette unknown to me. At length she was dragged off by three ordinary police, and after a prolonged struggle was led away under arrest. Before that contest was over, I saw Mrs. Brailsford charging the main cordon (here drawn up three deep), and returning again and again to the assault unaided. She then climbed the railings and crossed the grass, but I think her arrest came later, and at a different point in the square.

So the isolated attacks continued, one woman after another flinging herself in vain against those thickly serried lines, like waves against a cliff. The worst part of the struggle was about 8:30, and I think it was about this time that my friend Dr. Soskice, the well-known Russian who has suffered years in Russian prisons for liberty, was arrested. Mr. Victor Duval was also arrested there for climbing the railings onto the grass and taking the number of a policeman. On the whole, however, the behaviour of the police showed great improvement since last year. Some women were hurt—one or two badly—but I heard no complaint against the police for wilful or malignant violence. As to the crowd, it was helpless, as usual in London, swaying to and fro, rushing hither and thither in terror of the horses and police.

Miss Billinghurst

But, with hardly an exception, it was strongly sympathetic with the women, and cheered them with real enthusiasm. Of course, many had come from mere curiosity, and one at least maintained his enthusiasm by more substantial considerations, for he took my watch. But the general sympathy and behaviour proved how wise the Union was in holding the demonstration at night, among working people, instead of among the idle and wealthy classes of the afternoon.

The contest continued for nearly an hour; but at nine o'clock the police advanced in lines, led by the mounted detachments, and gradually cleared the square of most of the crowd. The traffic had not been entirely stopped at any time, and it now began to pass freely. Taking advantage of taxis and motors, many of the women succeeded in approaching the main cordons again, and there they renewed the isolated attacks. When I say attacks, I do not mean that they used any personal violence. They merely did their utmost to force the lines by rushing through them. Usually, they were arrested after a short struggle, and the report that the police had orders to make no arrests were thus, happily, contradicted. Going to Cannon Row between nine-thirty and ten I found arrested women being brought in there every few minutes. The numbers in that station alone had reached 180 by nine-fifty. Just at that time, as I was returning to Whitehall, I met Miss Billinghurst, that indomitable cripple, being carried shoulder high by four policemen in her little tricycle or wheel-cart that she propels with her arms. Amid immense cheering from the crowd, she followed the rest into the police station.

In Whitehall and Parliament Street themselves a continuous excitement was maintained all through the evening, because no one knew where the next window might be broken. One would hear a crash, and in the midst of the crowd some silent and self-possessed woman would suddenly be seized and rushed away. Many of the window breakers, however, escaped arrest, owing to the density of the crowd itself, and a few escaped by strategy. In Whitehall, I think the Treasury suffered most—no doubt in compliment to the Chancellor of the Exchequer. The Scottish Education Office suffered, too, owing to its proximity rather than its demerits. The War Office, which I at first thought escaped lightly, was roughly treated also, one leading Suffragette having broken five windows on her own, and there were many others there engaged. But all suffered, and the National Liberal Club, the savage den of manhood suffrage, was not forgotten.

As I went to work in Fleet Street soon after ten, a grey-haired lady beside me suddenly dashed a stone through a window of the Charing Cross post-office and stood stock still until a policeman led her off to Bow Street. Her example was at once followed by two others, but only one of them was captured. That was the last I was able to see of the demonstration, and I think it was one of the last actions of the 220, or whatever the exact number may be.

EMMELINE PETHICK-LAWRENCE: The total number of those arrested was 223, including four men. Bow Street police court was blocked. It took several days to dispose of all the cases. Meanwhile the police gave the hospitality of their billiard-room to the women awaiting their trial. Anybody who for the next two or three days entered the room would have been surprised at the light-hearted talk and laughter as stories were told of individual experience.

Finally some two hundred of us found ourselves together in a wing of Holloway Prison specially reserved for Suffragettes. Six who had thrown stones were committed for trial at the next London Quarter Sessions.

In prison a curious experience awaited me.

We had unconsciously and indirectly brought off a revolution in prison. All the prisoners were now treated under Mr. Churchill's Prison Rule 243A.* The authorities of Holloway Prison might or might not have become friendly, but with such numbers in prison at the same time and with the former experience of the hunger-strike in their memory, they were ready to give us the moon if we demanded it. Rule 243A gave us something of the status of political prisoners. We wore our own clothes, exercised together in perfect freedom, played a sort of football in the yard, got ourselves up in fancy dress, and joked with the wardresses and behaved as though we were at a house party.

On my release I wrote in our paper:

We of the W.S.P.U. have dared to affirm the human and divine equality of man and woman. On that affirmation we are prepared to stake our honour, our liberty, and our life. Upon that affirmation, we take our stand against all material and spiritual forces of negation and denial.

The temper of the whole Union was now at white heat. Letters poured into our office, of which the following is a sample: "Lloyd George rouses the most timid to militancy. Please put my name down for the next protest."

In December, Suffragettes succeeded in completely silencing Mr. Asquith at a meeting held in the City Temple. After a quarter of an hour spent in the vain endeavour to complete a sentence, he left the platform, and the meeting proceeded without disturbance.

EMMELINE PANKHURST: One individual protest deserves mention because of its prophetic character. In December Miss Emily Wilding Davison was arrested for attempting to set fire to a letter box at Parliament Street post-office. In court Miss Davison said that she did it as a protest against the Government's treachery, and as a demand that women's suffrage be included in the King's Speech. "The protest was meant to be serious," she said, "and so I adopted a serious course. In past agitation for reform the next step after window-breaking was incendiarism, in order to draw the attention of the private citizens to the fact that this question of reform was their concern as well as that of women."

Miss Davison received the severe sentence of six months' imprisonment for her deed.

* Prison Rule 243A. The new regulation was as follows: In the case of any offender of the second or third division whose previous character is good, and who has been convicted of, or committed to prison for, an offence not involving dishonesty, cruelty, indecency, or serious violence, the Prison Commissioners may allow such ameliorations of the conditions prescribed in the foregoing rules as the Secretary of State may approve in respect of the wearing of prison clothing, bathing, hair-cutting, cleaning of cells, employment, exercise, books, and otherwise. Provided that no such amelioration shall be greater than that granted under the rules for offenders of the first division.

WOMEN'S WAR

CHRISTABEL PANKHURST: "I cannot start the New Year without putting my name down for the next protest against the policy of the Government." "I fully realise that the only way to get the vote is to fight for it." "Please enter my name for the next protest. I should like to help to hasten the day when we shall have votes for women."

Messages such as these came thick and fast to the W.S.P.U. headquarters as 1912 began. Rumours appeared in the Press that it would be "impossible" for pro-suffragist and anti-suffragist Ministers of the Government to oppose one another on the public platform by speaking, some for and others against votes for women, although the pro-suffrage Ministers had undertaken to campaign in favour of the women's amendment.

Women noticed in the New Year a strange silence as to votes for women on the part of their "friends in the Cabinet." Mr. Lloyd George at Cardiff, Lord Haldane at Nottingham, Lord Grey at Sunderland, Mr. Runciman at Newcastle said not one word of the cause they had promised to advocate in order to assure its inclusion in the reform bill. If the Suffragettes had not been present to heckle them, they would not even have mentioned votes for women.

Mother had now returned from her tour in Canada and the United States, where she had travelled ten thousand miles and spoken in many different places. At a welcome meeting in London she applauded the protest we had made in her absence against the Government's "gross breach of their pledge regarding the Conciliation Bill." She announced that she would again lead a protest against this policy.

A grave incitement to militancy was now delivered by a Cabinet Minister, Mr. Hobhouse, at a speech in Bristol, the scene of the great franchise riots prior to the Reform Act of 1832. He declared that in the case of votes for women there had not been the kind of popular sentiment uprising which accounted for the burning of Nottingham Castle in 1832 or the tearing up of the Hyde Park railings in 1867. In fact, there had been "no ebullition of popular feeling."

This sensational challenge to women by a responsible Minister of the Crown had a decisive effect on the future course of the woman suffrage movement.

"So fully," said Mrs. Pethick-Lawrence, "did the Government, the Peers, and the King understand the argument of arson and destruction, that the Reform Bill became law a few months afterward, namely, in June 1832."

By holding up to women the example of men's methods of winning the vote, Mr. Hobhouse was taking the very grave responsibility of inciting them, said Mrs. Pethick-Lawrence, "to serious forms of violence, compared to which Mrs. Pankhurst's exhortation is mildness itself."

Mrs. Pankhurst issued a handbill to men and women: "I invite you to come to Parliament Square, Monday, March 4, 1912, at eight o'clock, to take part in a great protest meeting against the Government's refusal to include women in their Reform Bill."

March 1, 1912

EMMELINE PANKHURST: We had planned a demonstration for March 4, and this one we announced.

We planned another demonstration for March 1, but this one we did not announce. Late that afternoon, I drove in a taxi-cab, accompanied by the Hon. Secretary of the Union, Mrs. Tuke, and another of our members, to No. 10 Downing Street, the official residence of the Prime Minister. It was exactly half-past five when we alighted from the cab and threw our stones, four of them, through the window panes. As we expected, we were promptly arrested and taken to Cannon Row Police Station.

The hour that followed will long be remembered in London. At intervals of fifteen minutes relays of women who had volunteered for the demonstration did their work. The first smashing of glass occurred in the Haymarket and Piccadilly, and greatly startled and alarmed both pedestrians and police. A large number of the women were arrested, and everybody thought that this ended the affair. But before the excited populace and the frustrated shop owners' first exclamation had died down, before the police had reached the station with their prisoners, the ominous crashing and splintering of plate glass began again, this time along both sides of Regent Street and the Strand.

A furious rush of police and people toward the second scene of action ensued. While their attention was being taken up with occurrences in this quarter, the third relay of women began breaking the windows in Oxford Circus and Bond Street. The demonstration ended for the day at half-past six with the breaking of many windows in the Strand.

DAILY GRAPHIC, Saturday, March 2, 1912
WAR ON WINDOWS
SUFFRAGETTE RAID ON WEST END SHOPS
WIDE-SPREAD DAMAGE
MORE THAN A HUNDRED WOMEN ARRESTED

The West End of London last night was the scene of an unexampled outrage on the part of the militant suffragists. The women "furthered their cause" by doing thousands of pounds' worth of damage to the windows of West London shopkeepers.

Bands of women paraded Regent Street, Piccadilly, the Strand, Oxford Street, and Bond Street, smashing windows with stones and hammers.

In all quarters the outrage, carefully planned and organised, occurred with startling suddenness, and shopkeepers found their property damaged and destroyed before any steps could be taken to prevent the onslaught.

By seven o'clock practically the whole of the West End of London was a city of broken glass. Shutters were put up and in some cases temporary barricades erected. In nearly all cases the work of destruction was executed with hammers, which the women carried concealed under their clothes. Many of the rioters were young girls, and were terribly nervous when the crucial moment arrived.

One of the most noteworthy factors in the scene was the general attitude of the crowds which collected with astonishing rapidity. Bitter hostility to the women was expressed on all sides, and there is no doubt that had any recurrence of the outrages been attempted later in the evening the women would have been severely handled in spite of the presence of the police.

In all about 120 women, including Mrs. Pankhurst, were arrested.

DOWNING STREET

The most daring raid took place on the Prime Minister's house at No. 10 Downing Street. Just after five-thirty p.m. a private motor-car drove up Downing Street, and as it reached the Prime Minister's house three women jumped out and immediately began throwing stones at the house opposite them. Two windows were broken on each side of the door downstairs, four panes in all. The police patrols were taken by surprise, but before the women could do any further damage the constables had run through them and seized their arms. All three were taken to Cannon Row police station, but as Mrs. Pankhurst was being led past the Home Office she suddenly wrenched her arm free and threw a stone through one of the windows. About the same time another woman broke two windows at the Local Government Board Office.

At the Home Office a clerk who was sitting writing had a narrow escape, a heavy stone flying over his head.

THE STRAND

Between St. Clement Danes and Charing Cross the array of broken windows presented a remarkable spectacle. The southern side of the Strand was singled out for attack; the other side, with a few exceptions, escaped.

Directly the women started operations the police telephoned the jewellers in the West End warning them, and advising them to remove all valuables from their windows. The police stated that within an hour 4,000 extra men would be drafted in from the suburbs, and asked the jewellers whether they would require any special guard. It was feared that looting hooligans might follow the smashing of the windows.

REGENT STREET AND PICCADILLY

About 100 women made their way to Piccadilly, Regent Street, and neighbourhood. In many cases the windows were of large size and a complete hole was made in them. In other instances the thick glass was simply splintered, but none the less rendered useless.

Throughout the whole length of Coventry Street, Regent Street, as far as Oxford Street, along Bond Street and the greater part of Piccadilly, the women continued the wreckage, apparently indiscriminately. The well-known firm of Swan and Edgar had some seven or eight windows smashed. The Regent Street post-office and Hope Brothers' establishment also suffered. By seven o'clock nearly sixty of the delinquents had been conveyed to Vine Street police station.

March 4, 1912

EMMELINE PANKHURST: A hundred or more women walked quietly into Knightsbridge and walking singly along the streets demolished nearly every pane of glass they passed. Taken by surprise the police arrested as many as they could reach, but most of the women escaped.

For that two days' work something like two hundred Suffragettes were taken to the various police stations, and for days the long procession of women streamed through the courts.

It was a stormy imprisonment for most of us. A great many of the women had received, in addition to their sentences, "hard labour," and this meant that the privileges at that time accorded to Suffragettes, as political offenders, were withheld.

March 5, 1912

The panic-stricken Government did not rest content with the imprisonment of the window-breakers. They sought, in a blind and blundering fashion, to perform the impossible feat of wrecking at a blow the entire militant movement. Governments have always tried to crush reform movements, to destroy ideas, to kill the thing that cannot die. Without regard to history, which shows that no Government have ever succeeded in doing this, they go on trying in the old, senseless way.

Our headquarters in Clement's Inn had been under constant observation by the police, and on this evening an inspector of police and a large force of detectives suddenly descended on the place, with warrants for the arrest of Christabel Pankhurst and Mr. and Mrs. Pethick-Lawrence, who with Mrs. Tuke and myself were charged with "conspiring to incite certain persons to commit malicious damage to property." When the officers entered they found Mr. Pethick-Lawrence at work in his office, and Mrs. Pethick-Lawrence in her flat upstairs. My daughter was not in the building. The Lawrences, after making brief preparations, drove in a taxi-cab to Bow Street station, where they spent the night. The police remained in possession of the offices, and detectives were despatched to find and arrest Christabel. But that arrest never took place. Christabel Pankhurst eluded the entire force of detectives and uniformed police, trained hunters of human prey.

The offices in Clement's Inn were thoroughly ransacked by the police, in a determined effort to secure evidence of conspiracy. They went through every desk, file and cabinet, taking away with them two cab loads of books and papers, including all my private papers, photographs of my children in infancy, and letters sent me by my husband long ago. Some of these I never saw again.

The police also terrorised the printer of our weekly newspaper, and although the paper came out as usual, about a third of its columns were left blank. The headlines, however, with the ensuing space mere white paper, produced a dramatic effect.

Most eloquent of all was the editorial page, which was absolutely blank except for the headline, "A CHALLENGE!" and the name at the foot of the last column, Christabel Pankhurst.

"Silk, thistle, pansy, duck, wool, E.Q."

EMMELINE PANKHURST: On March 14 Mr. and Mrs. Pethick-Lawrence, Mrs. Tuke, and myself were brought up for preliminary hearing on the charge of having, on November 1, 1911, and on various other dates, "conspired and combined together unlawfully and maliciously to commit damage, etc." The case opened on May 15 in a crowded court-room in which I saw many friends. Mr. Bodkin, who appeared for the prosecution, made a very long address, in which he endeavoured to prove that the Women's Social and Political Union was a highly developed organisation of most sinister character.

His voice sank to a scandalised half-whisper as he stated the fact that we had presumed to include the sacred persons of the Government in our private code. "We find," said Mr. Bodkin portentously, "that public men in the service of His Majesty as members of the Cabinet are tabulated here under code names. We find that the Cabinet collectively has its code word, 'Trees,' and individual members of the Cabinet are designated by the name, sometimes of trees, but I am also bound to say the commonest weeds as well." Here a ripple of laughter interrupted.

The deadly possibilities of the code were illustrated by a telegram found in one of the files. It read: "Silk, thistle, pansy, duck, wool, E. Q." Translated by the aid of the code book the telegram read: "Will you protest Asquith's public meeting to-morrow evening but don't get arrested unless success depends on it. Wire back to Christabel Pankhurst, Clement's Inn."

Mr. Pethick-Lawrence and I spoke in our own defence, and Mr. Healey, M.P., defended Mrs. Pethick-Lawrence. Mr. Lawrence spoke first at the opening of the case. He began by giving an account of the suffrage movement and why he felt the enfranchisement of women appeared to him a question so grave that it warranted strong measures in its pursuit. He sketched briefly the history of the Women's Social and Political Union, from the time when Christabel Pankhurst and Annie Kenney were thrown out of Sir Edward Grey's meeting and imprisoned for asking a political question, to the torpedoing of the Conciliation Bill. "The case that I have to put before you," he said, "is that neither the conspiracy nor the incitement is ours; but that the conspiracy is a conspiracy of the Cabinet who are responsible for the Government of this country; and that the incitement is the incitement of the Ministers of the Crown." And he did this most effectually not only by telling of the disgraceful trickery and deceit with which the Government had misled the suffragists in the matter of suffrage bills, but by giving the plain words in which members of the Cabinet had advised the women that they would never get the vote until they had learned to fight for it as men had fought in the past.

When it came my turn to speak, realising that the average man is profoundly ignorant of the history of the women's movement—because the Press has never adequately or truth-fully chronicled the movement—I told the jury, as briefly as I could, the story of the forty years' peaceful agitation before my daughters and I resolved that we would give our lives to the work of getting the vote for women, and that we should use whatever means of getting the vote that were necessary to success.

"We founded the Women's Social and Political Union," I said, "in 1903. Our first intention was to try and influence the particular political party, which was then coming into power, to make this question of the enfranchisement of women their own question and to push it. It took some little time to convince us—and I need not weary you with the history of all that has happened—but it took some little time to convince us that that was no use; that we could not secure things in that way. Then in 1905 we faced the hard facts. We realised that there was a Press boycott against women's suffrage. Our speeches at public meetings were not reported, our letters to the editors were not published, even if we implored the editors; even the things relating to women's suffrage in Parliament were not recorded. They said the subject was not of sufficient public interest to be reported in the Press, and they were not prepared to report it. Then with regard to the men politicians in 1905: we realised how shadowy were the fine phrases about democracy, about human equality, used by the gentlemen who were then coming into power. They meant to ignore the women—there was no doubt whatever about that."

I went over the whole matter of our peaceful deputations, and of the violence with which they were invariably met; of our arrests and the farcical police-court trials, where the mere evidence of policemen's unsupported statements sent us to prison for long terms; of the falsehoods told of us in the House of Commons by responsible members of the Government—tales of women scratching and biting policemen and using hatpins—and I accused the Government of making these attacks against women who were powerless to defend themselves because they feared the women and desired to crush the agitation represented by our organisation.

"Now it has been stated in this court," I said, "that it is not the Women's Social and Political Union that is in the court, but that it is certain defendants. The action of the Government, gentlemen, is certainly against the defendants who are before you here to-day, but it is also against the Women's Social and Political Union. The intention is to crush that organisation.

"Now, a movement like that, supported like that, is not a wild, hysterical movement. It is not a movement of misguided people. It is a very serious movement. Women, I submit, like our members, and women, I venture to say, like the two women, and like the man who are in the dock to-day, are not people to undertake a thing like this lightly. May I just try to make you feel what it is that has made this movement the gigantic size it is from the very small beginnings it had? It is one of the biggest movements of modern times. A movement which is not only an influence, perhaps not yet recognised, in this country, but is influencing the women's movement all over the world.

"Now I want to say this deliberately as a leader of this movement. We have tried to hold it back, we have tried to keep it from going beyond bounds, and I have never felt a prouder woman than I did one night when a police constable said to me, after one of these demonstrations, 'Had this been a man's demonstration, there would have been bloodshed long ago.' Well, my lord, there has not been any bloodshed except on the part of the women themselves—these so-called militant women. Violence has been done to us, and I who stand before you in this dock have lost a dear sister in the course of this agitation.

"I say it is not the defendants who have conspired, but the Government who have conspired against us to crush this agitation; but however the matter may be decided, we are content to abide by the verdict of posterity. We are not the kind of people who like to brag a lot; we are not the kind of people who would bring ourselves into this position unless we were convinced that it was the only way. I have tried—all my life I have worked for this question—I have tried arguments, I have tried persuasion. I have addressed a greater number of public meetings, perhaps, than any person in this court, and I have never addressed one meeting where substantially the opinion of the meeting—not a ticket meeting, but an open meeting, for I have never addressed any other kind of a meeting—has not been that where women bear burdens and share responsibilities like men they should be given

An artist's impression of the Suffragette window-smashing raid

**Christabel and Emmeline Pankhurst on their release from prison,
December 22, 1908**

the privileges that men enjoy. I am convinced that public opinion is with us—that it has been stifled—wilfully stifled—so that in a public Court of Justice one is glad of being allowed to speak on this question."

The jury was absent for more than an hour, showing that they had some difficulty in agreeing upon a verdict. When they returned it was plain from their strained countenances that they were labouring under deep feeling. The foreman's voice shook as he pronounced the verdict, guilty as charged, and he had hard work to control his emotion as he added: "Your Lordship, we unanimously desire to express the hope that, taking into consideration the undoubtedly pure motives that underlie the agitation that has led to this trouble, you will be pleased to exercise the utmost clemency and leniency in dealing with the case."

A burst of applause followed this plea.

Lord Coleridge said: "You have been convicted of a crime for which the law would sanction, if I chose to impose it, a sentence of two years' imprisonment with hard labour. There are circumstances connected with your case which the jury have very properly brought to my attention, and I have been asked by you all three to treat you as first-class misdemeanours.* If in the course of this case I had observed any contrition or disavowal of the acts you have committed, or any hope that you would avoid repetition of them in future, I should have been very much prevailed upon by the arguments that have been advanced to me."

No contrition having been expressed by us, the sentence of the Court was that we were to suffer imprisonment, in the second division, for the term of nine months, and that we were to pay the costs of the prosecution.

On our way to prison on May 22 we told one another that our sentences could not stand. Public opinion would never permit the Government to keep us in prison for nine months, or in the second division for any part of our term. We agreed to wait seven Parliamentary days before we began a hunger-strike protest.

So much pressure was brought to bear that within a few days the Home Secretary announced that he felt it his duty to examine into the circumstances of the case without delay. Ultimately, which in this case means shortly before the expiration of the seven Parliamentary days, we were all three placed in the first division.

We all had the privilege of furnishing our cells with comfortable chairs, tables, our own bedding, towels, and so on. We had meals sent in from the outside; we wore our own clothing and had what books, newspapers, and writing materials we required. We were not

---

* In requesting to be treated as "first-class misdemeanours," the defendants wished to be classed as political prisoners. Though this would mean first division treatment and privileges during their imprisonment, it was not requested as a privilege. This was an important public definition of their actions against the Government. It was to show the world that they were not common criminals but prisoners whose actions had been directed toward the political goal of votes for women.

permitted to write or receive letters or to see our friends except in the ordinary two weeks' routine. Still we had gained our point that suffrage prisoners were politicals.

We had gained it, but, as it turned out, only for ourselves. When we made the enquiry, "Are all our women now transferred to the first division?" the answer was that the order for transference referred only to Mr. and Mrs. Pethick-Lawrence and myself. Needless to say, we immediately refused to accept this unfair advantage, and after we had exhausted every means in our power to induce the Home Secretary to give the other suffrage prisoners the same justice that we had received, we adopted the protest of the hunger-strike.

The word flew swiftly through Holloway, and in some mysterious way travelled to Brixton, to Aylesbury, and Winson Green, and at once all the other suffrage prisoners followed our lead. The Government then had over eighty hunger-strikers on their hands, and, as before, had ready only the argument of force, which means that disgusting and cruel process of forcible feeding. Holloway became a place of horror and torment. Sickening scenes of violence took place almost every hour of the day, as the doctors went from cell to cell performing their hideous office.

I was lying in bed, very weak from starvation, when I heard a sudden scream from Mrs. Pethick-Lawrence's cell, then the sound of a prolonged and very violent struggle, and I knew that they had dared to carry their brutal business to our doors. I sprang out of bed and, shaking with weakness and with anger, I set my back against the wall and waited for what might come. In a few moments they had finished with Mrs. Pethick-Lawrence and had flung open the door of my cell. On the threshold I saw the doctors, and back of them a large group of wardresses. "Mrs. Pankhurst," began the doctor. Instantly I caught up a heavy earthenware water jug from a table hard by, and with hands that now felt no weakness I swung the jug head high.

"If any of you dares so much as to take one step inside this cell I shall defend myself," I cried. Nobody moved or spoke for a few seconds, and then the doctor confusedly muttered something about to-morrow morning doing as well, and they all retreated.

I demanded to be admitted to Mrs. Pethick-Lawrence's cell, where I found my companion in a desperate state. She is a strong woman, and a very determined one, and it had required the united strength of nine wardresses to overcome her. They had rushed into the cell without any warning, and had seized her unawares, else they might not have succeeded at all. As it was she resisted so violently that the doctors could not apply the stethoscope, and they had very great difficulty in getting the tube down. After the wretched affair was over Mrs. Pethick-Lawrence fainted, and for hours afterward was very ill.

The wholesale hunger-strike created a tremendous stir throughout England, and every day in the House the Ministers were harassed with questions.

Mr. Asquith, forced against his will to take part in the controversy, rose and said that it was not for him to interfere with the actions of his colleague Mr. McKenna, and he added, in his own suave, mendacious manner: "I must point out this, that there is not one single prisoner who cannot go out of prison this afternoon on giving the undertaking asked for by the Home Secretary." Meaning an undertaking to refrain henceforth from militancy.

Shocked to the depths of his soul by the insult thrown at our women, Mr. Lansbury strode up to the Ministerial bench and confronted the Prime Minister, saying again: "That was a disgraceful thing for you to say, Sir. You are beneath contempt, you and your colleagues. You call yourselves gentlemen, and you forcibly feed and murder women in this fashion. You ought to be driven out of office. Talk about protesting. It is the most disgraceful thing that ever happened in the history of England. You will go down to history as the men who tortured innocent women."

ESCAPE

CHRISTABEL PANKHURST: I was alone facing a great problem, a crisis for the movement. Those who had shared the responsibility were prisoners. What best use could I make of the few remaining minutes of freedom to guard against the evident dangers? At any moment the police would come.

I did not sleep at all that night for thinking. Suddenly, in the small hours, I saw what I must do! Escape! The Government should not defeat us. They should not break our movement. It must be preserved and the policy kept alive until the vote was won. My law studies had not been in vain. They had impressed indelibly upon my mind the fact that a political offender is not liable to extradition. Long before, when actually a prisoner in Holloway, that thought had come to me, in my prison cell, as a matter of purely academic interest. "Of course, if one ever did wish to avoid imprisonment, one could escape to a foreign country and as a political offender be able to stay there." Not an academic matter now, but one of vital, practical, political concern! I must get to Paris, control the movement from there—and from there keep the fight going, until we won!

I could hardly wait for the morning! As soon as I could venture to rouse my kind hostesses I told them my purpose. Would they see Miss — and ask if she could arrange for me to drive in her car to the boat instead of travelling by train? One of them went to enquire. It was impossible, she learned, for reasons of possible recognition, but she returned with money for my needs. This was helpful indeed, for approach to my own bank might be imprudent. I must risk taking the train, and risk it was, for a Suffragette speaker was known by sight to thousands, and the morning newspapers gave the news that I was "wanted by the police." One of these friends said she would go with me to Paris. I borrowed a black coat and a black cloche hat. My face was sufficiently disguised by an unaccustomed pallor. We drove to Victoria Station. The boat train was crowded, for the coal strike had reduced the service. I bought fashion papers, as providing a non-political screen, and sat quietly in a corner. The train started. Safety so far! Opposite me sat a lady writing letter after letter, but not too busy, it seemed, to look at me intently every now and again. The train reached Folkestone town and stopped. The lady opposite crossed the compartment, put her head out the window and called: "Policeman!" My heart stood still. She gave him her letters to post! The train moved on to the boat station. I went aboard. "Don't come any further with me," I said to my kind companion. "Take this letter back with you and see that Annie Kenney gets it." She left me. The boat started . . . arrived! My foot touched the soil of France. We were saved. We would win.

ANNIE KENNEY: Two days went past. No news worth having. We had visits from many mystifying people who said they knew where she was or who suspected others were sheltering her. On the third day a mysterious woman came to my office. "I have a letter for you from Christabel." She guessed my thoughts. "I know you don't believe me, but I left her safe, and she wants you to join her with the greatest speed." I opened the letter. It read:—

Beloved Annie,—The bearer of this note is a good friend of the Cause. She, with another friend, helped me to escape. She will tell you where I am and give you an address that will find me. Keep this a secret. I ask it for reasons I will explain when we meet. I write this in case you cannot get away at once (but do so if you can, as I have much to tell you). I want you to take supreme charge of the whole Movement during my absence, and while Mother and Mr. and Mrs. Lawrence are in prison. There may be people who consider that they have far more political experience than you, but ignore this. I absolutely trust your simple way of looking at things and arriving at the right answer to all questions. Your keen intuition has always appealed to me. I know that no member or members of the Cabinet would swerve you an inch from the policy laid down. Be brave under your great responsibilities. Be firm under the many pressing arguments that will be brought to bear on you, in the hope of weakening you in your work. I trust you implicitly and I give you complete control over the whole Movement until the leaders are released and we are all once again united. Come quickly, and bring with you a member who understands the language of the country that I am sheltering in. Disguise yourself, and watch closely for Scotland Yard men. Let your friend do all the talking, as you are so well known. I have good reason for mystifying the authorities. What a day when women win the Vote! Press on and give all our loyal ones my love and my faith that each one will obey orders that will be sent through you by me, and by unity we shall win through. Come to me at the first possible moment.
                                                                —Christabel

CHRISTABEL PANKHURST: Longing for news, I walked for miles about Paris, thinking over the position and laying plans of action.

At last Annie came, having travelled by circuitous route in careful disguise.

The Government had resolved to crush the movement, to end not only window-breaking, but also deputations to the Prime Minister and other Ministers, and "interrupted speeches and spoilt perorations!" Repression had been the Government's policy for the first six years, and now their policy was repression intensified, combined with a new and subtle attempt to confuse and confound, divide and disintegrate, the movement.

I was now in solitary command of the W.S.P.U. For the moment the prison position of the leaders and of the large number of other prisoners was the dominant issue. Yet at the same time the fight must continue, and the political situation must be watched. Through our paper, *Votes for Women*, I could keep the trumpet sounding, and messengers and letters passing to and fro between Paris and London enabled continuous control. The search for me continued, with all its humour for us and its exasperation for the foe.

ANNIE KENNEY: When the leaders were released after having done a hunger-strike my work seemed to grow and not diminish. Each had instructions to give, each had messages to send to Paris. They were ill and needed rest and change. Scores of the rank and file were still in prison and had to be got out. Had it not been for Mrs. Drummond, my sister Jessie, Margaret Cameron, Mrs. Sanders, Miss Kerr, Mrs. Archdale, and that splendid Mr. Arthur Marshall, the movement would have been weakened and discredited. We survived the storm.

About this time I recalled Grace Roe from the provinces. Grace Roe had played a unique part in the fight. Her power of tenacity, her love and loyalty to her chosen leader will never be equalled. Charming in appearance, soft in speech, gracious in manner, no wonder she got passports and passed barriers whilst others were waiting, stool in hand and lunch in pocket. Her daring was a marvel.

From now until April 8, 1913, when I was again arrested, my work lay chiefly in visiting Paris, reading proofs of the paper, making speeches, interviewing militants, and in training Grace, who was to take my place in case of my arrest.

I had to meet militants at my private flat at midnight, to discuss future plans with organisers, and last but not least, to take the place of Mrs. Pethick-Lawrence and become the money-raiser for the Union.

It was at this time that the burning of empty houses was resorted to. Both Christabel and her mother were against the taking of human life, but Christabel felt the times demanded sterner measures, and burning she knew would frighten both the public and Parliament. "But no life must be taken on our side," she said. "We alone are the ones who are prepared to give our lives, if necessary."

Those to whom this fiery method appealed came forth willingly. It demanded more than courage; it demanded pluck. It was dangerous to the burner, and awful punishment awaited those caught. They only carried amateur materials: a bit of cotton-wool, a small bottle of paraffin, a few shavings, and a box of matches. The rest depended on themselves.

The sentences passed on those captured were very heavy.

We did risk human life when we burnt houses, in spite of the care we took to see that all buildings were untenanted, but Providence protected us. No life was lost except on the militants' side.

Mr. and Mrs. Lawrence also questioned the wisdom of militancy which might mean the loss of life. To question policy with Christabel meant everything. Once people questioned policy her whole feeling changed toward them.

EMMELINE PETHICK-LAWRENCE: It was now openly announced that Christabel Pankhurst was in Paris. The Government sought for her extradition,* but this was refused on the ground of the political nature of her offence. As soon as Mrs. Pankhurst could travel she joined her in Paris. They asked us to come to Boulogne to confer with them. Mrs. Pankhurst met us with the announcement that she and Christabel had determined upon a new kind of campaign. Henceforward she said there was to be a widespread attack upon public and private property, secretly carried out by Suffragettes who would not offer themselves for arrest, but wherever possible would make good their escape. As our minds had been moving in quite another direction, this project came as a shock to us both. We considered it sheer madness to throw away the immense publicity and propaganda value that the demonstration followed by the State trial had brought to our cause. The facts elicited and made public during the course of the trial and the influential memorials for the mitigation of the sentences had given the movement a political status which it had been considered purpose of the Government during the past six years to deny.

* On September 13, 1912, the *Daily Sketch* made public the details of Christabel's whereabouts.

Christabel Pankhurst in Paris

The task before us, as we saw it, was to organise a great campaign of popular demonstrations which should outdo anything achieved before. The people were eager to see us and to hear us and to support us. A few obstinate reactionary statesmen could not stand against an overwhelming popular demand. We urged that now that the three of us were free, Christabel should return and challenge the Government to arrest her. If they chose to adopt this course, her trial would be the sensation of the day. If not, she would be acclaimed by crowded audiences wherever she chose to speak. At by-elections as well as at outdoor and indoor meetings, our appeal to the populace would be irresistible.

Although we had been at one with Mrs. Pankhurst in her objective of women's political emancipation, and for six years had pursued the same path, there had always been an underlying difference between us that had not come into the open, mainly because of the close union of mind and purpose between ourselves and Christabel. Mrs. Pankhurst had accepted with extreme reluctance the temporary truce of militancy and had little use for the exercise of patience. "I want to be tried for sedition," she often exclaimed. Excitement, drama, and danger were the conditions in which her temperament found full scope. She had the qualities of a leader on the battlefield. While Christabel lived with us she agreed that we had to advance in militancy by slow degrees in order to give the average person time to understand every move and to keep pace.

To our surprise, Christabel, once so politically minded, was at one with her mother in resisting these suggestions. She informed us that she did not intend to return but to remain in Paris and direct the movement from there. It had never occurred to us for one moment that she would not be eager to come back at the first moment. Nerves frayed by the recent ordeal, we found ourselves for the first time in something that resembled a family quarrel.

After our return to England, we received a letter from Mrs. Pankhurst telling us that she had decided to remain abroad during August and September to recover from the effects of imprisonment; she would return for the great welcome which the Union proposed to give us at the Albert Hall in October. She urged us to make a trip to Canada to visit my brother Harold, who was in Vancouver Island, saying that she did not think we should wish to return to public life without her. We agreed to this suggestion and accordingly embarked without delay for Montreal.

While we were in Canada we received from Mrs. Pankhurst a surprising letter. She urged us to remain in Canada and make our domicile there and to remove our private property from our bank in London to safety beyond the reach of confiscation by the Government. After giving the suggestion full consideration, we wrote in reply that having staked our health and life for the vindication of the principle of human equality, we could not renounce it because of risk to our property.*

We picked up a paper one morning and saw that because the expenses of the trial had not been paid, the Government had put bailiffs into our home in Surrey. We returned to take our part in the welcome at the Albert Hall which was to inaugurate the coming winter campaign.

* The defendants in the conspiracy trial were ordered to pay the costs of the Crown and witnesses—approximately £1,100. As the only defendant with assets, Frederick Pethick-Lawrence was held responsible for this debt. He refused to pay the costs, stating, "The warfare between us and the Government has now been carried on to the financial plane, and the only course consistent with my principles is to fight every inch of the way."

The contents of their house were auctioned by the bailiffs, raising £300. In April 1913 the Government brought a civil action against Frederick Pethick-Lawrence to recover the balance of the claim due to the Public Prosecutor and a petition in bankruptcy was then filed.

In June 1913 several civil actions against Emmeline and Frederick Pethick-Lawrence from firms whose windows had been damaged in the window-smashing raids of March 1912 came before Mr. Justice Darling, in one civil case the jury returning a verdict in favour of the plantiffs for the full sum.

After payment had been taken from his estate for the Government's claim and that of the other creditors, Frederick Pethick-Lawrence's bankruptcy was annulled.

ARSON

MARY RICHARDSON (alias "Polly Dick"): "Arson!" I
cried. I felt limp. The word had haunted me for so long. I
had known I should not escape in the end. I must pay the
full price demanded of a Suffragette.

"Yes, arson," this seemingly callous young creature
repeated.

"Where?" I asked.

"Oh, it's a wonderful old mansion, quite near London,
uninhabited, of course, for years, and away from
everything. You see what's happened is this," she went on.
"The girl who was to work on the job with Millicent is ill,
and Christabel feels we must put on the pressure now we
have the Government in a bit of a bother with the
insurance companies. You'll come up tomorrow, say, for
the details?"

"Yes," I said. "I will come up; but I'll go home."

"Right," she said. "We'll get in touch with you there; but,
for heaven's sake, don't get arrested on the way."

I could not smile. I had been through all the horrors; she
had not. Yet I did try to understand her light-heartedness. I
knew the worth of a carefree spirit in such a movement as
ours.

Mary Richardson

My dejection returned when I found myself sitting in that district railway carriage. I stared vaguely at my fellow-passengers and kept muttering to myself. "Green cloak. The plan." It was as if I had become an automaton and was mechanically memorising my instructions.

Thick fog greeted me when I got outside the station. Near the entrance in the yellowish light cast by one of the station lamps I saw my accomplice. I knew Millicent, not by the colour of her cloak, for the fog had made it colourless, but because the cloak was bulging out with whatever she was carrying beneath it. She knew me at once.

"Take the tin of stuff from my right hand," she said. "My arm feels as if it is breaking."

I did so and realised from the weight and the shape of the tin that it contained some of our highly inflammable liquid. We then walked on in silence. Neither of us had anything to say, for we were complete strangers to one another. When Millicent did speak at last she made her feelings plain enough.

"I'm terrified," she said.

I smiled. I seemed to be looking on the whole business with indifference.

"This fog," she said, "makes everything very difficult; but I have studied the plan so I know we can reach the mansion."

"You must lead then," I told her. "I'm walking quite blind as to direction."

At this stage, therefore, she took command.

"We go diagonally across a five-acre field," I heard her say. "Then we have to skirt a small meadow and keep right. We keep going right until we see our objective. There are two towers at the east and west ends."

"It all sounds quite nice and easy," I retorted fiercely. I was impatient suddenly, and wanted to walk more quickly; but Millicent, who was older, was content to trudge along as we were going.

"I'm terrified," she said again as we were going round the meadow. And when at last the two towers could just be discerned through the fog she stopped in her tracks. "I—I feel paralysed," she told me. "I know I should never have volunteered for such a job."

I walked on and left her to make up her mind. To my dismay I saw there was a stout thorn hedge between us and the mansion. Millicent had come up to me, her face pale, sheer terror in her eyes.

"Goodness!" she cried. "That makes it hopeless, doesn't it?"

But I was not going to give up so quickly.

"There's only one way," I said. "That's for us to charge into the hedge like a bull, head foremost, and so ram a gap in it that we can crawl through."

This suggestion stupefied Millicent. So I took off my tweed jacket, stepped back a few paces and wrapped the jacket round my head; then I charged full pelt into the hedge. I came out on the far side with my hands badly scratched; but otherwise I was all right. I saw Millicent staring through the gap at me. I picked myself up off the grass, put on my jacket again and said, "Are you coming through?"

"No. No," she said. "I'll hand you the parcels. I'll wait here and watch."

I took the things from her and went on to the mansion. The putty of one of the ground-floor windows was old and broke away easily, and I had soon knocked out a large pane of the glass. When I climbed inside into the blackness it was a horrible moment. The place was frighteningly strange and pitch dark, smelling of damp and decay. I had to feel my way along, step by step, encumbered, as I was, by the three heavy parcels I had slung round my neck. After much groping I reached the hallway and knew I was near my objective. This was a cupboard under the main staircase.

To get the cupboard door to open was no easy thing. The hinges were rusted and they creaked and groaned ominously. A ghastly fear took possession of me; and, when my face wiped against a cobweb, I was momentarily stiff with fright. But I knew how to lay a fire—I had built many a camp fire in my young days—and that part of the work was simple and quickly done. I poured the inflammable liquid over everything; then I made a long fuse of twisted cotton wool, soaking that too as I unwound it and slowly made my way back to the window at which I had entered.

I climbed outside before setting a light to the fuse. For a moment I stood and watched the tiny flame run a few feet; then I hurried off to find the gap in the thorn hedge. When I did find it and crawled through, Millicent had fled.

I bumped into Millicent as she was hurrying back to find me.

"I'm terribly sorry," she explained. "I just couldn't. . . ." She stopped short and looked back behind us; I looked back, also. The red glow had grown into a huge red mushroom.

"We must get away quickly," I gasped. "We'd better separate. If we're alone it'll look less suspicious; and it'll be easier for one to get a lift in a market-gardener's cart going to Covent Garden. I'll go this way; you make your way back to the road."

Millicent clutched at my arm and burst into tears. "Oh no. No! No! Please let me come with you. I'd never find my way alone. Oh please, I feel so frightened."

"Very well," I said. "But it's a risk. And we'll have to hurry."

We went as fast as we could; but we were both groggy from fatigue and the mental strain of the whole, ugly business. After a while we heard the clanging of the bells on the fire-engines. We staggered on and made renewed efforts to get as far away as we could. For a long time we seemed to be walking along outside a high wall.

"It must be a gasworks," I said.

We kept on walking beside the wall. Millicent was unable to answer me or even to say yes or no. The fog was becoming denser; and we were still outside the wall. I began to feel we were condemned to walk beside it for ever in punishment for our sins. But at last we came to what seemed to be a residential quarter. There were some small houses in long rows. I sighed with relief as I turned the corner; then I cried, "Look!"

"What?"

"That blue light," I said.

"Blue light?" said Millicent in a puzzled way. "What is it? What . . . ?"

But she was unable to finish her question before two tall figures loomed out of the fog and were upon us.

"Aren't you two out a bit late?" one of the policemen said.

"Yes. Yes—we missed the last bus back to town," I stammered.

Suffragette Helen Ogston, having successfully interrupted Lloyd George's speech
to the Women's Liberal Federation at the Albert Hall, London, December 5, 1908,
uses a whip as a means of resisting the stewards who attempt to eject her from the meeting.

"I should say you did," said the man. "Just step across the road. We've been looking for you for the past hour."

We seemed to be the cause of some mild jubilation in the police station. Probably this was because we had been so speedily arrested. But it was the fog that had beaten us, and not the vigilance of the law.

SYLVIA PANKHURST: Militancy was now assuming a new and serious aspect. In December 1911 and March 1912, Emily Wilding Davison and Nurse Pitfield had committed spectacular arson on their own initiative, both doing their deeds openly and suffering arrest and punishment. In July 1912, secret arson began to be organised under the direction of Christabel Pankhurst. When the policy was fully under way, certain officials of the Union were given, as their main work, the task of advising incendiaries, and arranging for the supply of such inflammable material, house-breaking tools, and other matters as they might require. A certain exceedingly feminine-looking young lady was strolling about London, meeting militants in all sorts of public and unexpected places, to arrange for perilous expeditions. Women, most of them very young, toiled through the night across unfamiliar country, carrying heavy cases of petrol and paraffin. Sometimes they failed, sometimes succeeded in setting fire to an untenanted building—all the better if it were the residence of a notability—or a church, or other place of historic interest. Occasionally they were caught and convicted; usually they escaped.

When Asquith visited Dublin, on July 18, Irish suffragists met him by boat at Kingstown, and shouted to him through megaphones. They rained Votes for Women confetti upon him from an upper window as he and Redmond were conducted in torchlight procession through the streets, but when they attempted poster parades and an open-air meeting close to the hall where he was speaking, a mob attacked them with extraordinary violence. Countess Markievicz and others were hurt; every woman who happened to be in the streets was assailed. Many unconnected with the movement had to take refuge in shops and houses. The Ancient Order of Hibernians was abroad, determined to punish womanhood for the acts of militant women from England. Mary Leigh had rushed to the carriage in which John Redmond and the Prime Minister were riding and had dropped into it a small hatchet. She was mobbed, but escaped, and afterward she and Gladys Evans had made a spectacular show of setting fire to the Theatre Royal, where Asquith was to speak. They had attended a performance at the theatre, and as the audience was dispersing, Mary Leigh, in full view of numbers of persons, had poured petrol onto the curtains of a box and set fire to them, then flung a flaming chair over the edge of the box into the orchestra. Gladys Evans set a carpet alight, then rushed to the cinema box, threw in a little handbag filled with gunpowder, struck matches, and dropped them in after it. Finding they all went out as they fell, she attempted to get under the wire fencing into the box. Several small explosions occurred, produced by amateur bombs made of tin canisters, which, with bottles of petrol and benzine, were afterward found lying about.

Declaring it his duty to pass a sentence calculated to have a deterrent effect, Justice Madden sentenced both Mary Leigh and Gladys Evans to five years' penal servitude. He expressed the hope that when militancy were discontinued the term would be reduced. "It will have no deterrent effect upon us," responded Mary Leigh in defiant tones.

In Dublin the suffrage prisoners were on hunger-strike; the English were denied political treatment, and the Irish were striking in sympathy with them. All were released without resort to forcible feeding, save Mary Leigh and Gladys Evans, who were repeatedly warned that on no consideration would they be set free.

The East End Campaign   October 1912

SYLVIA PANKHURST: I regarded the rousing of the East End as of utmost importance. My aim was not merely to make some members and establish some branches, but the larger task of bringing the district as a whole into a mass movement, from which only a minority would stand aside. The need of our cause I believed to be such a movement. This was the meaning of Herbert Gladstone's challenge to the suffragists in 1908, and the still more pointed challenge of Hobhouse in February 1912, which had caused so much excitement. Not by the secret militancy of a few enthusiasts, but by the rousing of the masses, could the gage be taken up which not merely some Cabinet Ministers, but history itself had flung to us. The East End was the greatest homogeneous working-class area accessible to the House of Commons by popular demonstrations. The creation of a woman's movement in that great abyss of poverty would be a call and a rallying cry to the rise of similar movements in all parts of the country.

I induced the local W.S.P.U.'s to assist in organising it: Kensington, Chelsea, and Paddington made themselves responsible for shops in Bethnal Green, Limehouse, and Poplar respectively, and Unions, even so far afield as Wimbledon, sent speakers and canvassers. W.S.P.U. headquarters agreed to be responsible for the rent of a shop in Bow. An intensive campaign like that of an election, to include deputations to local M.P.'s, was to culminate in a demonstration in Victoria Park.

Strange women of the underworld came to us eagerly: "I have seen the Suffragettes in Holloway. They have made things better there! I remember you. I saw you when you was there." One of these poor ones came asking for me in my absence and left her address. I went to seek for her, and knocked at the door with the given number in a neighbouring alley. From the window, close beside me, an old man leant out, wrapped in a filthy blanket, displaying his naked breast and shoulders. He shouted and swore at me, and looked so evil and menacing that I fled precipitately; but chiding myself for cowardice, returned to knock again. Thereto came no response, but fearing the woman might be in trouble, I went again later in the day. Again the old fellow appeared at the window, extending a bare arm from his blanket to shake his fist in my face with horrible epithets. From others I learnt he was the landlord of a common lodging-house, expressing his objection to being disturbed during the day. The woman, who usually slept there, had merely left the address in case I should want to see her. For some time she was an eager attender at the meetings, then ceased to come. I learnt she was again in prison.

Above: Sylvia Pankhurst addresses a meeting in the East End of London.

Women in sweated and unknown trades came to us, telling their hardships: rope-makers, waste-rubber cleaners, biscuit-packers, women who plucked chickens, too often "high," for canning, and those who made wooden seeds to put in raspberry jam. Occupants of hideously unsavoury tenements asked us to visit and expose them. Hidden dwellings were revealed to us, so much built round that many of their rooms were as dark as night all day. Exorbitant rents were charged in wretched barracks for so-called furnished rooms, containing nothing but a dilapidated bedstead with the poorest of covering, and a couple of chairs. In one such, I met a fragile orphan girl earning seven shillings a week and her food, minus threepence insurance, for washing up in a city restaurant until nine each night, and paying six shillings a week in rent. It was "hard to keep straight," she said. I procured for her an offer of better work, but when I returned she was gone. I could find no trace. Her words haunted me. In a one-roomed dwelling were a crowd of little children, and a man lying ill on a heap of rags. He had been a blackleg in the dock strike, and the strikers had thrown him from the Embankment. His leg had been broken and had not recovered. His wife had just been released from prison, where she had served a sentence for begging. She had been standing in the gutter offering bootlaces for sale, but several people had given her pennies without troubling to take the laces. The policeman declared her trading merely a blind to cover appeals for alms.

Women flocked to our meetings; members joined in large numbers. I at once began urging them to speak, taking classes for them indoors, and inducing them to make a start outdoors by taking the chair for me at a succession of short meetings in the side streets where the workers lived, or by the market stalls in the shopping hours.

A family in the East End

The Lansbury* policy, which was in fact the policy of Christabel Pankhurst, was that the Labour Party should go into opposition, and vote against the Government in any and every division, on all questions, until the Government should introduce a measure for women's suffrage.

Lansbury spoke at the usual W.S.P.U. "At Home" in the London Pavilion, and there announced his intention to resign his seat in support of what he then deemed "*the* movement in the world," and "the biggest fight socially that is going on in our country." Only after making this public declaration, which was immediately reported in the Press, did he consult his sponsors, the Poplar Labour Party, a fact which caused great dissatisfaction amongst its members, and especially its officials.

The election having been called, it was important for suffragists of all schools that it should be won. Lansbury was in close accord with the W.S.P.U. The other suffrage organisations merely came down to hold independent meetings and sell their papers. The proper course for the W.S.P.U. was to place itself in contact with and work under the local Labour Party which was responsible for Lansbury's candidature.† The proper course for the Labour Party was to assume control of the campaign, putting the W.S.P.U. workers to the best possible use. Unfortunately both organisations were possessed of wholly incompetent officials, who immediately took up an attitude of acute hostility toward each other.

* George Lansbury was Labour Member of Parliament for Bow and Bromley.
† Lansbury's majority of 863 was reduced to a minority of 730 and he lost his seat in the House.

George Lansbury in the East End of London

THE SUFFRAGETTE, November 22, 1912

RALLY ROUND LANSBURY
THE FIGHT FOR WOMAN SUFFRAGE
IN BOW AND BROMLEY

The by-election of Bow and Bromley will stand out in history as a great political landmark in the fight for women's freedom. Not since the days of Plimsoll has a man taken the stand which George Lansbury is taking. A man of the people, he went to Parliament in 1910 to represent the people of Bow and Bromley, the people meaning to him voteless women as well as men.

All through his Parliamentary career George Lansbury has stood for equality and justice for women. He found that the House of Commons, with a majority in favour of Woman Suffrage, treated the women's demand for the vote with indifference, and the levity of an occasional lip service and a meaningless vote. The active protests of unrepresented women were met by long sentences of imprisonment as common criminals, followed by hunger-strikes and the horrors of forcible feeding. This at last became more than George Lansbury could stand as an honest man and a true democrat. Last April the renewal of the forcible feeding of suffrage prisoners so roused his indignation that what was regarded by the Press as a "regrettable incident" occurred one day in the House of Commons.

After a callous and cynical remark from the Prime Minister to the effect that suffrage prisoners undergoing forcible feeding could be released if they undertook never to be militant again George Lansbury crashed through the conventions of a respectably insincere House of Commons and strode up to Mr. Asquith. "It is disgraceful that the Prime Minister of England should make such a statement," said Mr. Lansbury. "You will go down in history as a man who tortured innocent women. I tell you commons of England you ought to be ashamed of yourselves." These and other hard-hitting truths were flung at the Prime Minister and the House of Commons before Mr. Lansbury was suspended by the Speaker.

AN APPEAL TO THE MEN OF BOW AND BROMLEY FROM MRS. LANSBURY

From her home in St. Stephen's Road, Bow, Mrs. Lansbury has sent the following short manifesto to the "men and women of Bow and Bromley":

Dear Friends,

My husband and I are one in this great fight for women.

We both of us believe that men and women, united as friends and comrades, can and will save our country from the horrors of destitution, prostitution, and misery.

You know the years he has toiled for you, and I feel I have done my part in supporting him by every means in my power. But now at this time, when he is standing almost alone, I want you to know and realise that he is fighting this fight all over again for you, and I want you to stand behind him in his tremendous task of breaking down evil and establishing good. So will you come out and help? We shall win, and you will help us, and, by so doing, make Bow and Bromley once more take first place in the struggle of the poor upward to a fuller life.

With every good wish, yours always,
Elizabeth J. Lansbury

HEARTILY SICK OF THIS POLITICAL FARCE

Mr. Lansbury, after deep deliberation, decided that he must go to his constituents and get from them a mandate as to his action on the subject of Votes for Women, and seek election as an independent Suffrage candidate. On November 14 he resigned his seat, and the by-election at Bow and Bromley is now in full swing.

THE SPLIT

EMMELINE PETHICK–LAWRENCE: At the landing-stage we were met by a friend who as my home-companion had nursed many of the Suffragettes after hunger-strike and therefore without taking part in the political side of the movement was everybody's friend. Instead of the smiles that we expected, sadness was written upon her face. I rallied her on her serious and grave aspect, and at last we asked her plainly: "Is anything the matter?" "Wait until we get home," she replied. "Well, now! what is it?" I demanded as soon as the door was shut. "They are going to turn you out of the Women's Social and Political Union," she said. "I don't believe it! Impossible! Incredible! You are dreaming!" was my vehement exclamation. "It is true," she said, very firmly and sadly, "and I want you to take it in before you see Mrs. Pankhurst."

It was well that I had received this warning. For the next day Mrs. Pankhurst told me that she had severed her connection with me. For a moment I was stunned.

My husband and I were not prepared to accept this decision as final. We felt that Christabel, who had lived for so many years with us in closest intimacy, could not be a party to it.

But when we met again to go further into the question, Christabel was present. Disguised, she had made a daring trip across the Channel in order to express in person her complete agreement with her mother. She made it quite clear that she had no further use for us. The sole reason given for her decision was that she intended to direct the Union from Paris. She said that we could speak as announced in the forthcoming meeting in the Albert Hall if we chose, but in that case neither Mrs. Pankhurst nor any other official of the Union would be there. She suggested that we should continue to edit *Votes for Women*, but it would no longer be the organ of the W.S.P.U.*

I was at first inclined to resist this ultimatum, but my husband saw clearly that to attempt to do so would prove disastrous to our cause. "We can no longer be creative in the movement, though we can be destructive. If we appeal to the Union we shall split the ranks. Is it worth while?" I saw that he was right. I felt that we could with advantage continue to edit the paper, which would represent our attitude toward the political world, but that it was unthinkable that we should appear on the Albert Hall platform with Mrs. Pankhurst, the head of the W.S.P.U., absent and hostile. We informed her of these decisions and a final consultation took place at Boulogne to arrange all the details connected with the separation.

We drew up a statement which all signed in the hope that if both sides refused to go beyond it, or to say anything further on the subject, the damage to the woman's movement might be reduced to a minimum.

* On October 18, the first issue of *The Suffragette*, edited by Christabel Pankhurst, appeared. *The Suffragette* now became the official weekly newspaper of the Women's Social and Political Union.

Emmeline and Frederick Pethick-Lawrence

DAILY GRAPHIC, October 18, 1912

SUFFRAGIST SPLIT
MR. AND MRS. P. LAWRENCE LEAVE THE W.S.P.U.
CAUSE OF TROUBLE
LEADERS' DISAGREEMENT ON MILITANT POLICY

"At the first re-union of the leaders after the enforced holiday, Mrs. Pankhurst and Miss Christabel Pankhurst outlined a new militant policy, which Mr. and Mrs. Pethick-Lawrence found themselves altogether unable to approve.

"Mrs. Pankhurst and Miss Christabel Pankhurst indicated that they were not prepared to modify their intentions, and recommended that Mr. and Mrs. Pethick-Lawrence should resume control of the paper *Votes for Women* and should leave the Women's Social and Political Union.

"Rather than make schism in the ranks of the Union, Mr. and Mrs. Pethick-Lawrence consented to take this course.

"In these circumstances, Mr. and Mrs. Pethick-Lawrence will not be present at the meeting at the Royal Albert Hall on October 17.

> Emmeline Pankhurst
> Emmeline Pethick-Lawrence
> Christabel Pankhurst
> F. W. Pethick-Lawrence."

The above announcement, under the heading "Grave Statement by the Leaders," appeared simultaneously yesterday in *Votes for Women* and a new weekly journal entitled *The Suffragette*. It means that a serious split has taken place in the ranks of the militant suffragists. Mr. and Mrs. Pethick-Lawrence, who threw themselves into the movement six years ago, and undoubtedly helped with their money to put the Women's Social and Political Union on its present basis, have withdrawn entirely and will in future conduct the paper *Votes for Women* as an independent organ.

MRS. LAWRENCE INTERVIEWED

Mr. and Mrs. Pethick-Lawrence, in an interview with a *Daily Graphic* representative yesterday, emphatically denied that their withdrawal could be construed as a split in the ranks.

"We withdrew," declared Mrs. Pethick-Lawrence, "so that there should be no split. If we had remained and the opinions of Mrs. and Miss Pankhurst and my husband and myself had not coincided, as they have in the past, it would have meant disruption. That is what we did not desire. We have the cause at heart and we thought it best to work separately.

"We are," she continued, "as militant at heart as anyone. It was on the question of the expediency of a certain militant policy which was discussed a few days ago that we disagreed. That is all. We shall run no organisation of any kind. We shall control and edit our paper, *Votes for Women*, upon the lines which we think best for the cause."

The women's suffrage movement during the early months of its existence was organised entirely from the sitting-room of Mr. and Mrs. Pethick-Lawrence's flat in Clement's Inn. The four leaders met there daily, and from this room the actual movement sprang.

"SHORT OF TAKING HUMAN LIFE"

Mrs. Pankhurst told a *Daily Graphic* representative that the withdrawal would not affect the work of the union. "The organ of the W.S.P.U. in future," she said, "will be *The Suffragette*, which has come into existence since last Monday. Mr. and Mrs. Pethick-Lawrence disagreed with what we considered the best policy, and we decided it was best that they should take the paper they founded, *Votes for Women*, and run it on their own lines."

"This is our policy," continued Mrs. Pankhurst slowly. "Short of taking human life we shall stop at no step we consider necessary to take."

"And that is the cause of the difference of opinion?"

"I cannot," she replied, "say anything more than I have said. Our militant policy is fixed and unalterable."

Mrs. Pankhurst has succeeded Mrs. Pethick-Lawrence as hon. treasurer of the W.S.P.U. and Mrs. Tuke becomes hon. secretary in succession to Mrs. Pankhurst. The W.S.P.U. is now in a strong financial position, having a reserve of £10,000.

October 17, 1912

CHRISTABEL PANKHURST: Mrs. Pankhurst appeared alone on the Albert Hall platform, without the hitherto invariable presence by her side of Mrs. Pethick-Lawrence. To her and to the assembled thousands of women this was a grief—as it was an evidence of the gravity of the hour and of the sternness of the fight to come. These women knew that Mother had not lightly parted from her who for the past six years had shared the immense moral and material responsibility of the movement. Formerly, Mother and Mrs. Pethick-Lawrence and I had triply held the fort at these great meetings. Now Mother held it alone. I was in exile, Mrs. Pethick-Lawrence, alas, with us no more! Pale, sorrowful, for all her brave determination, she knew what ruthless force she was defying for the sake of women, because the alternative to advance was, in her judgment, surrender.

EMMELINE PANKHURST: Whenever I stand upon this platform in the Albert Hall I can never feel that I am speaking to an ordinary political meeting. It seems to me rather that I am assisting at a review, and to-night I feel more than ever that we are reviewing our forces. We are considering and measuring our strength, we are seeing where we stand, considering the force of the opposing army, and deciding how our campaign is to be pursued. One thing is essential to an army, and that thing is made up of a two-fold requirement. In an army you need unity of purpose. In an army you also need unity of policy. In the Women's Social and Political Union, from its initiation until quite recently, we have had complete unity of purpose, and we have had complete unity of policy. That unity of purpose is still the same. I cannot continue my speech without referring to a statement which has been published, by the agreement of all parties concerned. That statement is signed by four persons, by Mr. and Mrs. Pethick-Lawrence, by my daughter and myself. When unity of policy is no longer there, then I say to-night, as I have always said, a movement is weakened and so it is better that those who cannot agree, who cannot see eye to eye as to policy, should set themselves free, should part, and should be free to continue their policy, as they see it, in their own way, unfettered by those with whom they can no longer agree. I give place to none in appreciation and gratitude to Mr. and Mrs. Pethick-Lawrence for the incalculable services that they have rendered to the militant movement for woman suffrage, and firmly believe that the women's movement will be strengthened by their being free to work for woman suffrage in the future as they think best, while we of the Women's Social and Political Union shall continue the militant agitation for woman suffrage initiated by my daughter and myself and a handful of women more than six years ago.

CHRISTABEL PANKHURST: Property meant much to the Government, said Mother, and it was through property that the Suffragettes would reach the Government. She wanted citizens who owned property to go to the Government and say: "Examine the cause that leads to the destruction of property. Remove the discontent; then women will return to what they formerly were, the most law-abiding half of the community."

"I incite this meeting to rebellion!" Mother went on. "And my last word is for the Government. You have not dared to take the leaders of the Ulster rebellion for their incitement. Take me, if you will. But I tell you this: that so long as those who incite to armed rebellion and the destruction of human life are at liberty, you shall not keep me in prison. Women in this meeting, although the vote is not yet won, we who are militant are free. Remember only the freedom of the spirit and join this magnificent rebellion of the women of the twentieth century."

GUERILLA MILITANCY

SYLVIA PANKHURST: The brief truce before the withdrawal of the Franchise Bill and its amendments was followed by destructive militancy on a hitherto unparallelled scale, petty injuries and annoyances continuing side by side with large-scale damage. Street lamps were broken, "Votes for Women" was painted on the seats at Hampstead Heath, keyholes were stopped up with lead pellets, house numbers were painted out, chairs flung in the Serpentine, cushions of railway carriages slashed, flower-beds damaged, golf greens all over the country scraped and burnt with acid. A bowling green was cut in Glasgow, the turf in Duthie Park, Aberdeen. A mother and daughter, bearing an ancient name, spent much of their time travelling in trains in order to drop pebbles between the sashes of carriage windows, hoping the glass would smash on being raised. Old ladies applied for gun licences to terrify the authorities. Bogus telephone messages were sent calling up the Army Reserves and Territorials. Telegraph and telephone wires were severed with long-handled clippers; fuse boxes were blown up, communication between London and Glasgow being cut off for some hours. There was a window-smashing raid in West End club-land, the Carlton, the Junior Carlton, the Reform Club, and others being attacked.

VOTES FOR WOMEN
PROTEST MEETING
OUTSIDE
HOLLOWAY PRISON
TO-DAY at 3 P.M.

A large envelope containing red pepper and snuff was sent to every Cabinet Minister; the Press reported that they all fell victims to the ruse. Boat-houses and sports pavilions in England, Ireland, and Scotland, and a grand-stand at Ayr race-course were burnt down. Mrs. Cohen, a Leeds member of the deputation to Lloyd George, broke the glass of a jewel-case in the Tower of London. Works of art and objects of exceptional value became the target of determined militants. Thirteen pictures were hacked in the Manchester Art Gallery. Refreshment pavilions were burnt down in Regent's Park and Kew Gardens, where the glass in three orchid houses was smashed, and the plants, thus exposed, were broken and torn up by the roots. Empty houses and other unattended buildings were systematically sought out and set on fire, and many were destroyed, including Lady White's house near Staines, a loss of four thousand pounds, Roughwood House, Chorley Wood, and a mansion at St. Leonard's valued at ten thousand pounds. There were fires at several houses in Hampstead Garden Suburb, at the Suburb Free Church, at Abercarn Church, Monmouthshire, in the Shipcoat Council Schools, at South Bromley Station on the London underground, and in a wood yard at Walham Green. Hugh Franklin set fire to an empty railway carriage; he was imprisoned and forcibly fed. An old cannon was fired near Dudley Castle, shattering glass and terrifying the neighbourhood. Bombs were placed near the Bank of England, at Wheatley Hall, Doncaster, at Oxted Station, and on the steps of a Dublin insurance office.

Where a capture was effected, the punishment varied considerably: up to nine months for breaking windows or the glass covering pictures; eighteen months or two years for arson.

Detectives examine a damaged train set on fire by Suffragettes,
April 26, 1913.

"Black Jennie"

MARY RICHARDSON (alias "Polly Dick"): There was not long to wait before I heard what my new task was to be. Once again my companion [*most likely Lilian Lenton under the alias of Lilian Mitchell*] and I were called upon for the almost superhuman effort of remaining calm and collected while all the time the hot terror of what lay in front of us burned in our brains. I doubt if there is anything much more difficult than to play the part of a normal, quiet individual when one is thoroughly involved in the most abnormal activities.

It was small wonder that neither my companion nor myself was able just to sit down quietly in the comfortable armchairs in that well-furnished drawing-room in Birmingham where we found ourselves on the following evening.

Our hostess, as had been pre-arranged, was unexpectedly absent from home. At least that was the excuse given us by the maid who had shown us to our bedrooms and taken us down afterward to the drawing-room. She had also volunteered the additional useful information that "Master will be late. Dinner will be put forward an hour to eight o'clock, instead of seven."

We had thanked her and were now roaming that luxurious room like caged animals. I think we both dreaded having to meet our host. Eventually he arrived and our ordeal commenced. He was a stout, middle-aged business man. It was in a business-like way that he greeted us.

"Miss Dick?"

"Yes," I said.

"Miss ——?"

"Miss Mitchell," my companion, Lilian Mitchell, replied.

"Well, Miss Dick and Miss Mitchell, I must start by apologising for the absence of my wife, who has been called very unexpectedly to London this morning by her sister, who, I understand, is ill. I hope my housekeeper, Mrs. Banks, has made you welcome. Just ask for anything you may require. I'm only sorry you are unable to remain until my wife returns. I understand you will be here for to-night only. Just taking a glance at our city, eh?"

I looked at Lilian, who replied to our host naturally and pleasantly. "Yes, I'm sorry it can only be for one night. It's very kind of you to put us up."

"Oh, I'm delighted," he said. "I'm only sorry that I'm so busy at the moment. I must rush away to a meeting after dinner, and I have to be off early in the morning, too."

That was fortunate, I thought to myself.

Dinner was then announced; and I was fearful that this would mean we would be asked questions about why we were paying our lightning visit to Birmingham.

The dining-room and the dinner were a delight; but I sat there dumb all through the meal. Almost the only words I uttered were in the nature of a lame excuse for my lack of appetite. But Lilian and our host seemed to get on, as they say, famously. Nevertheless I think she was as relieved as I was when the meal came to an end and we went into the library. There, almost as soon as he had sat down, our host noticed the time and glanced regretfully at Lilian; he got up, apologised again, and took his leave.

Lilian and I stared at each other. We were both thinking the same thing. She spoke first.

"At least, now he's gone, we can be ourselves and look our job closely in the eye. Have you studied the plan?"

"Yes," I said. "But I can't remember a single detail except something about a cinder path."

"Never mind, you've been through the mill more than I have," she said. "Shall I boss the show?"

"Nothing would please me better."

"I memorised the plan," she began. "It is—oh, bother the plan. We won't rehearse it yet; it'll do after we get into bed. I'm rather like those French students who say they can think more clearly when they're lying flat or have their feet in the air."

We sat there for a long time in silence and then Lilian suggested we might read one of the books in the big bookcase.

"You read," I said. "I can't."

And that was what she did until the marble clock on the mantelpiece struck ten.

"Time for bed," she said, and closed her book. "Shall we?"

Mrs. Banks came in at that moment. It was evidently her wish to go to bed, too. "Is there anything I can do for you young ladies before I go upstairs?" she asked.

"No, thank you, Mrs. Banks," Lilian said.

She seemed surprised that we should know her name; then she smiled. "The Master's told you my name?"

"Yes."

"He's a very kind man, the Master—and Madam, too, of course. I've been with them for thirty years. It's a pity Madam couldn't be here. You're quite sure you won't have a cup of tea—China tea?"

At that I came to life. "Oh, China tea!" I cried. "Yes. Oh yes, please. Could we have it upstairs in our bedroom, Mrs. Banks, or would that give you extra trouble?"

Lilian thought otherwise. "No, Dickiebird," she said. "It would be cosier here by the fire."

So we had it there; and I enjoyed it. Lilian explained why she had asked Mrs. Banks for tea by the fire. "I was afraid Black Jennie would be making too much noise. I'd put her in the wardrobe."

I shuddered. "Yes, you were quite right," I said.

The first thing that Lilian did when we reached our bedroom at last was to have a look in the wardrobe. "She's quiet enough now," she remarked.

I didn't care. I looked forward miserably to a sleepless night or, at any rate, a sleepless three hours for, in three hours, the time would have arrived for us to do our job. But I quickly fell asleep. It seemed to be no time at all before I found Lilian was patting my cheek to wake me up. As, I suppose, I must still have been drowsy, she leaned over and whispered in my ear, "Wake up, Polly. Black Jennie is spluttering." As she probably expected, that roused me at once. "Not a sound," she cautioned.

We dressed by the light of the street lamp outside.

"I'll draw the curtains when we get back," she said.

"If we get back," I said, gloomily.

"Of course, we'll get back. It will be all over in an hour. Cheer up!"

I tried vainly to do so. We were soon ready. Lilian opened the wardrobe door. "You carry Jennie," she said, casually.

I looked at Jennie in alarm. She was certainly spluttering and hissing. I felt my last moment had come, and that the thing would explode the moment I touched it. To pick up that black bag with the home-made time bomb inside terrified me. I took the strings of the bag carefully in my fingers and lifted. The splutterings increased.

"Don't drop her, whatever you do," Lilian said. She led the way. We chose the front staircase as it was farther from the servants' quarters and, though near our host's bedroom, it was best. We had been given to understand that he was a heavy sleeper and only hoped it was so.

As we left the house Lilian began muttering aloud the instructions she had memorised. "Along the left edge of the field." We managed that without mishap. "Down a steep cutting on to the railway track." That, we found, was a little more difficult owing to the additional instructions at all costs to leave no footprints.

"Wise woman," was Lilian's quiet comment. "She doesn't want our footprints traced back to her house."

"Yes," I said.

"Now we're supposed to turn right where we come in and follow the cinder track to the picnic grounds."

I was forced to smile. Lilian's carefree way of carrying out a dangerous job was a lesson to me I was never afterward to forget.

As we went along the cinder path the picnic grounds came into view, and also the newly built railway station. We were creeping cautiously nearer to the place when Lilian whispered, "The roof's not on. That's good. I can climb in that way. There'll be no need to break a pane of glass."

We reached the platform of the little station and stopped to listen for a moment. All we heard or all we could hear was the spluttering and hissing coming from the bag I was carrying.

"I think I'd better climb up over the wall now. Jennie sounds restive. I'll unlock the door of the ticket office and you can hand her in to me."

I nodded. I stood there, shivering in the cold night air, listening hard for any possible pursuer. I was filled suddenly with horrible fear when Jennie seemed to bounce once inside the bag. Lilian, impeded as she was by her long skirts, was as good as any acrobat. She was soon over the wall and had the door open. Her hand came out.

"Take Jennie out of the bag," she said.

I was trembling as I did this—she was making a great fuss for a mere, everyday marmalade pot. But Jennie was not the pot; she was whatever it was inside. Lilian had placed the thing in position and, before I could decide whether I was going to laugh or cry to be rid of my burden, she was over the wall again and standing at my side.

"That's that," she said. "But don't relax yet. The moon's come up so we'd better keep in the shadows. You follow me."

I was so relieved by then that I think I would have followed her anywhere. Slowly, more cautiously than ever, we retraced our steps. We did not speak again until we reached the house; then Lilian tip-toed over to the grandfather clock in the hallway.

"It's one forty-five," she told me. "The bang should come about two-thirty."

To get into bed and cover my head over with the bedclothes as quickly as possible was the one idea in my mind. And a few minutes afterward this was just what I was able to do. Neither Lilian nor I were curious to hear the explosion and we ensured ourselves against this by taking double doses of aspirin.

We did not hear Jennie; but we started up suddenly when we heard the door open. It was only Mrs. Banks. She went over and drew back the heavy curtains. It was daylight. She had brought in a tray with our early morning tea.

"Sugar, Miss Bird?" she asked me.

I smiled. So did Lilian. Mrs. Banks had evidently heard Lilian call me "Dickiebird" when we were in the library. She lingered and seemed to want to talk.

"I hope both you young ladies slept well last night," she said.

"Oh, very well indeed," Lilian replied gaily.

"Quite well," I said.

"I'm glad of that. Cook said she heard a terrible bang about three o'clock this morning. I didn't hear it; but Cook said it was loud enough to wake the dead."

Lilian smiled; but we were both too busy drinking our tea to say anything. When Mrs. Banks finally left the room Lilian murmured seriously, "Loud enough to wake the dead." Then in her broadest Scots dialect, in a dour, ministerial manner, she chanted,

> She spake with the tongue of wisdom,
> Who nought of wisdom knew.

She laughed. "Yes, we do make bangs to wake the dead, we who are living. Mrs. Banks spoke more truly than she knew."

"Is the little proverb original?" I asked her.

"Oh yes," she said. "Quite, quite original."

My feeling of relief was making me almost too joyous. We were up, dressed, and downstairs punctually by eight o'clock. We found our host in the breakfast-room, standing with his back to the fire and lifting his coat tails to let it warm his plump posterior in the manner of most elderly gentlemen of those days.

"Good morning, you ladies," he said, and bowed to us.

"Good morning," we chimed in together.

"I hope you feel refreshed after a good night's rest."

"Indeed we do," Lilian said with a merry smile.

"Splendid!" he said. "Shall we sit down? Breakfast is quite ready."

We sat at the table and ate heartily. To us it was a kind of celebration breakfast. Lilian and our host discussed golf. I ate. When we had finished, our host consulted his watch and remarked as he snapped the watch-case closed again, "The newspapers are late this morning. That is what always happens when I'm in a hurry."

But a moment later, to our discomfiture, the newspapers were brought in by the amiable Mrs. Banks. Our host picked one off the pile.

"Put the others in my despatch-case, Mrs. Banks," he told her.

"Yes, sir."

"You will excuse me if I glance through my paper," he said to us.

"Certainly," we said. It was Lilian who really spoke. Once again I found I had become tongue-tied.

Suddenly, so suddenly that both Lilian and I jumped, he exclaimed angrily, "Those blasted women again! Our new station practically demolished." The news so enraged him that he folded his newspaper, slapped it hard on the table, and leapt to his feet, exclaiming once again, "Those blasted women!"

When he observed our looks of mild agitation he apologised at once for his wrathful outburst, and then bade us goodbye. We watched him go down the pathway and could see that he was still angry by the way he kept slapping the newspaper against his leg.

"I think we ought to be on our way," Lilian observed, quietly.

I thought so, too.

We packed our bags, said goodbye to Mrs. Banks, and left the house. We purposely travelled by the tramcar into the city and then by taxi to the railway station.

"I'll buy the tickets," I said. "You be on the look-out for anyone who looks like a detective."

But our luck held. We were soon in the train and rushing toward London. For two hours we didn't speak until at last we found ourselves alone in the carriage. Lilian moved closer to me and said, "No more home-made bombs in marmalade pots for me, thank you."

"For me neither."

We started to laugh.

But there were no more for any of us. The woman chemist who made them had been apprehended, and she was sentenced to five years' penal servitude. That she was a brave woman who had done what she felt was her duty was proved by her words to her daughter who had come to bid her farewell.

"Pat, dear," she had said. "No tears. Think of me as being in America having a grand holiday."

February 24, 1913

CHRISTABEL PANKHURST: Meantime, guerilla militancy was proceeding. Many militants had been restive for some time, considering that it would be more dignified to anticipate the sorry outcome of the Government's now broken pledge than await it passively. As leaders, we had felt bound to restrain this eagerness, but now there was no reason for

delay. Nor were the women willing to return to the former ways of militancy, which led them in droves to prison and left Cabinet Ministers sneering at methods so relatively untroublesome to themselves, though so great a trial to the women.

One woman, however, could not avoid arrest—Mother! Already, Members of Parliament were asking the Government whether they intended to arrest Mrs. Pankhurst for the many acts of other Suffragettes.

Years of imprisonment, with or without hunger-strike—that was Mother's fate and she knew it!

Heroine! That is the name for her and I say it, though I am her daughter. How small we all look in comparison, except the other women who took upon themselves the sterner deeds and also faced long years of imprisonment.

The ingenuity and the pertinacity of the Suffragette guerillists were extraordinary. Never a soul was hurt, but the struggle continued. Golf greens suffered on one occasion by the carving on the turf of "Votes Before Sport" and "No Votes, No Golf"! The editor of *Golfing* complained on the plea that "golfers are not usually very keen politicians." "Perhaps they will be now," said the Suffragettes.

The damage done to property was more spectacular than serious. Museums began to be closed, here and there, with preventive caution, to the vexation of American visitors. Mr. Lloyd George's house at Walton Heath paid the price of its owner's deed. It was uninhabited and, indeed, not yet completely built.

Mother was thereupon arrested. Especially sensitive to any act that directly affected themselves, the Government indiscreetly made the first casualty to property owned by one of their members the occasion for arresting her.

She was taken to Scotland Yard and thence to Leatherhead. Next morning at the Epsom police court she was charged with "counselling and procuring" the act of the "unknown persons" who had damaged the house in course of building for Mr. Lloyd George, at Walton Heath. The accusation was based upon Mrs. Pankhurst's declared acceptance of responsibility for what the militant women might do in the struggle for enfranchisement. She had not known beforehand of the Lloyd George house affair, but as a matter of principle she was determined to stand by those who were pursuing militancy in the way facts had convinced her was the only effectual protest against the Government.

Mother reserved her defence and was committed for trial at the summer assizes to be held at Guildford in May. Bail she would not apply for as it meant giving an undertaking as to her activities. If the King's Speech did not promise a measure of votes for women, she must maintain her freedom of action. She would refuse bail and go to prison, but she would at once adopt the hunger-strike. "Therefore," said she, "if I am alive to be tried at the summer assizes, you will try a dying person." Could she not be tried elsewhere, she asked, so that the trial might take place without delay? But the prosecution "were afraid not."

She was taken to Holloway Prison and began the hunger-strike. There were suffrage prisoners already there, and one, Lilian Lenton, had only just been released, seriously ill with pleurisy, due to the entrance of liquid into her lung during forcible feeding. Sylvia, Joyce Locke, Miss Bennett, Miss Lambert, Miss Hall, and others were prisoners at this time and were hunger-striking and being fed by force.

Realising that Mother's hunger-strike would mean her death long before the three months had ended, or else her early release, the Government found within twenty-four hours that an early trial at the Central Criminal Court in London would after all be possible. Mother therefore gave an undertaking for this short time and was released on bail.

Emmeline Pankhurst is supported by Dame Ethel Smyth and Nurse Pine is in attendance
on the occasion of her re-arrest under the Cat and Mouse Act, May 26, 1913.

"Over One Thousand Women Have Gone to Prison"
April 2, 1913

EMMELINE PANKHURST: When I entered Old Bailey to be tried for inciting to commit a felony, the court was packed with women. A great crowd of women who could not obtain the necessary tickets remained in the streets below for hours waiting news of the trial.

Mr. Bodkin opened the case by explaining the "Malicious Damages to Property Act" of 1861, under which I was charged, and after describing the explosion which had damaged the Lloyd George house at Walton, said that I was accused of being in the affair an accessory before the fact. It was not suggested, he said, that I was present when the crime was committed, but it was charged that I had moved and incited, counselled and procured women whose names were unknown to carry out that crime. It would be for the jury to decide, after the evidence had been presented, whether the facts did not point most clearly to the conclusion that the women, probably two in number, who committed the crime were members of the Women's Social and Political Union, which had its office in Kingsway in London, and of which the defendant was the head, moving spirit, and recognised leader.

In reply to Mr. Bodkin, Emmeline Pankhurst spoke in her own defence.

"Over one thousand women have gone to prison in the course of this agitation, have suffered their imprisonment, have come out of prison injured in health, weakened in body, but not in spirit. I come to stand my trial from the bedside of one of my daughters, who has come out of Holloway Prison, sent there for two months' hard labour for participating with four other people in breaking a small pane of glass. She has hunger-struck in prison. She submitted herself for more than five weeks to the horrible ordeal of feeding by force, and she has come out of prison having lost nearly two stone in weight. She is so weak that

Above: Emmeline Pankhurst in a horse-drawn cab arrives at Holloway Prison.

she cannot get out of her bed. And I say to you, gentlemen, that is the kind of punishment you are inflicting upon me or any other woman who may be brought before you. I ask you if you are prepared to send an incalculable number of women to prison—I speak to you as representing others in the same position—if you are prepared to go on doing that kind of thing indefinitely, because that is what is going to happen. There is absolutely no doubt about it. I think you have seen enough even in this present case to convince you that we are not women who are notoriety hunters. We could get that, heaven knows, much more cheaply if we sought it. We are women, rightly or wrongly convinced that this is the only way in which we can win power to alter what for us are intolerable conditions, absolutely intolerable conditions.

"From the moment I leave this court I shall quite deliberately refuse to eat food—I shall join the women who are already in Holloway on the hunger-strike. I shall come out of prison, dead or alive, at the earliest possible moment; and once out again, as soon as I am physically fit I shall enter into this fight again. Life is very dear to all of us. I am not seeking, as was said by the Home Secretary, to commit suicide. I do not want to commit suicide. I want to see the women of this country enfranchised, and I want to live until that is done." [*Mr. Justice Lush passed sentence on Mrs. Pankhurst of three years' penal servitude.*]

As soon as the sentence was pronounced the intense silence which had reigned throughout the trial was broken, and an absolute pandemonium broke out amongst the spectators. At first it was merely a confused and angry murmur of "Shame. Shame." The murmurs quickly swelled into loud and indignant cries and then from gallery and court there arose a great chorus uttered with the utmost intensity and passion. "Keep the flag flying," shouted a woman's voice, and the response came in a chorus: "We will," "Bravo," "Three cheers for Mrs. Pankhurst." Then the women filed out, singing the "Women's *Marseillaise*":

> March on, march on
> Face to the dawn
> The dawn of liberty.

At three o'clock, when I left the court by a side entrance in Newgate Street, I found a crowd of women waiting to cheer me. With the two wardresses I entered a four-wheeler and was driven to Holloway to begin my hunger-strike. Scores of women followed in taxicabs, and when I arrived at the prison gates there was another protest of cheers for the cause and boos for the law. In the midst of all this intense excitement I passed through the grim gates into the twilight of prison, now become a battleground.

**Suffragettes outside Holloway Prison sing
the "Women's Marseillaise."**

THE CAT & MOUSE ACT

CHRISTABEL PANKHURST: The Government's new plan was formulated in the Cat and Mouse Act, a statutory memorial, unfortunately ineffaceable, of their lamentable treatment of women and their cause. It was a revolutionary constitutional innovation. Yet a Liberal Government preferred this unprecedented measure of repression to giving women the vote.

The Home Secretary had argued that the alternative to forcible feeding was "to let the prisoners die." He assured the House that women were prepared to die for the cause. "It has been said," he said, "that not many women would die, but I think you would find that thirty, forty, or fifty would come up, one after another." Finally, he foreshadowed the introduction of a new legislative act to deal with the matter. This proved to be the Cat and Mouse Act, as it was quickly named by critics of the Government.

This new way of coercion was meant for Mrs. Pankhurst. Her trial and the passing of the Cat and Mouse Act came together.

The Government prepared for their new fight against her by introducing this new measure, framed with the purpose of making her serve, in spite of the hunger-strike, every single day of the long sentence.

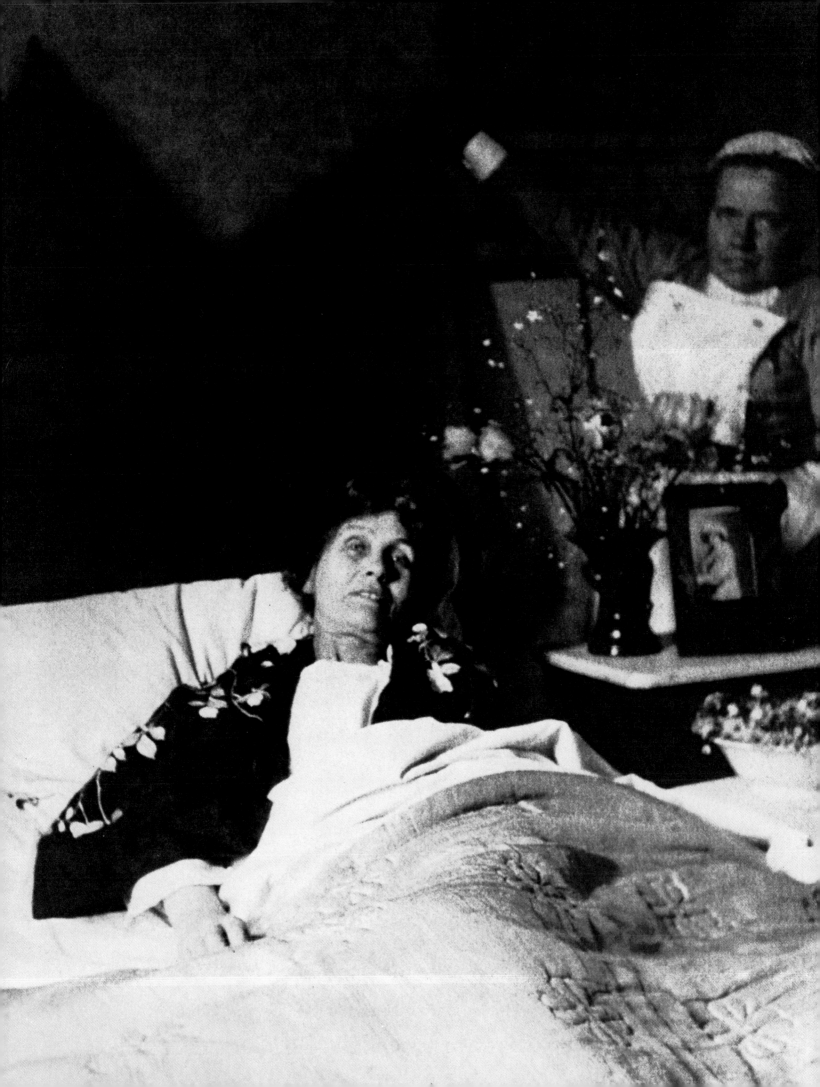

Ostensibly divided in theory on the question of votes for women, the Government united in coercing, more and more harshly, the women who demanded the vote. The Cat and Mouse Act is a memorial to the self-sacrifice of Mother and the numbers of other women who suffered under its cruel procedure.

"I have not the necessary powers," complained the Home Secretary, when he introduced the bill, "to deal with an unprecedented set of circumstances. Our former laws have been adequate in dealing with ordinary prisoners, but a new set of prisoners have come." Dropping his former claim that forcible feeding was "medical treatment," he admitted "that forcible feeding, whether for those who suffer it or for those who administer it, is a most objectionable practice." Other means ought to be sought, means which, he claimed, the Cat and Mouse Act would provide. A moment later he asked the House to leave him the power of forcible feeding, to be used at his will and pleasure. So the Cat and Mouse Act was not an alternative to "the most objectionable practice of forcible feeding"! It was an addition to it. Yet another extra weapon he sought: "the power to release without remission of sentence." The ticket-of-leave, known to the existing law, involved remission of sentence for the time it was in operation. The Home Secretary could not accept that Mrs. Pankhurst's fifteen days' sick leave from prison should be deducted from her three years' term of penal servitude. The Home Secretary claimed that if Parliament would carry this act, they would be saved the spectacle, which they now saw, of women defying the law and saying publicly that they would commit militant acts, be sent to prison, be out again in a few days, and be militant again:

> The period of temporary discharge may, if the Secretary of State thinks fit, be extended on a representation of the prisoner that the state of her health renders her unfit to return to prison. If such representation be made, the prisoner shall submit herself, if so required, for medical examination by the medical officer of the above mentioned prison, or other registered medical practitioner appointed by the Secretary of State.
>
> The prisoner shall notify to the Commissioner of Police of the Metropolis the place of residence to which she goes on her discharge. She shall not change her residence without giving one clear day's notice in writing to the Commissioner, specifying the residence to which she is going, and she shall not be temporarily absent from her residence for more than twelve hours without giving a like notice.

EMMELINE PANKHURST: The idea of militant suffragists respecting a law of this order is almost humorous, and yet the smile dies before the pity one feels for the Minister whose confession of failure is embodied in such a measure. Here was a mighty Government weakly resolved that justice to women they would not grant, knowing that submission of women they could not force, and so willing to compromise with a piece of legislation absolutely contrary to all of their avowed principles.

Of course the act was, from its inception, treated by the Suffragettes with the utmost contempt. We had not the slightest intention of assisting Mr. McKenna in enforcing unjust sentences against soldiers in the army of freedom, and when the prison doors closed behind me I adopted the hunger-strike exactly as though I expected it to prove, as formerly, a means of gaining my liberty.

That struggle is not a pleasant one to recall. Every possible means of breaking down my resolution was resorted to. The daintiest and most tempting food was placed in my

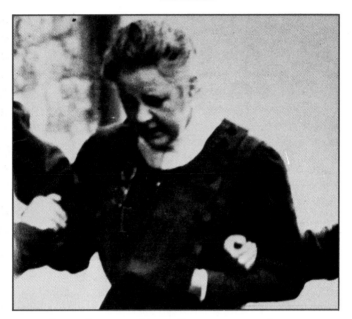

An unknown hunger-striking Suffragette prisoner taking exercise
in Holloway Prison yard

cell. All sorts of arguments were brought to bear against me—the futility of resisting the Cat and Mouse Act, the wickedness of risking suicide—I shall not attempt to record all the arguments. They fell against a blank wall of consciousness, for my thoughts were all very far away from Holloway and all its torments. I knew, what afterward I learned as a fact, that my imprisonment would be followed by the greatest revolutionary outbreak that had been witnessed in England since 1832.

Lying in my lonely cell in Holloway, racked with pain, oppressed with increasing weakness, depressed with the heavy responsibility of unknown happenings, I was sadly aware that we were but approaching a far goal. The end, though certain, was still distant. Patience and still more patience, faith and still more faith, well, we had called upon these souls' help before and it was certain that they would not fail us at this greatest crisis of all.

Thus in great anguish of mind and body passed nine terrible days, each one longer and more acutely miserable than the preceding. Toward the last, I was mercifully half unconscious of my surroundings. A curious indifference took possession of my overwrought mind, and it was almost without emotion that I heard, on the morning of the tenth day, that I was to be released temporarily in order to recover my health. The Governor came to my cell and read me my licence, which commanded me to return to Holloway in fifteen days, and meanwhile to observe all the obsequious terms as to informing the police of my movements. With what strength my hands retained I tore the document in strips and dropped it on the floor of the cell. "I have no intention," I said, "of obeying this infamous law. You release me knowing perfectly well that I shall never voluntarily return to any of your prisons."

They sent me away, sitting bolt upright in a cab, unmindful of the fact that I was in a dangerous condition of weakness, having lost two stone in weight and suffered seriously from irregularities of heart action. As I left the prison I was gratefully aware of groups of our women standing bravely at the gates, as though enduring a long vigil. As a matter of fact, relays of women had picketed the place night and day during the whole term of my imprisonment. The first pickets were arrested, but as others constantly arrived to fill their places the police finally gave in and allowed the women to march up and down before the prison, carrying the flag.

THE SUFFRAGETTE, April 4, 1913
ARTIFICIAL v. "FORCIBLE" FEEDING

By C. W. Mansell-Moullin, M.D., F.R.C.S.,
Vice-President of the Royal College of Surgeons
VERBATIM REPORT OF A SPEECH DELIVERED AT KINGSWAY HALL,
TUESDAY, MARCH 18, 1913

Last summer there were 102 Suffragettes in prison; 90 of those were being forcibly fed. All sorts of reports were being spread about what was being done to them. We got up a petition to the Home Secretary, we wrote him letters, we interviewed him so far as we could. We got absolutely no information of any kind that was satisfactory; nothing but evasion. So three of us formed ourselves into a committee—Sir Victor Horsley, Dr. Agnes Savill, and myself, and we determined that we would investigate these cases as thoroughly as we could. I don't want to be conceited, but we had the idea that we had sufficient experience in public and hospital practice and in private practice to be able to examine those persons, to take their evidence, to weigh it fully, and to consider it. And we drew up a report, and that report was published in *The Lancet* [the journal of the British Medical Association—ed.] and in the *British Medical*, at the end of August last year.

We stand by that report. There is not a single thing in that report that we wish to withdraw. There are some few things that we might put more strongly now than we did then. Everything that has happened since has merely strengthened what we said, and has confirmed what we predicted would happen.

Now Mr. McKenna has said time after time that forcible feeding, as carried out in His Majesty's prisons, is neither dangerous nor painful. Only the other day he said, in answer to an obviously inspired question as to the possibility of a lady suffering injury from the treatment she received in prison, "I must wait until a case arises in which any person has suffered any injury from her treatment in prison." I got those words from *The Times*—of course, they may not be correctly reported. Well, of course, Mr. McKenna has no personal knowledge. Mr. McKenna has never, as far as I know, made any enquiry for himself, nor do I think if he did it would have had any effect one way or the other. He relies entirely upon reports that are made to him—reports that must come from the prison officials, and go through the Home Office

to him, and his statements are entirely founded upon those reports. I have no hesitation in saying that these reports, if they justify the statements that Mr. McKenna has made, are absolutely untrue. They not only deceive the public, but from the persistence with which they are got up in the same sense, they must be intended to deceive the public.

STATEMENTS ABSOLUTELY UNTRUE
I don't wish to exonerate Mr. McKenna in the least. He has had abundant opportunity—in fact, it has been forced upon his notice—of ascertaining the falsehood of these statements, and if he goes on repeating them after having been told time after time by all sorts of people that they are not correct, he makes himself responsible for them whether they are true or not. And in his own statements in the House of Commons he has given sufficient evidence of his frame of mind with regard to this subject. Time after time has he told the Members of the House that there was no pain or injury, and almost in the same breath—certainly in the same evening—he has told how one of these prisoners has had to be turned out at a moment's notice, carried away in some vehicle or other, and attended by a prison doctor, to save her life. One or other of these statements must be absolutely untrue.

Now I come to the question of pain. Mr. McKenna says that there is none. Let me read you an account of how they manage. Of course, the prison cells are ranged down either side of a corridor. All the doors are opened when this business is going to begin, so that nothing may be lost. "From 4:30 until 8:30 I heard the most dreadful screams and yells coming from the cells." This is the statement of a prisoner whom I know and who I know does not exaggerate: "I had never heard human beings being tortured before, and I was never courageous. I sat on my chair with my fingers in my ears for the greater part of that endless four hours. My heart was thumping against my ribs, as I sat listening to the procession of the doctors and wardresses as they came to and fro, and passed from cell to cell, and the groans and cries of those who were being fed, until at last the procession paused at my door. My turn had come."

THE SCREAMS OF A PERSON IN AGONY

That is a statement. I hope none of you has ever been so unfortunate as to be compelled to listen to the screams of a person when you are yourself in perfect health—the screams of a person in agony, screams gradually getting worse and worse, and then, at last, when the person's strength is becoming exhausted, dying down and ending in a groan. That is bad enough when you are strong and well, but if you come to think that these prisoners hear those screams in prison, that they are the screams of their friends, that they are helpless, that they know those screams are being caused by pain inflicted without the slightest necessity—I am not exaggerating in the least, I am giving you a plain statement of what goes on in His Majesty's prisons at the present time—then it becomes a matter upon which it is exceedingly difficult to speak temperately.

FOOD DRIVEN INTO LUNGS

Then they say there is no danger. In one instance—that of an unresisting prisoner in Winson Gaol, Birmingham—there is no question but that the food was driven down into the lungs. The operation was stopped by severe choking and persistent coughing. All night the prisoner could not sleep or lie down on account of great pain in her chest. She was hastily released next day, so ill that the authorities when discharging her obliged her to sign a statement that she left the prison at her own risk. On reaching home she was found to be suffering from pneumonia and pleurisy, caused from fluid being poured into her lungs. The same thing happened only the other day in the case of Miss Lenton. For-

tunately, she is steadily recovering, and the Home Secretary may congratulate himself that these two cases—there have been others—are recovering, and that there will not have to be an inquest.

Then with regard to Miss Lenton. The Home Secretary wrote that she was reported by the medical officer of Holloway Prison to be in a state of collapse, and in imminent danger of death consequent upon her refusal to take food. This statement is not true. "Three courses were open—to leave her to die; to attempt to feed her forcibly, which the medical officer advised would probably entail death; and to release her on her undertaking to surrender herself at the further hearing of her case." That implied that she was not forcibly fed. She had been, but that fact was suppressed—suppressed by the Home Secretary in the statement he published in the newspapers, suppressed because the cause of her illness was forcible feeding. That has been proved absolutely.

As regards the moral and mental deterioration that has been already alluded to by Mr. Forbes Robertson and Mr. Bernard Shaw, I will only say this one thing. It shows itself everywhere where forcible feeding is practised. It shows itself in the prisons, where the medical officers, I am sorry to say, have on more than one occasion laughed and made stupid jokes about "stuffing turkeys at Christmas." It shows itself in the prison officials, in the reports they have drawn up. It shows itself in the Home Secretary in the untrue statements that he has published and the evasions that he has made; and it shows itself, too, in the ribald laughter and obscene jokes with which the so-called gentlemen of the House of Commons received the accounts of these tortures.

EXCELSIOR !

THE SUFFRAGETTE THAT KNEW JIU-JITSU.

THE SUFFRAGETTE, April 18, 1913
"THE OUTRAGETTES"
AN APPEAL TO THE GOVERNMENT FROM A LEADING NEWSPAPER

(The following article appeared as a leader in *The Weekly Dispatch* of April 13.)

A new kind of woman has been created by the present Government, and the sooner she disappears the better for law and order and national dignity. This new woman is the Outragette. She began simply as one asking that women should have votes. Later she became a Suffragette and then a Militant, and finally, exasperated by the pettifogging evasions which are possible under our so-called system of representative government, she became an Outragette, a window-smasher, a rioter, wrecker, and incendiary.

The Outragettes are now a formidable, though small, section of the women's movement, and not the least element of their strength is that they have in Mrs. Pankhurst a leader capable of heroism and martyrdom. No one who followed her trial the other day at the Central Criminal Court will ever forget the burning passion of her defence, the high resolution which she proclaimed, just as have all those men and women who in the past have fought and suffered for our liberties. No one can condone an organised attack on society, but dull would we be of mind if we could not thrill at the spectacle of a brave woman defying the whole force of government and law.

Mrs. Pankhurst was never intended to be a law-breaker. Surely her qualities of devotion to the good of her fellow-women marked her out to be a law-maker. Yet the Government, led by men whose chief cleverness lies in evasion and their ability to play tricks with Parliamentary procedure, have made Mrs. Pankhurst a law-breaker, have called into existence this wild tumult of Outragettes, women only in name and form, so completely have they been transformed into furies.

If we believe in democracy, in the moral truth that every human being is an end in itself, and does not exist to serve another's purpose, there is not and cannot be a single sound argument against admitting women to the full right of citizenship. The democrat is not going to be put off by the disgusting nonsense which has been put forward in the name of medical science, by such hopelessly confused arguments as were some time ago stated with a great parade of learned jargon by Sir Almroth Wright. Votes for Women is no more a question to be settled by physiologists than by lawyers or political intriguers.

The Liberal Party have always been ready to raise an outcry on behalf of oppressed peoples; and yet they refuse, through their leader, Mr. Asquith, to apply their own principles in the cause of the liberation of the millions of women who are the mothers, wives, and daughters of the world's greatest nation. Never was the utter insincerity of Liberalism made clearer, and never has its lip-loyalty to democracy had worse consequences than the transformation of decent Englishwomen into the wild tribe of Outragettes. The smallest gleam of political insight would show our muddle-minded politicians that the cause of Votes for Women is irresistible, despite the excesses of a section of its supporters. In the name of common sense and national honour, we ask the Government to try for once to put its belief in democracy to the test and confer on the women the full rights of citizenship.

"RAIDED!"

CHRISTABEL PANKHURST: This one word appeared blackly on the front page of our paper. The Government had completed their coup by raiding Lincoln's Inn House and seizing Rachel Barrett, assistant editor. They also arrested members of the office staff, Miss Kerr, Mrs. Sanders, wife of Alderman Sanders, and the Misses Lennox and Lake, though they had no part in militancy and no responsibility in connection with it. Documents were seized and taken to Scotland Yard. The Government had thus, as they thought, demolished the W.S.P.U. as an effective force, isolated me, and broken my control of the movement.

Mother wrote from her sick-bed to her women, telling them to be calm:

"Be strong. Be faithful to one another, and to the Union, and all will be well."

Annie and the General and all the raid prisoners appeared at Bow Street. They were charged with "having conspired with Mrs. Pankhurst, Miss Christabel Pankhurst, and others" to cause damage to property.

THE
FRAGETTE
May 2. 1913
1d
CHRISTABEL PANKHURST
AIDED!
THE
SUFFRAGETTE
1d
May 2. 1913
1d
EDITED BY CHRISTABEL PANKHURST
RAIDED!
THE
SUFFRAGETTE
1d
May 2. 1913
1d
EDITED BY CHRISTABEL PANKHURST
RAIDED!

The Trial

May 5, 1913

The Counsel for the prosecution said: "Mrs. Pankhurst is not before the Court for excellent reasons. Miss Christabel Pankhurst has been for over a year a fugitive from justice, but actually supports the work of the Union from the seclusion of Paris. Police finds at W.S.P.U. headquarters included," he said, "a large number of hammers and a letter suggesting that sneeze-producing powder should be spread in public gatherings." He did not know, he solemnly said, whether this was the cause of a recent epidemic of sneezing at the Central Criminal Court. It wasn't, but the suggestion roused General Drummond's risibility and there was an epidemic of laughter in Court.

Mr. Justice Phillimore, in spite of the jury's recommendation for mercy, gave heavy sentences to:

B. Clayton	*Analytical chemist*	*21 months*
Annie Kenney		*18 months*
Miss Kerr	*General office manager*	*15 months*
Mrs. Sanders	*Financial secretary*	*12 months*
Rachel Barrett	*Assistant editor of* The Suffragette	*9 months*
Geraldine Lennox	*Sub-editor*	*6 months*
Agnes Lake	*Business manager of* The Suffragette	*6 months*

CHRISTABEL PANKHURST: But again they failed. Again the Union rose phoenix-like from its Government-wrought ruins. The line of control between Paris and London was never broken. Annie Kenney and I had foreseen the Government's intention and we were ready! At the moment of the former raid, Annie had come forward as chief organiser. Now there stepped into the breach another unexpected and powerful personality—Grace Roe! We had told her beforehand to be ready to follow Annie. With quiet courage she had accepted the dangerous post. It had been a hushed secret until then that she would take Annie's place. Not a breath of it must get out, or the enemy might hear

Above: left, Documents being removed from the W.S.P.U. headquarters; centre, Suffragettes at Bow Street court; right, W.S.P.U. headquarters in Kingsway, London

and she would be arrested with Annie, instead of being free to replace her.

Grace was in command at headquarters. She and our splendid members, rallying as they always did, no matter what the Government's onslaughts might be, sent the wheels of the organisation smoothly round again. The paper appeared, meetings were held. Militant women were here, there, and everywhere throughout the country. Grace Roe's successor was appointed and in readiness, but we kept her identity a secret. Grace would be arrested eventually as Annie had been. She knew that well, but she went steadily on.

ANNIE KENNEY: We were all found guilty. My guilt lay chiefly in making inflammatory speeches, which I had decidedly done, but the interesting thing about them was that they were copies of speeches made by Sir Edward Carson,* only I had changed "Irish" to "Woman." I cross-examined the detective with great gusto over one speech that was read out, asking him if he considered such a speech merited arrest. "Certainly," was the reply. Then, I said, issue a warrant for the arrest of Sir Edward Carson, for the speech is his, the alterations alone being mine.

Prison. It was not prison for me. Hunger-strikes. They had no fears for me. Cat and Mouse Act. I could have laughed. A prison cell was quiet—no telephone, no paper, no speeches, no sea sickness, no sleepless nights. I could lie on my plank bed all day and all night and return once more to my day dreams.

Annie Kenney was moved to Maidstone Prison and was released after hunger-striking for three days.

I stayed one day in the hotel at Maidstone and then returned to London by ambulance. The local doctor demanded this. I may have been more ill than I thought. I was still very tired.

Mrs. Brackenbury, that beautiful character, who went to prison at seventy years of age, the wife of the late General Brackenbury, lent us her house at 2 Campden Hill Square. We called it Mouse Castle. All the Mice went there from all prisons and were nursed back to health and prepared for further danger work.

A few days elapsed and the one subject of talk was should we be rearrested under the Cat and Mouse Act. Rachel Barrett and I put it to the test. We went for a taxi ride. Nothing happened. The second time I ventured out I was arrested and taken back to prison but this time to Holloway.

When I arrived at Holloway I adopted the hunger-strike and was again released in three days. Before leaving I had the licence read to me, telling me to report myself at the prison in a week. I took the licence. I folded it carefully. I had an idea.

I waited a few more days. I escaped from Mouse Castle in the dead of night and I appeared at the weekly London Pavilion meeting. After my speech I pulled out my prison licence and put it up for auction. Being one of the first Mice who had received a licence from the Cat, it brought down the house. I banged the hammer at the first bidding for five pounds, which was proof that I was no business woman. On leaving the Pavilion I was rearrested.

* Sir Edward Carson (1854–1935) was a lawyer and politician. Known as the "uncrowned King of Ulster," he successfully led Northern Irish resistance to the British Government's attempts to introduce Home Rule for the whole of Ireland. In 1913 he recruited a private army that openly drilled for fighting, in the event that the Home Rule Bill was enacted, in preparation for a full-scale civil war.

On April 24, 1914, he successfully organised the landing of a large supply of weapons from Germany at Larne, County Antrim. The British Government began to make concessions to the Northern Irish, and in July 1914 Sir Edward Carson agreed to Home Rule for Ireland apart from Ulster (effectuated 1921).

"SHE DIED FOR WOMEN"

EMMELINE PANKHURST: Emily Wilding Davison was a character almost inevitably developed by a struggle such as ours. She was a B.A. of London University, and had taken first-class honours at Oxford in English Language and Literature. Yet the women's cause made such an appeal to her reason and her sympathies that she put every intellectual and social appeal aside and devoted herself untiringly and fearlessly to the work of the Union. She had suffered many imprisonments, had been forcibly fed and most brutally treated. On one occasion when she had barricaded her cell against the prison doctors, a hose pipe was turned on her from the window and she was drenched and all but drowned in the icy water while workmen were breaking down her cell door. Miss Davison, after this experience, expressed to several of her friends the deep conviction that now, as in days called uncivilised, the conscience of the people would awaken only to the sacrifice of a human life.

At one time in prison she tried to kill herself by throwing herself headlong from one of the upper galleries, but she succeeded only in sustaining cruel injuries. After that time she clung to her conviction that one great tragedy, the deliberate throwing into the breach of a human life, would put an end to the intolerable torture of women. And so she threw herself at the King's horse, in full view of the King and Queen and a great multitude of Their Majesties' subjects, offering up her life as a petition to the King, praying for the release of suffering women throughout England and the world. None can possibly doubt that that prayer can forever remain unanswered, for she took it straight to the Throne of the King of all the worlds.

MARY RICHARDSON: She stood alone there, close to the white-painted rails where the course bends round at Tattenham Corner; she looked absorbed and yet far away from everybody else and seemed to have no interest in what was going on round her.

A minute before the race started she raised a paper of her own or some kind of card before her eyes. I was watching her hand. It did not shake. Even when I heard the pounding of the horses' hoofs moving closer I saw she was still smiling. And suddenly she slipped under the rail and ran out into the middle of the racecourse. It was all over so quickly. Emily was under the hoofs of one of the horses and seemed to be hurled for some distance across the grass. The horse stumbled sideways and its jockey was thrown from its back. She lay very still.

SYLVIA PANKHURST: On the eve of the Derby she went with two friends to a W.S.P.U. bazaar in the Empress Rooms, Kensington, where, amid the trivial artificiality of a bazaar-fitter's ornamental garden, and the chatter of buying and selling at the stalls, she had joined in laying a wreath on the plaster statue of Joan of Arc, whom Christabel had called "the patron saint of Suffragettes." With a fellow-militant in whose flat she lived, she had concerted a Derby protest without tragedy—a mere waving of the purple-white-and-green at Tattenham Corner, which, by its suddenness, it was hoped would stop the race. Whether from the first her purpose was more serious, or whether a final impulse altered her resolve, I know not. Her friend declares she would not thus have died without writing a farewell message to her mother. Yet she had sewed the W.S.P.U. colours inside her coat as though to ensure that no mistake could be made as to her motive when her dead body should be examined. So she set forth alone, the hope of a great achievement surging through her mind. With sure resolve she ran out onto the course and deliberately flung herself upon the King's horse, Anmer, that her deed might be the more pointed. Her skull was fractured. Incurably injured, she was removed to the Epsom Cottage Hospital, and there died on June 8 without regaining consciousness. As life lingered in her for two days, Mansell-Moullin performed an operation, which, in surgeon's parlance, "gave great temporary relief," but the injured brain did not mend.

A solemn funeral procession was organised to do her honour. To the militants who had prepared so many processions, this was the natural manifestation. The call to women to come garbed in black carrying purple irises, in purple with crimson peonies, in white bearing laurel wreaths, received a response from thousands who gathered from all parts of the country. Graduates and clergy marched in their robes, suffrage societies, trade unionists from the East End, unattached people. The streets were densely lined by silent, respectful crowds. The great public responded to the appeal of a life deliberately given for an impersonal end. The police had issued a notice which was virtually a prohibition of the procession, but at the same time constables were enjoined to reverent conduct.

Mrs. Pankhurst intended to drive in the procession. Her licence had expired, and

Emily Wilding Davison, having rushed onto the Derby course and snatched the bridle of Anmer, the King's horse,
which struck her with its chest and then turned a complete somersault. The photograph shows Anmer
after its fall, with Jones (the King's jockey) and Emily Wilding Davison on the ground.

The funeral of Emily Wilding Davison

anxious lest she should be arrested on emerging from her flat, I went there to accompany her to the starting point. The detectives advanced to arrest her as she came out. She expressed her desire to attend the funeral; then silently accompanied them. I was shocked that with just a few of us to see it she should be taken away, thus quietly, without protest!

I marched with the hunger-strikers to the burial service at St. George's, Hart Street, the church of C. Baumgarten, a good friend of suffrage, and afterward to King's Cross, where the last of what was Emily Wilding Davison steamed away to be buried at her mother's home in Morpeth. Her tall shape flitted across my eyes; I could see her in imagination as she ran out unflinching across the course. The thought of her great courage and of that terrible agony which had ended her held my mind as in a vise.

Left: Emily Wilding Davison
Right: Anmer, the King's horse, with Jones up during the Derby Day Parade
Police leading Anmer after the accident

June 1913: Holloway Prison

The following was written about Mrs. Pankhurst's first hunger- and thirst-strike, after her arrest at Emily Wilding Davison's funeral.

EMMELINE PANKHURST: The hunger-strike I have described as a dreadful ordeal, but it is a mild experience compared with the thirst-strike, which is from beginning to end simple and unmitigated torture. Hunger-striking reduces a prisoner's weight very quickly, but thirst-striking reduces weight so alarmingly fast that prison doctors were at first thrown into absolute panic of fright. Later they became somewhat hardened, but even now they regard the thirst-strike with terror. I am not sure that I can convey to the reader the effect of days spent without a single drop of water taken into the system. The body cannot endure loss of moisture. It cries out in protest with every nerve. The muscles waste, the skin becomes shrunken and flabby, the facial appearance alters horribly, all these outward symptoms being eloquent of the acute suffering of the entire physical being. Every natural function is, of course, suspended, and the poisons which are unable to pass out of the body are retained and absorbed. The body becomes cold and shivery, there is constant headache and nausea, and sometimes there is fever. The mouth and tongue become coated and swollen, the throat thickens, and the voice sinks to a thready whisper.

When, at the end of the third day of my first thirst-strike, I was sent home, I was in a condition of jaundice from which I have never completely recovered. So badly was I affected that the prison authorities made no attempt to arrest me for nearly a month after my release.

July 13, 1913

I felt strong enough once more to protest against the odious Cat and Mouse Act, and, with Miss Annie Kenney, who was also at liberty "on medical grounds," I went to a meeting at the London Pavilion. At the close of the meeting, during which Miss Kenney's prison licence was auctioned off for twelve pounds, we attempted for the first time the open escape which we have so frequently since effected. Miss Kenney, from the platform, announced that we should openly leave the hall, and she forthwith walked coolly down into the audience. The police rushed in in overwhelming numbers, and, after a desperate fight, succeeded in capturing her. Other detectives and policemen hurried to the side door of the hall to intercept me, but I disappointed them by leaving by the front door and escaping to a friend's house in a cab.

July 21, 1913

Our ruse infuriated the police, and they determined to arrest me at my first public appearance, which was at the Pavilion. When I reached the Pavilion I found it literally surrounded by police, hundreds of them. I managed to slip past the outside cordon, but Scotland Yard had its best men inside the hall, and I was not permitted to reach the platform. Surrounded by plain clothes men, batons drawn, I could not escape, but I called out to the women that I was being taken, and so valiantly did they rush to the rescue that the police had their hands full for nearly half an hour before they got me into a taxi-cab that was bound for Holloway.

By this time I had made up my mind that I would not only resist staying in prison, I would resist to the utmost of my ability going to prison. Therefore, when we reached Holloway I refused to get out of the cab, declaring to my captors that I would no longer acquiesce in the slow judicial murder to which the Government were subjecting women. I was lifted out and carried into a cell in the convicted hospital wing of the gaol. The wardresses who were on duty there spoke with some kindness to me, suggesting that, as I was very apparently exhausted and ill, I should do well to undress and go to bed. "No," I replied, "I shall not go to bed, not once while I am kept here. I am weary of this brutal game, and I intend to end it."

Without undressing, I lay down on the outside of the bed. Later in the evening the prison doctor visited me, but I refused to be examined. In the morning he came again, and with him the Governor and the head wardress. As I had taken neither food nor water since the previous day my appearance had become altered to such an extent that the doctor was plainly perturbed. He begged me, "as a small concession," to allow him to feel my pulse, but I shook my head, and they left me alone for the day. That night I was so ill that I felt some alarm for my own condition, but I knew of nothing that could be done except to wait. On Wednesday morning the Governor came again and asked me with an assumption of carelessness if it were true that I was refusing both food and water. "It is true," I said, and he replied brutally: "You are very cheap to keep." Then, as if the thing were not a ridiculous farce, he announced that I was sentenced to close confinement for three days, with deprivation of all privileges, after which he left my cell.

Twice that day the doctor visited me, but I would not allow him to touch me. Later came a medical officer from the Home Office, to which I had complained, as I had complained to the Governor and the prison doctor, of the pain I still suffered from the rough treatment I had received at the Pavilion. Both of the medical men insisted that I allow them to examine me, but I said: "I will not be examined by you because your intention is not to help me as a patient, but merely to ascertain how much longer it will be possible to keep me alive in prison. I am not prepared to assist you or the Government in any such way. I am not prepared to relieve you of any responsibility in this matter." I added that it must be quite obvious that I was very ill and unfit to be confined in prison. They hesitated for a moment or two, then left me.

Wednesday night was a long nightmare of suffering, and by Thursday morning I must have presented an almost mummified appearance. From the faces of the Governor and the doctor when they came into my cell and looked at me I thought that they would at once arrange for my release. But the hours passed and no order for release came. I decided that I must force my release, and I got up from the bed where I had been lying and began to stagger up and down the cell. When all strength failed me and I could keep my feet no longer I lay down on the stone floor, and there, at four in the afternoon, they found me, gasping and half unconscious. And then they sent me away. I was in a very weakened condition this time, and had to be treated with saline solutions to save my life. I felt, however, that I had broken my prison walls for a time at least, and so this proved. It was on July 24 that I was released. A few days later I was borne in an invalid's chair to the platform of the London Pavilion. I could not speak, but I was there, as I had promised to be. My licence, which by this time I had ceased to tear up because it had an auction value, was sold to an American present for the sum of one hundred pounds. I had told the Governor on leaving that I intended to sell the licence and to spend the money for militant purposes, but I had not expected to raise such a splendid sum as one hundred pounds. I shall always remember the generosity of that unknown American friend.

CHRISTABEL PANKHURST: It was officially announced by the W.S.P.U. that "Mrs. Pankhurst has, by the advice of her doctor, left England to take a cure in order to recover from the effects of her experience under the Cat and Mouse Act. She will return in due course to resume her work for the movement as before."

Just before Parliament rose, the Attorney-General had vouchsafed an official excuse for the imprisonment of Mrs. Pankhurst and the freedom of Sir Edward Carson. This excuse was that Mrs. Pankhurst's words had led to the commission of deeds and Sir Edward Carson's words had not. But what of the recent rioting in Derry, we asked, when shots were actually fired?

The Government did not order Mrs. Pankhurst's arrest on her return to England, even though she spoke at two meetings,* and she decided during this lull in the fight to make another visit to America, giving herself the benefit of two restful voyages and the relative repose of speaking in full security from rearrest. She knew well that her suffering was destined to be renewed and that all her reserves of strength would be needed.

* Held at Kingsway Hall, August 5 and 11, 1913.

Above: Emmeline Pankhurst arrives at Ellis Island, New York, October 1913.

October 1913

EMMELINE PANKHURST: I sailed in the French liner *La Provence* for my third visit to the United States. My intention was published in the public press of England, France, and America. No attempt at concealment of my purpose was made, and in fact, my departure was witnessed by two men from Scotland Yard. Some hints had reached my ears that an attempt would be made by the immigration officers at the port of New York to exclude me as an undesirable alien, but I gave little credit to these reports. American friends wrote and cabled encouraging words, and so I passed my time aboard ship quite peacefully, working part of the time, resting also against the fatigue always attendant on a lecture tour.

We came to anchor in the harbour of New York on October 26, and there, to my astonishment, the immigration authorities notified me that I was ordered to Ellis Island to appear before a Board of Special Enquiry. The officers who served the order of detention did so with all courtesy, even with a certain air of reluctance. They allowed my American travelling companion, Mrs. Rheta Childe Dorr, to accompany me to the island, but no one, not even the solicitor sent by Mrs. O. H. P. Belmont to defend me, was permitted to attend me before the Board of Special Enquiry. I went before these three men quite alone, as many a poor, friendless woman, without any of my resources, has had to appear. The moment of my entrance to the room I knew that extraordinary means had been employed against me, for on the desk behind which the board sat I saw a complete *dossier* of my case in English legal papers. These papers may have been supplied by Scotland Yard, or they may have been supplied by the Government. I cannot tell, of course. They sufficed to convince the Board of Special Enquiry that I was a person of doubtful character, to say the least of it, and I was informed that I should have to be detained until the higher authorities at Washington examined my case. Everything was done to make me comfortable, the rooms of the Commissioner of Immigration being turned over to me and my companion.

I remained at Ellis Island two and a half days, long enough for the Commissioner of Immigration at Washington to take my case to President Woodrow Wilson, who instantly ordered my release.

A Speech Delivered at Madison Square Garden, New York
October 21, 1913

"Although you have a great deal of democracy, a great deal of representative government there, England is the most conservative country on earth; why, your forefathers found that out a great many years ago. If you had passed your life in England as I have, you would know that there are certain words which certainly, during the last two generations, certainly until about ten years ago, aroused a feeling of horror and fear in the minds of the mass of the people. The word 'revolution,' for instance, was identified in England with all kinds of horrible ideas. The idea of change, the idea of unsettling the established order of things.

"Why, then, should not I come to ask for help for British women? Whatever helps them is going to help women all over the world. It will be the hastening of your victory. It has not been necessary in the United States for women to be militant in the sense that we are, and perhaps one of the reasons why it is not necessary and why it may never be necessary is that we are doing the militant work for you. And we are glad to do that work. We are proud to do that work. If there are any men who are fighters in this hall, any men who have taken part in warfare, I tell you, gentlemen, that amongst the other good things that you, consciously or unconsciously, have kept from women, you have kept the joy of battle."

Americans, of all people, ought to see the logic of our reasoning. There is one piece of American oratory which has often been quoted from militant platforms. Patrick Henry summed up the causes that led to the American Revolution. He said: "We have petitioned, we have remonstrated, we have supplicated, we have prostrated ourselves at the foot of the throne, and it has all been in vain. We must fight—I repeat it, sir, we must fight."

Patrick Henry, remember, was advocating killing people, as well as destroying private property, as the proper means of securing the political freedom of men. The Suffragettes have not done that, and they never will. In fact the moving spirit of militancy is deep and abiding reverence for human life. In the latter course of our agitation I have been called upon to discuss our policies with many eminent men, politicians, literary men, barristers, scientists, clergymen. One of the last named, a high dignitary of the Church of England, told me that while he was a convinced suffragist, he found it impossible to justify our doing wrong that right might follow. I said to him: "We are not doing wrong—we are doing right in our use of revolutionary methods against private property. It is our work to restore thereby true values, to emphasise the value of human rights against property rights. You are well aware, sir, that property has assumed a value in the eyes of men, and in the eyes of the law, that it ought never to claim. It is placed above all human values. The lives and health and happiness, and even the virtue of women and children—that is to say, the race itself—are being ruthlessly sacrificed to the god of property every day of the world."

It was absolutely in this spirit that our women went forth to war.

Suffragettes picket Holloway Prison.

DAILY SKETCH, December 5, 1913
ALL THAT THE SUFFRAGETTES WHO RISKED DEATH TO "RESCUE" THEIR LEADER SAW OF MRS. PANKHURST'S ARREST

Mrs. Pankhurst is safe in gaol, and the police have the laugh for once of the Suffragettes. A party of Mrs. Pankhurst's followers risked being drowned by their small motor-boat being swamped in the rough sea, but the police tug reached the *Majestic* first, and the officers had Mrs. Pankhurst under arrest before the Suffragettes in their tiny craft came alongside the liner. All that the Suffragettes saw of their leader is shown in the above photograph taken from the *Majestic*—the tug racing for Plymouth with the Scotland Yard men and the local police officers on board, pleased that "the enemy" had been outwitted. The portrait (inset) of Mrs. Pankhurst was taken when she landed in New York. Her parting words to those on board were: "They may kill me, but we'll have the vote."

December 4, 1913

EMMELINE PANKHURST: The night before the White Star liner *Majestic* reached Plymouth a wireless message from headquarters informed me that the Government had decided to arrest me on my arrival. The arrest was made, under very dramatic conditions, the next day shortly before noon. The steamer came to anchor in the outer harbour, and we saw at once that the bay, usually so animated with passing vessels, had been cleared of all craft. Far in the distance the tender, which on other occasions had always met the steamer, rested at anchor between two huge grey warships. For a moment or two the scene halted, the passengers crowding to the deck rails in speechless curiosity to see what was to happen next. Suddenly a fisherman's dory, power driven, dashed across the harbour, directly under the noses of the grim war vessels. Two women, spray drenched, stood up in the boat, and as it ploughed swiftly past our steamer the women called out to me: "The Cats are here, Mrs. Pankhurst! They're close on you—" Their voices trailed away into the mist and we heard no more. Within a minute or two a frightened ship's boy appeared on deck and delivered a message from the purser asking me to step down to his office. I answered that I would certainly do nothing of the kind, and next the police swarmed out on deck and I heard, for the fifth time, that I was arrested under the Cat and Mouse Act. They had sent five men from Scotland Yard, two men from Plymouth and a wardress from Holloway, a sufficient number, it will be allowed, to take one woman from a ship anchored two miles out at sea.

Following my firm resolve not to assist in any way the enforcing of the infamous law, I refused to go with the men, who thereupon picked me up and carried me to the waiting police tender. We steamed some miles up the Cornish coast, the police refusing absolutely to tell me whither they were conveying me, and finally disembarked at Bull Point, a Government landing-stage, closed to the general public. Here a motor-car was waiting, and accompanied by my bodyguard from Scotland Yard and Holloway, I was driven across Dartmoor to Exeter, where I had a not unendurable imprisonment and hunger-strike of four days. Everyone from the Governor of the prison to the wardresses were openly sympathetic and kind, and I was told by one confidential official that they kept me only because they had orders to do so until after the great meeting at the Empress Theatre, Earl's Court, London, which had been arranged as a welcome home for me. The meeting was held on the Sunday night following my arrest, and the great sum of £15,000 was poured into the coffers of militancy. This included the £4,500 which had been collected during my American tour.

Several days after my release from Exeter I went openly to Paris to confer with my daughter on matters relating to the campaign about to open, returning to attend a W.S.P.U. meeting on the day before my licence expired. Nevertheless the boat train carriage in which I travelled with my doctor and nurse was invaded at Dover town by two detectives who told me to consider myself under arrest.* We were making tea when the men entered, but this we immediately threw out of the window, because a hunger-strike always began at the instant of arrest. We never compromised at all, but resisted from the very first moment of attack.

* During the year 1913 Mrs. Pankhurst was imprisoned under the Cat and Mouse Act six times. She was fifty-five years old.

Arrest	Hunger-Strike	Release		Arrest	Hunger-Strike	Release
April 3	9 days	April 12		July 21	3 days	July 24
May 26	4 days	May 30		December 4	3 days	December 7
June 14	2 days	June 16		December 13	4 days	December 17

Her periods of imprisonment were shorter than most hunger-striking Suffragettes', as Mrs. Pankhurst was never force-fed by the prison authorities.

The Bodyguard of Women

The reason for this uncalled-for arrest at Dover was the fear on the part of the police of the bodyguard of women, just then organised for the expressed purpose of resisting attempts to arrest me. That the police, as well as the Government, were afraid to risk encountering women who were not afraid to fight we had had abundant testimony. We certainly had it on this occasion, for knowing that the bodyguard was waiting at Victoria Station, the authorities had cut off all approaches to the arrival platform and the place was guarded by battalions of police. Not a passenger was permitted to leave a carriage until I had been carried across the arrival platform between a double line of police and detectives and thrown into a forty horse power motor-car, guarded within by two plain clothes men and a wardress, and without by three more policemen. Around this motor-car were twelve taxi-cabs filled with plain clothes men, four to each vehicle, and three guarding the outside, not to mention the driver, who was also in the employ of the police department. Detectives on motor cycles were on guard at various points ready to follow any rescuing taxi-cab.

THE SUFFRAGETTE, December 19, 1913

GOVERNMENT IN A PANIC

THEY DARE NOT FACE THE BODYGUARD

MRS. PANKHURST AGAIN BEATS
THE GOVERNMENT

SEIZED BEFORE EXPIRATION
OF LICENCE

RELEASED AFTER FOUR DAYS

THE BODYGUARD CREATES
POLICE PANIC

AMAZING SCENE AT VICTORIA STATION

SCOTLAND YARD LET LOOSE!

BATTALIONS OF POLICE GUARD
THE PLATFORM

VISITOR'S AMAZEMENT

That the Government are afraid to arrest Mrs. Pankhurst when the bodyguard are in attendance was demonstrated last Saturday, when on her return from France she was rearrested at Dover town before her licence had expired. However, the Government were only able to keep her in prison less than four days, and on Wednesday morning they were forced again to release her and to acknowledge themselves beaten.

Mrs. Garrud, a well-known Suffragette, demonstrates the methods of jujitsu she has taught the W.S.P.U. "bodyguard."

A Speech Delivered in Campden Hill Square
February 10, 1914

EMMELINE PANKHURST: Now, my friends, I want now to challenge the Government. I want to challenge this cowardly Government which makes war on defenceless and voteless women. I have returned to England in spite of them. When I came from America they sent battleships to meet me. I want you men, you taxpayers, to ask what it costs to deprive women of the vote; to ask what they pay for their armies of Continental police in plain clothes; ask what they pay for fire insurance; ask what it costs to protect Cabinet Ministers, these guardians of the public liberties. Well, if you like to pay, you men who call yourselves practical business men, go on paying. You will come to the conclusion at last that it is cheaper to give women the vote because I tell you that this fight is going on until we win the vote. Already it has cost millions. It will go on, and sooner or later the Britisher, whom we are told can only be touched through his pocket, will wake up and become a sensible man, and send these men who misgovern this country to the right-about, and give women the vote, to which they have as much right as the rest of you.

Now for my challenge. I have reached London in spite of the armies of police. I am here to-night, and not a man is going to protect me, because this is a woman's fight and we shall protect ourselves. I am coming out amongst you in a few minutes, and I challenge the Government to rearrest me. Let us see if they will dare do to me what they do not do to Labour leaders in my position, under the Cat and Mouse Act. You say that women are privileged! Yes, my friends, they are privileged to endure. [Voice: You ought to be deported as a mover of sedition!] I should come back again, my friend! Here is a man whose forefathers were seditious in the past, talking about sedition on the part of women, who are taxed but have no constitutional rights. Yes, my friends, I am seditious, and I shall go on being seditious until I am brought, with other women, within the constitution of my country.

March 9, 1914

I undertook a series of meetings outside London, the first of which was to be held in Glasgow, in the St. Andrew's Hall, which holds many thousands of people. In order that I might be free on the night of the meeting, I left London unknown to the police, in a motor-car. In spite of all efforts to apprehend me I succeeded in reaching Glasgow and in getting to the platform of St. Andrew's, where I found myself face to face with an enormous and manifestly sympathetic audience.

As it was suspected that the police might rush the platform, plans had been made to offer resistance, and the bodyguard was present in force. My speech was one of the shortest I have ever made. I said:

"I have kept my promise, and in spite of His Majesty's Government I am here to-night. Very few people in this audience, very few people in this country, know how much of the nation's money is being spent to silence women. But the wit and ingenuity of women is overcoming the power and money of the British Government. Our greatest task in this women's movement is to prove that we are human beings like men, and every stage of our fight is forcing home that very difficult lesson into the minds of men, and especially into the minds of politicians. I propose to-night at this political meeting to have a text. Texts are usually given from pulpits, but perhaps you will forgive me if I have a text to-night. My text is: 'Equal justice for men and women, equal political justice, equal legal justice, equal industrial justice, and equal social justice.' I want as clearly and briefly as I can to make it clear to you to-night that if it is justifiable to fight for common ordinary equal justice, then women have ample justification, nay, have greater justification, for revolution and rebellion, than ever men have had in the whole history of the human race. Now, that is a big contention to make, but I am going to prove it. You get the proof of the political injustice—"

As I finished the word "injustice," a steward uttered a warning shout, there was a tramp of heavy feet, and a large body of police burst into the hall, and rushed up to the platform, drawing their truncheons as they ran. Headed by detectives from Scotland Yard, they surged in on all sides, but as the foremost members attempted to storm the platform, they were met by a fusillade of flower-pots, tables, chairs, and other missiles. They seized the platform railing, in order to tear it down, but they found that under the decorations barbed wires were concealed. This gave them pause for a moment.

I had been surrounded by members of the bodyguard, who hurried me toward the stairs from the platform. The police, however, overtook us, and in spite of the resistance of the bodyguard, they seized me and dragged me down the narrow stair at the back of the hall. There was a cab waiting. I was pushed violently into it, and thrown on the floor, the seats being occupied by as many constables as could crowd inside.

I was kept in the Glasgow police-cells all night, and the next morning was taken, a hunger- and thirst-striking prisoner, to Holloway, where I remained for five memorable days. This was the seventh attempt the Government had made to make me serve a three years' term of penal servitude on a conspiracy charge, in connection with the blowing up of Mr. Lloyd George's country house.

The answer to that arrest had been swift and strong. In Bristol, the scene of great riots and destruction when men were fighting for votes, a large timber-yard was burnt. In Scotland a mansion was destroyed by fire. A milder protest consisted of a raid upon the house of the Home Secretary, in the course of which eighteen windows were broken.

The Rokeby Venus March 10, 1914

MARY RICHARDSON (alias "Polly Dick"): Law and its application reflected public opinion. Values were stressed from the financial point of view and not the human. I felt I must make my protest from the financial point of view, therefore, as well as letting it be seen as a symbolic act. I had to draw the parallel between the public's indifference to Mrs. Pankhurst's slow destruction and the destruction of some financially valuable object.

A painting came to my mind. Yes, yes—the Venus Velásquez had painted, hanging in the National Gallery. It was highly prized for its worth in cash. If I could damage it, I reasoned, I could draw my parallel. The fact that I had disliked the painting would make it easier for me to do what was in my mind.

I made my plans carefully and sent a copy of them to Christabel, setting out my reasons for such an action. The days, while I waited for her reply, seemed endless. But at last the message came, "Carry out your plan."

But it was always easier to make a plan than to carry it out. As the day approached when I should have to act I grew nervous. It was as though the task I had set myself was bigger than I could accomplish. I hesitated, hedged with myself, tried to say that someone else would be better able to do such a job than I. It will be difficult for anyone who has not known service in a great cause to understand my suffering.

The hours of hesitation were brought unexpectedly to an end by an announcement in the evening newspaper. "Mrs. Pankhurst taken from platform at Kensington [*Glasgow*] meeting." This made me act. Regardless of the immediate risk I went out to spend my last shillings on an axe. I mention that these were my last shillings to show that I, like other militants, lived on our own small incomes and were not able to draw on large sums of money from our headquarters, as was commonly reported. All we had given to us was care in sickness, hospitality during convalescence, and clothes to replace what were torn from our backs or lost.

The following morning I refused breakfast but sat for a while and enjoyed Mrs. Lyon's reading aloud from the newspapers. I told her I should be away for a fortnight or perhaps longer. She looked troubled. The pressure of her hand on mine when I bade goodbye to her half an hour later told me she had guessed the reason for my absence.

She surprised me by saying, "Your little room will be waiting for you when you come back. I shall not re-let it."

That was genuine kindness, for Mrs. Lyon could not have found it easy to make money from her boarders, whom she charged one pound a week for their full board and lodging. And I think I only paid fifteen shillings.

"You are very kind, Mrs. Lyon," I said; and I wanted to kiss her, but didn't dare.

"Take care of yourself, Polly Dick," she said.

They were strange sounds to my ear at that moment when I was embarking upon so serious a protest. I felt suddenly I was a stranger and apart from everyone else. Mrs. Lyon's words sounded like something in a foreign language I did not understand.

I left the house without saying goodbye to any of the others. My axe was fixed up the left sleeve of my jacket and held in position by a chain of safety-pins, the last pin only needing a touch to release it.

I walked rapidly and made my way by the side streets through Soho to Leicester Square, and then round to the back of the Gallery and so on to its front entrance.

It was a "free" day and there were many people going in. I kept with the crowds at first. On the first landing of the staircase where the stairs separated on the left and on the right I stopped and, from where I stood, I could see the Venus hanging on the north wall of the room on the right-hand side. Before the painting, guarding it, sat two broad-shouldered detectives. They were on the red plush seat in the centre of the room with their backs to me and seemed to be staring straight in front of them.

I turned away and wandered into the room on the left. This and several others I passed through, studying some of the paintings until, half an hour afterward, I found myself at the doorway of the room where the Venus was. To control my feelings of agitation I took out the sketch book I had brought with me and tried to make a drawing. Still with the open pad in my hand I entered the room and chose to stand in the far corner of it to continue my sketch. I found I was staring at an almond-eyed madonna whose beauty it was far beyond my powers to reproduce. Her smile, however, impressed itself sufficiently upon my senses to bring me a certain calmness of mind.

The two detectives were still between me and the Venus. I decided at last to leave the room and to wait for a while longer.

I studied the landscapes and watched the people who were passing; and, as I watched them, I felt I would have given anything to have been one of them. I spent an hour like this, in utter misery. It was getting near to mid-day, I knew. Chiding myself for having wasted two precious hours I went back to the Venus room. It looked peculiarly empty. There was a ladder lying against one of the walls, left there by some workmen who had been repairing a skylight. I had to pass in front of the detectives, who were still sitting on the seat, to approach the Velásquez painting. When I was near enough to it I saw that thick and possibly unbreakable glass had been put over it, no doubt as a protection. As I turned I saw there was a Gallery attendant standing in the far doorway. There were now three I must avoid.

I began to sketch again—this time I was a little nearer my objective. As twelve o'clock struck, one of the detectives rose from the seat and walked out of the room. The second detective, realising, I suppose, that it was lunch-time and he could relax, sat back, crossed his legs, and opened a newspaper.

That presented me with my opportunity—which I was quick to seize. The newspaper held before the man's eyes would hide me for a moment. I dashed up to the painting. My

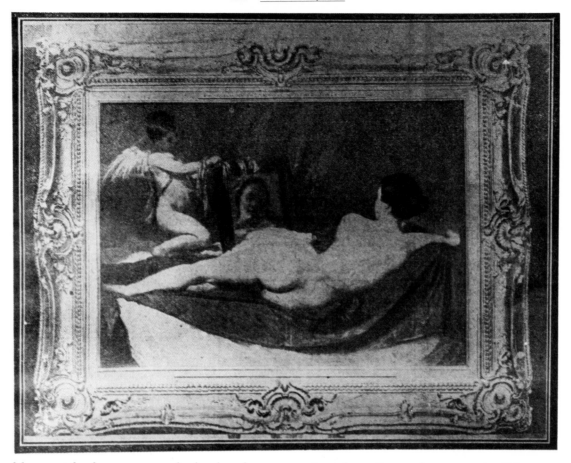

first blow with the axe merely broke the protective glass. But, of course, it did more than that, for the detective rose with his newspaper still in his hand and walked round the red plush seat, staring up at the skylight which was being repaired. The sound of the glass breaking also attracted the attention of the attendant at the door who, in his frantic efforts to reach me, slipped on the highly polished floor and fell face downward. And so I was given time to get in a further four blows with my axe before I was, in turn, attacked.

It must all have happened very quickly; but to this day I can remember distinctly every detail of what happened. . . .

Two Baedeker guide books, truly aimed by German tourists, came cracking against the back of my neck. By this time, too, the detective, having decided that the breaking glass had no connection with the skylight, sprang on me and dragged the axe from my hand. As if out of the very walls angry people seemed to appear round me. I was dragged this way and that; but, as on other occasions, the fury of the crowd helped me. In the ensuing commotion we were all mixed together in a tight bunch. No one knew who should or should not be attacked. More than one innocent woman must have received a blow meant for me.

In the end all of us rolled in an uncomfortable heap out of the room on to the broad staircase outside. In the scramble as we stumbled together down the stairs I was pillowed by my would-be attackers. Policemen, attendants, and detectives were waiting for us at the foot of the staircase, where we were all sorted out. I was discovered in the midst of the struggling crowd, more or less unharmed. They marched me quickly off along a corridor, down some stairs to a large basement. There, I was deposited in a corner and left to "cool off," as one detective put it. In fact I seemed to be the only one who did not need to cool off. The detectives, the police, even the police inspector who appeared, were purple in the face and breathing heavily, rushing backward and forward like ants which had been disturbed.

It was some minutes before I was dealt with; then the police inspector came up to me. He spoke breathlessly, "Any more of your women in the Gallery?" he demanded.

"Oh, I expect so," I replied, knowing full well that there were none.

"My God!" he shouted, and flung his cap down on the stone floor. He at once turned and ran from the room, pushing everybody else out of his way as he did so, in such great haste was he to give the order to "Clear the Gallery."

I felt tired all of a sudden and sat down weakly on the floor.

"You there! Stand up!" shouted a gruff voice; but I pretended not to hear, and remained where I was for what seemed a very long time. In fact it could not have been more than two hours before I was driven away in a police car. I saw people were still standing on the steps and on the pavement outside the Gallery, arguing together, and giving their views on the incident.

Once again I was taken back to Holloway.

This time I knew there would be a long term of forcible feeding to face. I was in comparatively good health. I had but two wishes, two hopes: one that Mrs. Pankhurst might be benefited by my protest, the other that my heart would give out quickly. It was strange to think that it was our heart that had brought us into the movement and that only its weakness could give us back our freedom.

EMMELINE PANKHURST: Miss Richardson, being placed on trial, made a moving address to the Court:

"I should like to point out that the outrage which the Government has committed upon Mrs. Pankhurst is an ultimatum of outrages. It is murder, slow murder, and premeditated murder. That is how I have looked at it. . . .

"How you can hold women up to ridicule and contempt, and put them in prison, and yet say nothing to the Government for murdering people, I cannot understand. . . .

"The fact is that the nation is either dead or asleep. In my opinion there is undoubted evidence that the nation is dead, because women have knocked in vain at the door of administrators, archbishops, and even the King himself. The Government have closed all doors to us."

PETITION TO THE KING

EMMELINE PANKHURST: We finally resolved on the policy of direct petition to the King because we had been forced to abandon all hope of successful petitioning to his Ministers. Tricked and betrayed at every turn by the Liberal Government, we announced that we would not again put even a pretence of confidence in them. We would carry our demand for justice to the throne of the Monarch. Late in December 1913, while I was in prison for the second time since my return to England, a great gala performance was given at Covent Garden, the opera being the "Jeanne d'Arc" of Raymond Rôze. The King and Queen and the entire court were present, and the scene was expected to be one of unusual brilliance. Our women took advantage of the occasion to make one of the most successful demonstrations of the year. A box was secured directly opposite the Royal Box, and this was occupied by three women, beautifully gowned. On entering they had managed, without attracting the slightest attention, to lock and barricade the door, and at the close of the first act, as soon as the orchestra had disappeared, the women stood up, and one of them, with the aid of a megaphone addressed the King.

Calling attention to the impressive scenes on the stage, the speaker told the King that women were today fighting, as Joan of Arc fought centuries ago, for human liberty, and that they, like the maid of Orleans, were being tortured and done to death, in the name of the King, in the name of the Church, and with the full knowledge and responsibility of established Government. At this very hour the leader of these fighters in the army of liberty was being held in prison and tortured by the King's authority.

The vast audience was thrown into a panic of excitement and horror, and amid a perfect turmoil of cries and adjurations, the door of the box was finally broken down and the women ejected. As soon as they had left the house others of our women, to the number of forty or more, who had been sitting quietly in an upper gallery, rose to their feet and rained suffrage literature on the heads of the audience below. It was fully three quarters of an hour before the excitement subsided and the singers could go on with the opera.

The sensation caused by this direct address to Royalty inspired us to make a second attempt to arouse the King's conscience, and early in January, as soon as Parliament re-assembled, we announced that I would personally lead a deputation to Buckingham Palace.

I wrote a letter to the King, conveying to him "the respectful and loyal request of the Women's Social and Political Union that Your Majesty will give audience to a deputation of women." The letter went on: "The deputation desire to submit to Your Majesty in person their claim to the Parliamentary vote, which is the only protection against the grievous industrial and social wrongs that women suffer; is the symbol and guarantee of British citizenship; and means the recognition of women's equal dignity and worth, as members of our great Empire.

"The deputation will further lay before Your Majesty a complaint of the mediaeval and barbarous methods of torture whereby Your Majesty's Ministers are seeking to repress women's revolt against the deprivation of citizen rights—a revolt as noble and glorious in its spirit and purpose as any of those past struggles for liberty which are the pride of the British race.

"We have been told by the unthinking—by those who are heedless of the constitutional principles upon which is based our loyal request for an audience of Your Majesty in person —that our conversation should be with Your Majesty's Ministers.

"We repudiate this suggestion. In the first place, it would not only be repugnant to our womanly sense of dignity, but it would be absurd and futile for us to interview the very men against whom we bring the accusations of betraying the Women's Cause and torturing those who fight for that Cause.

"In the second place, we will not be referred to, and we will not recognise the authority of men who, in our eyes, have no legal or constitutional standing in the matter, because we have not been consulted as to their election to Parliament nor as to their appointment as Ministers of the Crown."

I then cited as a precedent in support of our claim to be heard by the King in person, the case of the deputation of Irish Catholics, which, in the year 1793, was received by King George III in person.

I further said:

"Our right as women to be heard and to be aided by Your Majesty is far stronger than any such right possessed by men, because it is based upon our lack of every other constitutional means of securing the redress of our grievances. We have no power to vote for Members of Parliament, and therefore for us there is no House of Commons. We have no voice in the House of Lords. But we have a King, and to him we make our appeal.

"Constitutionally speaking, we are, as voteless women, living in the time when the

Suffragette arrested outside Buckingham Palace, May 21, 1914

power of the Monarch was unlimited. In that old time, which is past for men though not for women, men who were oppressed had recourse to the King—the source of power, of justice, and of reform.

"Precisely in the same way we now claim the right to come to the foot of the Throne and to make of the King in person our demand for the redress of the political grievance which we cannot, and will not, any longer tolerate.

"Because women are voteless, there are in our midst to-day sweated workers, white slaves, outraged children, and innocent mothers and their babes stricken by horrible disease. It is for the sake and in the cause of these unhappy members of our sex, that we ask of Your Majesty the audience that we are confident will be granted to us."

I had appointed May 21 for the deputation, in spite of the fact that the King had, through his Ministers, refused to receive us. Replying to this I had written, again directly to the King, that we utterly denied the constitutional right of Ministers, who, not being elected by women, were not responsible to them, to stand between ourselves and the Throne, and to prevent us from having an audience of His Majesty. I declared further that we would, on the date announced, present ourselves at the gates of Buckingham Palace to demand an interview.

Following the despatch of this letter my life was made as uncomfortable and as insecure as the Government, through their police department, could contrive. I was not allowed to make a public appearance, but I addressed several huge meetings from the balcony of houses where I had taken refuge. These were all publicly announced, and each time the police, mingling with crowds, made strenuous efforts to arrest me. By strategy, and through the valiant efforts of the bodyguard, I was able each time to make my speech and afterward to escape from the house. All of these occasions were marked by fierce opposition from the police and splendid courage and resistance on the part of the women.

The deputation to the King was, of course, marked by the Government as an occasion on which I could be arrested, and when, on the day appointed, I led the great deputation of women to the gates of Buckingham Palace, an army of several thousand police were sent out against us. The conduct of the police showed plainly that they had been instructed to repeat the tactics of Black Friday. Indeed, the violence, brutality, and insult of Black Friday were excelled on this day, and at the gates of the King of England. I myself did not suffer so greatly as others, because I had advanced toward the Palace unnoticed by the police, who were looking for me at a more distant point. When I arrived at the gates I was recognised by an inspector, who at once seized me bodily, and conveyed me to Holloway.

Before the deputation had gone forth, I had made a short speech to them, warning them of what might happen, and my final message was: "Whatever happens, do not turn back." They did not, and in spite of all the violence inflicted upon them, they went forward, resolved, so long as they were free, not to give up the attempt to reach the Palace. Many arrests were made, and of those arrested many were sent to prison. Although for the majority, this was the first imprisonment, these brave women adopted the hunger-strike, and passed seven or eight days without food and water before they were released, weak and ill as may be supposed.

In the weeks following the disgraceful events before Buckingham Palace the Government made several last, desperate efforts to crush the W.S.P.U., to remove all the leaders and to destroy our paper, *The Suffragette*. They issued summonses against Mrs. Drummond, Mrs. Dacre Fox, and Miss Grace Roe; they raided our headquarters at Lincoln's Inn House; twice they raided other headquarters temporarily in use, not to speak of raids made upon private dwellings where the new leaders, who had risen to take the places of those arrested, were at their work for the organisation. But with each successive raid the disturbances which the Government were able to make in our affairs became less, because we were better able, each time, to provide against them. Every effort made by the Government to suppress *The Suffragette* failed, and it continued to come out regularly every week. Although the paper was issued regularly, we had to use almost superhuman energy to get it distributed. The Government sent to all the great wholesale news agents a letter which was designed to terrorise and bully them into refusing to handle the paper or to sell it to the retail news agents. Temporarily, at any rate, the letter produced in many cases the desired effect, but we overcame the emergency by taking immediate steps to build up a system of distribution which was worked by women themselves, independently of the newspaper trade. We also opened a "*Suffragette* Defence Fund," to meet the extra expense of publishing and distributing the paper.

July 1914

Twice more [*July 8 and 16*] the Government attempted to force me to serve the three years' term of penal servitude, one arrest being made when I was being carried to a meeting in an ambulance. Wholesale arrests and hunger-strikes occurred at the same time, but our women continued their work of militancy, and money flowed into our Protest and Defence Fund. At one great meeting in July the fund was increased by nearly sixteen thousand pounds.

But now the unmistakable signs began to appear that our long and bitter struggle was drawing to a close. The last resort of the Government of inciting the street mobs against us had been little successful, and we could see in the temper of the public abundant hope that the reaction against the Government, long hoped for by us, had actually begun.

"Sisters to Separate" January 1914

SYLVIA PANKHURST: Messages had been reaching me that Mrs. Pankhurst and Christabel desired to see me in Paris.

The arrangements for the journey were made by Lincoln's Inn House. I was smuggled into a car and driven to Harwich. I insisted that Norah Smyth, who had become financial secretary of the Federation, should go with me to represent our members. My uncle, Herbert Goulden, always kind and thoughtful, to my surprise appeared to accompany me to the boat. He knew, I suppose, the reason for which I was summoned to Paris, though we did not discuss it. I was miserably ill in body, and distressed by the reason of my journey. A small private cabin had been booked for us in an assumed name. I reached it without mishap, but my uncle came down to tell us that detectives were on the boat. So ill that I almost wished I might die, I was tortured throughout the night by the thought that I should be seized on emerging from the cabin, and dragged back on the return voyage next morning. The detectives, however, were not seeking me, but on the trail of diamond thieves, and I landed at the Hook of Holland unmolested. The journey, which in other circumstances would have been delightful, seemed only excessively tiring.

As soon as we reached Paris the business was opened. Christabel, nursing a tiny Pomeranian dog, announced that the East London Federation of the W.S.P.U. must become a separate organisation; *The Suffragette* would announce this, and unless we immediately chose to adopt one for ourselves, a new name would be given to us. Norah Smyth was known both to Christabel and Mrs. Pankhurst. Like me, she desired to avoid a breach. Dogged in her fidelities, and by temperament unable to express herself under emotion, she was silent. I said she had accompanied me to represent our members and to report to them. Therefore she should be told the reason for our expulsion.

My presence at an Albert Hall meeting* had aroused the ire of Christabel. The *Daily Herald* made matters worse by observing:

> One great result of the militant Suffrage Movement has been to convince many people that the vote is not the best way of getting what one wants . . . every day the industrial rebels and the Suffrage rebels march nearer together. Thus one found Mrs. Despard, Mr. Pethick-Lawrence, and Miss Sylvia Pankhurst at the Albert Hall, demanding the release of Jim Larkin, which was contrary to W.S.P.U. policy.

I had gone to the Albert Hall to point out that "behind every poor man there stands a still poorer woman." To Christabel, Lansbury was a good fellow, of course, but his motto was: "Let them all come!" The W.S.P.U. did not want to be "mixed up with him." She added: "You have a democratic constitution for your Federation; we do not agree with that." Moreover, she urged, a working-women's movement was of no value: working women were the weakest portion of the sex: how could it be otherwise? Their lives were too hard, their

---

* This meeting was held to protest the imprisonment of Jim Larkin, leader of the Irish Transport Workers' Federation in Dublin, arrested on a charge of sedition.

education too meagre to equip them for the contest. "Surely it is a mistake to use the weakest for the struggle! We want picked women, the very strongest and most intelligent!" She turned to me. "You have your own ideas. We do not want that; we want all our women to take their instructions and walk in step like an army!" Too tired, too ill to argue, I made no reply. I was oppressed by a sense of tragedy, grieved by her ruthlessness. Her glorification of autocracy seemed to me remote indeed from the struggle we were waging, the grim fight even now proceeding in the cells.

Afterward, when we were alone together, Christabel said that sometimes we should meet, "not as Suffragettes, but as sisters." To me the words seemed meaningless; we had no life apart from the movement. I felt bruised, as one does, when, fighting the foe without, one is struck by the friend within.

DAILY SKETCH, February 7, 1914
SUFFRAGETTE SISTERS TO SEPARATE
MISS SYLVIA PANKHURST FORMS NEW ORGANISATION
"EXTENSION: NOT SPLIT"
MORE MILITANT METHODS TO BE USED BY NEW BODY

The movement in the East End of London, of which Miss Sylvia Pankhurst is hon. secretary, hitherto named the East London Federation of the W.S.P.U., has now become a separate organisation, entirely independent of the W.S.P.U.

MISS PANKHURST EXPLAINS
"It is not a split; it is an extension," Miss Sylvia Pankhurst told the *Daily Sketch* last night.

"We have only become in name what we were in fact before, an independent organisation.

"When we started work down here we had what we have now—an independent secretary and treasurer. You see, the movement has grown so large that it is difficult to work.

"Down here the conditions are different from what they are in other parts. We do different things. For instance, our 'no rent' strike which we are arranging for could not be carried out in any other part, but headquarters do not object to it, because they cannot do it themselves."

CONFINED TO EAST END
"The difference between our new organisation and the old one is that the East End movement is one restricted by a specific area, while the other has no boundary.

"Another difficulty is that down here we had become so large, and the conditions were peculiar to itself, that it was not always possible for headquarters to be able to give a decision at once and it was therefore thought it would be better if we were independent. You may say that our aims and objects will be the same as they always were."

SUGGESTED BY W.S.P.U.
"Did the suggestion that you should act independently come from headquarters?" asked the *Daily Sketch*.

Miss Sylvia pondered, and said: "Yes, you may state that it did."

What are the views of Miss Sylvia Pankhurst which are "not those of Miss Christabel Pankhurst"?

It is said that Miss Sylvia Pankhurst has for a long time adopted a militant policy of her own without consulting headquarters. One point of difference is that Miss Christabel Pankhurst has issued instructions that the W.S.P.U. was to be kept independent of all political parties, while the movement led by her sister has assumed strongly Socialist sympathies. Most of Miss Sylvia Pankhurst's supporters are avowed Socialists, and Miss Pankhurst has been working in close alliance with Mr. George Lansbury and other leaders of Labour in Bow and Bromley and adjoining constituencies.

"TERROR TO THE GOVERNMENT"
Miss Sylvia Pankhurst also established her "People's Army" for repelling police brutality, a departure from the Union policy. A third point is that the "Army" is open to both men and women, while the W.S.P.U. excludes men.

Miss Sylvia Pankhurst has figured in more than one street riot; and has been arrested in Whitehall, while leading men and women towards Downing Street. She boasts that the East End suffragists are "a terror to the Government."

SYLVIA PANKHURST: On reaching London we at once summoned a general meeting of the Federation. The members at first declared they would not be "thrown out" of the W.S.P.U., nor would they agree to a change of name. I persuaded them at last that refusal would open the door to acrimonious discussions, which would hinder our work and deflect attention from the cause. The name of our organisation was then debated. The East London Federation of the Suffragettes was suggested by someone, and at once accepted with enthusiasm. I took no part in the decision. Our colours were to be the old purple, white, and green, with the addition of red—no change, as a matter of fact, for we had already adopted the red caps of liberty. Mother, annoyed by our choice of name, hastened down to the East End to expostulate; she probably anticipated objections from Paris. "*We* are the Suffragettes! that is the name *we* are always known by," she protested, "and there will be the same confusion as before!" I told her the members had decided it, and I would not interfere.

In the East End, with its miserable housing, its ill-paid casual employment and harsh privations bravely borne by masses of toilers, life wore another aspect. The yoke of poverty oppressing all was a factor no one-sided propaganda could disregard. The women speakers who rose up from the slums were struggling, day in, day out, with the ills which to others were merely hearsay. Sometimes a group of them went with me to the drawing-rooms of Kensington and Mayfair; their speeches made a startling impression upon those women of another world, to whom hard manual toil and the lack of necessaries were unknown. Many of the W.S.P.U. speakers came down to us as before: Mary Leigh, Amy Hicks, Theodora Bonwick, Mary Paterson, Mrs. Bouvier, that brave, persistent Russian, and many others; but it was from our own East End speakers that our movement took its life. There was wise, logical Charlotte Drake of Custom House, who, left an orphan with young brothers and sisters, had worked both as barmaid and sewing machinist, and who recorded in her clear memory incidents, curious, humorous, and tragic, which stirred her East End audiences by their truth.

Melvina Walker was born in Jersey and had been a lady's maid; many a racy story could she tell of the insight into "High Life" she had gained in that capacity. For a long period she was one of the most popular open-air speakers in any movement in London. She seemed to me like a woman of the French Revolution. I could imagine her on the barricades, waving the *bonnet rouge*, and urging on the fighters with impassioned cries. When she was in the full flood of her oratory, she appeared the very embodiment of toiling, famine-ridden, proletarian womanhood.

Mrs. Schlette, a sturdy old dame, well on in her sixties, came forward to make a maiden oration without hesitation, and soon was able to hold huge crowds for an hour and a half at a stretch. Mrs. Cressell, afterward a Borough Councillor; Florence Buchan, a young girl discharged from a jam factory, the reason being given by the forewoman: "What do you want to kick up a disturbance of a night with the Suffragettes?"; Mrs. Pascoe, one of our prisoners, supporting by charing and home work a tubercular husband and an orphan boy she had adopted—but a few of the many who learnt to voice their claims.

March 1914

When our severance from the W.S.P.U. was complete, Zelie Emerson came to me in her most coaxing way. "I want you to start a paper." *The Suffragette* gave little attention to the special needs of women such as ours. Obviously we required an organ, and now that we had been cut off from the W.S.P.U., we were free to publish one. Our funds, however, were inadequate to the venture. Some of the provincial I.L.P. branches produced small propaganda sheets, paid for by advertisements, and distributed freely from door to door. I agreed to venture on such a sheet. Zelie Emerson consulted printers, and obtained from them estimates and dummy sheets, headed by the title which had occurred to me: *The Woman's Banner*. Finally we chose a sheet much larger than I had contemplated: eighteen inches by twenty-four inches, folded to make a four-page paper. We calculated that each inch of advertisement would pay for itself and an inch of news-matter. The idea was delightfully simple, but the plan did not work. Zelie secured only three inches of advertisement. At last she begged me to produce a specimen advance number, in order that she might have something better than a mere dummy to show. Nothing daunted, I agreed, and in the excitement of going to press, Zelie secured some large advertisements of Neave's Food and Lipton's cocoa to run for three months, her only success in the advertisement line. The paper was emphatically not an advertising medium.

A general meeting of the Federation was called to approve the scheme and select a title for the new paper. I think it was Mary Paterson who suggested the *Woman's Dreadnought*. It would not have been my choice, but the members generally acclaimed it, and I fell in with their view. I wished it had been *The Workers' Mate*, a name which occurred to me later. "Mate" was a favourite term of address with our people in the East End, and to my mind a most genial and sympathetic one.

The advance number of eight pages was published on March 8, the first regular issue on March 21, 1914. It was my earnest desire that it should be a medium through which working women, however unlettered, might express themselves, and find their interests defended. I took infinite pains in correcting and arranging their manuscripts, endeavouring to preserve the spirit and unsophisticated freshness of the original. I wanted the paper to be as far as possible written from life; no dry arguments, but a vivid presentment of things as they are, arguing always from the particular, with all its human features, to the general principle. No case of hardship came its way but the *Dreadnought* was eager to give it publicity, and if possible to muster help for its alleviation. How great was the need it sought to meet, how sure its appeal, could be measured by the response. From all over the East End, and much further afield, people in dispute with, or suffering under, employers, landlords, insurance agents, Government departments, local authorities, hospitals and asylums, lawyers, and railway companies brought their difficulties for publicity and solution.

The Victoria Park chained guard

May 24, 1914

It was often difficult for me to believe the Government really desired to rearrest me. I had spoken in Victoria Park in April unmolested; I had travelled to Budapest and returned in safety. Again we were organising a "Women's May Day" in Victoria Park on the second to last Sunday in May, three days after the deputation to the King. The procession was to halt for me at the door of the Women's Hall; I was to march in the centre of twenty women, chained to me and to each other; a spectacular guard, rather than a sure one. I was safer in a dense, closely packed crowd, with a substantial number of men, better able than women to resist the sheer weight of the police. Our stalwarts were carrying banners, attending to the carts of children, the maypoles, one of which was erected on each of the nine platforms, the literature, and so on. We could not seriously contemplate an attack. The detectives were not in sight, yet presently big men, dressed as costers, but of remarkably different build, began to appear from the side roads, pushing their way toward me. I knew them for detectives; there were fifty of them, it was said. At every step they were gaining their object, now insidiously, now roughly penetrating the crowd, drawing always more closely toward the chain-guard.

As we neared the park gates the police cleared a space amongst the waiting throng, as though to let the procession through, then made a fierce onslaught on the people, the coster-detectives laying about them with their sticks. Finally they dragged me and the chain-guard within the boating enclosure and locked its gates behind them. The inspector demanded the keys of the locks which held our chains together, whilst his subordinates tore at my neck, where they expected to find the keys hidden. Finally they smashed the padlocks with their truncheons. We received many a blow during the process, and any woman who attempted to hinder the work had her face pinched, her hair pulled, arms twisted and thumbs bent back, whilst her tormentors gave vent to most lurid epithets. The police were enraged; if the people showed turbulence in a strike they were accustomed to quell them with a good bludgeoning, but these crowds had been disciplined with the truncheon again and again, and still they reappeared. Outside the enclosure the people were charged by the horses and beaten with truncheons. Many were injured; a child had her knee broken. Sections of the crowd retaliated, calling for the gates to be opened, and presently broke down some of the railings, whereat the people poured into the park and the meeting was held.

As soon as the locks had been smashed I was flung on to the floor of a taxi-cab, with a good deal of swearing, pinching, and arm twisting; then four of the big men jumped in and occupied the seats, cursing the East End and its people. I was silent, and presently one of them insisted I should have a place on the seat. They began to question me: Why should I come to live amongst these "roughs" in the East End? I answered by reminding them that they had canvassed all the people in Ford Road, trying to get a room from which they could watch for me, and had offered "a small fortune" for it; yet at every house in the street they had been refused. "It's all in the game," one of my captors muttered shamefacedly. "You'll never get the vote," another jeered; but the best of them answered: "Oh, yes, they'll get it." I asked how it was that on the eve of the Poplar election and other occasions they had made no fight to take me; they answered: "The crowd was too strong!" When the more aggressive of them jumped out of the cab at the prison gates, one of the others said: "The best part of it all is the way the people fight for you and are willing to make sacrifices for the cause."

A Deputation to the Prime Minister

May 30, 1914

SYLVIA PANKHURST: I was free again with new resolutions for the struggle. The popular suffrage movement, with the East End as its most active centre, must make itself felt by the Cabinet. The objection of Asquith and others that the demand was not democratic, and the movement not of the masses, but of the classes, must be swept away. A deputation to the Prime Minister must be elected, not by the Federation, or any group of suffragists, but by great open rally meetings in the East End of London. These same open meetings should decide the terms of the demand. Asquith would probably refuse to receive the deputation. We should take no denial, but go in procession to interview him nevertheless. I should accompany the deputation: my licence having expired, I should be rearrested of course. Then I should not only repeat the usual hunger- and thirst-strike in prison, but continue it after release until the deputation should be received. Asquith might maintain his refusal to the bitter end; he had always been stubborn. In that case I must leave the others to carry on the fight. I did not want to die and leave all that we hoped to do—yet I was willing to die if it might help to ensure the victory.

June 10, 1914

I looked out on the throng, believing I might be seeing these crowds who had fought with me for the last time, their work-worn forms, their anxious, loving faces impressing themselves deeply upon my mind. I repeated my intention, striving to cheer and hearten them, beseeching them to keep up the fight should the issue prove fatal to me. They were earnest and silent, the men with bared heads, and the women with streaming tears. I was taken out on a long carrying chair, with poles for the bearers, on the shoulders of four of the men. The women wailed and stretched out their hands.

All happened as I expected: in Grove Road the detectives were gathering thickly to the left of us; our ranks were reduced by the narrowing of the road, and by a stationary taxi-cab to the right of us—placed there with intent. The plain clothes men swept inward with a quick, concerted movement; an inspector wheeled round his horse, and seized me by the wrists: "You are arrested, Miss Pankhurst!" The bearers were hurled aside. Nevinson clung to the carrying chair and was thrown to the ground. I was in the taxi with the detectives on my way to Holloway.

Above: Sylvia Pankhurst is carried to a meeting on a stretcher.

In prison the days crawled by, weary and painful from illness, yet otherwise calm. For the first time I made no fight to hasten release—the longer they kept me, the better for my purpose.

The prison was picketed night and day. Married women rose earlier and worked later, young factory girls gave up their leisure to take their share of the toil. Mrs. Mansell-Moullin organised a meeting of the Cymric* Suffrage Union at the Caxton Hall, where some of our East End women, with Lansbury, Nevinson, and Evelyn Sharp, voiced our demand. The United Suffragists lent their aid. Norah Smyth, who believed that Asquith would remain obdurate till my death, wrote, pleading with Mrs. Pankhurst to join the W.S.P.U. effort to ours. She replied that our action was not in conformity with W.S.P.U. policy; as to me, she said: "Tell her I advise her when she comes out of prison to go home and let her friends take care of her, as Annie Kenney and Mrs. Drummond have done." Norah Smyth was shocked by the reply. She knew me well enough to understand that I should not withdraw. Moreover she considered it would be humiliating to me and to the Federation to give way.

June 11, 1914

The hunger-strike was debated in the Commons. Lord Robert Cecil protested against forcible feeding, and urged his old scheme of deporting the militants. He asked whether the French Government could be induced to take action against Christabel. McKenna†, defending his administration, declared he had to deal with "a phenomenon absolutely without precedent in our history." He was advised to let the hunger-strikers die. The advice was given by those who believed the women would surrender their strike if told they would on no consideration be released:

> We have to face the fact, however, that they would die . . . in many cases they have got, in their refusals of food and water, beyond the point where they could help themselves. . . . There are those who . . . think that after one or two deaths in prison, militancy would cease. . . . So far from putting an end to militancy, I believe it would be the greatest incentive to militancy which could ever happen. For every woman who died, there would be scores who would come forward for the honour, as they would deem it, of the crown of martyrdom. . . . They have a courage, part of their fanaticism, which undoubtedly stands at nothing. . . . They would seek death; and I am sure that however strong public opinion outside might be to-day in favour of letting them die, when there were twenty, thirty, forty, or more deaths in prison, you would have a violent reaction of public opinion. . . . We should have woman after woman, whose only offence may have been obstructing the police, breaking a window, or even burning down an empty house, dying because she was obstinate. I do not believe that is a policy which, on consideration, will ever recommend itself to the British people, and I am bound to say for myself that I could never take a hand in carrying that policy out.

As to deportation: if the Suffragettes were sent to a distant island, it must either be treated as a prison, in which case they would hunger-strike as before, or the wealthy supporters of the militant movement would very quickly charter a yacht and bring the prisoners away. As to putting the prisoners into lunatic asylums, he made the startling admission:

* Welsh Suffrage Union.

† Reginald McKenna, Home Secretary, 1911–1915.

The "Bow Militants,"
Sylvia Pankhurst, George Lansbury, and Daisy Lansbury

"I have on many occasions . . . had the prisoners examined by doctors, but in no case have they been willing to certify them as lunatics."

As to giving them the franchise, that was not his province as Home Secretary. He did not think the suggestion could be seriously treated as a remedy for the existing state of lawlessness.

June 18, 1914

Release. The wardresses took me, as usual, in a taxi to Old Ford Road. A crowd had collected, for the pickets had telephoned I was coming. Norah Smyth had a motor at the door, waiting to take me to Westminster. Mrs. Payne helping me, I washed my face, changed the dress I had worn night and day in the prison, and came out immediately to take my seat in the car. The women were weeping. In a bodily sense I was weak, for this last hunger- and thirst-strike had followed only ten days after the preceding one, but I was cool and collected; only when I attempted to stand or sit upright I felt faint. I told Norah Smyth to call to the women to be of good cheer, and to drive with speed to the House of Commons. My mind was concentrated on the object, emotionless and uncaring, like one who is running a race.

The long summer evening was fading as we reached the House. A little crowd of our women were waiting for us there. We drew up near Richard Coeur de Lion's statue. Keir Hardie and Josiah Wedgwood came out to the car, both very gentle and kind. Keir Hardie said it would be best for me to go with them to wait in St. Stephen's Hall whilst they made efforts to communicate with Asquith. I smiled at his thoughtfulness: "I would, but they will not let me in," I told him. He went to arrange it, but came back saying that I was still black-listed for throwing a stone at the picture of Speaker Finch.* I must do, he told me, as Members of Parliament do when compelled to withdraw from the Chamber; I must write a letter to Mr. Speaker apologising for having "broken the rules of the House." It was simply a matter of form, he urged. To please him I consented. He returned with the news I expected: Mr. Speaker maintained his prohibition. "I must go to the steps; there is nothing else for it," I told him. He begged me to wait in the car a little while longer, and hurried away to get speech with Asquith. My companions, too, begged me to wait his return. I waited; the time seemed endless.

I called to my friends to help me, over-riding kind efforts to delay and obstruct me. Norah Smyth and the others supported me. They swerved from the Strangers' Entrance, unable, I saw, to face the policemen standing on the steps. Their instinct might be right—I should be moved immediately from that spot. I indicated the little square door to the left, nearer to Cromwell's statue, and there they laid me. A police inspector came forward to tell me I could not stay there. I replied I must wait there till the Prime Minister would consent to receive the deputation. There was some altercation. Policemen were bending to seize me, when Lansbury and Nevinson came running out to say that Asquith had agreed to receive us. I thought they might be mistaken, or saying it just to induce me to go away; to save me from being taken to prison. Then I saw Keir Hardie beside me. He told me, in his quiet way, that Asquith would receive six of our women on Saturday morning. I knew it was true; he would not lie. People began to cheer. Everyone was laughing and talking around me. Keir Hardie and Nevinson, Norah Smyth and Mrs. Watkins, dozens of people were helping me back to the car, amid waving of hands and handkerchiefs, congratulations and delight. "We are winning! At last we are winning!"

* John Finch, Speaker of the House of Commons from 1628 to 1629.

The East London deputation (left to right):
Mrs. Watkins, Mrs. Payne, Mrs. Savoy, Mrs. Bird, Mrs. Scurr, Mrs. Parsons

June 20, 1914

Next day I prepared a statement to be read by Mrs. Julia Scurr. She was to lead the deputation. I did not care to go. Let these working mothers speak for themselves; it was for this I had struggled. The statement would give them their cue and break the ice for them. I had put into it what I knew to be near their hearts.

Stout old Mrs. Savoy, the brush-maker, jolly and brave in spite of her dropsy and her palpitations—an example, indeed, to the *malades imaginaires*. "The best woman in Old Ford," George Lansbury called her. Motherly, anxious Mrs. Payne. Mrs. Bird, the wife of a transport worker, keeping a home for him and their six children on his wage of twenty-five shillings a week. Mrs. Parsons, a frail little woman, who, having a delicate father, had worked to help her mother to support her little brothers since she was twelve years of age; and now with a husband earning a small wage, was caring for her two little girls and an orphaned niece. Mrs. Watkins. Mrs. Scurr, who till the first advent of the Suffragettes in 1905–6, had been a "quiet housewife," but aroused by them to a sense of public duty, as she often told me, was now a vigilant Poor Law Guardian. They had been selected by the mass meetings as women known and respected in the districts where they lived.

They brought before the Prime Minister, in simple, moving phrases, the toilsome life of poor women.

Mrs. Savoy herself, who had worked forty-three years as a brush-maker, was only paid 1¼d. for a brush which took her nearly two hours to make. The Prime Minister and his companions started, as though it had been a bomb, when she put the brush, with its two hundred holes, on the table. "I do all the work; I keep my home; I ought to have a vote for it!" As a girl Mrs. Parsons had earned less than one shilling a day by packing cigarettes. Mrs. Bird, with her six children, declared herself better off than thousands of other wives, for thousands of husbands earned only eighteen shillings a week, and many had larger families than hers. "The husband scarcely knows how the money is spent," one of them urged. "A man brings his money home and lays it on the table, and then he is able to go out. There are all the expenses of rent, clubs and everything, and then clothes wear out; and you have to find clothes for the children, and the things that wear out in the home: it all has to come out of the weekly money; you do not get any extra." "You can tell we do not get a living, but an existence." They spoke of the housing conditions, so hideous in their district; the yards "only fit for a dirt pail." "We have to leave our children to the mercy of the street."

Mrs. Payne disclosed her great sorrow: "I have had to work at the side of my husband making shoes, and to look after my daughter and do everything for her. From the time she was born until she died she never combed her own hair; she was mentally deficient and lived to be twenty-seven. . . . Once when my girl was taken bad she went into the Poplar Workhouse. My husband thought he was compelled to let her go. When I got there next morning they had put her in a padded room. I asked the doctor why she was there. He told me I had no voice, I was not to ask the why or the wherefore—only the father had that right."

Always they returned to their demand for a place in the constitution:

We know there are some who belittle representative Government and declare the vote useless, but we cannot think that you, sir, as Prime Minister of this country, will assent to that view. . . .

Our demand is for the form of franchise for women you have repeatedly said you could best understand, and with which you would be most in sympathy. It is the form of franchise which you have declared your intention of establishing for men in the near future. It is the one for which your party is supposed to stand—a vote for every woman over twenty-one.

The great public demonstrations which elected us to speak to you to-day unanimously decided that we should lay before you the demand for an immediate Government measure for a vote for every woman over twenty-one. This demand is supported by an enormous volume of working-class opinion throughout the country, especially in our own district. . . . Organised labour has long made this demand, and for many years past the Trade Union Congress and later the Labour Party annual conferences have declared for it.

Asquith's reply revealed an unmistakable softening in his long hostility; almost he seemed to declare himself a convert:

. . . I tell you quite frankly that I have listened with the greatest interest to the statement read by Mrs. Scurr, and to . . . the special, individual experience of the various members of the deputation, by which the statement has been reinforced. I think it is a very moderate and well-reasoned presentation of your case and I will give it, you may be quite sure, very careful and mature consideration.

I am not going to enter into anything of argument, or to deal, so far as I can avoid it, with any controversial topic; but I think I am right in saying that the substance of the case you have to-day presented to me comes to this: that the economic conditions under which women labour in a community like, for instance, the East End of London, are such that either in the way of legislation, or perhaps in the way of administration, we cannot get substantial and intelligent reform unless women themselves have a voice in choosing representatives for Parliament. I think that is your case.

I think that fairly states the substance of it, and you have each of you given me special illustrations, drawn from your own experience, or from the experience of your leaders, to show that this is not a mere rhetorical statement, but does correspond to the actual facts of East End life. As I say, I am not going to argue, because I will take all these things into careful consideration.

WAR

EMMELINE PANKHURST: For the present at least our arms are grounded, for directly the threat of foreign war descended on our nation we declared a complete truce from militancy which was answered half-heartedly by the announcement that the Government would release all suffrage prisoners who would give an undertaking "not to commit further crimes or outrages." Since the truce had already been proclaimed, no suffrage prisoner deigned to reply to the Home Secretary's provision. A few days later, no doubt influenced by representations made to the Government by men and women of every political faith—many of them never having been supporters of revolutionary tactics—Mr. McKenna announced in the House of Commons that it was the intention of the Government, within a few days, to release unconditionally all suffrage prisoners. So ends, for the present, the war of women against men. As of old, the women become the nurturing mothers of men, their sisters and uncomplaining helpmates.

The struggle for the full enfranchisement of women has not been abandoned; it has simply, for the moment, been placed in abeyance. When the clash of arms ceases, when normal peaceful, rational society resumes its functions, the demand will again be made. If it is not quickly granted, then once more the women will take up the arms they to-day generously lay down. There can be no real peace in the world until woman, the mother half of the human family, is given liberty in the councils of the world.

VOTES FOR WOMEN
THE WOMEN'S SOCIAL AND POLITICAL UNION
OFFICES: LINCOLN'S INN HOUSE
KINGSWAY, W.C.

August 13, 1914

Dear Friend,

Even the outbreak of war could not affect the action of the W.S.P.U. so long as our comrades were in prison and under torture.

Since their release it has been possible to consider what should be the course adopted by the W.S.P.U. in view of the war crisis. It is obvious that even the most vigorous militancy of the W.S.P.U. is for the time being rendered less effective by contrast with the infinitely greater violence done in the present war not to mere property and economic prosperity alone, but to human life.

As for work for the vote on the lines of peaceful argument, such work is we know futile even under ordinary conditions to secure votes for women in Great Britain. How much less therefore will it avail at this time of international warfare!

Under the circumstances it has been decided to economise the Union's energies and financial resources by a temporary suspension of activities. The resumption of active work and reappearance of *The Suffragette*, whose next issue will be also temporarily suspended, will be announced at the right time. As a result of the decision announced in this letter, not only shall we save much energy and a very large sum of money but an opportunity will be given to the Union as a whole and above all to those members who have been in the fighting line to recuperate after the tremendous strain and suffering of the past two years.

As regards the war, the view the W.S.P.U. expresses is this: we believe that under the joint rule of enfranchised women and men the nations of the world will, owing to women's influence and authority, find a way of reconciling the claims of peace and honour and of regulating international relations without bloodshed; we nevertheless believe also that matters having come to the present pass it was inevitable that Great Britain should take part in the war and with that patriotism which has nerved women to endure torture in prison cells for the national good, we ardently desire that our country shall be victorious—this because we hold that the existence of all small nationalities is at stake and that the status of France and of Great Britain is involved.

It will be the future task of women, and only they can perform it, to ensure that the present world tragedy and the peril in which it places civilisation shall not be repeated, and therefore the W.S.P.U. will at the first possible moment step forward into the political arena in order to compel the enactment of a measure giving votes to women on the same terms as men.

I want in conclusion to thank with all my heart the generous and devoted women who have supported the W.S.P.U. until now, and to assure them of my confidence that at the present time and later when we resume active work that support will be continued.

Yours sincerely,

E. Pankhurst

**A tableau to the honour of Lord Kitchener's memory
in the Women's War Procession organised by the W.S.P.U., July 22, 1916**

The militant campaign was over. The war served to polarise the many attitudes within the suffrage movement previously hidden by the all-embracing demand for the vote.

Emmeline and Christabel Pankhurst had always opposed the Government because it denied women social and political justice. Now they saw their opportunity to take their place as de facto political leaders—as a crucial part of that same government in war time—by committing themselves and the W.S.P.U. to lead the women of Britain in National Service. They dedicated themselves to work in the national interest because they saw that women's playing an equal role in time of war would make their demand for the vote impossible to deny. On the one hand they lent their active support to Lloyd George; on the other, they undertook a propaganda campaign to encourage women to work in the munitions factories and essential services while men enlisted in the armed forces.

The Suffragette was renamed Britannia,* with a new dedication, "For King, for Country, for Freedom," that reflected Christabel's patriotic view of the war.

Sylvia Pankhurst continued to live and work amongst the poorest men and women in the East End of London. The increased privation caused by the war moved her to organise social services and facilities to reduce the suffering which surrounded her. In conflict with her mother and Christabel, she constantly attacked the Government for engaging in a "War of iniquity falsely extolled as the War to end War."

Emmeline Pethick-Lawrence, a former leader of the W.S.P.U., fully supported Sylvia's work and at the outbreak of war travelled to America to initiate an International Women's Peace Movement. She succeeded in uniting many women suffragists in Europe and America in an attempt to halt the hostilities, and her efforts culminated in the Women's Peace Conference at The Hague in April 1915.

Political power, poverty, and peace were the three major issues that now divided the original leadership of the Women's Social and Political Union.

* On October 15, 1915.

The East End

SYLVIA PANKHURST: War hardships arose immediately. The women in trouble came at once to the Women's Hall and asked for Sylvia. I was deeply impressed by their faith in the Federation and in me. They had fought with us and made sacrifices: I would strive to mitigate for them the burden of war. Our staff and members rose bravely to the occasion, the poor gallantly helping the poor. The East London Federation of Suffragettes acted as a Trade Union or a family solicitor on behalf of the people in need, approaching Government departments, magistrates, and local authorities as the case might require, and meanwhile, if other assistance were lacking, supplying the immediate sustenance required.

Prices rose in the first week to famine height; factories were shut down in panic; men and women thrown out of employment. Reservists were called up. Separation allowances were slow in coming, and when they came how meagre. Despairing mothers came to us with wasted infants. I appealed through the Press for money to buy milk, but the babies were ill from waiting; doctors, nurses, and invalid requirements were added, of necessity. Soon we had five Mother and Infant Welfare Centres in East End districts, and a toy and garment factory for unemployed women.

Before August 1914 was out we had opened our Cost Price restaurants, where two-penny meals to adults and penny meals to children were served to all comers, with free meal tickets for the destitute. The Gunmakers' Arms,* a disused public house, was turned into a clinic, day nursery, and Montessori school. We regarded our relief work as a lever for securing similar institutions from public funds, and were amongst the first to organise such work. We agitated by meetings, processions, and deputations to Government departments to protect the people from exploitation by profiteers, to secure that wages should rise with the cost of living, to gain, for the women soon flocking from all quarters into what had hitherto been masculine occupations, a rate of pay equal to that of men. We set up a League of Rights for Soldiers' and Sailors' Wives and Relatives to strive for better naval and military pensions and allowances. We toiled for the preservation of civil liberties, always so gravely attacked in war time. Votes for Women was never permitted to fall into the background. We worked continuously for peace, in face of the bitterest opposition from old enemies, and sometimes unhappily from old friends. To us came many tried militant stalwarts of the W.S.P.U. We were giving the lead to a substantial share of the Labour, Socialist, and Suffrage organisations. Much of this activity hung on me. I had often a stiff fight to keep going with the broken health left to me from the hunger-strikes.

When I first read in the Press that Mrs. Pankhurst and Christabel were returning to England for a recruiting campaign, I wept. To me this seemed a tragic betrayal of the great movement to bring the mother-half of the race into the councils of the nation.

* Renamed the Mothers' Arms.

Above: Women digging the roads

Above: The Cost Price Restaurant in the Old Ford Road
Families in the streets of the East End of London

Emmeline Pankhurst's letter of August 13 to members of the W.S.P.U. had notified them of "a temporary suspension of activities," so that "an opportunity will be given ... to those individual members who have been in the fighting line to recuperate after the tremendous strain and suffering of the past two years." This letter had given no indication of what the future policy of the W.S.P.U. would be during the war

It was only in September when Christabel Pankhurst returned to London and gave an interview to the Daily Telegraph *that their new goals and policy for the W.S.P.U. were publicly announced.*

DAILY TELEGRAPH, September 4, 1914

MISS C. PANKHURST & ENGLAND'S NEED

SPIRIT OF PATRIOTISM

SUFFRAGISTS' LOYAL CAMPAIGN

After an absence from England of about two and a half years, spent mainly in Paris, Miss Christabel Pankhurst has returned. She crossed the Channel, and is now in London, cheery and energetic as ever.

Speaking on behalf of the Women's Social and Political Union she said:

"We feel the best thing we can do is to try and put the case to others as we women see it ourselves. The people of this country must be made to realise that this is a life and death struggle, and that the success of the Germans would be disastrous for the civilisation of the world, let alone for the British Empire.

"Everything that we women have been fighting for and treasure would disappear in the event of a German victory. The Germans are playing the part of savages, overriding every principle of humanity and morality, and taking us back to the manners and methods of the Dark Ages.

"Among certain people there is a sort of idea that present events form part of evolution—that it is ordained that Germany shall supplant England. We suffragists do not by any means agree with them. We do not feel that Great Britain is in any sense decadent. On the contrary, we are tremendously conscious of strength and freshness. We feel that the future is ours; that there is a great future before our country; that in this tremendous crisis we must all be as strong as we can."

Christabel had come home. On September 8, 1914, she addressed a flower-garlanded welcome-home meeting at the London Opera House.

MANCHESTER GUARDIAN, September 9, 1914

MISS CHRISTABEL PANKHURST

From our London correspondent. By private wire.

LONDON, Tuesday Night

Miss Christabel Pankhurst celebrated her return tonight by addressing a big meeting in the London Opera House and making a sound recruiting speech. There were few possible recruits there, the audience being three parts women, and the men were mainly over the age. It was really a welcome-home meeting.

It was almost disconcertingly evident that as far as she is concerned the political truce will be thorough. There could not have been more amazing proof of the complete change brought about by the war than the use by Miss Pankhurst of such phrases as the following:

"In the English-speaking countries under the British flag and the Stars and Stripes woman's influence is higher. She has a greater political radius, her political rights are more extended than in any other part of the world.

"I agree with the Prime Minister that we cannot stand by and see brutality triumph

over freedom."

This last remark startled her followers into laughter such as greets a particularly bold piece of repartee.

Miss Pankhurst occasionally fell, as if by force of habit, into the sarcastic vein, and then her followers felt they were on familiar ground.

It was obvious that the Christabel Pankhurst who has come back radiant from exile is not quite the same lady as she who fled to France so long ago. For one thing she seemed to have lost a good deal of her fluency of speech; for another the whole tone and temper of her speech were so entirely different, and there seemed to be no more reason that it should have been made on a Women's Social and Political Union platform than on any other. The anger and indignation which used to be turned against the Government she now directed against Germany, for in Germany she thinks women's position is the lowest and most hopeless. She ended with a vigorous appeal to the men to go and join the army, her argument being that militant women ought to be able to do something to rouse the militant men.

She had a most affectionate welcome appearing alone on the huge stage with an olive green curtain as the background and a barrier of bouquets at her feet.

Her mother was present in one of the boxes. The flags of the Allies decorated the room, and a women's band played national airs.

Baroness T'Serclaes and Mairi Chisholm with their ambulance at the French Front

A woman stoker working at the furnaces of a large factory in South London

Christabel always sought to inspire and rouse in women a sense of their personal dignity and importance. She viewed the war as a great opportunity for women to achieve equality, to take power and work alongside men at every level in society, whether in the factories or at the Front. Christabel felt that pacifism and socialism must be denounced as small-time partisan squabbles in a time of national crisis and the question of votes for women suspended.

Many of the former militants of the W.S.P.U. were disillusioned and unconvinced by this policy. They had never questioned Christabel's leadership at the time of guerilla warfare against the Government because as individuals it was for the social and political emancipation of women that they fought. Now that Christabel wished to move their struggle into the arena of world war, many refused to support her call to arms. They felt that war was yet another form of male oppression in society, and so they began to move away from the W.S.P.U.

The leadership remained: Emmeline Pankhurst, Flora Drummond, Annie Kenney, Grace Roe, and Christabel. They ignored the dissenting membership of the Union and, with the zeal and passion with which they had led the militants, moved on to organise the women of England.

Emmeline Pankhurst travelled throughout England speaking on the war crisis and the German peril. With all her oratory, passion, and conviction she urged men to enlist and women to work in the factories. Her supporters, who were numerous, handed a white feather to every young man they encountered wearing civilian dress, urging them all to enlist immediately.

Emmeline Pankhurst, now fifty-six years old, had suffered ten hunger-strikes in the preceding eighteen months. Her last arrest had been as she was being carried on a stretcher to a W.S.P.U. meeting. The war and the suffrage truce most probably saved her life and Christabel's "radiant return from exile" inspired her to continue her work in the women's cause.

A Speech Delivered at Carnegie Hall
New York, October 25, 1914

CHRISTABEL PANKHURST: You must not suppose that because the Suffragettes fight the British Government for the sake of the vote, and because we have refused to allow the Government to crush our movement by imprisonment and by torture, you must not suppose that on that account the Suffragettes are not patriotic. Good heaven! Why should we fight for British citizenship if we do not most highly prize it?

Our view is that the very foundations of our movement for women's freedom are threatened. Our view is that if our country does not win, the value of British citizenship, if it is not absolutely destroyed, will be very much decreased. We want to see the strength of our country maintained, because we believe that that strength is more and more going to be used for the good of the whole world. Our country has made mistakes in the past—or, rather, the men have done so who governed the country. But we are going to do better in the future—above all, when British women co-operate with the men in the important work of Government.

What we Suffragettes aspire to be when we are enfranchised is ambassadors of freedom to women in other parts of the world, who are not so free as we are.

Britain is fighting for her own national existence. Britain is fighting for the existence of friendly nations who are as dear to us almost as our own country is, and Britain is fighting for great principles of freedom and self-government. I want to make this claim that we, the British, are fighting not only for our Allies; we are fighting for you.

Germany is hacking her way through.

Get hold of that expression. It is not mine, it is theirs. The Germans are hacking their way through. The hacking began on Belgium. Germany hacked her way through Belgium to France. She is hacking her way through France to Britain—if she can get there.

When she has hacked her way through Belgium, when she has hacked her way through France, when she has hacked her way through Britain, she will hack her way to you. Some of you, perhaps, do not think so. I know what it is. You think the Kaiser has a special partiality for America. Now, why should he love America any more than Great Britain? Can you see why he should? Don't you flatter yourselves. You are extremely nice people, but you are no nicer than we are.

Do not forget that point: that there is no difference between you and Great Britain from the German point of view. Why should there be?

One or two points are being made by certain peace advocates—they cannot love peace more than I do. You say Britain should have agreed to arbitration. I have dealt with that. We wanted to, but the other side would not have it. They chose the arbitrament of the gun. They chose the settlement of bloodshed. Some people are tempted to say that all war is wrong, and that both sides to every war must be in the wrong. I challenge that statement and deny it utterly, absolutely, and with all the power I have at my disposal. All wars are not wrong. Was your war against a British Government wrong? As an Englishwoman, I say that when you fought us for the principle of freedom, for the right of self-government, you did right. I am glad you fought us and I am glad you beat us.

I am glad, I say, that you fought us. You were in the right; we were in the wrong. We were as much in the wrong in that war as Germany is in the wrong today.

Christabel's attack on Germany shocked the New York suffrage societies. President Wilson had asked all citizens not to enter into partisan discussion.

CHRISTABEL PANKHURST: I know what the President has said for yesterday and today. Who can say what it may be necessary, in the interests of the country and in the interests of the world and humanity of the future, for him to say tomorrow? At present we are winning without you, and we are going to win without you. But suppose that were not so, what then. Think it over! It seems to me time that America listened to both sides. I notice everywhere the activities of the German Press Bureau. It is surely not worse to hear partisan arguments than to read them.

In direct opposition to Christabel, five days later Emmeline Pethick-Lawrence addressed a mass suffrage meeting at Carnegie Hall.

NEW YORK TRIBUNE, October 31, 1914

GREAT RECEPTION GIVEN TO MRS. PETHICK-LAWRENCE IN CARNEGIE HALL WOMEN OF WORLD IN LEAGUE TO END WAR GOV. GLYNN DROPS IN AT GATHERING, WHICH APPLAUDS APPEAL OF ENGLISH SUFFRAGETTE

It is to this country that Mrs. Pethick-Lawrence, the British Suffragette, looks to lead the world in her peace movement. She brought this message to a mass meeting of the Women's Political Union at Carnegie Hall last night.

The keynote of the meeting was woman's work in stopping war—not alone stopping the present European war, but preventing others. Behind the women on the platform hung a great placard bearing a message from Olive Schreiner, and Mrs. Pethick-Lawrence read another from the novelist, which ran:

"If the women of America start an International Woman's Peace Society I shall do all that lies in my power to assist in Europe or South Africa. It should be a society in which all women of all races on earth should equally find their place. It should overstep the miserable little bounds of nationality and race which lie at the root of the world's evil and war today. Its watchword should be 'humanity.'"

GOVERNOR GLYNN LOOKS ON

Mrs. Pethick-Lawrence, dressed in a semi-Eastern costume, with plenty of scarlet, vivid green and brown fur, and a black lace scarf, trimmed with gold embroidery, started out to paint a picture of some of London's war-time scenes, when Governor Glynn suddenly appeared and was greeted by the same girls' drum corps that had welcomed the Englishwoman to the platform.

The Governor lingered but a few minutes.

"America has especial qualifications for this task," said Mrs. Pethick-Lawrence. "She is the only great independent nation, untrammelled by traditions of the past and deliberately set with her face to the future. America has a great part to play in the new future. She alone can unite Italy and the neutral nations of Europe in the effort to limit the sphere of the present conflict, and at the first opportunity to arbitrate for peace." Mrs. Pethick-Lawrence gave many illustrations of the actual sorrow of the war. None produced a deeper effect than the story of the letter found inside the tunic of a dead German. His wife had written to him:

My dearest Heart:
When the little ones have said their prayers and prayed for their dear father, and have gone to bed, I sit and think of thee, my love, I think of the old days when we were betrothed, and I think of all our happy married life. Oh, Ludwig, beloved of my soul! Why are people fighting each other? I cannot think that God would wish it.

Jane Addams

Emmeline Pethick-Lawrence's pacifism and pleas for international understanding did not affect Christabel's arguments. For the next six months Christabel travelled throughout America addressing audiences on the Great War and woman's role in war time. These two women, who had been such close friends, movingly reflected the differences that divided many feminists at this time.

The Woman's Peace Party

As a result of Emmeline Pethick-Lawrence's Carnegie Hall appeal, Chrystal Eastman formed the Woman's Peace Party of New York.

EMMELINE PETHICK-LAWRENCE: Chrystal Eastman urged me if possible to see Miss Jane Addams, who was the most influential woman in America. I went to Chicago and Miss Addams invited me to stay at Hull House, the headquarters of her far-famed Social Settlement.

Jane Addams was one of the outstanding personalities of my epoch. Her character was unique in my experience. She was often called "America's first citizen." But she made herself of no account.

She was actuated by a deep and almost tragic sense of duty. She had a deep respect for the "humanity" that is common in each individual, and if worship is attested by self-surrender and sacrifice, it may be said that Jane Addams worshipped common "humanity." I entreated her to consent to be nominated for the presidency of the Woman's Peace Party. Although she had written books on the subject of universal peace and had confessed herself a pacifist since the age of eight, yet it seemed to be a presumption that women should dream of intervening in any way while a great world war was in progress.

However, she consented to come to the Washington Conference and when there yielded, as if with a sigh, to the unanimous wish of all who were present, and to her innate, unconquerable sense of duty. She took up the burden and did not lay it down again to the end of her life, and when America enlisted in the war in 1917, she became the object of national opprobrium and hate, which she accepted with the same demeanour as she accepted before and afterwards the nation's appreciation and praise.

In Holland a great suffrage pioneer and leader, Dr. Aletta Jacobs, had conceived an idea far more daring than mine. Her proposition was to bring together the women of Europe—of the belligerent as well as the non-belligerent countries—and the women of America, by calling them to a women's peace conference at The Hague.

Early in April 1915 more than fifty representatives from the National Women's Peace Party of America embarked [on the *Noordam*] for The Hague with the president, Jane

Addams. The mayor of New York presented us with a flag on which the word "PEACE" was emblazoned in great white letters on blue ground, and the captain had it hoisted as we left New York Harbour.

All was plain sailing until we reached Dover. There the *Noordam* was stopped by order of Great Britain, and for four days Jane Addams remained in communication with the American Ambassador. At last some very important-looking emissary came on board and conferred with Miss Addams. He told her that the American Ambassador could take no action in the matter. Two hours after that we were steaming across the Channel. We were given to understand that we steamed at our own risk.

There were only two British representatives besides ourselves [*Emmeline and Frederick Pethick-Lawrence*] at the conference. They were Chrystal Macmillan and Kathleen Courtney, who had remained in Holland since February to further the arrangements for the congress. The other British delegates, including Olive Schreiner and Sylvia Pankhurst amongst a hundred and fifty notable women, were not allowed to leave their own shores. Olive Schreiner sent a message to the congress expressing what all the delegates felt:

> The time has come now for the great step which humanity must take if it is to continue in its upward path—the step across the narrow bounds of nation and race in a larger and wider human fellowship.

When the congress opened on April 28, 1915, there were about fifteen hundred people present, representing Austria, Belgium, Canada, Denmark, Germany, Great Britain, Hungary, Italy, the Netherlands, Norway, Sweden, and the United States of America.

The place was swarming with reporters who expected "incidents," but the congress proceeded to hold its sessions in an atmosphere of sympathetic harmony. The preamble to the resolutions stated: "This international congress of women of different classes, creeds and parties is united in expressing sympathy with the suffering of all, whatever their nationality, who are fighting for their country or labouring under the burden of war. Since the mass of the people in each of the countries now at war believe themselves to be fighting not as aggressors but in self-defence, there can be no irreconcilable differences between them; and their common ideas afford a basis upon which an honourable peace might be established. The congress therefore urges the Governments of the world to put an end to bloodshed and begin peace negotiations." The congress did much more than pass resolutions. It brought into friendly association the women from the belligerent countries and made them realise that their fundamental interests were one and the same. Included in the resolutions was a provision that women should be made responsible citizens and be given a voice in deciding these vital questions of war and peace that affect them so deeply.

On the last day of the conference, the congress appointed envoys* to carry its message to the rulers of the belligerent and neutral countries.

They were received by several governments, in London, Berlin, Vienna, Budapest, Rome, Paris, Copenhagen, Christiania, Stockholm, Petrograd, and The Hague. They were also received by the Pope in Rome and in Washington by the President of the United States of America.

After these important interviews came to an end Jane Addams went back to America, and the thick barriers of war hid the people of the nations one from the other and all communication between them ceased. In each country the women who had been represented at The Hague congress carried out the promise that the delegates had given to each other to work in their own country for reconciliation.

---

* Among these envoys were Jane Addams and Emily Balch, from America, and Chrystal Macmillan and Kathleen Courtney, from England.

The Right to Serve

A Speech Delivered at the London Polytechnic, June 24, 1915

EMMELINE PANKHURST: The object of the women responsible for this meeting is to keep before the nation what they feel to be the real need for us here in Great Britain; the object we should be determined to attain if this war is to be won and if the ideals of which we have been thinking this afternoon are to be preserved.

Women are eating their hearts out with desire to see their services utilised in this national emergency. It is not a question with us of war bonuses; it is not a question of red tape, which has to be slowly untied. With us it is not a question of these things; but we realise that if this war is to be won, the whole energy of the nation and the whole capacity of the nation will have to be utilised in order to win.

And that is not the opinion of women alone; the Prime Minister said it weeks ago; Mr. Lloyd George has said it. But what is the outcome of all they have said? A week is to be spent and perhaps a minimum of money is to be spent on getting a comparatively small number of men trade unionists into hire on this question. . . . How is it that men can be so behind as not to see that the fire of patriotism burns in the hearts of women quite as strongly as it does in the hearts of men.

Imagine what women are thinking, when they find in Germany half a million women today are engaged in making ammunition—while 70,000-odd women who registered themselves at Easter at one single invitation of the Board of Trade are only being utilised to the number of 2,000 for national service.

Well, it is very difficult indeed for women to restrain their impatience and it is only because they realise how serious the situation is that their impatience is not being made more manifest than at present. . . . What I am saying this afternoon is not in unkind criticism of my native land. It is really because of my burning desire to make it plain to the only people who can deal with the situation that we are ready as a nation to be organised and to do our part.

I expect I am the biggest rebel in this meeting and I am one of the biggest rebels in the country. I am one of those people who, at the right time and in the proper place, are prepared to fight for certain ideals of freedom and liberty and would be willing to give my life for them; we are prepared to hold great organising meetings all over the country and enlist women for war service if they will only set us free to do it. We here and now this afternoon offer our services to the Government, to recruit and enlist the women of the country for war service, whether that war service is the making of munitions, or whether that war service is the replacing of skilled men who have been called up, so that the business of the country may go on.

The following day The Times carried a report of her speech. Three days later, on June 28, a letter was sent from Buckingham Palace to Lloyd George saying, "His Majesty the King was wondering whether it would be possible or advisable for you to make use of Mrs. Pankhurst."

Within a few days the W.S.P.U. received a £2,000 grant from Lloyd George to finance a parade asserting women's "Right to Serve." Emmeline Pankhurst and the W.S.P.U. finally had the official recognition they had been seeking during the past year. Now the brilliant organising abilities of Annie Kenney, Grace Roe, Flora Drummond, and Emmeline Pankhurst combined to create a monumental procession full of the famous Suffragette pageantry.

On July 17, 1915—less than three weeks after the letter from King George V—Lloyd George and Winston Churchill reviewed the Right to Serve parade of over 30,000 women. The Right to Serve demonstration was highly successful and put considerable pressure on employers and the Trade Union movement to admit women freely into industry. The Trade Union movement had fought bitterly through strikes and other forms of industrial action to secure higher wages and better working conditions for men. Trade unionists opposed employing women at lower wages as they felt this would undermine their own working conditions. The question of equal pay, which Sylvia was pressing for, seemed impossible to resolve even though the principle of equal pay for women had first been approved by the Trades Union Congress in the 1890's. The situation remained deadlocked.

A Speech Delivered at the London Pavilion, October 5, 1915

EMMELINE PANKHURST: I had hoped that I might be able to give to the willing thousands of women who have offered their services to the Government as munitions makers some definite information as to the time and as to how those services were to be utilised, but unfortunately I am not yet in that position.

I believe that the Minister of Munitions, Lloyd George, is undoubtedly exceedingly anxious to fulfill those pledges made to women when we waited upon him some weeks ago.

How is it then that we are not getting this work done? Well, it is our view that it is a duty to be absolutely frank about these matters, because the fate of our country is at stake, and so I want to say that the reason that women are not getting skilled training today is that it has been, and I think is still to a certain extent being, opposed by the organised skilled workmen.

Yes, there is opposition there, opposition and prejudice of a kind almost intolerable in time of peace, but which is something like treachery and traitorism in time of war. Women are exercising far more self-control and self-restraint than perhaps some people give them credit for, but it is extremely trying to their patience.

We hear of strikes and riots amongst men. Well, ladies and gentlemen, what if women lost patience and began to riot—not for money, not in order to have easier conditions, but because they were not allowed to work at the time of their country's need. We hope it won't come to that; and we do ask men in this country, both masters and men, to realise the situation, to understand that in a time of national crisis like this, all the old prejudices must go and all the old rules and regulations must go. In time of war the rules of peace must be set aside and we must put ourselves without delay upon a war basis, let the women stand shoulder to shoulder with the men to win the common victory which we all desire.

Women register to work in the munitions factories.

Inequality and Prejudice

The conflict, inequality, and prejudice shown in men's attitudes toward women workers were, however, much more significant than Emmeline Pankhurst chose to admit in her speech. Sylvia Pankhurst and the East London Federation of Suffragettes were strongly opposed to the exploitation of women as a cheap source of labour even in time of war. The Woman's Dreadnought *received many letters like this one about conditions in the factories:*

Dear Miss Pankhurst,

The first few women who entered the factory at which I work in Croydon (Government Contractors) received 12s.6d. a week, with the bait held out to them that under the premium bonus system which is in vogue the women would be able to earn £1 a week.

The new hands they are taking on are only to receive 8s. a week, with a promise that when they know their work they will have a rise!!!???

Take off the insurance 3d., and unemployment contribution 5d., and that reduces the women's wages horribly—already the women are coming to me to say they cannot live on them—some have children to keep.

Three weeks ago the firm closed the applications list with 500 on their books—this makes the employers very independent—at the same time it does not pay them to "sack" a hand that knows her work, and take on a fresh one.

The profits (I hear) all around are large, and the Government (so I am told) since Lloyd George has been in control of the Munitions Department is shovelling out the money to help contractors buy machinery.

You ask about the work done—we make bomb fuses.

Hours for all so far are 8:00 a.m. to 6:00 p.m. with one hour for dinner—no tea, no mid-morning lunch—eaten on the benches.

A Munitions Worker

SYLVIA PANKHURST: As the war dragged on, involving the entire population in its sacrifices, and as the imminence of conscription became apparent, it seemed to me that the claim of the whole people to enfranchisement could be urged with overwhelming logic. Again and again we took the lead in calling upon such suffrage and Labour organisations as were prepared to co-operate in joint demonstrations in Trafalgar Square, in Hyde Park, and in theatres and large halls. Whatever additional subjects such gatherings might strive to promote, human suffrage took always a prominent place. We formed an Adult Suffrage Joint Committee, with which more than seventy London Labour organisations were soon affiliated. We lobbied the House of Commons persistently. In March 1915 a Board of Trade circular was issued appealing to women to register at the Labour Exchanges for war service. Our East

London Federation immediately wrote to the President of the Board of Trade, as well as to Asquith and Lloyd George, demanding equal pay for women with men, and proper conditions and safeguards for women's labour.

On April 13, the Rt. Hon. Walter Runciman, President of the Board of Trade, called a conference of the women's organisations at the Board of Trade to encourage the registration of women war workers.

Mrs. Drake and I, on behalf of our federation, were the first to speak. We urged for women the vote and equal pay with men. Most of the other suffrage societies took the same line, but the National Union of Women's Suffrage Societies and the Women's Liberal and Conservative organisations promised unconditional co-operation with the Government. [*The Women's Social and Political Union were not present.*]

Down with Sweating!

**IF A WOMAN DOES A MAN'S JOB
SHE MUST HAVE A MAN'S PAY!**

Down with High Prices and Big Profits

**VOTES FOR WORKING WOMEN
GREAT JOINT DEMONSTRATION OF**

The East London Federation of the Suffragettes, United Suffragists, Forward Cymric Suffrage Union, Herald League, B.S.P., The Dockers' Union, and branches of the I.L.P. Amalgamated Toolmakers, Engineers and Machinists, Electrical Trade Union, National Union of Railwaymen, and others.

**IN TRAFALGAR SQUARE
SUNDAY, SEPTEMBER 26, 4 p.m.**

COME IN YOUR THOUSANDS AND SEND THE GOVERNMENT A BUDGET MESSAGE.

**Above: Women workers cleaning a train
Overleaf: A woman worker in the boatyards
Women wagon washers
A woman driving a steamroller**

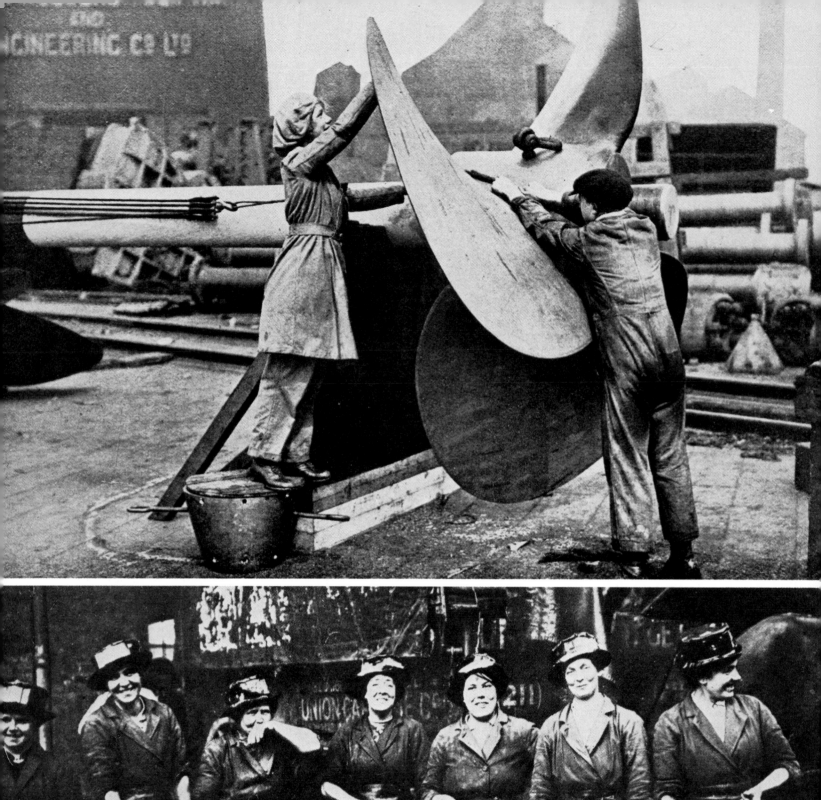

The Death of Keir Hardie

SYLVIA PANKHURST: It was at the great joint meeting we had organised in Trafalgar Square that the newsboys began crying "Death of Keir Hardie." The news stared at me from the posters in their hands. Shocked and trembling, I turned to W. C. Anderson, M.P., of the I.L.P., who stood beside me: "Is it true?" "It must be," he answered gently, and turned with practical mind to draft a resolution. "I will move it," he said; "he was our man."

The news of Keir Hardie's death, which was announced from the platform at the end of the meeting, cast a gloom over the audience, who passed the following resolution in silence:

> This meeting expresses deep sorrow at the news that has just come of the death of Keir Hardie, the veteran who from his childhood has fought the good fight of the people.
>
> Founder of the Labour Party, he had always remained true to his principles no matter what they cost him. His spirit remains fighting with us, so long as men, women and children are not secured the necessaries of life.

I knew that Keir Hardie had been failing since the early days of the war. The great slaughter, the rending of the bonds of international fraternity, on which he had built his hopes, had broken him. Quite early he had had a stroke in the House of Commons after some conflict with the jingoes. When he left London for the last time he had told me quietly that his active life was ended, and that this was forever farewell, for he would never return. In his careful way he arranged for the disposal of his books and furniture and gave up his rooms, foreseeing his end, and fronting it without flinching or regret.

I spent the day which followed his death writing an article about him for the *Dreadnought* and refusing to see anyone; my sole respite for mourning and tribute to this great friend.

WOMAN'S DREADNOUGHT, October 2, 1915

Keir Hardie has been the greatest human being of our time. When the dust raised by opposition to the pioneer has settled down, this will be known by all.

He was a child of nature akin to the Scotch moors. His father was a fisherman, and he too had the weather-fashioned look of those who follow the calling of the sea. He was built for great strength, his head was more grandly carved than any other; his deep-set eyes like sunshine distilled, as we see it through the waters of a pool in the brown earth.

The first Labour Member of Parliament, he was for years absolutely alone. He held to his independence, untouched by the temptations that assault lesser men. One of the outstanding features of his years of absolute isolation as the sole Labour Member was his fight for the unemployed. He marched with the workless men and women from East London and forced their need upon the hide-bound consciousness of Parliamentary ears. For his contention that workless men and women have a claim upon society to be provided with work, he was ridiculed and most angrily abused. But by the poor and those who understood him he was greatly loved. I remember, as a child, before I had ever seen Keir Hardie, hearing my father's voice thrilling with emotion in praising his struggle for the unemployed.

None had more reason to be grateful to him than the little band of women who broke out of the Independent Labour Party to fight for their enfranchisement, and to found a growing body of militant Suffragettes.

He collected funds for us, wrote leaflets for us, taught us Parliamentary procedure, introduced us to helpful men and women, spoke for the cause of women's enfranchisement, both in Parliament and out. He visited us in prison, and strove to procure ameliorations of our lot. When forcible feeding was started in 1909, he was filled with a horror and concern which made him physically ill. He was ridiculed for his protests in Parliament against the outrage, but he continued to raise the question persistently.

He toiled to awaken the members of the Parliamentary Labour Party, and the Labour movement as a whole, to the great need for the enfranchisement of women, and for the comradeship of working women with working men. He scarcely made a speech without dwelling upon this, and when enthusiasts asked him to write a motto, he would choose "VOTES FOR WOMEN AND SOCIALISM FOR ALL."

E. Sylvia Pankhurst

Then I was back in the surge of work, with the charge on my conscience to be doubly steadfast and true.

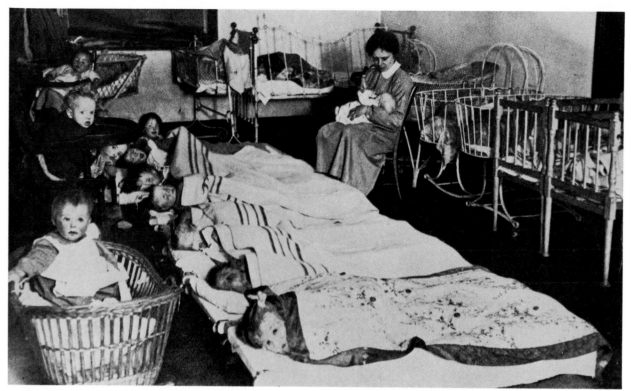

"Save the Children"

With renewed passion Sylvia launched a further appeal to "Save the Children." The doctor who was active in running the baby clinics backed this appeal with the current statistics of the infant mortality rate.

DR. BARBARA TCHAYKOVSKY: We are losing this year 100,000 to 170,000 babies out of our annual gift of 800,000. Shall we not save the nations at home while our youth is shedding its life's blood abroad? There is no time to be lost, for while we talk and deliberate, every half hour five babies die, and many more are maimed to grow up one day to swell the ranks of the millions now so unfit as to be unable to serve their country in its need.

Here in the East End we are doing all humanly possible with our restaurants, clinics for nursing and expectant mothers, and health talks, as well as our nursery, which has now thirty-five bonnie babies. The heaviest item is of course food and milk, and unfortunately it is impossible to secure Government grants for this. We are therefore entirely dependent on the practical sympathy of our subscribers.

The calls on our mother and baby centres, for milk, eggs, medicines, doctoring, and nursing care, are still very urgent. Will you help by sending us some money for this work? Will you send us new-laid eggs, arrowroot, barley, glaxo, or virol?

The following typical cases are helped at our mother and baby centres:

Destitute mother and child, father enlisted, no allowance yet, we supplied milk and dinners.

Mother, young baby, and four other children destitute, father enlisted three weeks ago, allowance not yet come through, we supplied dinners, milk, and maternity outfit.

Above: Children in the nursery of the Mothers' Arms

Delicate child of eight months, father a coach painter, enlisted, but was discharged as medically unfit, father now earning intermittently up to £1 a week, 5/– rent to pay, child requires glaxo and careful treatment, receiving these at Mothers' Arms.

Mother of eleven children; husband died before birth of last child, which is now seven months old; mother having milk and other help from Mothers' Arms.

Premature baby, very small, came under our care from day of birth. We are giving free milk and care from clinic, child now doing well. Mother was a widow with two children. She married a second time and was deserted by her husband six weeks after marriage. Mother is also under our care. More help needed.

A widow whose husband had worked sixteen years for the London County Council and died after six weeks in hospital, leaving his wife and three children absolutely penniless. The youngest child is two years old and the woman was expecting another almost immediately. The L.C.C. said it could not help. The two elder children went to relatives. We found a home for the youngest child and provided the mother with nourishment until the time of her confinement, when we arranged for her admission to a maternity home in the country. This woman nearly died at the time of her confinement, her serious condition resulting from grief at the loss of her husband. It will be several months before she will be able to undertake work of any kind. More help is needed.

Sylvia continued to fight against the suffering and injustice created by the war. Separation allowances, old-age pensions, unmarried mothers, war babies, sweated workers, the victimised enemy aliens and pacifists—all these came under her scrutiny and gained her support. She continued to badger the Government, lead deputations, write letters to every Government bureau, and publicise these inequities in her editorials for the Woman's Dreadnought.

Sylvia Pankhurst with a deputation of old-age pensioners

"Not Might, but Right!" April 8, 1916

SYLVIA PANKHURST: The militarists continued their agitation for "National Service" for all men and women "from 16–60 years of age," and a "Service Franchise" giving a vote to every soldier, sailor, and munition worker and disfranchising conscientious objectors. The women were to remain voteless till after the war.

We were to march from the East End to Trafalgar Square, to raise our opposing slogans: "Complete democratic control of national and international affairs!" "Human suffrage and no infringement of popular liberties." The *Daily Express*, the *Globe*, and many other newspapers, wherein appeared frequent incitement to violence against "peace talk," directed their battalions of invective against our meeting, denouncing it as "open sedition." As usual, friends saluted us on our march through the East End; crowds gathered to speed us; they had struggled with us for a decade; they supported us still, though our standard seemed now more Utopian, more elusively remote.

At Charing Cross we came into a great concourse of people, clapping and cheering. They welcomed our slender ranks as an expression of the old, old cry: "Not might, but right!"—a symbol of the triumph of the spirit over sordid materialism, and of their own often frustrated hopes and long unsatisfied desires. To them we were protestants against their sorrows, and true believers in the living possibility of a world of happiness. In their jolly kindness some shouted: "Good old Sylvia!" I gave my hands to many a rough grip. They pressed round me, ardent and gay, sorrowful, hopeful, earnest. Many a woman's eyes brimmed with tears as she met mine; I knew, by a sure instinct, that she had come across London, overweighted with grief, to ease her burden by some words with me.

As we entered the square a rush of friends, with a roar of cheers and a swiftness which forestalled any hostile approach, bore us forward, and hoisted a group of us on the east plinth, facing the Strand, whilst the banner-bearers marched on westward, where the banners were to be handed up; but the north side was packed with soldiers who fell upon the approaching banners and tore them to shreds. The law offered no protection; so few policemen had never been seen in the square at any demonstration. Far from assisting us to maintain order, they prevented our men speakers, and numbers of our members who wished to support us, from mounting the plinth, though we urged that they should come. We were left, a little group of women and a child or two, to deal with what might arise.

The Government had obviously given orders to leave us to the violence of the mob.

We were not afraid.

A small, hostile group had established itself by the plinth, prompted by the organisers of the disturbance, whom I recognised as old hands at such work; poor, shabby public house loafers, they shouted without pausing for breath till their red faces were purple. I continued in spite of them, by taking pains to speak clearly and not too fast. From the north the disturbers hurled at me roughly screwed balls of paper, filled with red and yellow ochre, which came flying across the lions' backs and broke with a shower of colour on anyone they chanced to hit. The reporters on the plinth had drawn near me to listen; thus, inadvertently, they intercepted the missiles aimed at me, and were covered with red and yellow. They sprang back to avoid a further volley, and Mrs. Drake's twelve-year-old daughter, Ruby, received a deluge of red full in her eyes. Crying, she buried her face in her mother's dress, while the "patriots" raised a cheer.

Always after such incidents, our mother and baby clinics, the day nursery, the restaurants, the factory, all our work for ameliorating distress suffered immediately from loss of donations. A cable repudiating me from Mrs. Pankhurst was published and helped to detach some of the old W.S.P.U. members who still supported us.

BRITANNIA, April 28, 1916

A MESSAGE FROM MRS. PANKHURST

Hearing of a demonstration recently held in Trafalgar Square,
Mrs. Pankhurst, who is at present in America, sent the following cable:
"STRONGLY REPUDIATE AND CONDEMN SYLVIA'S FOOLISH AND UNPATRIOTIC
CONDUCT. REGRET I CANNOT PREVENT USE OF NAME. MAKE THIS PUBLIC."

SYLVIA PANKHURST: My own activities were no more to their taste than theirs to mine. Families which remain on unruffled terms, though their members are in opposing political parties, take their politics less keenly to heart than we Pankhursts. Yet often in those days I woke in the night, hearing the words of the father who had guided our early thoughts: "My children are the four pillars of my house."

Some of the W.S.P.U. members who had been pacifists at the outbreak of war abandoned their position in the long, sad period when the armies were at a deadlock. The fear that their country might suffer defeat undermined the convictions of many who had counted themselves internationalists.

Daily distribution of milk at 20 Railway Street, Poplar

Women's War Work

The needs of the war were escalating, and in April 1916 conscription was introduced by the Government. As a result even more women were needed to fill jobs as men entered the armed forces.

Statement from the War Office, September 1916

The formation of large armies has necessarily had a far-reaching effect on the industrial and commercial life of the Nation, and in view of the increasing demand for men of military age to bear arms in the defence of liberty, it is incumbent on those not engaged in Military Service to make a supreme effort to maintain the output of Articles required for the War and the export trade.

It is considered that a more widespread knowledge of the success which has been attained by Women in nearly all branches of men's work is most desirable, and will lead to the release of large numbers of men to the Colours who have hitherto been considered indispensable.

Employers who have met the new conditions with patience and foresight readily admit that the results achieved by the temporary employment of Women far exceed their original estimates, and even so are capable of much further extension. If this is true in their case, how much greater must be the scope for such substitution by those Employers who have not attempted it from reasons of apprehension or possibly prejudice? The necessity of replacing wastage in our Armies will eventually compel the release of all men who can be replaced by women, and it is therefore in the interests of Employers to secure and train temporary substitutes as early as possible, in order to avoid any falling off in production.

Women of Great Britain, employers of labour, remember that:

(a) No man who is eligible for Military Service should be retained in civil employment if his place can be temporarily filled by a woman or by a man who is ineligible for Military Service.

(b) No man who is ineligible for Military Service should be retained on work which can be performed by a woman (for the duration of the War) if the man himself can be utilised to release to the Colours one who is eligible for Military Service, and who cannot be satisfactorily replaced by a woman.

Women workers operating cranes
in a shell-filling factory

Men and women workers checking shells in a shell-filling factory

In England, Ireland, Scotland, and Wales the Board of Trade had over six hundred Labour Exchanges, where women registered for factory and office work and were referred to suitable employment. In the rural areas the Board of Trade appointed Women Agricultural Officers to work with the farmers recruiting and training women to work on the land.

Women effectively replaced men as workers in semi-skilled and labouring trades throughout England. However, they were excluded from the more intellectual pursuits of management, administration, and highly skilled jobs, which were retained by men. For example, in newspaper and magazine publishing the recommended jobs for women were copy-holding, cutting for the printers, despatch, folding, letterpress machine work, machine ruling, numbering, reading proofs, stitching, and sub-editing.

The War Office also carefully defined this work as "Trades and Processes in which Women are successfully employed in temporary replacement of Men."

In further support of the Government's policy, on July 22, 1916, the Women's Social and Political Union organised a Women's War Procession to demand a still greater national war effort and war service for women, especially in munitions factories.

The work that women undertook in the munitions and aeroplane factories was extremely hazardous and badly paid. Sylvia, again in opposition to her mother and Christabel, launched a public attack on the dangerous working conditions.

SYLVIA PANKHURST: Occasionally in some obscure news paragraph the death of a worker or two from the poisonous dust and gases in the munitions factories was recorded. The explosive powders with which shells were filled were highly injurious to all who handled them. The Press referred humorously to the "yellow girls" who worked with the T.N.T., because their skin soon became a bright mustard yellow. The T.N.T. workers wore caps and overalls, and were instructed to wash their hands before taking a meal; but such precautions were but conscience-smoothers, for it was medically recognised that the main danger to the workers was inhalation through the lungs and absorption by the skin. In October 1916, at an inquest on Lydia Gibson, an examiner at a munitions factory who died from T.N.T. poisoning, the managing director of the factory stated that so injurious was T.N.T. that some workers could not work an hour with it.

The Medical Inspector of Factories issued a notice: "High explosives may cause skin irritation; no danger to life."

The contrary was the case. T.N.T. was brought into the factory in the form of powder, it was heated and mixed with a nitrate and poured into the shells in liquid form. The powder blowing about the factory, and the fumes from the hot liquid being inhaled by the workers caused symptoms similar to pneumonia, jaundice, and pitch cancer. As in white lead and other dangerous processes, all the workers in T.N.T. suffered to a greater or lesser extent, though only a minority died. The enthusiasm with which thousands of women had flocked to the factories, appealing to be allowed to help the men at the Front, was not wholly proof against the conditions prevailing there.

I was approached by women working at a London aircraft works; they were painting aeroplane wings with dope varnish at a wage of 15s. a week, for which they had to work from 8 a.m. to 6:30 p.m. They were frequently expected to work on till 8 p.m. and were paid only bare time rates for this overtime. There was no mess-room and meals were often taken in the horrid atmosphere of the workshop. It is an axiom that fatigue and insufficient nourishment invite all industrial poisoning. It was common, they told me, for six or more of the thirty women dope painters to be lying ill on the stones outside the workshop, for half an hour, or three-quarters, before they were able to return to their toil. During a part of this period they were unconscious, and they suffered the agonising sensations of fainting, in losing and regaining consciousness. If the spell outside the workshop were not excessively prolonged, their pay was not stopped for an attack of illness. If, as often happened, they were obliged to absent themselves for a day, they were not allowed to return for a week, and their pay was docked. Illness frequently compelled them to remain at home for a fortnight.

By dint of agitation I secured some ameliorations, both in wages and conditions; the women gave thanks very handsomely:

> We, the working women and girls, employed by Messrs. . . . beg to tender our thanks to the Editor of the *Woman's Dreadnought* for agitating on our behalf for better conditions; and we hereby pledge ourselves to support the paper and bring it to the notice of all working women.

Poor girls, they sorely needed support. They were working under the grip of the Munitions Act; they could not change their employment or their employer without permission, and were liable to punishment for absence from their unwholesome toil, unless excused on the ground of illness. Some of the active spirits amongst them were struggling to get their fellow-employees into a Trade Union, the management employing coercion and strategy to prevent them.

So it rolled on, the war of iniquity, falsely extolled as "the war to end war." In 1917, America came into the war; the high and dearly cherished hopes of President Wilson's exalted mediation, his promises of a peace without victory and without rancour came tumbling down, like a mere house of cards, amid the disillusion and sorrow of a multitude. Then Russia, her people oppressed by intolerable burdens, burst into revolution, whereof the reverberations, huge and far-reaching, were to influence the whole course of the war.

Russia

In March 1917 there was deep concern in England that Russia might withdraw her troops from the war as a result of the revolution, thus seriously weakening the position of England and her allies. Emmeline Pankhurst had continued to work closely with Lloyd George, now Prime Minister, and on June 1, 1917, she wrote to him requesting permission to travel to Russia.

June 1, 1917

Dear Mr. Lloyd George,

We have come to the conclusion that it is the duty of our Union to send immediately to Russia representatives who will explain to the Russian people the opinions as to the war and the conditions of peace held by us as patriotic British women, loyal to the national and Allied cause.

I therefore write to you to ask that the necessary passports and permits be given to myself and my colleagues who are to accompany me to Russia on this patriotic mission.

The British Government, according to a statement appearing in today's papers, are sincerely desirous of enabling the Russian Government and people to have an opportunity of hearing at first hand the opinions of all sections of British thought and, therefore, the necessary facilities for myself and my colleagues to travel to Russia will, we know, in accordance with this policy, be given at once.

Considering that Mr. J. R. MacDonald and other representatives of factions described in the Press of today as "not over-enthusiastic in a vigorous prosecution of the War" are allowed to visit Russia and preach their unpatriotic and fatal doctrines, there could be no excuse for preventing or delaying the visit to Russia of ourselves, the representatives of a patriotic movement.

The great burden of responsibility which you, as Prime Minister, have assumed will only be increased and your task of saving the nation by victory rendered more difficult by the activities of Mr. MacDonald and his friends during their stay in Russia. Our purpose as patriots and as friends and champions of freedom is the very opposite of theirs.

Of your own approval of our mission, we are sure, and we shall be very greatly obliged if you will give the necessary directions to the departments concerned, so that we may at once proceed on our journey to Russia.

I am,

Yours faithfully,
Emmeline Pankhurst

Permission was granted. Emmeline Pankhurst and Jessie Kenney sailed from Aberdeen to Norway and travelled overland to Petrograd.

**Above: Madame Botchkareva,
Commandant of the Women's Battalion of Death**

"For a short time, Mrs. Pankhurst and Miss Kenney stayed in the Hotel Astoria, which had become the headquarters of the Allied Military and naval staff in Petrograd. . . . Madame de Chabanov, President of the All Russian Women's Union, arranged a series of meetings in private houses, and Miss Kenney spoke at one large outdoor meeting of women factory workers. . . . Mrs. Pankhurst wanted to hold a whole series of mass outdoor meetings, but this was not allowed. Starvation and uncertainty and fear had created an atmosphere in which anything might happen, and though Mrs. Pankhurst was willing to take risks, the provisional government was not. It was a big disappointment. Anxious to make a supreme effort to energize the Russian people, she found herself restricted to preaching to the converted and entertaining the fashionable.

"Journalists hurried to interview her, and she did not mince her words—this was her best chance of reaching a wider audience."*

NOVOE VREMIA (NEW TIMES), July 13, 1917

EMMELINE PANKHURST: I came to Petrograd with a prayer from the English nation to the Russian nation, that you may continue the war on which depends the fate of civilisation and of freedom.

I have been told that the Russian nation ignores foreign public opinion. I do not believe it. I do not believe that Russians want to be isolated from the rest of the world. I cannot admit that the cry of despair of the widows and orphans and the slavery of the peoples in the territories occupied by Germany do not touch the heart of the Russian nation.

I believe in the kindness of heart and the soul of Russia. It is necessary for the Russian nation to know how the British look on this war, how not only men, but women of all classes are taking part in the work. Girls with a university education are working on the lathes on Government work. Ladies of the highest classes are replacing the working women on Sundays. In England we are anxious for our own country and for Russia. We are afraid lest Russia, now free from slavery, should fall into the hands of Germany.

From the very beginning of my public life I was in the ranks of Socialists, together with my husband. But I soon found how narrow were the interests with which I was concerned. I thus devoted myself to the cause of women. I consider that as a revolutionist, who has been sixteen times in prison, I deserve the sympathy of those people who have been at the head of the revolution in Russia. Fourteen times I organised a food-strike in prison, and was only thus let out of prison, having been condemned for three years' penal servitude for having organised a political plot.

"The Russian press was sharply divided about Mrs. Pankhurst. Left-wing writers saw her as a capitalist tool, a prestigious puppet. Right-wing journalists went into rhapsodies over her. 'I wondered,' wrote one of them, 'if there was anything feminine left in this woman rebel. Yet she has remained essentially feminine. It gives her figure a soft, romantic character. She is not a chauvinistic Valkyrie. Her patriotism is impersonal and nationalistic, able to lift the soul to the highest summits of morality. She is a new woman.' The provisional government was now in a desperate situation. Deserters continued to stream back from the fronts and Kerenski† made an extensive personal tour of the armies in an attempt to restore morale. In a last effort to conjure an outburst of patriotism, he created the Women's Battalions. Would not the sight of them, with their cropped hair, smart uniforms, eager faces, shame the Army into courage?"‡

* This invaluable record of Mrs. Pankhurst's and Miss Kenney's movements was compiled by David Mitchell in his book *Women on the Warpath* (published in the U.S. as *Monstrous Regiment*), page 69, from interviews with and the diaries of Jessie Kenney.
† Leader of the provisional government.
‡ *Women on the Warpath*, page 67.

BRITANNIA, August 3, 1917

LONG LIVE RUSSIA!   LONG LIVE THE ALLIES!

TELEGRAM RECEIVED FROM MRS. PANKHURST

FIRST WOMEN'S BATTALION NUMBER TWO HUNDRED AND FIFTY
TOOK PLACE OF RETREATING TROOPS. IN COUNTER ATTACK MADE ONE
HUNDRED PRISONERS INCLUDING TWO OFFICERS. ONLY FIVE WEEKS' TRAINING.
THEIR LEADER WOUNDED. HAVE EARNED UNDYING FAME, MORAL
EFFECT GREAT. MORE WOMEN SOLDIERS TRAINING, ALSO MARINES.
PANKHURST

ILLUSTRATED LONDON NEWS, August 4, 1917

THE WOMEN'S BATTALION OF DEATH

At a time when part of the Russian Army, under the misguiding influence of agitators, was showing a disinclination to continue the war, a band of patriotic women set a fine example by forming themselves into an armed force to go the front. A Reuter message from Petrograd of July 4 stated:

"The colours of the Petrograd Women's Contingent were blessed today in the square of St. Isaac's Cathedral. The colours of the Contingent are of light gold, with black lettering and a cross in the centre, with the name of Madame Botchkareva, the Commandant, in one of the corners.

"The first detachment consisted of over 200 women and girls, with hair cropped, and with full men's uniform and rifles.

Madame Botchkareva has already won two St. George's Crosses for bravery at the front, where she has led more than one desperate enterprise. Amongst the women's banners were two bearing the inscriptions 'Death is better than shame' and 'Women, do not give your hands to traitors.'

"Mrs. Pankhurst, who was present at the blessing of the colours, has described the movement as 'the greatest thing in history since Joan of Arc.'

"Madame Botchkareva is a Siberian peasant whose husband was killed in the war. Having obtained permission to take his place, she joined the regiment at the front, and saw fighting before she formed the women's battalion."

Above: Mlle. Kudatgora,
who received the Russian Military Order of Valour

A Speech Delivered at the Army and Navy Hall Petrograd, August 1917

EMMELINE PANKHURST: I want to speak to you as a woman. I have seen the Regiment of Women to the Death, who in a few days' time are going to the Front to fight for their country. We have always been told that it is the duty of women to care for their homes. They risk their lives to bring children into the world, and this has been the battlefield in life. We have also been told that it is the duty of men to protect their homes and to protect national liberty and honour. The day has come when the duty of women in Russia has become twofold. For the women must not only care for their home; they must also fight. The women of the world are looking to you men of Russia, and they are wondering what part you will play now that the liberty of the world is at stake. I honour these women who are setting such an example to their country. When I looked at their tender bodies I thought how terrible it was that they should have to fight besides bringing children into the world. Men of Russia, must the women fight, and are there men who will stay at home and let them fight alone?

One thing women say: Never will we be slaves to Germany. Better that we should die fighting than be outraged and dishonoured like the women in France, in Belgium, in Serbia, in Montenegro and other invaded countries. Better to die than to live in slavery.

What is it that the Allies are fighting for? They are fighting for national freedom and for national honour. They are fighting to save the world from enslavement to Germany. Let us fight together as faithful Allies until the end.

> On her return to London from Russia, Emmeline Pankhurst, with Annie Kenney, Flora Drummond, and Christabel Pankhurst, on behalf of the Women's Social and Political Union declared the the W.S.P.U. would in future be known as The Women's Party. This announcement was made public on November 2, 1917, in Britannia, as was The Women's Party programme during the war and following it.

Emmeline Pankhurst salutes the Women's Battalion of Death.

The Women's Party

BRITANNIA, November 2, 1917

THE WOMEN'S PARTY VICTORY, NATIONAL SECURITY, AND PROGRESS

THE WAR

(1) War till victory, followed by a Peace imposed upon the Germans and their allies which, by withdrawing subject populations from their control and by reducing their mineral and their other warlike resources, will make it physically impossible for the Germans to wage another war with any prospects of success. The Peace terms to include those indicated in the Allies' note to President Wilson as follows:

The restitution of provinces formerly torn from the Allies by force or against the wish of their inhabitants; the liberation of the Italians, as also of the Slavs, Roumans, and Czech-Slovaks from foreign domination; the setting free of the populations subject to the bloody tyranny of the Turks and the turning out of Europe of the Ottoman Empire as decidedly foreign to Western Civilisation.

(2) The adoption of more radical and vigorous war measures, with a view to securing complete and speedy victory.

Such measures include:

(a) FOOD RATIONS accompanied by the development of communal kitchens, so as to economise domestic labour, reduce food waste, and guarantee to the people the best possible food at the lowest possible prices, cooked in the most skilful way, so that its full nutritive value may be secured.

(b) ALL NON-ESSENTIAL INDUSTRY to be now reduced and even prohibited in order to liberate additional labour power for ag-ricultural and war industry and fighting power for the trenches.

(c) EFFICIENT AND LOYAL PUBLIC SERVICE to be guaranteed by ridding all Government Departments of officials having enemy blood or connections, and of officials who have pacifist and pro-German leanings or have displayed lack of the necessary zeal and competence.

(d) BETTER CO-ORDINATION of the military, naval, and aerial efforts of the Allies. Such co-ordination to be based on the principle of pooling the honour and the resources of the Allies.

SPECIAL WOMEN'S QUESTIONS

Equal pay for equal work.

Equal marriage laws, including equal conditions of divorce.

Equality of parental right as between mother and father, the interest of the child in every case to be supreme.

The age of consent to be raised so that the girl's person is as fully protected as her property.

Equal opportunity of employment.

Equality of rights and responsibilities in regard to the social and political service of the nation.

MATERNITY AND INFANT LIFE

The community to guarantee, where necessary, to the expectant and nursing mother the food and other conditions required to enable the bearing and rearing of healthy children. Financial contribution to be made by both parents as may be reasonable, having regard to the facts of each individual case.

Above: Flora Drummond speaking in Hyde Park

EDUCATION

Every child to be guaranteed by the community from birth until it becomes fully grown and self-supporting member of society the material conditions of life, the medical supervision and treatment, and the general education followed by specialised education necessary to render the child a worthy citizen.

HOUSING QUESTION

All state and state-subsidised housing schemes to be framed and carried out in accordance with modern and improved ideas of architecture, sanitation, and domestic economy. In particular the handicap of over-work and undefined hours of labour, which constitute the special burden of the married woman, to be reduced to a minimum by adopting the principle of co-operative housekeeping. The system of co-operative housekeeping to be carried out in such a way as to guarantee the privacy of the family and of the individual, while introducing into the housekeeping industry the combined advantages of division and co-operation of labour which have already revolutionised other branches of industry and have enabled an enormous increase in the productivity of non-domestic labour. The present non-co-operative system of housing involves injustice to the housewife and an incalculable waste of national wealth.

TRUE LIBERTY

The Women's Party maintains that the internal dangers that threaten the existence of democratic nations at the present time are due to a failure to realise that freedom does not mean the absence of control and discipline, but really means self-control and self-discipline. The Women's Party is of the opinion that in the mind of every British man and woman a sense of national duty and responsibility must go together with the sense of individual political and economic rights. The Women's Party calls upon all British women to join its ranks and work for the achievement of its objects in order to defend the great heritage that has been handed down to us, and to hand it on enriched and glorified to the generations to come.

For The Women's Party,
EMMELINE PANKHURST
CHRISTABEL PANKHURST
ANNIE KENNEY
FLORA DRUMMOND

A Speech Delivered at the Queen's Hall
November 7, 1917

CHRISTABEL PANKHURST: We believe that it is imperative to form a women's party in these days when certain influences are seeking to herd women voters into the wrong political camps. We who long before the war were fighting for votes for women, and meeting in certain quarters—where now a great interest is displayed in women's political ideas—with very little assistance in our hard struggle are the people upon whom falls the duty and responsibility of starting The Women's Party.

We believe that The Women's Party may succeed in avoiding the mistakes which the men's parties have made. At least it will be our humble and earnest endeavour to do that.

Our Women's Party is based upon no sort of sex antagonism. There never could be in our minds a question of sex antagonism except in so far as the men rear barriers of exclusion from right and responsibility against us. In so far as these barriers are now to be broken down, the political antagonism of sex naturally disappears. At the same time we feel that, as women have long been onlookers at the political game, they are in a position to set an example to the men who have got into false political grooves, and that, therefore, it would be wrong for women, with the special political contribution they have to make at this stage in our national history, to merge their political identity in the worn-out parties of the past, or even with some of the new parties which men may form today and tomorrow.

Christabel Pankhurst also spoke at great length on the war as outlined in The Women's Party manifesto. The formation of The Women's Party was greeted with enthusiasm by the members of the Women's Social and Political Union.

THE VOTE

One of the most important effects of the W.S.P.U. militant campaign was to bring women into the non-militant suffrage societies in large numbers. The issue of votes for women had been politely broached by the constitutional societies through the years, but with very little success and minimal interest. The controversial tactics of the W.S.P.U. and their widespread news coverage revitalised the question of votes for women and the non-militant suffrage societies became stronger and more powerful.

In April 1916 the Liberal and Unionist War Committees had demanded a vote for every soldier in the trenches. To be eligible to vote, the existing franchise laws required men to be qualified as householders and to have occupied a dwelling for at least one year prior to the fifteenth day of the July preceding an election. As a result of these qualifications, the enormous numbers of men serving abroad in the armed forces and the men who had moved to different parts of the country to undertake war work had by accident lost their voting rights.

The Non-Militants

Millicent Garrett Fawcett, as president of the large non-militant National Union of Women's Suffrage Societies—representing 500 to 600 non-militant groups—though pledged to "unconditional co-operation with the Government," now became concerned that if the question of electoral reform was raised by the Government, votes for women should be included in this reform. In May she wrote to the Prime Minister, the Rt. Hon. Herbert Henry Asquith.

May 4, 1916

Dear Mr. Asquith,

I am venturing once more to address you on the subject of the enfranchisement of women.

A very general rumour has prevailed since last autumn supported by statements made by responsible persons, and by its own inherent reasonableness, that the Government will, before the general election following the end of the war, find it necessary to deal with the franchise question in order to prevent the hardship and injustice which would arise if men who have been serving their country abroad, or in munitions areas in parts of this country other than those where they usually reside, should in consequence be penalised by losing their votes.

This has caused a certain amount of restlessness and anxiety among the 500 or 600 societies forming the N.U.W.S.S. as well as among other suffrage organisations. Not, of course, that any of us is in any degree hostile to the enfranchisement of men who have been suffering and working for our country, but it is feared that the suffrage may be dealt with in a manner prejudicial to the future prospects of the enfranchisement of women. To allay this feeling of restlessness and anxiety we desire to bring certain considerations before you and to ask you for an expression of your opinion upon them.

When the Government deals with the franchise, an opportunity will present itself of dealing with it on wider lines than by the simple removal of what may be called the accidental disqualification of a large body of the best men in the country. We trust that you may include in your bill clauses which would remove the disabilities under which women now labour. An agreed bill on these lines would, we are confident, receive a very wide measure of support throughout the country. Our movement has received very great accessions of strength during recent months, former opponents now declaring themselves on our side, or, at any rate, withdrawing their opposition. The change of tone in the Press is most marked.

These changes are mainly consequent on the changed industrial and professional status of women, and the view has been widely expressed in a great variety of organs of public opinion that the continued exclusion of women from representation will, on these grounds, be an impossibility after the war.

If I refer to what the N.U.W.S.S. has done in the way of service to the country since the war began, it is not that I claim for it any greater degree of patriotism than has been shown by practically all women. I only mention it because I can speak with personal knowledge of it. Within two days of the declaration of war, the N.U.W.S.S. determined to suspend its ordinary political activities, and to devote its organisation and money-raising powers to alleviate distress arising out of the war, and to other work calculated to sustain, as far as might be, the vital energies of the nation during the struggle which lay before it.

In this work we have had a considerable measure of success, but I will not trouble you with any detailed recital of it. We know from our own experiences, and we trust that you also realise, that women of all classes are eager to bear their full share of the work and the suffering demanded from the country, and that whatever opportunity has been given them they have devoted themselves with whole-hearted eagerness to the national work they have found to do. The record of our own Scottish Women's Hospitals bears proof of this fact, which is now widely recognised throughout the country.

We believe that it is the recognition of the active, self-sacrificing and efficient national service of women which has caused the recent access of strength to the movement we represent.

We should greatly value an expression of your views upon the subject of the possibility of the Government dealing with the franchise question in the direction indicated above.

Believe me, dear Mr. Asquith,

Yours very faithfully,
Millicent Garrett Fawcett

On Behalf of the National Union of Women's Suffrage Societies.

Dear Mrs. Fawcett,

I have received your letter of the 4th. I need not assure you how deeply my colleagues and I recognise and appreciate the magnificent contribution which the women of the United Kingdom have made to the maintenance of our country's cause.

No such legislation as you refer to is at present in contemplation; but if and when it should become necessary to undertake it, you may be certain that the considerations set out in your letter will be fully and impartially weighed, without any prejudgement from the controversies of the past.

Yours very faithfully,
H. H. Asquith

Members of Unit VII, First Aid Nursing Yeomanry, wearing their gas masks.
This unit served with the French forces at Epernay.

On July 16, Asquith announced that a Select Committee would be set up to consider registration and franchise, but the House did not support the motion and it was withdrawn on July 19. The Government still intended to introduce legislation of some kind, and the N.U.W.S.S.—now with the support and backing of twelve other strong non-militant suffrage organisations—requested that a deputation be received to discuss the impending electoral reform. This was refused.

Again they wrote to Asquith.

August 4, 1916

Sir:

While much regretting that you are unable to see us personally, we now, as suggested by your letter of the 1st inst., have the honour to submit the following statement of the principal points which we desired to lay before you.

We desire to make it plain that this issue is not of our raising, but it has been forced upon us by the declared intention of the Government to deal with questions of registration possibly including electoral reform.

If these intentions are limited to ensuring that men who are already on the Parliamentary Register should not be disqualified by reason of absence on war service, we should not oppose such legislation.

But if the proposals made are such as to establish a new qualification, or by means of changes in the period of residence to add a number of new names to the register, then we feel that our own issue is inextricably involved, and that we cannot stand aside. Our reasons for holding this view are, briefly, as follows:

(1) Parliament does not lightly touch the thorny question of electoral reform, and if dealt with now a fresh consideration may be indefinitely postponed.

(2) The inclusion of great numbers of new men voters intensifies the injustice and anomaly of the exclusion of all women.

(3) The injustice of such exclusion—always great and for long keenly felt—will become more intolerable than ever after the war, when the problem of the re-

adjustment of men's and women's labour has to be faced. It is impossible to ignore the fact that the entry of large numbers of women into skilled occupations hitherto closed to them, and the discovery by employers of the great value of their labours, may possibly produce an apparent clashing of interests between the sexes, and that in solution of the problems that will arise the aid of Parliament may be invoked. It is contrary to every principle of British justice, as well as of democratic government, that such an issue should be dealt with by a body upon which two or three parties to the dispute—employers and the men workers—are fully represented, but over which the women workers have no control.

If a new qualification is to be established based on services in the war, we claim the right of women to a direct influence upon Parliament.

Upon this and other problems of reconstruction after the war, we claim the right of women to a direct influence upon Parliament.

If a new qualification is to be established based on services in the war, then the claim of women to share in such a qualification cannot be ignored. The services they have rendered to the country have been so amply acknowledged, both by the Ministers mainly responsible for the direct conduct of the war and by those responsible for the maintenance of the country's industry, that we need not labour this point. We cannot believe that the compliments that have been paid to women have been empty words.

But there is another body of women who deserve, we think, even better of the country than the munitions and industrial workers and field labourers, and they are the women who have given their husbands and sons ungrudgingly to its defence.

Our organisations remain unweakened and our belief in our cause, inspired as it has always been by our desire for fuller service, has only deepened in intensity during this time of trial.

In the settlement of the problems that lie in the future we claim our share, and we claim that women have proved themselves worthy of it.

We have, sir, the honour to be

Your obedient servants,

SIGNED:

MARY WHITTY	ACTRESSES' FRANCHISE LEAGUE
FLORENS ROCH	CATHOLIC WOMEN'S SUFFRAGE LEAGUE
F. SHEWELL COOPER	CHURCH LEAGUE FOR WOMEN'S SUFFRAGE
MAUD SELBORNE	CONSERVATIVE AND UNIONIST WOMEN'S FRANCHISE ASSOCIATION
JANE E. STRICKLAND	CHURCH LEAGUE FOR WOMEN'S SUFFRAGE
J. SPRING RICE	IRISH WOMEN'S SUFFRAGE FEDERATION
EVA McLAREN	LIBERAL WOMEN'S FORWARD UNION
HERBERT JACOBS	MEN'S LEAGUE FOR WOMEN'S SUFFRAGE
EVELYN M. L. ATKINSON	NATIONAL UNION OF WOMEN'S SUFFRAGE SOCIETIES
ADELINE M. CHAPMAN	NEW CONSTITUTIONAL SOCIETY FOR WOMEN'S SUFFRAGE
ANNIE G. FERRIER	SCOTTISH CHURCHES LEAGUE FOR WOMEN'S SUFFRAGE
FRANCES H. SIMSON	SCOTTISH UNIVERSITY WOMAN SUFFRAGE UNION
BERTHA BREWSTER	UNITED SUFFRAGISTS

Franchise and Electoral Reform

THE RT. HON. HERBERT HENRY ASQUITH
THE HOUSE OF COMMONS, AUGUST 14, 1916
House of Commons Debates, Vol. 85

"The moment you begin a general enfranchisement on these lines of State service, you are brought to face to face with another most formidable proposition: What are you going to do with the women? I do not think I shall be suspected—my record in the matter is clear that I have no special desire or predisposition to bring women within the pale of the franchise—but I have received a great many representations from those who are authorised to speak for them, and I am bound to say that they presented to me not only a reasonable, but, I think, from their point of view, an unanswerable case. They say they are perfectly content, if we do not change the qualification of the franchise, to abide by the existing state of things, but that if we are going to bring in a new class of electors, on whatever ground of State service, they point out—and we cannot possibly deny their claim—that during this War the women of this country have rendered as effective service in the prosecution of the War as any other class of the community.

"It is true they cannot fight, in the gross material sense of going out with rifles and so forth, but they fill our munitions factories, they are doing the work which the men who are fighting had to perform before, they have taken their places, they are servants of the State, and they have aided, in the most effective way, in the prosecution of the War. What is more, and this is a point which makes a special appeal to me, they say when the War comes to an end and when these abnormal and, of course, to a large extent transient conditions have to be revised, and when the process of industrial reconstruction has to be set on foot, have not the women a special claim to be heard on the many questions which will arise directly affecting their interests, and possibly meaning for them large displacement of labour?

"I cannot think that the House will deny that, and I say quite frankly that I cannot deny that claim. It seems to me, and it seems to all my colleagues—although I do not profess for a moment that we are in agreement on all these points as to who ought or ought not to be enfranchised—that nothing could be more injurious to the best interests of the country, nothing more damaging to the prosecution of the War, nothing more fatal to the concentration of the national effort, than that the floodgates should be opened on all those vast complicated questions of the franchise, with an infinite multiplicity of claimants, each of whom can make a perfectly plausible if not irresistible case for themselves, and that at this stage of the War that that should be thrown on the floor of the House of Commons, and into the arena of public discussion outside, and that we should be diverted from that which ought to be our supreme and sole purpose to what is practically a review of the whole basis of our electoral constitution ... at this stage of War."

Despite the contradictory elements in Asquith's speech, a Conference on Electoral Reform was set up, comprising thirty-two members of the House from all parties, to consider the question of electoral reform and report back to the House.

Above: Mairi Chisholm driving the Baroness T'Serclaes in their motor-cycle and side-car.
Pervyse, France, September 9, 1917

DAILY GRAPHIC, January 31, 1917

NEW CHARTER FOR VOTERS
Sweeping Changes Proposed by the Speaker's Conference: Redistribution of Seats
VOTES FOR WOMEN OVER 30

Drastic changes in the franchise and electoral laws have been recommended by the Speaker's Conference, the report of which was issued last night.

The most important proposals include the following:

Qualifying period six months.

All existing franchises are swept away and a residual vote is substituted, together with an occupier's vote for business premises of the yearly value of £10.

Representation of universities to remain.

Redistribution of seats.

London (excluding the City) to be treated as a single area and divided into constituencies returning from three to five members.

Proportional representation.

All elections on one day.

Votes for soldiers and sailors.

Votes for women, ages 30 and 35 preferred.

The recommendations do not affect Ireland. They apply only to the House of Commons of Great Britain.

LONDON CONSTITUENCIES WITH 3 TO 5 MEMBERS

The Speaker in his report to the Prime Minister recalls the circumstances under which the Conference was called into being, and concludes by bearing witness to the admirable temper and conciliatory disposition shown by the members of the Conference in grappling with the difficulties confronting them.

All the recommendations of the Conference were agreed to unanimously, with the exception of women's suffrage, the resolutions in this case being the opinions of the majority.

The Conference on Electoral Reform recommended that unmarried women on the Local Government Register and the wives of men on the register should be entitled to vote, but only at a specified age. Various ages were discussed, with thirty and thirty-five receiving the most favourable response. The proposed age qualification was stipulated to avoid the establishment of a total female majority.

Queen Mary's Army Auxiliary Corps camped in Crécy Forest,
France, June 7, 1918.

THE RT. HON. HERBERT HENRY ASQUITH
THE HOUSE OF COMMONS, MARCH 28, 1917
House of Commons Debates, Vol. 92

"I beg to move, 'That this House records its thanks to Mr. Speaker for his services in presiding over the Electoral Reform Conference, and is of the opinion that legislation should promptly be introduced on the lines of the Resolutions reported from the Conference.'

"My opposition to woman suffrage has always been based, and based solely, on considerations of public expediency. I think that some years ago I ventured to use the expression 'let the women work out their own salvation.' Well, Sir, they have worked it out during this War. How could we have carried on the War without them? Short of actually bearing arms in the field, there is hardly a service which has contributed, or is contributing, to the maintenance of our cause in which women have not been at least as active and as efficient as men, and wherever we turn we see them doing with zeal and success, and without any detriment to the prerogatives of their sex, work which three years ago would have been regarded as falling exclusively within the province of men. But what I confess moves me still more in this matter is the problem of reconstruction when this War is over. The questions which will then necessarily arise in regard to women's labour and women's functions and activities in the new ordering of things—for, do not doubt it, the old order will be changed—are questions in regard to which I, for my part, feel it impossible, consistently either with justice or with expediency, to withhold from women the power and right of making their voice directly heard. And let me add that, since the War began, now nearly three years ago, we had no recurrence of that detestable campaign which disfigured the annals of political agitation in this country, and no one can now contend that we are yielding to violence what we refused to concede to argument. I, therefore, believe—and I believe many others who have hitherto thought with me in this matter are prepared to acquiesce in the general decision of the majority of the Conference—that some measure of woman suffrage should be conferred. In regard to the form which this recommendation takes, I understand it has been prompted partly by a desire to prevent a preponderance of female as compared with male voters, and partly by a feeling that a discrimination by way of age was fairer than the setting up of any special class or business qualification. I say nothing on the delicate point of age or ages which are suggested."

The same evening the House of Commons voted on the legislation proposed by the Conference on Electoral Reform and it was approved by the large majority of 341 to 62.

Women drivers in the First Aid Nursing Yeomanry,
Calais, January 1917

Mechanics of the Women's Royal Air Force working on the fuselage of an AVRO biplane

A Speech Delivered at the Queen's Hall
April 23, 1917

EMMELINE PANKHURST: We have to make sure that before the bill passes through the House of Commons to the House of Lords the women's suffrage clause shall be an integral part of the bill, and that the Government shall make it clearly understood that the whole measure stands or falls by the acceptance of every clause in the measure.

What we want to proclaim to this meeting is that we want the bill, the whole bill, and nothing but the bill. We are prepared, as we told the Prime Minister when a deputation waited upon him a little while ago, to take the measure of enfranchisement which the Government in its wisdom thinks will be acceptable to the majority of Parliament and can be passed without friction or delay.

It will be fifty years on the seventeenth of May since John Stuart Mill introduced the first women's suffrage bill into the House of Commons. Fifty years is a long time and it seems to me that fifty years of agitation that has seen men and women going from the cradle to the grave, hoping and longing to see this thing pass, is altogether too long a time even in a conservative country like England.

Men have said kind and gracious things about the part women have played in this war. But women think of what we have done as simply doing our duty, and our regret is that it has taken so long for opportunities to be given to us, and that even now in the third year of the war, the organisation of women for essential war work is far from complete.

We want the vote so that we may serve our country better. We want the vote so that we shall be more faithful and more true to our allies. We want the vote so that we may help to maintain the cause of Christian civilisation for which we entered this war. We want the vote so that in future such wars if possible may be averted.

We recognise as women that this war has to be fought out to the bitter end, that the spirit which led to it has to be crushed, that German ambitions of world conquest have to come to an end.

Members of the Women's Land Army

Representation of the People
Committee Stage

The women's suffrage bill was debated in the House of Commons at the committee stage before being referred to the House of Lords. On this occasion in the debate, Ramsay MacDonald summarised the prevailing sentiment regarding votes for women.

JAMES RAMSAY MacDONALD
THE HOUSE OF COMMONS, JUNE 19, 1917
House of Commons Debates, Vol. 94

"It is pretty evident from the course the Debate has taken that this matter has already been fought and won. Some hon. members are prepared, like gallant gentlemen, to go down with flags flying; others, like more cautious businessmen, without changing their opinions have declared that they have changed their side. I think the House ought to be quite certain that it is doing the right thing, and that a mere majority decision is not an affair either of a passing emotion, which we will regret a little later on, or a matter of expediency, in view of the fact that at the next election we shall probably have women voters. Therefore, I listened with a good deal of pleasure and interest to the speech, for instance, of the hon. Member for Westminster — Mr. Burdett-Coutts — my hon. friend's speech was an echo from very far distant times. It brought me back to a somewhat mid-Victorian frame of mind. His conception of the relation between man and woman is a relationship in which the woman is inferior to the man in everything except moral character and moral inspiration. Surely there never was a time at any period in history when that was less true than it is at the present time. He admitted that the relations between man and woman have recently very much improved. I would venture to suggest to him that improvement upon the fanciful, mythical and romantic relationship in which woman is morally superior but in everything else inferior has been steadily going on until today there is far more equality between men and women in the economic, in the social, and in the intellectual field than there has ever been."

The vote was taken and the bill passed the committee stage by 385 to 55.

Members of the Women's Forage Corps feeding a hay baler

The Earl of Loreburn introduced an amendment to the bill.

Representation of the People Bill

THE HOUSE OF LORDS, JANUARY 9, 1918
House of Lords Debates, Vol. 27

THE EARL OF LOREBURN:

"The purpose of the amendment is to stop that part of the Bill which bestows the vote upon women for the Imperial Parliament.... My view simply is that it is not in the true interests of the State, or in the interest of women themselves that they should have power in Imperial matters."

THE MARQUESS OF CREWE:

"The atmosphere after the conclusion of the war is by common admission uncertain but one thing about it I think must be agreed—it cannot be in the political sense calm. It may be very much the contrary. A great number of questions exciting controversial feelings among all Parties will emerge suddenly, will rise to the surface, and will be freely discussed, without any of the patriotic checks which all men, however keen their desires, wish to apply to political discussion at this moment. I therefore venture to ask those who believe that the consideration of this question could properly be postponed, what advantages can be expected from its postponement?

"I recall the political position on this subject as it existed just before the war. We all know how high feelings ran. It is literally true that it would have been no surprise to us, the members of the Government of that day, if any one of our colleagues in the House of Commons who had taken a prominent line either for or against the grant of the vote to women had been assassinated in the street. Nor, I venture to say, would it have been the slightest surprise to Scotland Yard.

"It is quite true that the various leaders of the women's party had drawn the line at murder, although they did not draw it at any other kind of outrage for the propagation of their ideas. But we all know that every period of political agitation is liable to have its Invincible wing, and nobody was certain that some enthusiastic supporters of the movement might not take the life, either of one of the Ministers who declared himself in strong opposition to the Bill, or of one of those who was known to be strongly in favour of it, on the ground that he was acting as a traitor in remaining a member of the Government which refused the vote. That is an atmosphere, if the grant of the vote is refused, which will undoubtedly be re-created, one of these days."

VISCOUNT HALDANE:

"Women are taking a tremendous part in this war. They are sacrificing their health, their lungs, they are sacrificing everything, to throw themselves into the work, and they have thrown themselves into it with an integrity of purpose and with a determination to make the right prevail which certainly does not put them anywhere behind the other sex. My noble friend spoke as if women had not imperilled their lives in this war."

THE EARL OF LOREBURN:

"I never said that."

VISCOUNT HALDANE:

"A good many have died. There have been women, like Edith Cavell, whose names will not be forgotten, women who have died under shell fire, died under bombardment, died by bullet wounds just the same as men have died."

THE LORD BISHOP OF LONDON:

"I should not have ventured to take part in the debate at all had I not thought I could contribute a certain amount of experience from a quarter which is not specially familiar to your Lordships—that is, the working class quarters of the great cities.

I have known them for twenty-nine years, and although for many years I was very doubtful as to the support of woman suffrage—it was hardly a tactful way to convert us by burning down our Churches or putting bombs in our homes and Cathedrals—I have been wholly converted to the support of this movement by the belief that we need women in the reconstruction of the world after the war."

Women's Royal Air Force motor-cyclist

DAILY MIRROR, January 11, 1918

VOTES FOR WOMEN PASSED BY LORDS
MANY PEERESSES LISTEN TO GRAVE WARNINGS
MAJORITY OF 63
EARL CURZON FEARS SOCIALISTIC INFLUENCES
BISHOPS SUPPORT BILL

"Hurrah! It's a fine ending to a long fight."

This exclamation was made over the telephone by an official of The Women's Party when told of the House of Lords' decision last night on Lord Loreburn's amendment to the Reform Bill to omit the clauses giving the vote to 6,000,000 women.

The division resulted as follows:

For the amendment	71
Against	134
Majority against	63

The division was taken in a fairly large House and amidst much interest. A large number of peeresses were present and many ladies also keenly interested in the question occupied seats on the floor of the House below the bar.

On the steps of the Throne and in other parts of the House were a number of M.P.s.

Lord Curzon and Lord Crawford were among the peers who abstained from voting.

VICTORY FOR WOMEN

"Hurrah! It's a fine ending to a long fight," said a member of The Women's Party when told of the House of Lords' decision to grant the vote to over eight million women. It was a victory for the married woman and the spinster alike—a victory for all those imprisoned by a society that totally denied women any human rights. The House of Lords' decision represented the end of a long struggle by both the militant and the non-militant suffragists, always united in their belief in the essential equality of men and women. It was a victory for the three generations of women who had fought and strived for the vote using every tactic from the most genteel persuasion to the most violent confrontation. More than one thousand Suffragettes had been imprisoned for demanding that women should have the most basic and simple right to vote. Solitary confinement, hard labour, brutality, broken health, and ultimately death were the price paid by women of dedication and conscience for their belief that all women should be free.

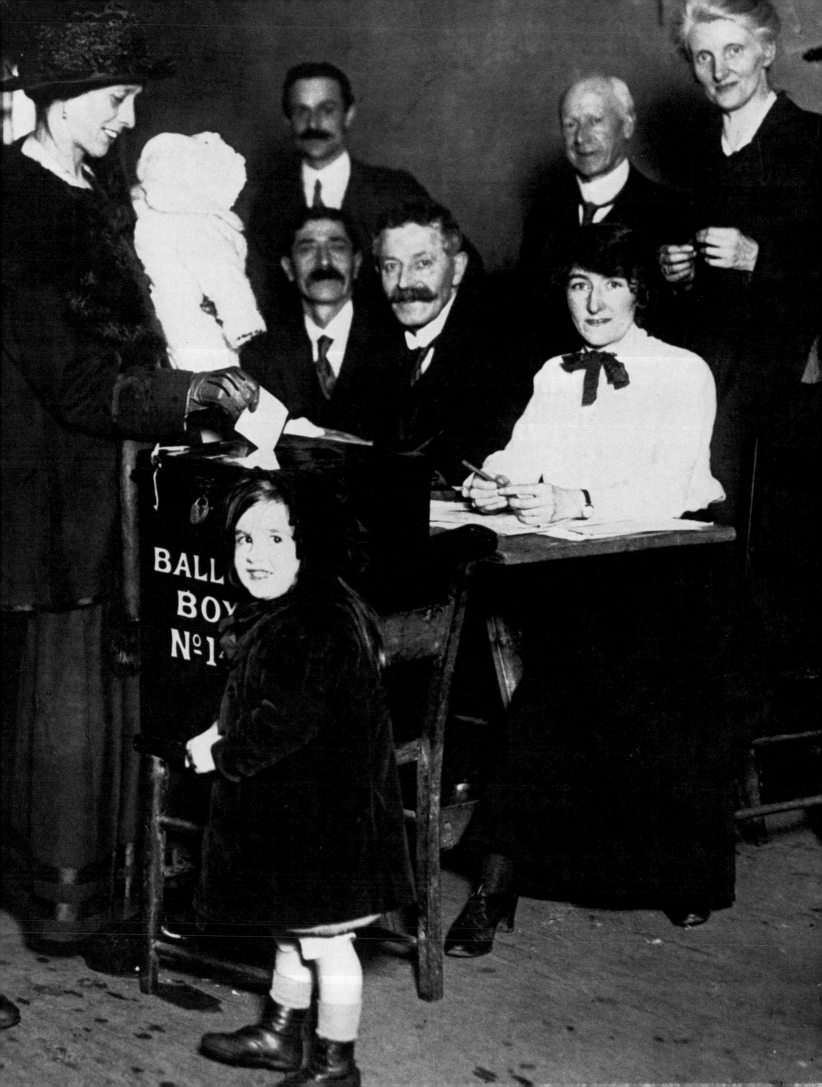

SOURCE MATERIAL

BRITISH MUSEUM: NEWS-PAPERS AND PERIODICALS

Britannia
Common Cause
Daily Graphic
Daily Mirror
Daily News
Daily Sketch
Graphic
Illustrated London News
Manchester Evening Chronicle
Labour Leader
Labour Record
New York Tribune

Punch
Sketch
The Standard
The Suffragette
Suffragette News Sheet
The Times
Vote
Votes for Women
The Weekly Dispatch
Woman's Dreadnought
Women's Franchise
Women's Suffrage Journal
Women's Suffrage Record

ARCHIVES

British Museum, State Papers: Parliamentary Reports.
British Museum, Gladstone Papers MSS. 45985 (Royal Correspondence). Ponsonby to H. Gladstone, Marienbad, August 13, 1909. Arthur Davidson to H. Gladstone, Rufford Abbey, September 11, 1909.
E. S. Pankhurst Papers, International Instituut voor Sociale Geschiedenis, Amsterdam.
State Archives: Cabinet Papers, Public Record Office. Home Office Papers, Public Record Office. Metropolitan Police Reports, Public Record Office.
Women's Service Collection, Fawcett Library, London.
Women's Suffrage Collection, London Museum.
Women's Suffrage Collection, Manchester Public Library.

PAMPHLETS

America and the War, Christabel Pankhurst, Carnegie Hall, October 25, 1914. London Museum 50.82.339.
The Importance of the Vote, Emmeline Pankhurst, London, 1907.
The New Crusade, Emmeline Pethick-Lawrence, London, 1907.
Women, the Unions and Work, Selma James, Women's Liberation Workshop, London, 1972.
Women's War Work, issued by HMSO, War Office, September 1916. Fawcett Library, London 396.5:940.3.

BIBLIOGRAPHY

BILLINGTON-GREIG, THERESA. THE MILITANT SUFFRAGE MOVEMENT. London, 1911.

BLACKBURN, HELEN. RECORD OF WOMEN'S SUFFRAGE. London, 1902.

COLMORE, GERTRUDE. THE LIFE OF EMILY DAVISON. The Woman's Press, London, 1913.

DANGERFIELD, GEORGE. THE STRANGE DEATH OF LIBERAL ENGLAND. First published, London, 1935; Reprinted, MacGibbon & Kee Ltd, 1966.

FAWCETT, MILLICENT GARRETT. THE WOMEN'S VICTORY—AND AFTER: PERSONAL REMINISCENCES, 1911-1918. London, 1920.

_____. WHAT I REMEMBER. London, 1924.

FULFORD, ROGER. VOTES FOR WOMEN. London, 1957.

GAIR WILKINSON, LILY and MRS. WIBAUT. WOMEN IN REBELLION, 1900. Independent Labour Party, London, 1973.

GORE-BOOTH, EVA. THE WOMEN'S SUFFRAGE MOVEMENT AMONG TRADE UNIONISTS, IN BROUGHAM GILLIERS, THE CASE FOR WOMEN'S SUFFRAGE. London, 1907.

KENNEY, ANNIE. MEMORIES OF A MILITANT. London, 1924.

LANSBURY, GEORGE. MY LIFE. London, 1928.

LYTTON, CONSTANCE. PRISONS AND PRISONERS. London, 1914.

_____. LETTERS OF CONSTANCE LYTTON. Ed. by Betty Balfour. London, 1925.

MARRECO, ANNE. THE REBEL COUNTESS: THE LIFE AND TIMES OF CONSTANCE MARKIEVICZ. London, 1967.

MITCHELL, DAVID. WOMEN ON THE WARPATH. London, 1966. Published in the U.S. as MONSTROUS REGIMENT by Macmillan Publishing Co., Inc.

_____. THE FIGHTING PANKHURSTS. London, 1967.

MITCHELL, HANNAH. THE HARD WAY UP. London, 1968.

MONTEFIORE, DORA. FROM A VICTORIAN TO A MODERN. London, 1927.

NEVINSON, HENRY WOODD. MORE CHANGES, MORE CHANCES. London, 1925.

NEWSOME, STELLA. WOMEN'S FREEDOM LEAGUE, 1907-1957. London, 1958.

PANKHURST, DAME CHRISTABEL. UNSHACKLED. London, 1959.

PANKHURST, EMMELINE. MY OWN STORY. London, 1914.

PANKHURST, E. SYLVIA. THE SUFFRAGETTE. London, 1911.
_____. THE SUFFRAGETTE MOVEMENT. London, 1931.
_____. THE HOME FRONT. London, 1932.
_____. THE LIFE OF EMMELINE PANKHURST. London, 1935.

PETHICK-LAWRENCE, EMMELINE. MY PART IN A CHANGING WORLD. London, 1938.

PETHICK-LAWRENCE, FREDERICK WILLIAM. FATE HAS BEEN KIND. London, 1943.

RAEBURN, ANTONIA. THE MILITANT SUFFRAGETTES. London, 1973.

RICHARDSON, MARY. LAUGH A DEFIANCE. London, 1953.

ROSEN, ANDREW. RISE UP, WOMEN! London, 1974.

ROWBOTHAM, SHEILA. HIDDEN FROM HISTORY. London, 1973.

SINCLAIR, ANDREW. THE BETTER HALF. London, 1966.

SMYTH, ETHEL. FEMALE PIPINGS IN EDEN. London, 1933.

SNOWDEN, PHILIP (Viscount Snowden of Ickornshaw). AN AUTOBIOGRAPHY, Vols. 1, 2. London, 1934.

STEWART, WILLIAM. J. KEIR HARDIE: A BIOGRAPHY. London, 1921.

STRACHEY, RAY. THE CAUSE. London, 1928.

SYKES, CHRISTOPHER. NANCY: THE LIFE OF LADY ASTOR. London, 1972.

WRIGHT, SIR ALMROTH E. THE UNEXPURGATED CASE AGAINST WOMAN SUFFRAGE. London, 1913.

PICTURE SOURCES

published in the *Daily Mirror*, July 13, 1909.

119. George Bernard Shaw. Radio Times Hulton Picture Library.

120-1. "Pageant of Great Women," presented at the Scala Theatre, November 10, 1909. Originally published in the *Daily Mirror*. Inset photographs by Miss Leon, London.

123. An artist's impression of forcible feeding. Originally published in the *Illustrated London News*, April 27, 1912.

125. Suffrage demonstration outside Bingley Hall, Birmingham, September 7, 1909. Originally published in the *Daily Graphic*, September 20, 1909.

126. W.S.P.U. drum and fife band. The London Museum.

127. Mary Leigh. Originally published in *Votes for Women*, August 30, 1912.

129. A *Daily Sketch* photograph depicting a re-enactment of forcible feeding. Originally published May 1, 1913.

131. J. Keir Hardie. The London Museum.

134. Lady Constance Lytton in Newcastle shortly before throwing a stone at Sir Walter Runciman's car, October 8, 1909. Originally published in *The Suffragette*, by E. Sylvia Pankhurst.

137. Amelia Brown and Alice Paul in court, November 10, 1909. Originally published in the *Daily Mirror*.

139. Members of the W.S.P.U. selling copies of their newspaper *Votes for Women*. The London Museum.

140. W.S.P.U. members advertising their newspaper *Votes for Women*. Originally published in *The Suffragette* by E. Sylvia Pankhurst.

141. General Drummond. Midge Mackenzie Collection.

142. Emmeline Pankhurst and Mrs. Stanton Blatch. Originally published in the *New York Tribune*, October 21, 1909.

143. American suffragists advertise Emmeline Pankhurst's appearance at the Academy of Music, New York. Originally published in *Votes for Women*.

144. Harry Pankhurst. International Instituut voor Sociale Geschiedenis.

147. Lady Constance Lytton disguised as Jane Warton. The London Museum.

148. Mary Gawthorpe, Leslie Hall. The London Museum.

149. Vera Holme, chauffeuse, with A. Flatman, Geraldine Lister, and Georgina Brackenbury during the Cheltenham by-election. The London Museum.

151. Elsie Howey. The London Museum.

152. Lady Constance Lytton. Originally published in the *Daily Mirror*.

155. Lady Constance Lytton. Originally published in *Prisons and Prisoners*, by Constance Lytton.

157. Emmeline Pankhurst, 1910. The London Museum.

158. W.S.P.U. demonstration in support of the Conciliation Bill, June 18, 1910. The London Museum.

159. W.S.P.U. demonstration in support of the Conciliation Bill, June 18, 1910. Originally published in the *Daily Sketch*, June 20, 1910.

161. W.S.P.U. demonstration in Hyde Park, July 23, 1910. The London Museum.

163. A member of the W.S.P.U. deputation to the House of Commons is hurled to the ground during the violent confrontation with the police on Black Friday, November 18, 1910. Originally published in the *Daily Mirror*, November 19, 1910.

164. Black Friday, November 18, 1910. Originally published in the *Daily Mirror*, November 19, 1910.

165. W.S.P.U. deputation members arrested, Black Friday, November 18, 1910. Originally published in the *Daily Sketch*, November 19, 1910.

166. Police line, Black Friday, November 18, 1910. Originally published in the *Daily Mirror*, November 19, 1910.

167. Dr. Garrett Anderson and Emmeline Pankhurst, November 18, 1910. The London Museum.

168. A sympathiser is arrested, November 18, 1910. Originally published in the *Daily Mirror*, November 19, 1910.

169. Black Friday, November 18, 1910. Originally published in the *Daily Mirror*, November 19, 1910.

170. Mary Clarke. The London Museum.

171. Sylvia Pankhurst. The London Museum.

172. King George V. Originally published in the *Daily Graphic*, June 22, 1911.

173. The census "stop-out." The London Museum.

174. Miss Marjorie Bryce, niece of the British Ambassador to the United States, as Joan of Arc in the Women's Suffrage Procession, June 17, 1911. The London Museum.

175. The Women's Suffrage procession, June 17, 1911. The London Museum.

176. Emmeline Pankhurst leaving for America, October 4, 1911. Originally published in *The Standard*, October 5, 1911.

178. Members of the women's suffrage deputation to the Prime Minister outside 10 Downing Street, November 17, 1911. Originally published in the *Daily Mirror*, November 18, 1911.

181. Miss Billinghurst. The London Museum.

183. Emily Wilding Davison letter. The London Museum.

185. A damaged store after the window-smashing raid, March 1912. The London Museum.

191. An artist's impression of the window-smashing raid. *Illustrated London News*.

192. Christabel and Emmeline Pankhurst on their release from prison, December 22, 1908. Originally published in *Votes for Women*, December 31, 1908.

195. Suffragettes mobbed and beaten by an angry crowd while attempting to question Lloyd George on Votes for Women, Llanystymdwy, Wales, September 21, 1912. Originally published in the *Daily Mirror*, September 23, 1912.

198. Christabel Pankhurst in Paris. Originally published in the *Daily Sketch*, September 13, 1912.

201. A timber yard in Devonport burnt down by Suffragettes. Originally published in the *Daily Graphic*, December 16, 1913.

202. Mary Richardson. The London Museum.

204. Suffragette Helen Ogston. Originally published in the *Illustrated London News*, December 12, 1908.

206. Sylvia Pankhurst addresses a meeting in the East End of London. The London Museum.

207. A family in the East End. Radio Times Hulton Picture Library.

208. George Lansbury in the East End of London. Tower Hamlets Central Library.

209. George Lansbury. Originally published in *The Suffragette*, November 22, 1912.

211. Christabel and Emmeline Pankhurst with Emmeline Pethick-Lawrence. The London Museum.

212. Emmeline and Frederick Pethick-Lawrence. Originally published in the *Illustrated London News*, April 6, 1912.

214. Emmeline Pankhurst. The London Museum.

217. Members of the W.S.P.U. in prison costume demonstrate outside Holloway Prison during the imprisonment of Emmeline and Christabel Pankhurst, November 1908. Originally published in the *Daily Graphic*, November 16, 1908.

218. Detectives examine a damaged train set on fire by Suffragettes. Originally published in the *Daily Graphic*, April 18, 1913.

219. Mary Richardson, alias "Polly Dick." The London Museum.

223. Emmeline Pankhurst. Originally published in *The Suffragette*, April 11, 1913.

225. Emmeline Pankhurst is supported by Dame Ethel Smyth and Nurse Pine is in attendance on the occasion of her re-arrest under the Cat and Mouse Act, May 26, 1913. The London Museum.

226. Emmeline Pankhurst in a horse-drawn cab arrives at Holloway Prison. Originally published in the *Daily Mirror*, April 4, 1913.

227. Suffragettes outside Holloway Prison sing the "Women's Marseillaise." Originally published in the *Daily Mirror*, April 4, 1913.

229. Emmeline Pankhurst, recovering from a hunger-strike, attended by Nurse Pine. The London Museum.

231. An unknown hunger-striking Suffragette prisoner taking exercise in Holloway Prison yard. The London Museum.

232. Cat and Mouse poster created by the W.S.P.U. The London Museum.

234. *Punch* cartoon. Originally published in *Punch*, July 13, 1910.

235. *Punch* cartoon. Originally published in *Punch*, July 6, 1910.

236. W.S.P.U. supporter sells copies of *The Suffragette*'s "Raided!" issue, May 2, 1913. Originally published by the *Daily Mirror*, May 3, 1913.

237. Interior of the W.S.P.U. offices after a police raid on April 30, 1913. The London Museum.

238. Documents being removed from the W.S.P.U. headquarters. Suffragettes at Bow Street court. W.S.P.U. Headquarters in Kingsway, London. Originally published in the *Daily Mirror*, May 1, 1913.

239. Annie Kenney. Originally published in *The Suffragette*, April 11, 1913.

240. Emily Wilding Davison. The London Museum.

241. Emily Wilding Davison funeral cortege, June 14, 1913. The London Museum.

243. Emily Wilding Davison on the Derby course. Originally published in the *Daily Mirror*, June 5, 1913.

244-5. Emily Wilding Davison funeral cortege, June 14, 1913. The London Museum.

246. Emily Wilding Davison. Anmer, the King's horse, with Jones up during

the Derby Day parade. Police leading Anmer after the accident. Originally published in the *Daily Mirror*, June 5, 1913.

249. Emmeline Pankhurst, Ellis Island, New York, October 1913. The London Museum.

251. Suffragettes picket Holloway prison. Originally published in the *Daily Sketch*, December 16, 1913.

252. A tug carrying Emmeline Pankhurst from the liner *Majestic* to Plymouth. Inset picture of Emmeline Pankhurst. Originally published in the *Daily Sketch*, December 5, 1913.

255. Mrs. Garrud, a well-known Suffragette, demonstrates jujitsu. Originally published in the *Sketch*, July 6, 1910.

256. Emmeline Pankhurst speaking from a balcony in Campden Hill Square. The London Museum.

258. Mary Richardson. Originally published in the *Daily Mirror*, March 11, 1914.

260. The Rokeby Venus. Originally published in the *Daily Mirror*, March 11, 1914.

261. Statement by Mary Richardson. Originally published in the *Daily Mirror*, March 11, 1914.

263. Emmeline Pankhurst picked up bodily by Inspector Rolse outside Buckingham Palace while leading the W.S.P.U. deputation to the King, May 21, 1914. Originally published in the *Daily Sketch*, May 21, 1914.

265. Suffragette arrested outside Buckingham Palace, May 21, 1914. Radio Times Hulton Picture Library.

266–7. Arrested Suffragette escorted by police across the bridge in St. James's Park. Radio Times Hulton Picture Library.
Mounted police hold back the crowds on Constitution Hill (inset). Originally published in the *Graphic*, May 30, 1914.

269. Sylvia Pankhurst in the East End. The London Museum.
Christabel Pankhurst in Paris. Originally published in the *Daily Sketch*, September 13, 1912.

272. The Victoria Park chained guard. Originally published in the *Woman's Dreadnought*.

274. Sylvia Pankhurst being carried to a meeting on a stretcher. Originally published in the *Daily Mirror*, June 11, 1914.

276. The "Bow Militants," Sylvia Pankhurst, George Lansbury, and Daisy Lansbury. Originally

published in *The Suffragette*, February 21, 1913.

278. The East London deputation: Mrs. Watkins, Mrs. Payne, Mrs. Savoy, Mrs. Bird, Mrs. Scurr, Mrs. Parsons. Originally published in *The Suffragette Movement*, by E. Sylvia Pankhurst.

281. The British Fleet is despatched to protect the French coast. Originally published in the *Daily Mirror*, August 4, 1914.

283. A tableau to the honour of Lord Kitchener's memory in the Women's War procession organised by the W.S.P.U., July 22, 1916. Originally published in the *Daily Graphic*, July 24, 1916.

284. Women digging the roads. Originally published in *The Home Front*, by E. Sylvia Pankhurst.

285. Cost Price Restaurant, 400 Old Ford Road. East End families. Originally published in *The Home Front*, by E. Sylvia Pankhurst.

287. Baroness T'Serclaes and Mairi Chisholm with their ambulance at the French Front. The Imperial War Museum.

288. A woman stoker. The War Office.

291. Jane Addams. Bettmann Archive.

293. The "Right to Serve" demonstration, July 17, 1915. Originally published in the *Daily Sketch*, July 19, 1915.

295. Women register to work in the munitions factories. The London Museum.

296. Women workers. The War Office.

297. Women washing a train. The War Office.

298. Woman working on a boat propeller. Wagon washers. The War Office.

299. Woman driving a steamroller. The War Office.

300. Woman factory worker. The War Office.

301. Symbol of international labour solidarity. Originally published in the *Woman's Dreadnought*.

302. Children at the Mothers' Arms. Originally published in *The Home Front*, by E. Sylvia Pankhurst.

303. Sylvia Pankhurst with a deputation of old-age pensioners. Originally published in *The Home Front*, by E. Sylvia Pankhurst.

304. Trafalgar Square, April 8, 1916. Originally published in *The Home Front*, by E. Sylvia Pankhurst.

305. Daily distribution of milk to children. Originally published in *The Home Front*, by E. Sylvia Pankhurst.

306. Women working in a shell-filling factory. The Imperial War Museum.

307. Women workers operating cranes in a shell-filling factory. The Imperial War Museum.

308-9. Men and women workers in a shell-filling factory. The Imperial War Museum.

310. Recruiting poster. The Imperial War Museum.

312. Madame Botchkareva, Commandant of the Women's Battalion of Death. Originally published in *Britannia*, August 3, 1917.

314. Mlle. Kudatgora. Originally published in *Britannia*, June 29, 1917.

315. Emmeline Pankhurst salutes the Women's Battalion of Death. Originally published in *Britannia*, August 10, 1917.

316. Flora Drummond speaking in Hyde Park. Originally published in the *Daily Sketch*, June 4, 1915.

319. Women ambulance drivers at the French Front. The Imperial War Museum.

320. Millicent Garrett Fawcett. Midge Mackenzie Collection.

322. Members of Unit VII, First Aid Nursing Yeomanry, who served with the French Forces at Epernay. The Imperial War Museum.

324. Mairi Chisholm driving the Baroness T'Serclaes in their motor-bike, Pervyse, September 9, 1917. The Imperial War Museum.

325. Queen Mary's Army Auxiliary Corps camped in Crécy Forest, France, June 7, 1918. The Imperial War Museum.

326. Women drivers in the First Aid Nursing Yeomanry, Calais, January 1917. The Imperial War Museum.

327. Mechanics of the Women's Royal Air Force working on the fuselage of an AVRO biplane. The Imperial War Museum.

328. Members of the Women's Land Army. The Imperial War Museum.

329. Members of the Women's Forage Corps feeding a hay baler. The Imperial War Museum.

331. Women's Royal Air Force motor-cyclist. The Imperial War Museum.

333. An unknown woman casting her vote at the first election. Radio Times Hulton Picture Library.

Endpapers. Originally published January 24, 1913, in the *Daily Graphic*.

Hard-cover illustration. *Punch* cartoon originally published January 23, 1918.

INDEX

ABOUT MIDGE MACKENZIE

Midge Mackenzie is an award-winning film director and producer who has worked extensively in both America and Europe. Born in London and educated both there and in Dublin, she entered film production in 1960. In 1964, after two years as a producer in her own right, she moved to America and worked on a series of television specials for the B.B.C. that focused on the New York art world of the sixties.

Having shot several films on civil rights issues, first for the B.B.C., then for the Democratic Party in the 1968 campaign, she made *Women Talking*, the first film to concern itself with the "New Wave" of feminist thinking in America. Her work on the image of women in films, undertaken for the British Film Institute, led to an invitation from the Massachusetts Institute of Technology to lecture on the same subject in America. Since 1968, when she filmed the Golden Jubilee of Women's Suffrage in London, she has continued to direct and produce a number of successful films (including a significant profile of Jane Fonda) while researching the history of the fight for the vote—both for the 6-part television series *Shoulder to Shoulder*, which she developed, edited, and co-produced, and for this book.

GRAPHIC CREDITS

The display type for this book, Korinna, was set in film and is based on drawings originally executed at H. Bethold AG in 1904. The contemporary Korinna type family was relettered into a useful series of four weights by Ed Benguiat, Vic Caruso, and the staff of Photo-Lettering, Inc. The text type, Trump Medieval, is a film version of the typeface designed by Georg Trump in 1954.

This book was photo-composed in film by New England Typographic Service, Inc. The double-dot reproductions were made by The Alderman Studios, Inc., the printing in two colors was done by Rigby Corporation, and the binding was handled by Interstate Book Manufacturers, Inc.

Production and manufacturing coordination was directed by Ellen McNeilly. The photographs in this volume were reproduced from various archive materials by Stephen Prockter and printed by Modernage and Jonathan Lumley.

Graphics were directed by R. D. Scudellari.

Book design and layout were styled by Louise Fili.

Manuscript and proof coordination was handled by Sally Rogers.